DISCARD

W9-BNG-212

COLD WAR CHRONOLOGY
SOVIET-AMERICAN RELATIONS
1945-1991

COLD WAR CHRONOLOGY
SOVIET-AMERICAN RELATIONS
1945-1991

Kenneth L. Hill

Congressional Quarterly Inc.
Washington, D.C.

Cover Design: Carol Crosby Black

Copyright © 1993 Congressional Quarterly, Inc.
1414 22nd Street, N. W., Washington, D. C. 20037

Printed in the United States of America.

Library of Congress Cataloging-in-Publication Data

Hill, Kenneth L.
    Cold War chronology : Soviet-American relations, 1945-1991 /
Kenneth L. Hill.
        p.   cm.
    Includes bibliographical references and index.
    ISBN 0-87187-921-2
    1. United States--Foreign relations--Soviet Union--Chronology.
    2. Soviet Union--Foreign relations--United States--Chronology.
    3. Cold war--Chronology.   I. Title.
E183.8.S65H55   1993
327.73047--dc20   93-34140
                                                                  CIP

For Gregory, Susan, David, and Kyle

Preface

A study of the chronology of events in Soviet-American relations since 1945 reveals some interesting insights and patterns. One revelation is the range of conflict between the superpowers, including: the deployment of nuclear weapons; arms control; the alleged use of chemical and biological weapons; trade; disinformation; assassinations; the role of the United Nations and the composition of the UN Secretariat; defections by artists on cultural tours; and Premier Nikita Khrushchev's desire to visit Disneyland, which he was not permitted to do.

The geographical reach of the superpower competition was equally broad. No region of the world was untouched. The cold war started in Europe and the Near East, but it eventually spread to Asia, the Middle East, Africa, Latin America, even outer space. President Ronald Reagan's decision to develop his Strategic Defense Initiative rankled the Soviets because of the potential for the United States to acquire a first-strike capability within the framework of the SDI system.

One pattern that recurs again and again through four decades of cold war involves conflicting interpretations of treaties signed by the United States and the Soviet Union. The Yalta and Potsdam treaties were particularly contentious, and the different interpretations soured Soviet-American relations immediately after World War II. Forty years later the pattern was unchanged; President Reagan consistently complained of Soviet treaty violations, and he established a special committee to study and monitor them. For years the United States insisted that a Soviet radar site at Krasnoyarsk violated the Anti-Ballistic Missile treaty. The Soviets just as insistently rejected the American allegation. In 1989 the Soviets admitted that the site did in fact violate the treaty, and the following year General Secretary Gorbachev agreed to dismantle the radar.

There was also a cyclical characteristic to Soviet-American relations. Despite the bitter rivalry, the danger of a nuclear confrontation compelled both Moscow and Washington to moderate their competition at times and search for areas of agreement. Periods of crisis were usually followed by efforts to reduce tensions. The partial Nuclear Test Ban treaty, for example, was agreed to shortly after the Cuban missile crisis. Leonid Brezhnev, Yuri Andropov, Konstantin Chernenko, and Mikhail Gorbachev all denounced President Reagan's 1981 proposal to eliminate intermediate-range nuclear weapons in Europe, but in 1987 the United States and the Soviet Union signed a treaty doing just that.

During President Reagan's first term in office, the superpower relationship was tense and hostile. Then in 1985 Reagan and Gorbachev met in Geneva for the first of four summit meetings. At the last summit meeting in 1988 President Reagan met with dissidents, artists, and religious leaders in Moscow and talked about human rights. President Richard Nixon and General Secretary Brezhnev held three summit meetings, the first of which convened while the United States was waging a war in Southeast Asia against North Vietnam, a Soviet ally. At the 1972 Moscow summit, the United States and the Soviet Union agreed to a set of principles designed to regulate their relations. These principles failed to diminish the superpower rivalry but were symbolically important in that they demonstrated a desire to regulate Soviet-American competition to help avoid direct confrontations.

Some Soviet-American differences lasted for a long time. Berlin remained a problem long after the resolution of the Berlin blockade in 1949. Cuba was a thorn in Soviet-American relations until the breakup of the Soviet Union in 1991. The chronology also confirms a point often made by former secretary of state Dean Rusk, namely, that most Soviet-American differences were the result of multilateral rather than bilateral problems. It was Soviet-American rivalry for influence in Afghanistan, Angola, Berlin, or Cuba that generated superpower tensions. As a result of the rapprochement that occurred after the first Reagan-Gorbachev summit, regional problems, while not resolved, at least became a topic for discussion between the leaders of the superpowers, thus lessening superpower tensions.

Each entry is accompanied by a short description or analysis. The abbreviation that follows the entry directs the reader to a source if additional information is needed. The index at the back of the book enables the reader to find quickly all the entries for a particular topic.

Some rather important events have shorter entries than others, because the significant events can be more easily researched. Due to space limitations, not all events have been included in the chronology. Depending on the source used, some events are referred to by different names or have different dates because of time zone differences. For example, the Budapest Youth Festival that met in August 1949 is also known as the International Youth Festival. The author has endeavored to eliminate as many of these differences and inconsistencies as possible, but undoubtedly a few still remain.

It is the author's hope that students, scholars, news organizations, and journalists studying Soviet-American relations will find this book useful.

Many people contributed to the completion of this work. The reference librarians at La Salle University did an outstanding job of locating many sources that made this book possible. In particular, I would like to thank Ellen Wall, W. Steven Breedlove, and Ithne C. Bearden.

A number of people assisted in the research, including Lois Kazniki, a graduate student at Harvard University, and Aimee Tagert, Lynn Zikoski, Michele Sherikijan, and Cindy Herrle.

I would also like to thank professors Joseph Brogan, Robert Courtney, and Edward Turzanski of the Political Science Department at La Salle University for their encouragement and support. I owe special thanks to Janet Amacher, a Philadelphia lawyer.

Any faults and errors are my own.

Kenneth L. Hill
Professor of Political Science
La Salle University

Sources

Following are titles and publishers of the sources in the chronology. Roman numerals indicate volumes and Arabic numbers indicate page numbers of citations.

AFP	*American Foreign Policy 1950-1955 II* (New York: Arno Press)
AFPBD	*American Foreign Policy Basic Documents* (Washington, D.C.: Department of State)
AFPBD 1977-1980	*American Foreign Policy Basic Documents 1977-1980* (Washington, D.C.: Department of State)
AFPCD	*American Foreign Policy Current Documents* (Washington, D.C.: Government Printing Office)
AFRADR	*American Foreign Relations: A Documentary Record* (New York: New York University Press)
CDSP	*Current Digest of the Soviet Press*
DAFR	*Documents on American Foreign Relations* (New York: Harper and Brothers). Princeton University was the publisher from 1945 to 1946. Harper was the publisher from 1955 to 1966. Simon and Schuster was the publisher from 1967 to 1987.
DIA	*Documents on International Affairs* (New York: Oxford University Press)
DOD	*Documents on Disarmament* (Washington, D.C.: Arms Control and Disarmament Agency)
DOG 1944-1959	*Documents on Germany 1944-1959* (Washington, D.C.: Office of the Historian, Bureau of Public Affairs)
DOG 1944-1985	*Documents on Germany 1944-1985* (Washington, D.C.: Office of the Historian, Bureau of Public Affairs)
DOGUO 1945-1954	Beate Ruhm von Oppen, *Documents on Germany Under Occupation 1945-1954* (New York: Oxford University Press, 1955)
DSB	*Department of State Bulletin*
FA	*Foreign Affairs*
FRUS	*Foreign Relations of the United States* (Washington, D.C.: Government Printing Office)
NT	*New Times*
NYT	*New York Times*
PP	*Public Papers of the Presidents of the United States* (Washington, D.C.: Government Printing Office)

Sources

USDSD   *United States Department of State Dispatch*
VS   *Vital Speeches*
WCPD   *Weekly Compilation of Presidential Documents* (Washington, D.C.: Government Printing Office)

Abbreviations

Following are abbreviations for principle terms used throughout the chronology.

ABM	Anti-Ballistic Missile (treaty)
ASEAN	Association of Southeast Asian Nations
BPA	Basic Principles Agreement
CDE	Conference on Confidence- and Security-Building Measures and Disarmament in Europe
CFE	Conventional Forces in Europe
CSCE	Conference on Security and Cooperation in Europe
ECOSOC	Economic and Social Council (United Nations)
EDC	European Defense Community
FRG	Federal Republic of Germany (West Germany)
GDR	German Democratic Republic (East Germany)
IAEA	International Atomic Energy Agency
ICBM	Intercontinental ballistic missile
INF	Intermediate-range Nuclear Forces
MBFR	Mutual and Balanced Force Reductions
MFN	Most favored nation
NATO	North Atlantic Treaty Organization
OECS	Organization of Eastern Caribbean States
PNE	Peaceful Nuclear Explosion (treaty)
SDI	Strategic Defense Initiative
START	Strategic Arms Reduction Talks
TTB	Threshold Test Ban (treaty)
UN	United Nations
WTO	Warsaw Treaty Organization

1945

September 1   V-J Day   President Harry S. Truman declared September 2
V-J Day, the day of Japan's formal surrender. Although the Allied
powers were hopeful that an era of peace had begun, Soviet-American
differences were growing and developed into the cold war. (PP 257)

September 3   Democracy in Bulgaria   Maynard Barnes, the American representative in Sofia, wrote to Secretary of State James Byrnes regarding
elections in Bulgaria. The Soviets, he said, were interfering in Bulgaria's
internal affairs to make certain the government remained subservient to
the Soviet Union. Barnes did not think a democracy could be established in Bulgaria while Soviet military forces were present and the
Allied Control Commission, composed of the United Kingdom, the
United States, and the Soviet Union, continued to function on the basis
of the unanimity rule. Barnes thought the Yalta and Potsdam agreements would prove to be worthless if the situation in Bulgaria did not
change. (FRUS IV 317)

September 4   Secret Yalta Agreements   Secretary of State Byrnes, in response to a question at a news conference, said the Soviet claim to the
Kurile and Sakhalin islands, taken from Japan at the end of World War
II, was an issue that would be settled at a future date, but he did not
oppose the Soviet claim. Byrnes was alluding to secret agreements made
at Yalta by Roosevelt and Stalin. (DSB 9/9/45 370)

September 7   Soviet Activities in Iran   Wallace Murray, the American ambassador to Iran, informed Washington that Soviet troops occupying the
northern province of Azerbaijan would not allow Iranian military forces
to enter the area. The United States consistently supported the Iranian
government in its efforts to have the Soviet troops withdrawn, and this
became a major source of friction between the United States and the
Soviet Union. (FRUS VIII 402)

September 8   Iran and the London Conference   Acting Secretary of State
Dean Acheson notified Secretary of State Byrnes that the Iranian
government believed it had the right to participate in the forthcoming
London meeting of the Council of Foreign Ministers when it dealt with
the issue of foreign troops in Iran. The Iranian government wanted the
Soviets to withdraw their troops as quickly as possible. (FRUS VIII 404)

September 8   The U.S. Accused   An editorial in *Izvestia* accused the United
Kingdom and the United States of interfering in Romania's internal
affairs. London and Washington wanted the government of Petru Groza

in Bucharest, supported by the Soviet Union, to become more representative of the people. The Soviet Union was determined to do whatever was necessary to retain control over Romania's government. (NYT 9/9/45 23)

September 10 *The Fatherland Front in Bulgaria* The American embassy in Sofia sent a report to Secretary of State Byrnes based on the observations of Reuben Markham of the *Christian Science Monitor*. Markham, who was knowledgeable about Bulgaria, reported that the Fatherland Front, the ruling body in Bulgaria, was dominated by the communists, who used the same tactics as those employed by the supporters of Adolf Hitler, namely, terror and murder. Markham did not think the Bulgarian government would permit genuinely free elections. (FRUS IV 322)

September 11 *Ukrainians to the Soviet Union* Arthur Lane, the American ambassador to Poland, reported to the State Department on the forcible transfer of Ukrainians from Poland to the Soviet Union. According to Lane, about one million Ukrainians were being transferred. (FRUS V 371)

September 11 *Council of Foreign Ministers* The first meeting of the Council of Foreign Ministers convened in London. The council, composed of the foreign ministers representing China, France, the Soviet Union, the United Kingdom, and the United States, could consider territorial questions or any other issues resulting from World War II. Each of the Big Five could participate in the peacemaking process, but voting was limited to those nations that signed armistice agreements with the defeated countries. Every member of the council had the right to veto if it had the right to vote. (DSB 9/16/45 392)

September 12 *The Groza Government* Assistant Secretary of State Dean Acheson, in a note to Secretary of State Byrnes, said there was "irrefutable evidence" that Andrei Vishinsky, the Soviet vice commissar of foreign affairs, was responsible for putting the Groza government into power in Romania. (FRUS V 618)

September 14 *Kennan Reports on Iran* George Kennan, the American *chargé d'affaires* in Moscow, notified Washington that the Soviet press was publicizing a declaration issued by groups in northern Iran opposed to the Teheran government. Kennan thought the publicity indicated Soviet support for the rebels. (FRUS VIII 407)

September 18 *Soviets Desire Oil Concession* Ambassador Wallace Murray reported to Washington on a conversation he had with Anushiravan Sepahbodi, the Iranian minister of foreign affairs. Murray said the Soviet government had failed to respond to the numerous notes from

Iran about conditions in the northern part of the country. Sepahbodi claimed the Soviets would cooperate with Iran only if it granted the Soviet Union an oil concession. (FRUS VIII 411)

September 22 *Council of Foreign Ministers* Viacheslav Molotov, the Soviet foreign minister, abruptly demanded a reorganization of the conference format of the London meeting of the Council of Foreign Ministers. He insisted that China could participate only in the discussions about Japan, and France could take part only in the negotiations for an Italian peace treaty. The United States assumed that although voting rights were limited, each of the Big Five would nevertheless be able to participate in all the talks. Molotov disagreed. Secretary of State Byrnes objected to the Soviet stance, but it remained firm. (FRUS II 313)

September 25 *Soviet Demands on Turkey* Edwin Wilson, the American ambassador to Turkey, informed Secretary of State Byrnes that the Soviet Union was making demands on Turkey pertaining to the Dardanelles Straits, which connect the Sea of Marmara with the Aegean. Wilson thought the Soviets wanted to bring about a change of government in Ankara, one that would be more friendly to the Soviet Union. If this occurred, he said, the Soviets would dominate the Dardanelles and Western influence in Turkey would dwindle. Wilson thought the demands made by the Soviet Union were a facade to conceal the Soviet desire to subjugate Turkey. The United States consistently supported the Turkish government in its various conflicts with the Soviet Union, and this became a major source of friction between the two superpowers. (FRUS VIII 1248)

September 25 *Soviet Activities in Iran* Ambassador Wallace Murray, in a message to the State Department, said the Soviet Union might want to annex the northern provinces of Iran and establish a government in Teheran controlled by Moscow. He suggested it was time for the United States to take a firm stand opposing Soviet actions. (FRUS VIII 417)

September 27 *Murray and Maximov* Ambassador Wallace Murray reported to the State Department on a conversation he had with M. A. Maximov, the Soviet ambassador to Iran. Maximov initiated the conversation, according to Murray, to reveal the hostility of the Iranian government toward the Soviet Union despite Moscow's alleged efforts to improve relations between the two countries. (FRUS VIII 420)

September 30 *Atomic Energy* George Kennan, the American *chargé* in Moscow, sent Washington a memorandum prepared by Thomas Whitney, the head of the American embassy's economic research center. According to Whitney, the Soviets would do whatever was necessary to learn the secrets of atomic energy, and he expected them to be successful. He did not think, given the nature of the Soviet system, that normal channels could be used to keep abreast of Soviet advances. (FRUS V 884)

October 2 *Foreign Ministers End Meeting* The London meeting of the Council of Foreign Ministers ended. The United States and the Soviet Union disagreed on many issues, including peace treaties for the defeated nations of World War II, the occupation of Japan, the disposition of Italy's colonies, the British presence in Greece, the nature of the Bulgarian and Romanian governments, territorial boundaries, and reparations. Procedural and substantive differences brought the London conference to a close. (NYT 10/3/45 1)

October 3 *Molotov on London Conference* Foreign Minister Molotov issued a statement at a news conference blaming the Western powers for the breakup of the London meeting of the Council of Foreign Ministers. He denied Secretary of State Byrnes's assertion that the conference ended to enable the Soviet delegation to consult with Stalin. (NYT 10/4/45 1)

October 4 *Kennan on London Conference* George Kennan, the American *chargé* in Moscow, in a note to Secretary of State Byrnes, said the Soviet Union might respond to the results of the London meeting of the Council of Foreign Ministers by accusing the American and British governments of being dominated by reactionaries hostile to the Soviet Union. If Moscow took that path, said Kennan, Stalin would have to make the Soviet people aware that the wartime cooperation among the Big Three was a thing of the past. Kennan suggested that Moscow might again use the idea of *capitalist encirclement* to explain Western policies. (FRUS V 888)

October 5 *Byrnes on London Conference* Secretary of State Byrnes addressed the nation on the results of the London meeting of the Council. of Foreign Ministers. The Soviets, he said, were unwilling to compromise on questions of procedure and this led to the breakup of the conference. He said the conference would not have resolved any issues if it continued to meet because differences were so fundamental. Despite this assessment, he said the United States was determined to continue efforts to conclude agreements with the Soviet Union on contentious issues. (DSB 10/7/45 507)

October 8 *Soviet-Turkish Relations* George Kennan, the American *chargé* in Moscow, reported to Washington about rumors in the Soviet Union suggesting the possibility of war with Turkey. He said Moscow might be responsible for spreading the rumors to frighten the Ankara government into making concessions in relation to the Dardanelles. (FRUS VIII 1252)

October 10 *Ethridge to the Balkans* Secretary of State Byrnes announced that Mark Ethridge of the *Louisville Courier-Journal* would travel to Bulgaria and Romania as his special representative to determine if their governments were generally representative of their populations as called for in the Yalta Declaration on Liberated Europe. (DSB 10/14/45 583)

October 13 *Soviet-Hungarian Trade Pact* The United Kingdom and the United States sent notes to the Soviet Union objecting to the five-year Soviet-Hungarian trade pact that was about to be concluded. The effect of the transaction was to tie the Hungarian economy to that of the Soviet Union. The United Kingdom and the United States favored multilateral rather than bilateral agreements with those nations that signed armistice terms with the victorious Allies. (FRUS IV 888)

October 23 *Assessment of Soviet Policy* Ambassador Averell Harriman sent Secretary of State Byrnes a general assessment of Soviet foreign policy prepared by Counselor of Embassy George Kennan and Second Secretary of Embassy John P. Davies at the American embassy in Moscow. Soviet foreign policy was, according to the study, fluid but also aggressive. Dominating Turkey and the Black Sea was thought to be a major Moscow priority. The study suggested that the Soviets would do all they could to exploit irredentist and nationalist sentiments in neighboring countries if this would advance the interests of the Soviet Union. (FRUS V 901)

October 23 *Truman to Joint Session of Congress* President Truman appeared before a joint session of Congress urging the legislators to adopt a program of universal military training. He said the United States must remain powerful because modern weapons had compromised America's "geographical security." The president insisted that America's strength would be used to help enforce the authority of the United Nations. (PP 404)

October 24 *Harriman Meets Stalin* Ambassador Averell Harriman and Josef Stalin discussed the breakdown of the London meeting of the Council of Foreign Ministers. After reviewing the positions of both countries, the Soviet leader said he was sure the two sides could reach a compromise agreement on convening a conference to write peace treaties for the nations defeated in World War II. (FRUS II 567)

October 27 *Turkey Endangered* Ambassador Edwin Wilson notified the State Department of a conversation he had with Hasan Saka, Turkey's minister of foreign affairs. The minister reported a substantial number of Soviet troops moving into Romania and Bulgaria toward the Turkish border, and he thought war might occur in two weeks. Alternatively, the troop movements, he said, might be intended to frighten Turkey into supporting various demands made by the Soviet Union. The United States was supporting Turkey in its conflict with the Soviet Union. (FRUS VIII 1260)

October 27 *Truman on U.S. Foreign Policy* President Truman, in an address in New York City, listed twelve fundamental principles to guide American foreign policy. The president alluded to Soviet-American difficulties that had developed in 1945, but he hoped the two countries could resolve their differences and cooperate in building a peaceful world order. Nevertheless, he stressed the necessity for remaining militarily strong if freedom were to be protected. He also announced that the United States would not share with other nations "the process of manufacturing the atomic bomb or any other instruments of war." (PP 431)

October 30 *Ethridge Reports on Bulgaria* Special representative Mark Ethridge notified Secretary of State Byrnes that the Bulgarian government was not representative of the people and therefore was in violation of the Yalta Declaration on Liberated Europe. He said the government was dominated by the communists, who were controlled by the Soviet Union. He did not expect the elections scheduled for November to be a free expression of the people's will. (FRUS IV 357)

October 31 *Byrnes on Eastern Europe* Secretary of State Byrnes, in an address delivered before the New York Herald-Tribune Forum, spoke about the relationship between the Soviet Union and the nations of Eastern Europe. He recognized the legitimacy of the Soviet Union's security concerns, which were considered in the occupation arrangements made with the defeated nations. He insisted, however, that people should enjoy the right of self-determination and that governments must be responsive to the governed. The secretary warned against spheres of influence that resulted in regions of the world becoming cut off from nations outside their region. Soviet domination of the Eastern European nations became a major source of Soviet-American tensions after World War II. (DSB 11/4/45 709)

November 2 *Soviet-Hungarian Trade Pact* The Soviet Union replied to the American note of October 13 regarding the Soviet-Hungarian trade pact tentatively agreed to in August. The Soviets rejected the American arguments opposing the trade agreement. (FRUS IV 901)

November 3 *Demands on Turkey* Ambassador Edwin Wilson notified the State Department of a conversation he had with Sergey Vinogradov, the Soviet ambassador to Turkey. Wilson said the Soviet Union would insist on having military bases in Turkey to better protect the Dardanelles. He believed the Soviets wanted the bases to dominate Turkey, not to protect it. (FRUS VIII 1271)

November 4 *Hungarian Elections* Elections were held in Hungary, and the Smallholders party won 246 seats, a majority; the Communist party won 70 seats. According to the American embassy in Budapest, the elections were genuinely free. (FRUS IV 904)

November 6 *Molotov on Foreign Policy* Foreign Minister Molotov, in a speech in Washington, extolled the achievements of the Soviet Union in dealing with German aggression and stressed the need to rebuild the Soviet economy so it could support the nation's military needs. His tone toward the United States was generally conciliatory, but he warned against using the discovery of atomic energy for achieving foreign policy goals. (VS XII:3 70)

November 12 *Turkey and the Dardanelles* The Turkish government notified the United States that its proposal, made on November 2, for revising the 1936 Montreux Convention was an acceptable basis for negotiations. That convention dealt with passage through the Dardanelles Straits in times of peace and war and Turkey's right to fortify the straits. The Soviets wanted a new regime rather than a revised one, and they wanted to share with Turkey military responsibility for protecting the straits. American and Turkish officials believed the Soviets wanted to ultimately dominate Turkey, and this was one factor that led to the formulation of the Truman Doctrine in 1947. (FRUS VIII 1275)

November 12 *Harriman on Korea* Ambassador Averell Harriman wrote to Secretary of State Byrnes about the Soviet Union and Korea. The ambassador said that Moscow viewed Korea in much the same way as it viewed Finland, Poland, and Romania: geographical areas that could be used by adversaries to attack the Soviet Union. Harriman believed the Soviets might want to establish a friendly government in North Korea, even if that meant the continued partition of the country. (FRUS VI 1121)

November 14 *Ethridge in Moscow* Mark Ethridge, special representative to the secretary of state, reported to Washington on a meeting he had in Moscow with Andrei Vishinsky, the assistant people's commissar for foreign affairs. In their conversation, Ethridge said the scheduled November elections in Bulgaria would not produce a representative government. Ethridge accused the Soviets of interfering in Bulgaria's internal affairs through the Fatherland Front, a communist-dominated coalition running the government. He suggested delaying the November elections to give the opposition candidates more time to campaign. Vishinsky denied all the allegations and opposed delaying the elections. (FRUS IV 374)

November 14 *Soviet-American Friendship* Assistant Secretary of State Dean Acheson, in a speech to the National Council of American-Soviet Friendship, declared there was nothing in the historical background of the United States and the Soviet Union that should prevent them from developing a relationship based on mutual understanding. He agreed that the Soviet Union needed friendly neighbors, but they must, he said, enjoy the right of self-determination. (DSB 11/18/45 787)

November 15 *Discontent in the Soviet Union* Ambassador Averell Harriman sent a message to Washington on conditions in the Soviet Union. He said there was widespread discontent among the population because of poor economic conditions and the nature of the government bureaucracy. He thought the dissatisfaction of the population would lead to a feeling of resignation rather than to any kind of organized uprising in support of reforms. (FRUS V 916)

November 16 *Byrnes on World Cooperation* Secretary of State Byrnes, in a speech in South Carolina, spoke about the dangers of atomic war. He said civilization could not survive the destruction of an atomic war, and he called on the United Nations to create a commission to regulate the use of atomic energy for peaceful purposes. He added that, in the past, American and Russian interests had never clashed and did not think there was any reason why they should in the future. (DSB 11/18/45 783)

November 16 *Lithuanians Ask for Help* President Truman received a telegram from Lithuanian exiles living in Paris. They alleged that the Soviet government was systematically exterminating large numbers of Lithuanians in the Soviet Union, and the émigrés asked the president to help prevent the slaughter. (FRUS V 887)

November 18 *Bulgarian Elections* Elections were held in Bulgaria; according to Maynard Barnes, the American representative, they were rigged. The Fatherland Front, dominated by the communists, claimed it received 88 percent of the votes. (FRUS IV 390)

November 19 *Soviet Activities in Iran* Hussein Ala, the Iranian ambassador to the United States, reported that the uprising in Azerbaijan was the work of the Soviet Union. He maintained that if Soviet troops withdrew from Iran, the government would be able to control the rebel forces. (FRUS VIII 434)

November 20 *Fighting in Azerbaijan* Ambassador Wallace Murray reported to Washington that Moscow was responsible for the antigovernment uprising taking place in Azerbaijan. He said the Soviets should be requested to remove all their troops from Iran by January 1. The State Department accepted Murray's suggestion and sent a note to the Soviet Union on November 24. (FRUS VIII 436)

November 22 *The Soviets and Iran* Ambassador Wallace Murray reported that General Sovyetnikov, a Soviet military official in Iran, had warned an Iranian commander that if his troops attempted to advance to connect with Iranian forces in the northern part of the country, the attempt "would be regarded as an attack on the Soviet Union." (FRUS VIII 442)

November 22 *Russian Intellectuals* Ambassador Averell Harriman reported to the State Department about Russian intellectuals and their attitudes toward the United States. Many of them, said Harriman, believed America had become hostile toward the Soviet Union and was determined to block Soviet efforts to bring democracy to the Balkans. The animus of the intellectuals was in part the result of the Soviet media depicting America as bellicose and aggressive. (FRUS V 921)

November 23 *Invitation to Talk* Secretary of State Byrnes wrote to Foreign Minister Molotov asking if he would be willing to host a Big Three foreign ministers meeting. Byrnes hoped a meeting in Moscow would enable the ministers of the Big Three to resolve some of their differences. On November 24 Molotov agreed to host the meeting. France was not invited to attend the conference, and the French government was displeased with the United Kingdom and the United States. (FRUS II 578)

November 23 *The Soviets and Iran* Ambassador Wallace Murray reported to the State Department on a conversation he had with Ahad Yakubov, the Soviet *chargé* in Teheran. Murray said the movement of Iranian forces into the northern part of the country was of concern only to the Soviet Union, not to other countries. He claimed that what was going on in Azerbaijan was a "democratic movement," not an uprising. (FRUS VIII 445)

November 26 *Ethridge Reports on Romania* Special representative Mark Ethridge reported to Washington on conditions in Romania. He said the Groza regime, supported by the Soviet Union, did not represent the people as required by the Yalta Declaration on Liberated Europe. Political opposition groups were unable to function because they were harassed by the communist-dominated government. (FRUS V 627)

November 27   Harriman Reports on Iran   Ambassador Averell Harriman reported to the State Department on a conversation he had with Marjid Ahy, the Iranian ambassador to Moscow. Soviet officials told Ahy that Iran's military units would not be welcomed in Azerbaijan province. The Soviets claimed that if Iranian forces entered the area, bloodshed would result, thus requiring the Soviets to dispatch more troops to quell any disturbances. (FRUS VIII 459)

November 27   Atomic Weapons and the Soviets   Ambassador Averell Harriman wrote to Secretary of State Byrnes about the impact on the Soviet Union of America's possession of atomic weapons. Harriman said the Soviets, as a result of the Red Army victories over Nazi Germany, were feeling secure for the first time since 1917. Then the United States developed the atomic bomb and the Soviets again felt insecure. The ambassador suggested that this condition influenced the foreign policies of the Soviet Union. (FRUS V 922)

November 29   Soviet Response on Iran   The Soviet Union responded to the November 24 American note on Iran. Moscow saw no reason to accept the suggestion for an early Soviet troop withdrawal and alleged that the people in Azerbaijan province were not rebelling; they were attempting to protect their "democratic rights." The Soviets said they prevented Iranian military forces from entering northern Iran because their presence would exacerbate current difficulties in the region. (FRUS VIII 468)

November 29   Truman on Potsdam   President Truman, in response to a question at a news conference, said efforts were being made to revise the Potsdam Declaration as it pertained to the unanimity rule governing Germany. The rule gave the Soviet Union veto power on occupation policies. The Potsdam Declaration was not revised. (PP 510)

December 4   The Soviets and the Atom Bomb   Ambassador Averell Harriman reported to Washington that some officials in the Soviet Union believed "Anglo-American reactionaries" wanted to use the potential destructive capabilities of America's atomic arsenal to bring about changes in Soviet foreign policies that would benefit the West. (FRUS V 928)

December 7   Ethridge Reports to Byrnes   Special representative Mark Ethridge reported to Secretary of State Byrnes that the governments in Bulgaria and Romania were dominated by Moscow, and their economies were required to serve the interests of the Soviet Union. Secretary of State Byrnes intended to use the Ethridge report at the Moscow foreign ministers meeting as evidence that neither of the Balkan nations had a representative government as required by the Yalta Declaration on Liberated Europe. (FRUS V 638)

December 14 *The Atomic Energy Committee* Members of the Senate Atomic Energy Committee met with President Truman concerning proposals that Secretary of State Byrnes might make to the Soviets while attending the Big Three foreign ministers meeting in Moscow. The senators wanted to make certain the secretary did not propose sharing atomic secrets with the Soviet Union. The president assured the senators that secrets would not be shared. (FRUS II 609)

December 15 *The Moscow Conference* Secretary of State Byrnes arrived in Moscow to meet with his Soviet and British counterparts. Byrnes believed that a journey to the Soviet Union might break the deadlock that had developed in London the previous September. At the 1945 Yalta Conference the United Kingdom, the Soviet Union, and the United States agreed that their foreign ministers should meet periodically to discuss common problems. At Potsdam, the Council of Foreign Ministers was created to increase the number of nations participating in the peacemaking process. The December 1945 Moscow conference reverted to the policy of Big Three meetings. (NYT 12/16/45 1)

December 19 *Byrnes Meets with Stalin* Secretary of State Byrnes, while taking part in the Big Three foreign ministers meeting in Moscow, met with Josef Stalin. Among other things, the secretary and the Soviet leader discussed the peace treaty process for the nations defeated in World War II, foreign troops in Iran, and differences between the United States and the Soviet Union that emerged at the London meeting of the Council of Foreign Ministers in September. (FRUS II 680)

December 22 *Territorial Demands on Turkey* Ambassador Edwin Wilson in Turkey informed Secretary of State Byrnes that the Soviet press had printed a letter from two professors, residents of the Georgian Soviet Socialist Republic that has a common border with Turkey. They demanded that Turkey cede to the Soviet Union about 180 miles of territory along the Black Sea coast that had been under the control of czarist Russia. (FRUS VIII 1285)

December 23 *Byrnes Meets with Stalin* Secretary of State Byrnes met with Josef Stalin for a second time to discuss the situation in Iran, the possibility of the Teheran government bringing charges against the

Soviet Union at the United Nations, control of atomic energy, American troops in northern China, and the representative nature of the governments in Bulgaria and Romania. (FRUS II 750)

December 24 *Acheson on Iranian Crisis* Assistant Secretary of State Acheson instructed Ambassador Averell Harriman to inform Josef Stalin that if Iran brought charges against the Soviet Union to the United Nations and the evidence indicated the allegations had merit, the United States would have to support Iran. Acheson was concerned that the United Nations might be seriously impaired as a result of a Soviet-American split at the first session of the world organization. (FRUS VIII 512)

December 27 *Moscow Conference Communiqué* The United Kingdom, the Soviet Union, and the United States issued a communiqué at the conclusion of their meeting in Moscow. The communiqué noted agreements that had been reached, including completing peace treaties for the nations defeated in World War II, establishing commissions pertaining to the occupation of Korea and Japan, withdrawing military forces from China, taking steps to make the Romanian and Bulgarian governments more representative, and supporting a United Nations General Assembly resolution to establish an atomic energy commission. Although the ministers succeeded in reaching a number of agreements, subsequently there were conflicting interpretations as to how they should be implemented. As a result, some of the accomplishments achieved at Moscow proved ephemeral. (FRUS II 815)

1946

January 14 *State of the Union* President Truman, in his State of the Union address, pledged to support the principles of the United Nations Charter and reiterated the fundamental principles of U.S. foreign policy first articulated on October 27, 1945. He expressed the hope that democratic political systems would develop in Germany and Japan, and he alluded to the difficulty of reconciling the views of the Big Four concerning the occupation of Germany. (PP 41)

January 18 *Soviets and Turkey* Secretary of State Byrnes, in a note to Assistant Secretary of State Dean Acheson, commented on a conversation he had in London with Hasan Saka, Turkey's foreign minister. Saka said the Soviets were making demands for military bases in Turkey, and they wanted to take control of the Kars and Ardahan regions in the eastern part of the country. Saka informed Byrnes that if the Soviets attacked Turkey, it would fight rather than surrender. (FRUS VII 809)

January 19 *Soviets and Iran* At the first session of the United Nations, Iran formally charged the Soviet Union with interfering in its internal affairs. Moscow was supporting a secessionist movement in Azerbaijan province, and the Soviets would not permit Iran's military forces to enter the area. On January 25 Andrei Vishinsky, the Soviet representative to the United Nations, in a letter to the president of the Security Council, denied the allegations made by the Iranian government and said the Soviets would be willing to negotiate with Iran to resolve their differences. The United States supported Iran's desire to have the Security Council investigate the allegations. (FRUS VII 304)

January 29 *Yalta Agreements* Secretary of State Byrnes announced that President Roosevelt and Josef Stalin had concluded a number of secret agreements at the 1945 Yalta Conference. In return for Stalin's commitment to enter the war against Japan after Germany's surrender, the Soviets received the Kurile Islands, a naval base at Port Arthur, the southern half of Sakhalin Island, and the preservation of the status quo in Outer Mongolia. The secretary suggested that a treaty should be signed to formalize the Yalta agreements. (DSB 2/10/46 189)

January 29 *Kennan on Soviet Behavior* George Kennan, the American *chargé* in Moscow, reported to Washington on factors influencing Soviet thinking about international affairs. The Soviets, he said, were emphasizing two major ideas: the inevitable economic problems confronting the United States, particularly in the area of unemployment, and the notion that differences between the United States and the United Kingdom would become more acute as their economic interests clashed. (FRUS VI 683)

February 12 *Speech by Stalin* George Kennan sent to the secretary of state a commentary on the preelection speech of Josef Stalin on February 9. Stalin made a number of assertions that worried officials in Washington. He reiterated the Marxist idea that capitalism leads to war and he blamed the West for beginning both world wars. He extolled the power of the Red Army and pledged to increase its military might. Stalin's speech implicitly sanctioned the idea of a protracted conflict between the Soviet Union and the West led by the United States. (FRUS VI 694)

February 22 *Kennan's Long Telegram* George Kennan sent a "long telegram," eight thousand words, to the Department of State analyzing Soviet foreign policies. He began with an examination of the "basic features of post-war Soviet outlook." The Soviet Union, he said, had a "neurotic view of world affairs," believing it was being encircled by the capitalist countries. Furthermore, the Leninist idea of the inevitability of war between socialist and capitalist nations made it difficult for the Soviet leadership to accept the idea of an indefinite period of peaceful coexistence. This attitude, combined with what Kennan referred to as the paranoia in the Russian national character that led to distrust of foreigners, contributed to the developing tensions between the United States and the Soviet Union. Kennan's analysis of Soviet behavior became the foundation for America's policy of containment. (FRUS VI 696)

March 5 *The Iron Curtain* Winston Churchill, in a speech delivered at Westminster College in Fulton, Missouri, declared that "from Stettin in the Baltic to Trieste in the Adriatic, an iron curtain has descended across the Continent." There were, he said, certain facts that could not be ignored, including the Soviet domination of Eastern Europe and the transformation of East Germany into a procommunist state. The nations of Western Europe, he warned, particularly France and Italy, were being undermined by "Communist fifth columns." He did not believe the Soviets wanted war with the West, but he thought they desired "the indefinite expansion of their power and doctrines." To meet the Soviet challenge he called for a greater degree of cooperation between the United States and the United Kingdom, including the British Commonwealth. (VS XII:11 329)

March 17 *Kennan on Iran* George Kennan, the American *chargé* in Moscow, in a note to the secretary of state, said he expected the Soviets would try to install a friendly government in Teheran. Once this was accomplished, the Soviet Union could then be requested to keep its troops in Iran. He added that there was insufficient evidence to assume the Soviet Union had any immediate plans for a war with Turkey. He did say that a possible Soviet objective would be to have a friendly government installed in Ankara. (FRUS VII 362)

March 20 *U.S. Supports Iran* Secretary of State Byrnes, in a letter to Ambassador Wallace Murray in Iran, said the United States would support placing the Iranian complaint against the Soviet Union at the top of the United Nations Security Council agenda. (FRUS VII 367)

March 27 *Soviets Boycott Council* Andrei Gromyko, a Soviet delegate to the United Nations, announced that the Soviet Union would not participate in any debates regarding the Iranian complaint against the Soviet Union. (FRUS VII 388)

April 4 *Soviet-Iranian Agreement* The Soviet Union and Iran signed an agreement on three issues. All Soviet troops were to be withdrawn from Iran by May 6, 1946, a joint Soviet-Iranian oil company was to be established, and Azerbaijan was to be treated as an internal Iranian issue. (FRUS VII 405)

April 4 *The U.S. and Iran* Secretary of State Byrnes introduced a resolution to the United Nations Security Council deferring any action on the Iranian complaint against the Soviet Union until May 6, the date Soviet troops were scheduled to be out of Iran. The Soviet Union and Iran were instructed to keep the Security Council informed about the troop withdrawals. The resolution was approved. (FRUS VII 407)

April 5 *Smith Talks to Stalin* Walter Bedell Smith, who was confirmed by the Senate to be ambassador to the Soviet Union after Averell Harriman's resignation on February 14, reported to Washington on a conversation he had with Josef Stalin. Among other things, the ambassador told the Soviet leader that the United States was apprehensive about some of his foreign policies because they appeared to threaten the peace. Stalin, in turn, complained about some American policies he considered unfriendly toward the Soviet Union. The conversation ended with Stalin and Smith agreeing that both sides should make an effort to improve relations. Smith gave Stalin a letter from President Truman inviting the Soviet leader to visit the United States. (FRUS VI 732)

April 25 *Council of Foreign Ministers* The first session of the second meeting of the Council of Foreign Ministers met in Paris. The ministers had a rather long agenda, including the writing of peace treaties for the nations defeated in World War II. (NYT 4/26/46 1)

April 29 *The Byrnes Treaty*   At the Paris meeting of the Council of Foreign Ministers, Secretary of State Byrnes introduced a twenty-five-year treaty for the demilitarization and disarmament of Germany. The proposed treaty would have required the United States to protect the security of its European allies and the Soviet Union and would have necessitated keeping American military forces in Europe indefinitely, a historic shift in U.S. foreign policy. (DSB 5/12/46 815)

May 1 *Stalin's Order of the Day*   Josef Stalin, in an "Order of the Day," declared that some international forces were preparing for another war and therefore the Red Army had to be diligent in protecting the peace. His order set the tone for the May Day celebrations. (VS XII:15 451)

May 27 *Molotov on Paris Meeting*   Foreign Minister Molotov, during a recess in the Paris peace negotiations, accused the United Kingdom and the United States of attempting to impose their will on the Soviet Union. He rejected the suggestion of Secretary of State Byrnes that if the Paris meeting produced no peace treaties for the nations defeated in World War II, the issue should be taken to the United Nations. (DOGUO 138)

May 31 *Smith on Soviet Satellites*   Ambassador Walter Bedell Smith, in a message to the State Department, said the Soviets would do whatever was necessary to keep the Eastern European countries subservient to Moscow. He went on to say that Europe was being divided between the communist nations controlled by the Soviet Union and the free nations of Western Europe. (FRUS VI 758)

June 14 *The Baruch Plan*   The United States, at the first meeting of the United Nations Atomic Energy Commission, presented the Baruch Plan, named after Bernard Baruch, an adviser to President Truman, for the control and supervision of atomic energy. The plan was designed to promote the peaceful uses of atomic energy. The American proposal called for the establishment of an International Atomic Development Authority with no nation having the right to veto. The United States promised to share its nuclear technology with other nations and to destroy its nuclear weapons once the authority was established. The Soviets rejected the Baruch Plan because they would have been denied the right of veto. (DSB 6/23/46 1057)

June 21 *Litvinov's Analysis*   Ambassador Walter Bedell Smith notified Washington of a conversation between Richard C. Hottelet, a correspondent for CBS, and Maxim Litvinov, the former Soviet ambassador to the United States. Litvinov was uncharacteristically frank in his assessment of Soviet-American relations. He said differences between the United

States and the Soviet Union were now so great they could not be reconciled. He predicted Germany would remain divided and Moscow would not accept the safeguards called for in the Baruch Plan. (FRUS VI 763)

July 4   Convening a Peace Conference   The Council of Foreign Ministers agreed to convene a peace conference on July 29 to be attended by the Big Five foreign ministers and representatives from sixteen nations that had made a substantial contribution to the defeat of the European Axis powers. (FRUS II 769)

July 10   Molotov Speech on Germany   Foreign Minister Molotov, at the Council of Foreign Ministers meeting in Paris, responded to the German treaty proposed by Secretary of State Byrnes on April 29. Molotov criticized the proposal and said the treaty would not promote the major objectives of the occupation. Molotov's speech indicated wide differences between the United States and the Soviet Union on the question of a German peace treaty. (DOGUO 144)

July 12   Paris Meeting Ends   The Council of Foreign Ministers ended its meeting in Paris after it succeeded in reaching a number of agreements. Trieste was made a free territory under the supervision of the United Nations, thereby at least temporarily resolving that issue. Italy had to yield its former colonies to the Big Four, who would try to reach an agreement on how to finally dispose of them. The ministers agreed on Italy's reparations to the Soviet Union, and peace treaties were completed for Bulgaria, Finland, Hungary, Italy, and Romania. (NYT 7/13/46 1)

July 15   Byrnes on Paris Meeting   Secretary of State Byrnes, in a speech before the opening of the Paris Peace Conference, declared that the recently concluded Council of Foreign Ministers meeting had resolved a number of issues. He was pleased with the agreements reached, but he chided the Soviet Union for its uncompromising attitude on many problems that divided the Soviet Union and the United States. He was critical of Moscow's rejection of his proposed treaty for Germany, saying that if such a treaty had existed earlier, both world wars could have been avoided. The secretary also expressed disappointment with the lack of progress in completing an Austrian peace treaty. (DSB 7/23/46 167)

July 29   The Paris Peace Conference   Representatives from the Big Five plus sixteen other nations met in Paris to discuss the peace treaties agreed to by the Council of Foreign Ministers the previous month. The sixteen other nations could suggest changes in the treaties for Bulgaria, Finland,

Hungary, Italy, and Romania, but the council was not compelled to accept the changes. The Paris Peace Conference concluded on October 15 after agreeing to treaties for each of those five defeated nations in World War II. (FRUS III 26)

August 7 *The Soviet Union and Turkey* The Soviet Union proposed to Turkey that a new regime be established for the Dardanelles Straits. The Soviets wanted to participate in the administration of the straits, and Moscow suggested that Turkey and the Soviet Union should "organize by joint means the defense of the straits." Moscow's proposal would have excluded the United States and the United Kingdom from participation in a new regime but would have included Romania and Bulgaria. By putting the straits under a joint Turkish-Soviet command, the Soviet Union would have been able to dominate the straits militarily and thereby endanger Turkey's security. Turkey, with the backing of the United States, rejected the Soviet proposal. (DSB 9/1/46 420)

August 12 *U.S. Concern Over Turkey* Ambassador Edwin Wilson sent a note to Secretary of State Byrnes suggesting that Turkey's independence had become a vital American national interest. The ambassador warned that Soviet domination of Turkey would enable the Soviet Union to extend its power toward the Persian Gulf and Suez. (FRUS VII 836)

September 6 *Speech by Byrnes* Secretary of State Byrnes in a speech in Stuttgart, Germany, broadcast to the German people, responded to the statements made by Foreign Minister Molotov on July 10. The secretary delivered a comprehensive analysis of American policy vis-à-vis Germany, specifying certain aims to be achieved. He called for the establishment of a German provisional government to enable the Germans to play a more active role in their own affairs, and he wanted the Ruhr and the Rhineland to remain a part of Germany. The secretary wished to increase Germany's level of production, and he proposed eliminating economic barriers between the German zones of occupation. He said the final decision on the German-Polish border would have to wait until a peace treaty for Germany was completed. The United States was willing, he said, to merge its zone with that of any other occupying power to help improve economic conditions. (DSB 9/15/46 496)

September 24 *Stalin Replies to Questions* Josef Stalin replied to questions put to him by Alexander Worth, a reporter for the *London Sunday Times.* When asked if the American monopoly of atomic weapons threatened the peace, Stalin said it did not. Atomic bombs, he said, could not decide the outcome of a war, nor did he believe the American monopoly would last much longer. (FRUS VI 784)

November 4   *Council of Foreign Ministers*   The third meeting of the Council of Foreign Ministers convened in New York. The principal function of the meeting was to complete peace treaties for Bulgaria, Finland, Hungary, Italy, and Romania. On December 12 the ministers gave final approval to treaties for each of those five nations. The treaties were to go into effect in September 1947. (FRUS II 988)

December 2   *The Berlin Fusion Agreement*   The United Kingdom and the United States signed an agreement to merge their zones in West Germany on January 1, 1947. The fusion agreement, creating a single zone called *Bizonia*, was intended as a first step leading to the economic unification of West Germany. (DOGUO 195)

December 3   *Greece Wants Investigation*   The Greek government requested the United Nations Security Council to investigate conditions on the northern frontier that Greece shared with Albania, Bulgaria, and Yugoslavia. The three communist countries were supporting the Greek rebels in their efforts to overthrow the government. Communist efforts to win control of the Greek government became a major source of friction between the United States and the Soviet Union. (FRUS VII 272)

December 12   *Iran and Azerbaijan*   The Iranian government regained control over Azerbaijan province. The following day, Ambassador George Allen, in a note to the State Department, attributed the collapse of the communist regime in Azerbaijan to the firm backing of the Teheran government by the United States. (FRUS VII 561)

1947

January 5 *Elections in Poland* The United States sent notes to the United Kingdom and the Soviet Union about the activities of the Polish government. The United States objected to the obstacles erected by the Polish authorities to hamper the electoral efforts of individuals not associated with the communists. The provisional government was accused of relying upon violence, including murder, to eliminate political opponents. These activities, Washington charged, violated the Yalta and Potsdam accords. (DSB 1/9/47 134)

January 6 *State of the Union* President Truman, in his State of the Union address, said that America's policies toward the Soviet Union were based on the same principles that applied to all nations. The president acknowledged differences between the United States and the Soviet Union, but he emphasized the need for cooperation between the two to complete peace treaties for Germany and Austria. (PP 9)

January 7 *Marshall Appointed Secretary of State* President Truman accepted the resignation of Secretary of State Byrnes. The president then nominated General George C. Marshall as his successor. He was confirmed by the Senate on January 8 and took the oath of office on January 21. (PP 12)

January 16 *The Soviets and Poland* An article in the Soviet publication *New Times* was critical of the United States for allegedly interfering in Poland's internal affairs. The article pointed out that the forthcoming elections were in keeping with the Potsdam agreement, and any changes in Poland's western frontier were categorically rejected. The United States contended that the border between Germany and Poland was temporary pending the completion of a German peace treaty. (NT 1/16/47 1)

January 21 *Elections in Poland* Ambassador Arthur Lane reported to Washington on the Polish elections conducted two days earlier. He said the claim made by the governing coalition that it won more than 80 percent of the votes was false. The nature of the Polish government became a contentious issue in Soviet-American relations. (FRUS IV 410)

March 5 *Bela Kovacs Arrested* The United States, in a note to the Soviet chairman of the Allied Control Commission for Hungary, protested the arrest of Bela Kovacs, the former secretary general of the Hungarian Smallholders party that won a majority of votes in the November 1945 elections. He was arrested by the Soviets because he had parliamentary immunity and therefore could not be detained by the Hungarian government. The United States wanted the Allied Control Commission, composed of representatives of the Big Three, to investigate the incident. According to American officials, by arresting Kovacs the Soviet Union was interfering in Hungary's internal affairs. On March 8 the Soviets rejected the American protest. (DIA 329)

March 12 *The Truman Doctrine* President Truman appeared before a joint session of Congress to announce what came to be known as the Truman Doctrine. His recommendations were a response to specific conditions in Greece and Turkey and the general deterioration of Soviet-American relations since 1945. The essence of his doctrine was the decision to provide economic and military assistance to those nations threatened by communism. Greece was in the throes of a civil war, and the insurgent forces there were supported by the communist regimes in Albania, Bulgaria, and Yugoslavia. Turkey was being pressed by the Soviet Union to bring the Dardanelles under some form of joint Soviet-Turkish control, and Moscow was demanding the return of territory lost to Turkey by the czars. In his message, the president emphasized the ideological dimension of the conflict: "Totalitarian regimes imposed on free peoples, by direct or indirect aggression, undermine the foundations of international peace and hence the security of the United States." In May President Truman's request for $400 million to aid Greece and Turkey was approved by Congress. (PP 176)

March 21 *Marshall and Germany* Secretary of State Marshall, at the meeting of the Council of Foreign Ministers that convened in Moscow on March 10, proposed establishing a provisional German government. He thought a central government was necessary to cope with the national problems outside the authority of the individual German states. He said a written constitution protecting political parties, free elections, and freedom of speech, religion, and assembly was necessary. The Soviets rejected Marshall's proposal. (DSB 3/30/47 569)

May 22 *Truman Doctrine Criticized* Elbridge Durbar, the American *chargé d'affaires* in Moscow, reported on the Soviet propaganda offensive against Truman's proposal to aid Greece and Turkey. The Soviet campaign, according to Durbar, was particularly vicious; the people were told that American capitalists had maintained contacts with German businesspeople during World War II and that the capitalists were now planning for a new war. The Soviets charged that American aid was extended to needy nations to eventually subjugate them. (FRUS IV 562)

June 5 *The Marshall Plan* Secretary of State Marshall, in a speech at Harvard University, presented the administration's proposal to help meet the needs of war-devastated Europe: the Marshall Plan, or as it was officially entitled, the European Recovery Program. American policy, Marshall said, was not directed against any country or doctrine, and he opposed giving aid on a piecemeal basis; a comprehensive plan was necessary. Finally, he warned that any country that sought to block the economic recovery of other countries would not receive assistance. (DSB 6/15/47 1159)

July 2 *Molotov on the Marshall Plan* Foreign Minister Molotov announced in Paris that the Soviet Union would not participate in the Marshall Plan. The Soviet decision contributed to the division of Europe. (DIA 51)

July (no date) *The Mr. X Article* *Foreign Affairs* published an article by George Kennan entitled "Sources of Soviet Conduct." For a brief period the authorship was unknown because Kennan signed the article with the letter X. Some of the article was based on Kennan's February 22, 1946, "long telegram." The article helped legitimate President Truman's efforts to contain the Soviet Union. (FA 7/47)

August 26 *Unification of Korea* The United States, in a note to the Soviet Union, presented a seven-point proposal designed to bring about the unification of Korea. The United States suggested holding elections in Korea before establishing a provisional government. On September 4, Foreign Minister Molotov rejected the American proposal. (DIA 693)

August 30 *U.S. Note on Petkov* The United States, in a note to the Soviet Union, protested the death sentence given to Nikola Petkov on August 16. He was the leader of the Agrarian Union party in Bulgaria. In particular, Washington rejected the Soviet position that his case was a Bulgarian internal affair. The United States charged that Petkov's arrest and the dissolution of his Agrarian Union political party violated the Yalta agreements and was therefore a proper concern to the signatories of those agreements. At the time, the Soviet Union was in the process of eliminating all opposition to communist rule in Eastern Europe. (FRUS IV 178)

September 18 *Vishinsky at the UN* Deputy Foreign Minister Andrei Vishinsky, in an address to the United Nations General Assembly in support of a Soviet-sponsored resolution on "warmongering," specifically charged the United States, Turkey, and Greece with engaging in "criminal propaganda for a new war." He criticized the Truman Doctrine and the Marshall Plan, and he accused the United States of engaging in an arms race. He said West Germany was being used by the United States to expand America's power in Europe, and he criticized Secretary of State Marshall for alleging that Soviet allies were supporting the communist rebels in Greece. (VS XIII:24 741)

September 25 *Protest on Behalf of Truman* Ambassador Walter Bedell Smith delivered a letter to Foreign Secretary Molotov protesting the anti-American statements in the Soviet press. Smith particularly objected to the "libelous" attack on President Truman contained in an article in *Literaturnaya Gazeta* written by Boris Gorbatov in which he compared President Truman to Adolph Hitler. On September 28 the Soviets rejected the American protest. (FRUS IV 588)

October 5 *Cominform Established* *Pravda* announced that representatives of the Communist parties of Bulgaria, Czechoslovakia, France, Hungary, Italy, Poland, Romania, the Soviet Union, and Yugoslavia met in Poland from September 21 to September 28. They agreed to establish a Communist Information Bureau (the Cominform), which the Soviet Union used as an instrument to dominate the policies of the Eastern European satellites and Communist parties throughout Europe. (NYT 10/6/47 1)

October 5 *Cominform Manifesto* The Cominform nations issued a manifesto declaring that the United Kingdom and the United States wanted Germany and Japan defeated in World War II to eliminate them as economic competitors. London and Washington were accused of supporting imperialism, opposing democracy, and preparing for another war. The manifesto urged Communist parties everywhere to take the lead in opposing U.S. policies on as many fronts as possible. Left-wing political parties, such as the socialists, were denounced as tools of the capitalists. Following the publication of the manifesto, many left-wing noncommunist political leaders in Eastern Europe were arrested and executed. (DAFR 623)

October 21 *Balkan Committee Established* The United Nations General Assembly voted to establish a Special Committee on the Balkans to help resolve the conflicts between Greece and its three communist neighbors, Albania, Bulgaria, and Yugoslavia. The Soviet Union voted against the resolution; the United States supported it. (DIA 320)

October 22 *Warmongers Criticized* Deputy Foreign Minister Vishinsky, in an address to the Political and Security Committee of the United Nations General Assembly, again criticized American "warmongers." He cited, among others, Secretary of Defense James Forrestal, Secretary of Commerce Averell Harriman, and former secretary of state James

Byrnes. He berated the magazines *Field Artillery Journal* and *Successful Farming* for recent articles the Soviets found objectionable. (NYT 10/23/47 1)

October 22   The Zhdanov Two-Camp Theory   *Pravda* published the contents of a speech given by Andrei Zhdanov, a member of the Soviet Politburo, at the conference establishing the Cominform. According to Zhdanov, the world was divided into two camps, the imperialist and the anti-imperialist. All nations were in one camp or the other, thus there could be no neutrality. He urged communists to oppose U.S. imperialism in the form of the Marshall Plan, calling it an instrument to make Europe the forty-ninth state. (FRUS IV 597)

November 6   The U.S. Criticized   Foreign Minister Molotov, in a speech in celebration of the thirtieth anniversary of the October 1917 revolution, accused the United States of being an imperialist power seeking to expand its control over other nations by giving economic assistance and establishing military bases. In contrast, he said the Soviet Union was committed to a policy of peace. (VS XIV:3 73)

December 19   The London Conference   Secretary of State Marshall, in an address to the American people on the results of the Council of Foreign Ministers meeting in London from November 25 to December 15, said the negotiators were unable to agree on peace treaties for Germany and Austria. The secretary labeled the results of the conference "disappointing," and he accused the Soviet Union of wanting to retain control over East Germany. (DSB 12/28/47 1244)

1948

January 3 *U.S. and Iran* Robert Lovett, the acting secretary of state, told Ambassador George Allen to inform the Iranian government that the United States considered Iran as important to American security interests as Greece and Turkey. At the time, Iran, Greece, and Turkey were coping with different types of communist threats, but only Greece and Turkey were included in the Truman Doctrine. As a result, Iran feared renewed Soviet pressure. (FRUS V 88)

January 7 *State of the Union* President Truman, in his State of the Union address, emphasized the growing interdependence of nations. When any nation loses its independence, he said, that affects the United States. To keep America militarily strong, he asked Congress to approve a universal military training bill, and he urged the lawmakers to authorize funds for the European Recovery Program. (PP 7)

January 17 *U.S. Aid and Military Bases* Secretary of State Marshall issued a statement refuting the charge, frequently made by the Soviet Union, that there was a relationship between the United States granting economic aid to European allies and those allies giving military base rights to the United States. (DSB 1/25/48 115)

February 13 *Soviets Protest London Meeting* The Soviet Union, in notes to France, the United Kingdom, and the United States, protested the decision to convene a meeting later in the month in London to discuss the future of Germany. The Soviets argued that any agreement pertaining to occupation policies in Germany not agreed to by the four occupying powers would violate the Potsdam agreement. On February 21 the United States rejected the Soviet protest. (DIA 554)

February 23 *The London Conference* Because the Soviet Union and the Western powers were not making any progress in completing a German peace treaty, France, the United Kingdom, and the United States convened a meeting of their foreign ministers in London to explore solutions pertaining to the division of Germany and to discuss European security issues. On the first day of the meeting, an invitation was extended to the Benelux nations to join the negotiations; they did so on February 26. (DSB 3/21/48 380)

February 25 *The Czech Coup* A new government was formed in Czechoslovakia and, in what amounted to a coup d'état, the communists removed all their rivals from political power. The coup proved that the Soviet Union was unwilling to tolerate a coalition government, though it was dominated by the communists. The coup was a major event in the cold war, and the actions of the Czech communists, as dictated by Stalin, helped persuade the Senate and House of Representatives to pass the Marshall Plan and the Senate to adopt the Vandenberg Resolution, which supported the establishment of a collective European defense pact. (FRUS IV 736)

February 26 *The Czech Coup Protested* The British, French, and American governments issued a joint declaration condemning the February 25 communist coup in Czechoslovakia. (FRUS IV 738)

March 20 *Soviets Quit Allied Control Council* The Soviet Union, in protest against the decisions taken at the London conference, withdrew from the Allied Control Council created at the Yalta Conference for governing Germany after its surrender. The control council consisted of the supreme commanders representing France, the United Kingdom, the Soviet Union, and the United States. The withdrawal of the Soviet Union in effect ended any hope for a quadripartite control system as envisioned in the Potsdam agreement. (DIA 574)

March 27 *Norway Accused* The Soviet newspaper *Izvestia* accused Norway of planning to lease military bases to the United States. (NYT 3/28/48 1)

March 28 *Soviets Accuse Sweden* Newspapers in the Soviet Union accused Sweden of building military bases to be used by the United States. (NYT 3/29/48 1)

April 3 *The Marshall Plan* President Truman signed into law the European Recovery Program (the Marshall Plan). (PP 203)

April 3 *Greece and the Italian Elections* Robert Lovett, the acting secretary of state, recommended to the American embassy in Greece that the government there should be encouraged to consider announcing its intention not to accept any more reparations from Italy. American officials felt that such a policy would help the democratic forces in the forthcoming Italian elections. The United States had information that the Soviet Union was considering renouncing reparations to assist the Italian Communist party. (FRUS IV 68)

April 18 *Italian Elections* Elections were held in Italy, and the Christian Democratic party won a majority of seats in the Chamber of Deputies and won the largest bloc of seats in the Senate. The communists and their allies won about 30 percent of the seats in both chambers, fewer than expected. The United States considered the victory of the Christian Democratic party over the communists a major advance for democracy in Italy. (NYT 4/20/48 1)

April 29 *Smith to Meet Molotov* Secretary of State Marshall instructed Ambassador Walter Bedell Smith to seek a meeting with Foreign Minister Molotov to inform him about American foreign policy objectives. The Soviets were expected to alter their policies because of the passage of the European Recovery Program earlier in the month and the defeat of the Italian Communist party in the April elections. Smith was instructed to warn the Soviet minister against any acts of aggression and to assure him the United States had no hostile intentions vis-à-vis the Soviet Union. (FRUS IV 840)

May 2 *Support for Soviet Policies* The Soviet journal *Literaturnaya Gazeta* printed a letter from thirty-two American artists expressing support for Soviet foreign policies. (NYT 5/3/48 1)

May 4 *Smith Meets Molotov* Ambassador Walter Bedell Smith met with Foreign Minister Molotov to discuss Soviet-American relations. The ambassador charged the Soviet Union with a number of offenses, including violating agreements reached during World War II regarding Eastern Europe. He accused the Soviets of seeking to expand their power while at the same time interfering in the internal affairs of nations aligned with the United States. Ambassador Smith said American policies were basically defensive, were supported by the American people, and did not threaten the Soviet Union. The policies the Soviets objected to, said Smith, were often nothing more than a reaction to Soviet activities in various parts of the world. (FRUS IV 845)

May 9 *Molotov Responds to Smith* Foreign Minister Molotov responded to the May 4 statement of Ambassador Smith. Molotov denied the charges made by the American ambassador, and the foreign minister defended what he termed the "resurgence of democratic forces" in Eastern Europe after the defeat of Germany. He accused the United States of being responsible for Soviet-American tensions. (FRUS IV 851)

May 11 *Molotov and Smith* *New Times,* a Soviet journal, published the exchange of views between Ambassador Smith and Foreign Minister Molotov. American officials had assumed the exchange of views would be considered confidential. (NT SUPPLEMENT 5/26/48 1)

May 11 *Wallace Letter to Stalin* Henry Wallace, the former secretary of commerce in the Truman administration, wrote an open letter to Josef Stalin. Wallace was one of the leaders of the left-wing Democrats that believed President Truman was betraying the ideals of Franklin Roosevelt. Wallace and his supporters assumed that Stalin was eager to have good relations with the United States but, they charged, the Truman administration was hostile toward the Soviet Union. In his letter,

Wallace called for an end to the cold war, and he listed steps that both countries could take to achieve that result. (DIA 160)

May 12   Reason for Soviet Disclosure   Members of the State Department's policy planning staff evaluated the Soviet decision to make public the record of the Smith-Molotov talks. The staff concluded that the actions of the Soviet Union indicated it was more interested in scoring a propaganda victory than in seriously attempting to resolve Soviet-American differences. (FRUS IV 865)

May 24   Forced Labor   The United States charged the Soviet Union with kidnapping people for forced labor. The United States estimated that twenty-five thousand to thirty thousand East Germans had been kidnapped to work in uranium mines in East Germany and ten thousand Czechs had been kidnapped to work in uranium mines in Czechoslovakia. (NYT 5/26/48 3)

May 28   Marshall on Democracy   Secretary of State Marshall, in a speech in Portland, Oregon, criticized the Soviets for distorting facts, events, and communications. He referred to the recent diplomatic exchange between Ambassador Walter Bedell Smith and Foreign Minister Molotov. Marshall said the Soviet Union, without consulting the United States, not only made the diplomatic exchange public but also edited it for propaganda reasons. (DSB 6/6/48 744)

June 6   Soviet Treaty Violations   The *Department of State Bulletin* published a list of Soviet violations of international agreements, including those pertaining to Austria, Bulgaria, Germany, Hungary, Korea, Manchuria, Poland, and Romania. The list was made public because of a Senate inquiry. (DSB 6/6/48 738)

June 7   London Conference Communiqué   Six days after the close of the London conference on West Germany that began on February 23, the Western foreign ministers issued a communiqué describing agreements that had been reached. France, the United Kingdom, and the United States decided to lay the foundations for a unified West German state with more control given to an elected German government after the approval of a constitution. Agreements were also reached with respect to the occupation rights to be retained by the three Western powers after a West German government was organized. Finally, there was a separate agreement on international control of the Ruhr. The London agreements led to the creation of West Germany in September 1949. (DSB 6/20/48 807)

June 11   *The Vandenberg Resolution* The United States Senate passed the Vandenberg Resolution by a 64-to-4 margin. Senator Arthur Vandenberg, the Republican chairman of the foreign relations committee, introduced his resolution because President Truman needed bipartisan backing for his foreign policies after the Republicans won control of Congress in 1946. With the passage of the resolution, the president could be more confident that if the United States joined a military alliance, the Senate would recommend ratification of the treaty. (DSB 7/18/48 79)

June 12   *Truman on Foreign Policy* President Truman, in an address in California, criticized the Soviet Union for its rejection of the Marshall Plan, excessive use of the veto in the United Nations Security Council, indirect aggression in Eastern Europe, and interfering in the internal affairs of nations. The president outlined steps the United States had taken since World War II to achieve peace, including a plan for controlling atomic energy, various economic assistance programs, and support for the United Nations. (PP 336)

June 22   *Western Currency in Berlin* The British, French, and American commandants in Berlin announced that they intended to introduce a new currency to be distributed in West Berlin. (DOG 1944-1959 446)

June 24   *The Berlin Blockade* Soviet forces implemented a blockade of Berlin halting all railroad traffic, the major means of transporting food and fuel into the city. The blockade was a response to the Western currency reform announced on June 22, the decisions taken at the London conference earlier in the month that established the foundation for West Germany, and the Soviet desire to drive the three Western powers out of Berlin. (NYT 6/24/48 1)

June 24   *The Soviet Bloc Ministers* The foreign ministers from the eight Soviet bloc nations attended a conference in Warsaw to forge a unified reply to the agreements reached at the six-power London conference pertaining to Germany. They issued a communiqué that, among other things, accused France, the United Kingdom, and the United States of wanting to keep Germany divided while at the same time rebuilding West Germany's military might. (DIA 566)

June 25   *Clay on Blockade* General Lucius Clay, the U.S. military governor for Germany, suggested to Washington that a military convoy be sent from West Germany to West Berlin to break the Soviet blockade. Clay did not think the Soviets would challenge the convoy. (FRUS II 917)

June 26   *Berlin Airlift* The United States announced that an expanded airlift would begin to carry food and supplies into Berlin. The airlift became the major instrument for supplying the people of Berlin with the necessities of life during the course of the blockade. (DOG 1944-1959 447)

July 1 *The Allied Kommandatura* The Soviets announced their withdrawal from the Allied Kommandatura, and it then ceased to function as the four-power instrument for governing Berlin. (DIA 585)

July 6 *Note to Soviets on Berlin* France, the United Kingdom, and the United States, in identical notes to the Soviet Union, objected to the Berlin blockade and the dangerous situation created because of it. The Soviets were reminded that the Western powers rejected the claim that West Berlin was a part of the Soviet zone of occupation. They expressed a willingness to negotiate differences with the Soviet Union but not until the blockade was lifted. (FRUS II 959)

July 14 *Soviets Respond to Protest on Berlin* The Soviet Union, in notes to France, the United Kingdom, and the United States, insisted that Berlin was within the Soviet zone of occupation. The three Western powers were told they had no rights in Berlin because their policies violated the 1945 Potsdam agreement on Germany. (DIA 589)

July 14 *Soviet Plan for Korea* Ambassador Walter Bedell Smith notified Washington that the Soviet Union was in the process of establishing a government in North Korea, and the decision would not be influenced by anything the United Nations Temporary Commission on Korea might do pertaining to South Korea. (FRUS VI 1240)

July 30 *Aide-Mémoire to the Soviets* Ambassador Smith, along with his British and French counterparts, delivered an aide-mémoire to the Soviet government dealing with the Berlin issue. The United States rejected the Soviet contention that the three Western powers no longer had occupation rights in Berlin. Smith requested that Molotov and Stalin meet with the American, British, and French ambassadors to discuss the Berlin situation. (FRUS II 995)

August 3 *Smith Meets with Stalin* Secretary of State Marshall received a report from Ambassador Smith on his meeting with Josef Stalin and Foreign Minister Molotov to discuss the Berlin crisis. The British and French ambassadors also attended the meeting. Smith told Stalin that the three Western powers were in Berlin by right, and they intended to remain there. He said the Western Big Three were eager to resolve differences with the Soviet Union, but no negotiations could take place while the blockade remained in effect. (FRUS II 998)

August 6 *Smith Meets with Molotov* Ambassador Smith and the British and French ambassadors met with Foreign Minister Molotov to discuss details of a possible agreement on Berlin. They presented Molotov with a revised draft agreement based on discussions during the meeting with Stalin on August 2. At the close of the meeting, Molotov said he wanted to draw up a counterproposal, which he would then present to the three Western powers. (FRUS II 1018)

August 9 *Western Proposal Rejected* The Soviet Union rejected the proposal on Berlin put forward by France, the United Kingdom, and the United States on August 6. Foreign Minister Molotov suggested a partial lifting of the blockade, the acceptance of the Soviet currency throughout Berlin, a delay in implementing the London conference decisions, and a four-power meeting to discuss Berlin and German issues. (FRUS II 1024)

August 12 *Meeting with Molotov* The ambassadors from France, the United Kingdom, and the United States again met with Foreign Minister Molotov, and they rejected the proposals he put forth at the August 9 meeting. Ambassador Smith insisted that the three Western powers had juridical rights in Berlin that could not be terminated by the Soviet Union. (FRUS II 1035)

August 16 *Meeting with Molotov* Ambassador Smith reported to Washington on the meeting he and his British and French counterparts had with Foreign Minister Molotov concerning Berlin. Smith said he consistently emphasized two points. First was that the Western powers were in Berlin by right and not at the sufferance of the Soviet Union, and second was that the decisions taken at the London conference would not be suspended or delayed. Molotov rejected the position of the Western powers and insisted they had no juridical rights in Berlin. After the meeting with Molotov, Ambassador Smith was instructed to seek another meeting with Josef Stalin. (FRUS II 1042)

August 23 *Meeting with Stalin* Ambassador Smith, along with the British and French ambassadors, met with Josef Stalin and Foreign Minister Molotov to discuss Berlin issues. A tentative agreement between the two sides was reached regarding the currency issue, but the arrangements for its implementation were to be worked out by the military governors in Berlin. Smith said he would have to consult with Washington to determine if the agreement were acceptable. (FRUS II 1065)

August 27 *Berlin Directive* Ambassador Smith, along with his French and British counterparts, met with Foreign Minister Molotov. They agreed on a directive regarding the Berlin crisis based on the preliminary agreement reached on August 23 but left the four military governors in Berlin with the responsibility for reaching a detailed agreement based on the principles agreed to in Moscow. (FRUS II 1085)

September 7 *Disagreement on Berlin* The four military governors in Berlin announced they could not reach an agreement based on the August 27 directive. (NYT 9/8/48 1)

September 12 *The Berlin Negotiations* Washington instructed Ambassador Smith to seek another meeting with Molotov or Stalin to present an aide-mémoire regarding the Berlin negotiations. (FRUS II 1151)

September 14 *Disagreement on Berlin* The ambassadors from France, the United Kingdom, and the United States delivered an aide-mémoire to the Soviet government regarding negotiations conducted by the four military governors in Berlin. The Western powers said that Marshal Vasiliy Sokolovsky, the Soviet military governor, had deviated from the principles agreed to in Moscow on August 27. (FRUS II 1152)

September 18 *Soviet Aide-Mémoire on Berlin* The Soviet Union responded to the September 14 aide-mémoire from the Western Big Three. The Soviets said it was the Western military governors in Berlin who had deviated from the principles agreed to in Moscow on August 27, not the Soviet military governor. Ambassador Smith believed the Soviet response indicated that Moscow was no longer interested in resolving the Berlin problem. (FRUS II 1162)

September 22 *The Berlin Negotiations* France, the United Kingdom, and the United States responded to the September 18 Soviet aide-mémoire. The Western nations said the differences between the two sides on the Berlin issues involved principles rather than technical disagreements. The Western nations insisted on knowing whether the Soviets were prepared to lift the blockade. They were not. (FRUS II 1180)

September 25 *Vishinsky Criticizes the U.S.* Deputy Foreign Minister Andrei Vishinsky, in an address to the United Nations General Assembly, said the United States "is now attempting to realize plans for world domination." He accused President Truman of changing America's policy from one of fighting fascism to one of supporting fascist regimes. According to Vishinsky, the United States had become an expansionist power with a "true worship of the atom bomb. . . ." (VS XV:2 38)

September 25 *Soviets and Berlin* The Soviet Union rejected the positions taken by the three Western powers in their September 22 note regarding Berlin. The Soviets said the Western powers had to assume responsibility for the failure to resolve the Berlin problems. (FRUS II 1181)

September 29 *Berlin and the UN* France, the United Kingdom, and the United States sent identical letters to the secretary general of the United Nations informing him that the Berlin situation constituted a threat to world peace as defined in Chapter VII of the United Nations Charter. The Western powers requested that the Berlin issue be taken up by the Security Council as quickly as possible. (DIA 611)

October 3 *The Soviets and Berlin* The Soviet Union responded to the decision of the three Western powers to take the Berlin issue to the United Nations. The Soviets said the United Nations lacked jurisdiction regarding the issue and recommended instead convening a meeting of the Council of Foreign Ministers. (DIA 610)

November 6 *Molotov Speech* Foreign Minister Molotov, in a speech to Communist party officials in Moscow, accused the Western nations of preparing for another war and said that war had been avoided only because of the power of the Soviet Union and the nations of Eastern Europe. He accused the United States of not wanting to eliminate atomic weapons and of violating treaties negotiated during World War II. (DIA 147)

November 13 *War Preparations* Soviet Deputy Foreign Minister Andrei Vishinsky, in an address to the United Nations General Assembly's Political Committee, accused the United States of preparing an attack against the Soviet Union similar to that on Pearl Harbor. (NYT 11/14/48 4)

November 27 *UN Balkan Resolution* The United Nations General Assembly approved a resolution introduced by China, France, the United Kingdom, and the United States on October 26 calling on Albania, Bulgaria, and Yugoslavia to cooperate with the Special Commission on the Balkans, established in October 1947, to better enable it to carry out its mandate. The three communist nations were supporting the communist insurgency in Greece. The Soviet Union opposed the resolution. (DSB 12/5/48 696)

December 5 *Elections in West Berlin* Elections were held in West Berlin, and they proved to be a test of strength between communists and noncommunists. In spite of the communists' opposition to holding the elections and encouragement to their supporters not to participate, more than 85 percent of the eligible voters cast ballots. The Social Democratic party received approximately two-thirds of the vote. (FRUS II 1276)

1949

January 4 *Prisoners of War* The State Department released to the press the contents of a note to the Soviet Union inquiring about German prisoners of war still being held by the Soviet Union. At the April 1947 Council of Foreign Ministers meeting, the participants agreed that prisoners of war should be repatriated by December 1948. France, the United Kingdom, and the United States had complied with the deadline but, allegedly, not the Soviet Union. (DSB 1/16/49 77)

January 5 *State of the Union* President Truman, in his State of the Union address, committed the nation to a strong military posture in defense of peace. He called on Congress to pass a universal military training bill, and he said he was satisfied that aid to Greece and Turkey was being used well. (PP 6)

January 7 *Acheson Appointed Secretary of State* President Truman announced that Dean Acheson would succeed George Marshall as secretary of state. On January 18 Acheson was confirmed by the Senate, and on January 21 he took the oath of office. (PP 9)

January 15 *Soviet Peace Offensive* Foy Kohler, the American *chargé* in Moscow, reported to Washington on a "peace campaign" then being carried out by the Soviet Union. A basic theme of the campaign was America's responsibility for bringing about the cold war and pursuing policies that increased international tensions. The peace campaign emphasized the willingness of Stalin to meet with President Truman to resolve Soviet-American differences. (FRUS V 556)

January 24 *Soviets and Prisoners of War* The Soviet Union responded to the American request made on January 3 for information about prisoners of war. The Soviets refused to supply the information requested, but they did say that all prisoners would be repatriated by December 1949. The Soviets alleged that prisoners of war located in the Western-controlled zones of Germany were not repatriated as they should have been. (DSB 3/27/49 389)

January 30 *Stalin Replies to Questions* Josef Stalin responded to a number of questions put to him by J. Kingsbury Smith, the European general manager of the International News Service. In response to a question regarding Berlin, the Soviet leader said nothing about the currency issue, leading observers to believe he might be interested in resolving the Berlin problem. (FRUS V 562)

February 15 *Labor Camps* The United States introduced a resolution in the United Nations Economic and Social Council (ECOSOC) charging the Soviet Union with using slave labor. American officials estimated that between eight million and fourteen million people were being used as slave laborers. The resolution called for an investigation of labor conditions in the Soviet Union. The Soviets announced they would not cooperate with any commission created by the United Nations to study the allegation. (NYT 2/16/49 1)

March 4 *Molotov Replaced* Radio Moscow announced that Andrei Vishinsky was the new foreign minister replacing Viacheslav Molotov. (FRUS V 584)

March 24 *Soviets Deny Slave Labor Charge* *Pravda* denounced the United States for accusing the Soviet Union of using slave labor. In addition to denying the allegation, made at the ECOSOC meeting on February 15, the article accused the United States of using slave labor. (CDSP I:12 32)

April 1 *Soviets Protest NATO* The Soviet Union, in anticipation of the signing of the NATO treaty, sent notes of protest to Belgium, Canada, France, the United Kingdom, Luxembourg, the Netherlands, and the United States charging that NATO was an aggressive military alliance directed at the Soviet Union and the nations of Eastern Europe. The Soviets alleged that NATO violated the principles of the United Nations Charter and the 1945 Potsdam and Yalta agreements. (DAFR 607)

April 2 *NATO Foreign Ministers Meet* The foreign ministers of the twelve NATO nations met in Washington in preparation for the signing of the treaty. They agreed to issue a statement rebutting the Soviet assertion made on April 1 that NATO was an aggressive military alliance. (FRUS IV 271)

April 4 *Truman on NATO* President Truman signed the treaty creating the NATO military alliance. He said the alliance was in keeping with the United Nations Charter, was basically defensive in character, and was an instrument designed to prevent aggression. (DAFR 609)

April 20 *World Peace Congress* The World Congress of Partisans for Peace, a communist-front organization working in support of Stalin's peace offensive against the West, met in Paris for five days. Delegates from more than forty countries attended the congress. Paul Robeson, the leader of the American delegation, said African Americans would not participate in a war against the Soviet Union. (FRUS V 826)

April 20 *Kirk to the Soviet Union* President Truman selected Vice Admiral Alan G. Kirk to be ambassador to the Soviet Union. He replaced Walter

Bedell Smith, who had resigned in March. Kirk was confirmed by the Senate on May 20. (FRUS V 631)

April 21 *U.S. Reacts to Peace Congress* Michael J. McDermott, a State Department press officer, expressed the official U.S. position on the World Peace Congress meeting in Paris. He said the congress was used to support the Soviet campaign depicting the Soviet Union as favoring peace and the Western nations as being the cause of world tensions. (FRUS V 827)

May 4 *Four-Power Communiqué* France, the United Kingdom, the United States, and the Soviet Union issued a communiqué declaring that the Berlin blockade would be lifted on or before May 12 and a meeting of the Council of Foreign Ministers would convene in Paris on May 23. The Soviet effort to drive the Western powers out of Berlin had failed. (DSB 5/15/49 631)

May 16 *Acheson on Iran* Secretary of State Acheson wrote to Ambassador John Wiley on the subject of Soviet intentions vis-à-vis Iran. The ambassador feared the Soviets might seize the northern provinces of Iran, but Acheson did not think so because the Soviets realized such an action might lead to a war with the United States. He expected the Soviets to continue using tactics they had employed in the past to frighten the Teheran government into making concessions. (FRUS VI 519)

May 23 *Council of Foreign Ministers* The sixth meeting of the Council of Foreign Ministers convened in Paris to discuss problems pertaining to Berlin, Germany, and Austria. (FRUS III 915)

May 31 *Note to Soviets on Human Rights* The United States delivered a note to the Soviet Union stating that a dispute existed about the human rights provisions of the treaties of peace with Bulgaria, Hungary, and Romania. The United States was invoking those parts of each of the three treaties concerning controversies over interpretation. The note was sent to the Soviet Union because it was one of the signatories to each of the treaties. (FRUS V 247)

June 20 *Foreign Ministers Communiqué* At the conclusion of the Council of Foreign Ministers meeting in Paris, the ministers issued a communiqué on the negotiations carried out concerning Berlin and peace treaties for Germany and Austria. Deputies of the Big Four were given the responsibility of reaching an agreement on an Austrian peace treaty no later than September 1, 1949. The foreign ministers agreed to continue their discussions on a German peace treaty while attending the fourth session of the United Nations General Assembly scheduled to be convened in September. The ministers of the Western powers made little progress in reconciling their differences with the Soviet Union. (DSB 7/4/49 857)

July 1 *Human Rights Violations* The United States sent notes to Bulgaria, Hungary, and Romania charging each of them with violating the peace treaties signed after World War II. The United States invoked the relevant treaty articles for the settling of disputes. (DSB 7/11/49 29)

July 10 *Agents in East Germany* The *New York Times* reported that an American radio program beamed to East Germany identified individuals by name and address who were thought to be Soviet agents. (NYT 7/10/49 1)

July 13 *The Greek-Yugoslav Border Closed* Ambassador Cavendish Cannon reported to Washington that Yugoslavia had announced the closing of the Greek-Yugoslav border. This meant the Greek communists were no longer receiving aid from the Tito government. (FRUS VI 368)

July 19 *Truman on Foreign Policy* President Truman, in a speech in Chicago, compared the making of foreign policy in democratic and communist regimes. He pointed out that in a democracy policies must have the support of the people. He expressed confidence that in the long run the appeal of democracy would spread around the world and communism would be defeated. (PP 385)

August 14 *Budapest Youth Festival* The Budapest Youth Festival convened in Hungary and was attended by representatives from more than eighty nations. The purpose of the festival was to win support for Soviet foreign policies and to criticize those of the United States. (FRUS V 836)

September 21 *West Germany Established* The Federal Republic of Germany was officially established. (DSB 10/3/49 512)

September 23 *Soviet Resolution on War* Foreign Minister Vishinsky introduced a resolution to the United Nations General Assembly criticizing the United Kingdom and the United States for allegedly preparing for a new war. The resolution, a reaction to the establishment of NATO, condemned preparations for war, favored abolishing atomic weapons, and proposed that the permanent members of the Security Council negotiate a peace pact. (FRUS II 88)

September 23 *Truman Statement on Atomic Bomb* President Truman issued a statement informing the American people that the Soviet Union had tested an atomic bomb. On September 25 the Soviet Union announced that it had the atomic bomb but still favored abolishing all atomic weapons. (DIA 189)

October 1 *Soviets Protest on West Germany* The Soviet Union, in a note to the United States, protested the creation of the West German state. The Soviets said the United States had violated the Potsdam agreement and decisions taken at the Paris meeting of the Council of Foreign Ministers in May and June 1949. (DSB 10/17/49 590)

October 6 *U.S. Rejects Soviet Protest* James Webb, the under secretary of state, issued a statement rejecting the protests by the Soviet Union in its October 1 note regarding the West German state. (DSB 10/17/49 590)

October 8 *German Democratic Republic* The German Democratic Republic formally came into being, although the Soviet Union continued to exercise control over the government. (NYT 10/8/49 1)

October 16 *The Greek Civil War* The communist forces in Greece announced they were suspending military operations against the Greek government. The suspension was in part attributable to President Tito's decision to cease aiding the rebels after Yugoslavia's expulsion from the Cominform in 1948. (FRUS VI 434)

October 17 *Acheson on Greek Civil War* Secretary of State Acheson issued a statement asserting that the rebel cease-fire announcement in Greece reflected existing military conditions. For the first time since the civil war began, said Acheson, the Greek government controlled the northern borders of the country. Acheson accused the communist insurgents of having resorted "to every crime against humanity including murder and arson. . . ." (DSB 10/31/49 658)

October 24 *London Meeting of Diplomats* A number of State Department officials and the American chiefs of mission to the Eastern European countries met in London for a two-day conference. They discussed a number of policies to be followed regarding the satellite countries and Tito's break with Moscow. The officials agreed that a major American goal should be the "reduction and eventual elimination" of Soviet control over the Eastern European nations. (FRUS V 28)

November 6 *Malenkov Speech* Georgy Malenkov, a member of the Soviet Politburo, in an address to leaders of the Communist party in Moscow, accused the United States of using the Marshall Plan and NATO as instruments in preparation for another war. He praised the militancy of the Soviet-sponsored peace movement, emphasizing that it rejected pacifism as a basis for peace. He blamed the imperialist powers for beginning both world wars, and he asserted that capitalism would collapse should there be a third world war. (DIA 129)

November 14 *U.S. Responds to Soviet Proposal* Warren Austin, an American delegate at the United Nations, responded to the Soviet proposal for a five-power peace pact made on September 23. He did not think the Soviet proposal could be taken seriously considering its past record. He mentioned the Soviet alliance with Nazi Germany and the nonaggression pacts signed with Finland, Latvia, Estonia, and Lithuania. Austin suggested that if the Soviet Union were genuinely interested in peace, Moscow could halt the "hate campaign" directed at Western nations, particularly the United States. (DAFR 650)

November 29 *Cominform Communiqué* Radio Moscow broadcast a communiqué issued by the Cominform after a meeting in Hungary. The broadcast reaffirmed the Zhdanov line, first formulated in October 1947, as well as the thesis that the United Kingdom and the United States were preparing for another war. The Cominform members agreed to intensify the peace campaign throughout the world. (DAFR 652)

December 1 *Soviet Peace Plan Rejected* The United Nations General Assembly rejected the September 23 Soviet proposal to have the permanent members of the Security Council sign a peace pact. Concurrently, the General Assembly approved a British-American resolution that contained a number of principles intended to help ease international tensions. (DSB 1/2/50 5)

December 9 *The Soviet Peace Offensive* The Department of State prepared a study on the Soviet peace offensive. The study traced the background of the offensive, listed communist-dominated meetings that had been held in support of the peace drive, and enumerated basic themes contained in Soviet propaganda. (FRUS V 839)

December 21 *Molotov on Foreign Policy* Viacheslav Molotov, a member of the Politburo, at a celebration for Stalin's birthday, accused the United Kingdom and the United States of preparing for another war as a way of coping with their economic crises. (CDSP I:52 6)

December 30 *Japanese Prisoners of War* Secretary of State Acheson, in a note to the Soviet Union, sought its agreement to establish an international committee to investigate the question of Japanese prisoners of war still held by the Soviet Union. The Soviets said they held 95,000 Japanese as prisoners, but the Japanese government put the figure at more than 375,000. The Soviets rejected Acheson's proposal. (DSB 1/16/50 102)

1950

January 2 *Soviets Accuse Truman* *Pravda* accused President Truman of prolonging the Chinese civil war by supplying Taiwan with military equipment. According to Soviet sources, the American policies violated the Cairo Declaration signed at Potsdam on December 1, 1943. (CDSP II:2 22)

January 4 *State of the Union* President Truman, in his State of the Union address, called for a Point Four program to bring technological and financial assistance to the underdeveloped nations. He thought the program he recommended would eventually bring the benefits of democracy to millions of people, and thus communism would suffer another defeat. (PP 4)

January 6 *North Atlantic Council* The ministers attending the North Atlantic Council meeting in Washington issued a communiqué. They approved a strategic concept consisting of a set of principles for an integrated defense system for the North Atlantic area. The integrated system was intended to increase the political and military cooperation among the members of the alliance, thus making it more effective in responding to the Soviet threat. (DSB 1/16/50 104)

January 10 *Soviets Boycott Council* Ambassador Jacob Malik walked out of the United Nations Security Council and said the Soviet Union would not take part in any Security Council functions until the Nationalist Chinese government was expelled and the Beijing delegation seated. (NYT 1/11/50 1)

January 12 *Acheson Speech* Secretary of State Acheson, in a speech before the National Press Club, analyzed events in Asia since 1945 and America's response to them. He defined America's defense perimeter in Asia and said those nations outside it would, if militarily attacked, have to rely on their own resources and the United Nations. Critics said his speech led Moscow to believe that North Korea could attack South Korea without evoking an American response. (DSB 1/23/50 111)

January 24 *Kirk on Soviet Behavior* Ambassador Kirk sent a note to Secretary of State Acheson regarding Soviet bellicosity toward the United States. Kirk attributed the Soviet behavior to the belief that the West was getting weaker while communism, as evidenced by Mao's victory in China, was getting stronger. (FRUS IV 1083)

January 25   *Kirk on Pospelov's Speech* Ambassador Kirk sent to Washington an analysis of a January 22 speech by Peter Pospelov, a leading theoretician in the Soviet Communist party, in which he claimed that communism would triumph over capitalism. He predicted a major economic crisis for the West, and he expected communism to spread to other areas of Asia because of Mao's victory in China. Pospelov emphasized the important role played by peace groups supporting Soviet foreign policy objectives. (FRUS IV 1087)

January 26   *U.S. Aid to Korea* The United States and South Korea signed a mutual defense assistance agreement enabling South Korea to receive economic and military assistance. (AFP 1950-1955 II 2529)

January 31   *A Foreign Policy Review* President Truman ordered a comprehensive review of Soviet-American relations "in the light of the probable fission bomb capability and possible thermonuclear bomb capability of the Soviet Union." The policy assessment was designed to evaluate the nature and extent of the Soviet threat and to determine how the American government, given its resources, should react. The study was conducted by a committee under the leadership of Paul Nitze, the director of the policy planning staff at the Department of State. The conclusions of the study were contained in NSC-68, which was completed the following April. (FRUS I 141)

January 31   *The Hydrogen Bomb* President Truman announced he had directed the Atomic Energy Commission to continue work on the development of a hydrogen bomb. His decision was in part a reaction to the successful explosion of an atomic bomb by the Soviet Union in August 1949 and the assumption the Soviets would develop a hydrogen bomb when they acquired the technological know-how. (PP 138)

February 1   *The Japanese Emperor* The Soviet Union, in a note to the United States, proposed that the Japanese emperor and a number of military officers be tried as war criminals. The State Department rejected the Soviet proposal. (DSB 2/13/50 244)

February 8   *Acheson and the Soviets* Secretary of State Acheson, in response to a question at a news conference, commented on Soviet foreign policy objectives. He described the Soviet Union as being both ideological and imperialistic. When, however, the Soviets are confronted with strength as in Berlin, Greece, and Turkey, they will, he said, adjust their policies accordingly. (DSB 2/20/50 272)

February 8   *Soviet International Behavior* The State Department issued a memorandum analyzing Soviet behavior. It was described as more aggressive than in the past with the Soviets seemingly more willing to take risks, including the use of military force, to advance their foreign policy goals. The memorandum predicted more communist activity in Southeast Asia. (FRUS IV 1099)

February 10   The GDR   Secretary of State Acheson distributed to some State Department officials a position paper adopted by the United States and the five members of the Brussels Pact on December 15, 1949. They had decided not to give any recognition to the German Democratic Republic, which was established on October 7, 1949. (FRUS IV 942)

February 14   The Sino-Soviet Treaty   The Soviet Union and the People's Republic of China signed a thirty-year Treaty of Friendship, Alliance, and Mutual Assistance. The treaty was specifically directed against the Japanese and "any other state which should unite in any form with Japan in acts of aggression." At the time, Japan was still under the American occupation, thus the Sino-Soviet alliance was directed at the United States as well. The two communist nations pledged to assist each other if either was subject to a military attack, and they agreed to "develop and consolidate economic and cultural ties." (DIA 541)

February 15   On Negotiating with the Soviets   Charles Yost, director of the State Department's Office of Eastern European Affairs, wrote a memorandum analyzing the difficulties encountered in negotiating with the Soviet Union. He said because the differences between the United States and the Soviet Union involved their most important interests, negotiations were not likely to be successful. (FRUS I 153)

February 16   Acheson on Total Diplomacy   Secretary of State Acheson, in remarks made to a group at the White House, said the United States had to develop what he called a "total diplomacy." He wanted the United States to marshal all of its resources to enable the nation to deal with the Soviet Union from a position of strength. He thought this was the most effective way to meet the challenge of communism. (DSB 3/20/50 427)

February 22   The Czech Peace Resolution   The Czech National Assembly, as part of a worldwide propaganda campaign, passed a peace resolution accusing the United States of pursuing aggressive foreign policies that endangered world peace. (FRUS IV 309)

February 24   Acheson News Conference   Secretary of State Acheson issued a statement criticizing the Eastern European nations, particularly Bulgaria and Hungary, because of their civil rights records. He said the United States would continue to speak out on behalf of the people of Eastern Europe who were denied basic human rights. (DSB 3/6/50 377)

March 3 *Partisans for Peace* The State Department announced that a group representing the World Congress of Partisans for Peace would be refused admission to the United States. The Partisans for Peace was a communist-front organization that wanted to present the American Congress with a petition regarding armaments and atomic weapons. The State Department decision was supported by the Congress. (DSB 3/13/50 400)

March 15 *The Stockholm Peace Appeal* The Permanent Committee of the World Congress of Partisans for Peace convened in Stockholm for a four-day meeting. On March 19 the delegates approved the Stockholm Resolution declaring that the first nation to use atomic weapons would be committing a crime against humanity and members of that government would be treated as war criminals. The Stockholm Resolution was a part of the Soviet worldwide peace campaign to depict the Soviet Union as a peace-loving nation and the United States as a warmonger. The American and British governments were criticized for refusing to meet with representatives of the peace movement seeking support for the peace campaign. (CDSP II:12 21)

March 15 *Acheson on Asia* Secretary of State Acheson, in a speech in San Francisco, analyzed the recently concluded Sino-Soviet treaty and changes taking place in Asia. He said two dominant trends were emerging in Asia. One was a reaction against poverty and the second was opposition to foreign domination. The secretary emphasized American support for efforts to improve the quality of life in Asia, and he criticized the Soviets for the small amount of aid being granted to China. He said the special rights given to the Soviet Union in the Sino-Soviet treaty violated China's sovereignty. (DSB 3/27/50 467)

March 16 *Acheson on Soviet Policy* Secretary of State Acheson, in a speech at the University of California (Berkeley), compared the philosophies of the Soviet and American governments and said it was difficult to find a compromise between the two. He delineated Soviet-American differences in relation to a number of issues, including the use of force, the United Nations, the treatment of diplomatic representatives, and the control of atomic energy. (DSB 5/27/50 473)

March 19 *Pravda on Total Diplomacy* An article in *Pravda* said Secretary of State Acheson's concept of *total diplomacy* had come to replace atomic diplomacy and was intended to make the United States more aggressive. (CDSP II:12 17)

March 20 *Gubitchev Leaves Country* Valentin Gubitchev, who had been found guilty on March 7 of spying for the Soviet Union, left the United

States. He received a suspended sentence on condition that he leave the country and not return. (NYT 3/21/50 1)

April 7 NSC-68 President Truman received the policy review he ordered on January 31. The review, contained in NSC-68, described the Soviet Union as an expansionist power eager to support the world communist movement. The United States, according to the report, had to develop a global strategy to effectively cope with the communist threat backed by Soviet military might. The report rejected a preventive war as a way of dealing with the Soviet threat or a return to isolationism. NSC-68 advocated increasing defense spending substantially, building the hydrogen bomb, and strengthening America's conventional military capabilities. NSC-68 provided President Truman with a conceptual framework for analyzing the Soviet threat in the postwar world. (FRUS I 235)

April 11 The U.S. and Eastern Europe A study circulated by the State Department recommended policies the United States should pursue to reduce Soviet control over the Eastern European satellites. Some of these included supporting human rights, sustaining a propaganda campaign against the communist governments, and using the United Nations to advocate greater freedom for the satellite nations. (FRUS IV 14)

April 11 Soviets Charge Violation The Soviet Union, in a note to the United States, charged that an American military airplane had violated Soviet airspace on April 8. The American plane, allegedly after refusing to land, was fired on by Soviet fighters and then disappeared. On April 18 the United States accused the Soviet Union of shooting down outside Soviet territory an unarmed American Navy airplane carrying ten crew members. The United States demanded an apology and compensation. (DSB 5/1/50 668)

April 20 Truman on Foreign Policy President Truman, in an address to the American Society of Newspaper Editors, commented on the Soviet peace offensive. He accused the Soviets of using propaganda to cloak their acts of imperialism, and he emphasized the need for the United States to do a better job of explaining American values. The president said "we must make ourselves heard round the world in a great campaign of truth." (PP 260)

April 22 Acheson on Soviet Imperialism Secretary of State Acheson, in an address to the American Society of Newspaper Editors, presented his views on the Soviet threat to the United States. He said weakening the United States was a major Soviet goal, but he also pointed out that communism threatened Western civilization. The Soviets, Acheson said, hoped to achieve their goals by employing a tactic of divide and rule aimed at sowing disunity between the United States and its NATO allies. The secretary presented six proposals for dealing with the Soviet threat, and he again emphasized the idea of total diplomacy. (DSB 5/1/50 673)

April 22 Soviets and Japan The Soviet Union announced that all Japanese prisoners of war had been repatriated except those under investigation and those held as war criminals. Some Japanese prisoners were turned over to the People's Republic of China. Japan claimed that 370,000 Japanese prisoners of war were unaccounted for by the Soviets. The United States also did not accept the Soviet claim. (CDSP II:17 23)

April 25 Evaluating Soviet Policies Ambassador Kirk sent Washington an evaluation of Soviet foreign policy prepared by members of the United States embassy in Moscow. The Soviets were said to be pursuing a policy just short of going to war with the United States, an option they wanted to avoid. The Soviets were accused of exploiting the social and economic changes resulting from World War II and of launching a "revolutionary offensive" to extend their power. (FRUS I 292)

April 26 Soviets and Propaganda *Pravda* criticized President Truman and Secretary of State Acheson for their speeches to the American Society of Newspaper Editors a few days earlier. The two leaders were accused of attempting to intimidate the masses by using "total propaganda" and "atomic and hydrogen blackmail. . . ." (CDSP II:17 20)

May 9 Prisoners of War Tass, the Soviet news agency, declared that all German prisoners of war had been repatriated. The United States did not accept the Soviet claim. (DSB 6/19/50 1018)

May 9 Truman on Foreign Policy President Truman, in a speech at the University of Wyoming, said the Soviet Union wanted to divide the free nations of the world and to undermine their democratic institutions. The president declared that communism, regardless of tactics used by its leaders, would eventually be defeated because of the moral and material superiority of the free world. He warned, however, that defeating communism would take a long time. (PP 333)

May 14 London Foreign Ministers Meeting The foreign ministers of France, the United Kingdom, and the United States issued a declaration announcing their intention to continue to reduce their controls over West Germany and to establish a study group to explore further modifications in the West German Occupation Statute. The ministers proposed that German reunification should come about after the establishment of a freely elected government. The Soviets were accused of blocking German unification based on free elections. (DAFR 554)

May 23   U.S. Protests to Soviet Union   The United States, in a note to the Soviet Union, charged that it was developing an army in the German Democratic Republic, thus violating international agreements that called for the demilitarization of Germany. (DSB 6/5/50 918)

May 26   Western Big Three Call for German Elections   France, the United Kingdom, and the United States sent identical notes to General Vasiliy Chuikov, the Soviet military governor in East Germany, proposing that elections be held throughout Germany as a prelude to the establishment of an all-German government and the adoption of a formal peace treaty. The Soviets rejected the proposal. (DIA 162)

May 31   Acheson Talks to Congress   Secretary of State Acheson spoke to members of the House and Senate about his recent trip to Europe. He reported that the NATO allies were uniting and building their military strength to deter Soviet aggression. He accused the Soviets of blocking the completion of an Austrian peace treaty, and he expressed concern about the Soviet threats to Greece, Turkey, and Iran. He said all the NATO leaders recognized the necessity of defending the North Atlantic area and the need to build military strength to ensure that "the future belongs to freedom." (DSB 6/12/50 931)

June 9   On Repatriations   The United States again requested the Soviet Union to make available information about Japanese prisoners of war still held by the Soviets. A similar note was sent on December 30, 1949, but Moscow did not respond. (DSB 8/14/50 257)

June 22   Acheson on Soviet Policy   Secretary of State Acheson, in a speech to the Harvard Alumni Association, reviewed Soviet policies since 1945 and the American response to them. He recalled Soviet threats to Turkey and Iran, support for the communist insurgency in Greece, and governments imposed in Eastern Europe as a result of Soviet military might. The secretary referred to the "creative efforts" made by the free nations to build a North Atlantic community based on principles "which must eventually prevail in the wider world." (DSB 7/3/50 14)

June 25   The Korean War Begins   North Korean military units invaded South Korea, and two days later the United Nations Security Council passed a resolution, supported by the United States, calling for the withdrawal of the invading forces. On June 27 President Truman ordered United States air and naval units to assist the military forces of South Korea. The outbreak of the Korean War helped globalize the cold war and had a significant impact on Soviet-American relations. (DIA 631)

June 27   Korea Aided   The United Nations Security Council voted to send military units to help South Korea defend itself against North Korea. At the time, the Soviet Union was boycotting the council and thus could not veto the resolution. (AFP 1950-1955 II 2540)

June 27   Aide-Mémoire to the Soviet Union   The United States delivered an aide-mémoire to the Soviet Union asking it to disavow any responsibility for North Korea's attack on South Korea. The Soviets were asked to use their influence to have North Korean military forces withdraw from below the thirty-eighth parallel. On June 29 the Soviets responded by alleging that South Korea had invaded North Korea. (DIA 634)

June 29   Consequences of Korea   President Truman, in reaction to the outbreak of the Korean War, met with a group of advisors to determine those areas around the perimeter of the Soviet Union most in danger of a Soviet attack. According to his advisors, the most important danger spots were Iran, West Germany, and Yugoslavia. (FRUS I 324)

July 3   Soviet Treaty Violations   The *Department of State Bulletin* published a memorandum on Soviet violations of international treaties that brought up to date a similar document issued in June 1948. The memorandum accused the Soviets of violating international treaties whenever they thought it was in their interest to do so. (DSB 7/3/50 8)

July 7   Potato Bugs in Germany   The State Department released to the press a reply to a June 30 note from the Soviet Union accusing the United States of dropping potato bugs on East Germany to ruin its agricultural crops. The United States denied the charge. (DSB 7/24/50 134)

July 12   The Stockholm Resolution   Secretary of State Acheson, in a statement released to the press, denounced the Stockholm Resolution adopted on March 19 by the Partisans for Peace as communist propaganda. At the time of the Stockholm meeting, the Soviet Union considered the peace movement a major instrument for advancing Soviet foreign policy goals. (DSB 7/24/50 131)

July 19   Soviets Accuse the U.S.   *Pravda* again accused the United States of dropping potato bugs on East Germany to ruin its agricultural crops. The United States again denied the charge. (CDSP II:29 36)

August 8   Kennan on Korea   George Kennan, the counselor at the American embassy in Moscow, presented the secretary of state with an analysis of Soviet foreign policy objectives. Kennan did not believe the Korean conflict indicated the Soviet Union was willing to go to war with the

United States, nor did he think that Korea would be the first in a series of small wars directed by the Soviet Union. (FRUS I 361)

August 11 *Kirk on Soviet Intentions* Ambassador Kirk sent Secretary of State Acheson an analysis of Soviet intentions. The ambassador expected the Soviet Union to continue its support for the world peace movement and, at the same time, to exploit the fear that war might break out. (FRUS I 367)

August 15 *Forced Labor* Walter Kotschnig, a deputy U.S. representative to ECOSOC, accused the Soviet Union of failing to cooperate with United Nations efforts to investigate the use of forced labor in the Soviet Union and the nations of Eastern Europe. (DSB 9/25/50 510)

September 10 *Acheson on War* Secretary of State Acheson, in a television interview, said it was irresponsible to think that war with the Soviet Union was inevitable. He said war could be avoided if the United States dealt with the Soviet Union from a position of strength. He advocated strengthening NATO and unifying West Germany as a means to make the Western nations more secure against the communist threat. (DSB 9/18/50 460)

October 5 *Threat from Chou Enlai* Acting Secretary of State James Webb notified a number of diplomatic officials that Foreign Minister Chou Enlai of the People's Republic of China had threatened to send Chinese military forces into Korea if the United Nations forces crossed the thirty-eighth parallel. (FRUS VII 877)

November 5 *China Enters the War* General Douglas MacArthur, in a report to the United Nations Security Council, said Chinese troops had entered the Korean conflict on October 20. The Chinese "volunteer" forces were successful in driving the United Nations forces back toward the thirty-eighth parallel. (AFP 1950-1955 II 2581)

November 6 *Bulganin Speech* Nikolai Bulganin, vice chairman of the Council of Ministers, in a speech in Moscow celebrating the thirty-third anniversary of the October 1917 revolution, accused the United States of preparing for a new war in the expectation that it would lead to the collapse of the Soviet Union. Bulganin said the Soviets could defeat any aggression, and he boasted that communist influence was spreading throughout the world. He also accused the United States of committing aggression in Korea. (DIA 139)

November 20 *Soviets on Japanese Peace Treaty* The Soviet Union sent the United States an aide-mémoire regarding a Japanese peace treaty. Among other things, Moscow wanted to know whether the United

States intended to have military bases in Japan after a treaty was signed and whether the People's Republic of China would be consulted about the terms of the treaty. (DIA 616)

November 30 *Truman and the Bomb* President Truman caused a contro-versy when, in response to a question at a news conference, he said the United States was considering using the atomic bomb in Korea. He added that "there has always been active consideration of its use." His comments disturbed some NATO allies, and British prime minister Clement Attlee flew to Washington to consult with the president. (PP 727)

1951

January 3 *Acheson on Ministers Meeting* Secretary of State Acheson, in a statement at a news conference, commented on the exchange of notes between the United States and the Soviet Union regarding a meeting of the Council of Foreign Ministers. He said the last meeting of the council in May 1949 was a "process of fruitless negotiation," and as a result he wanted Soviet policies clarified before the Western nations would agree to convene another meeting. (DSB 1/15/51 90)

January 8 *State of the Union* President Truman, in his State of the Union address, identified the Soviet Union as a threat to all free nations in part because of its military might and subversive activities. He proposed a number of policies to cope with the Soviet threat, including economic and military assistance programs. (PP 7)

January 21 *Speech by Pospelov* Peter Pospelov, a member of the Politburo, in a speech in Moscow, accused the United States of preparing for another war. He said American leaders, since the time of President Wilson, had been plotting against the Soviet Union. (DSB 2/12/51 257)

January 23 *U.S. Responds to Soviet Note* The United States again rejected the Soviet call for convening a foreign ministers meeting without adequate preparations. The United States repeated its offer to have representatives of the Big Four meet to determine what issues could be discussed if a meeting were convened. The Soviets only wanted to discuss Germany, but the United States insisted on a broader agenda. (DSB 2/5/51 228)

February 5 *Soviet Note to the U.S.* The Soviet Union, in response to the January 23 note from the United States, accused France, the United Kingdom, and the United States of wanting to rearm West Germany. The Soviets repeated their demand to convene a meeting of the Big Four foreign ministers to discuss the demilitarization of Germany. (DSB 2/19/51 313)

March 19 *Forced Labor* The United Nations Economic and Social Council approved a resolution calling on the International Labor Organization to establish a committee to investigate the charge that nations were using forced labor as a means of political coercion. The United States had accused the Soviet Union of such a practice. (DSB 4/23/51 670)

April 14 *Truman Speech* President Truman, in a radio address to the nation, declared that the Soviet Union was a threat to every nation in the world, and he accused the Soviets of attempting to divide the democratic nations so they could be more easily defeated. According to the president, the Soviets ignored the needs of their own people so that resources could be used in support of the world communist movement. (PP 227)

April 30 *Acheson on Foreign Policy* Secretary of State Acheson, in a speech to the United States Chamber of Commerce, analyzed certain aspects of Soviet foreign policies and the American response to them. He said a basic Soviet objective was to win control over the industrial resources of Europe and the resources of Asia. He then outlined what the United States was doing to counter the Soviet challenge. (DSB 5/14/51 766)

June 10 *Japanese Peace Treaty* The Soviet Union, in a note to the United States, objected to the proposed peace treaty for Japan, alleging it would not be prevented from regaining its military might. The Soviets wanted all foreign troops withdrawn from Japan within one year after a treaty was signed and a prohibition against any nation having military bases in Japan. (DSB 7/23/51 138)

June 23 *U.S.-Soviet Trade Restrictions* The United States notified the Soviet Union of trade restrictions imposed by the U.S. Congress in the Trade Agreements Extension Act of 1951. As a result of the congressional action, the August 1937 Soviet-American trade agreement was nullified. The United States also cancelled trade agreements that had been in effect with Bulgaria, Hungary, and Poland. (DSB 7/16/51 95)

July 4 *Truman on the Soviet Threat* President Truman, in a speech in Washington, commented on the nature of the Soviet threat to the free world. He pointed out that in addition to Soviet military might, the communists used whatever instruments they could to further their aims. The president said the United States had to live up to its ideals and thereby set an example for the rest of the world if it were to meet the nonmilitary challenge of communism. (PP 370)

July 9 *U.S. Responds to Soviets* The United States responded to the June 10 note from the Soviet Union regarding a Japanese peace treaty. The American note rejected the Soviet protests and declared that Japan should not be denied the right of joining a collective defense pact sanctioned by the United Nations Charter. (DSB 7/23/51 143)

August 2 *National Intelligence Estimate* A National Intelligence Estimate report, written by individuals from various agencies in the intelligence community, analyzing probable Soviet policies to mid-1952 said the Soviet Union was unlikely to seek a general war with the United States because of America's superiority in atomic weapons. The report warned that a major Soviet objective was to divide the NATO nations and to prevent the rearmament of West Germany and Japan. (FRUS IV 1622)

September 8 *Japanese Peace Treaty* Forty-nine nations attending the San Francisco conference signed the Japanese peace treaty. The Soviet Union, Poland, and Czechoslovakia refused to sign. The treaty went into effect in March 1952, and Japan then regained its sovereignty. The Soviets said the treaty was illegal because Moscow did not sign it. (DIA 611)

October 5 *Kirk Meets with Vishinsky* Ambassador Kirk met with Foreign Minister Vishinsky to discuss Soviet-American relations in general and the Korean War in particular. Kirk said the Soviet Union was not helpful in bringing the Korean War to an end and, while the war lasted, Soviet-American relations were not likely to improve. He tried to assure Vishinsky the United States had no aggressive designs on the Soviet Union. (DSB 10/29/51 687)

October 15 *Vishinsky Responds to Kirk* Foreign Minister Vishinsky responded to the comments made by Ambassador Kirk on October 5. Vishinsky said it was the Soviet Union, not the United States, that was seeking to end the Korean War. He said American policies were the cause of international tensions, and if they were to be reduced, the United States would have to change its policies. (DSB 10/29/51 688)

November 8 *Acheson at the UN* Secretary of State Acheson, in an address to the United Nations General Assembly meeting in Paris, said there were a number of things the Soviets could do to demonstrate their desire to reduce international tensions. He called on the Soviets to establish a Korean cease-fire, to complete peace treaties for Austria and Germany, to allow Italy to become a member of the United Nations, and to respect human rights. (DSB 11/19/51 803)

November 21 *The Mutual Security Act* The Soviet Union, in a note to the United States, protested the passage of the Mutual Security Act on October 8, alleging that it violated the 1933 agreement between President Roosevelt and Foreign Minister Litvinov. In particular, the Soviet Union objected to the provision of the act that set aside $100 million to aid refugees from communist nations. The Soviets said the money could be used to support efforts to overthrow the Soviet government, a violation of the 1933 agreement. The United States rejected the Soviet protest. (DSB 12/3/51 910)

November 22 *The Paris Agreements* The foreign ministers of France, the United Kingdom, and the United States, after meeting with Chancellor Konrad Adenauer of West Germany in Paris, issued a statement containing an outline of some of the agreements they reached. These included abolishing the Occupation Statute and the Allied High Commission, thus allowing West Germany to regain much of its sovereignty. The implementation of these agreements required the solution of other problems, including the creation of a European army. (DSB 12/3/51 891)

November 24 *The Paris Agreements* *Pravda* criticized the November 22 Paris agreements. The Western nations were accused of wanting to keep Germany divided rather than supporting a unified, democratic Germany. (CDSP III:47 17)

December 26 *Kirk Resigns* President Truman announced that Admiral Kirk was resigning as ambassador to the Soviet Union and would be replaced by George Kennan, who was confirmed by the Senate the following March 13. (FRUS 1952-1954 VIII 962)

December 30 *Acheson on Foreign Policy* Secretary of State Acheson, in a speech in New York, reviewed foreign policy events of the past year. He said the North Atlantic nations were now more secure as a result of the growing strength of NATO. There were, he said, danger spots in the Near and Middle East the Soviets could exploit, but he thought that Greece and Turkey were now less endangered because of their intention to join the NATO alliance. (DSB 1/7/52 3)

1952

January 9 *State of the Union* President Truman, in his State of the Union address, reviewed events of the past year and was satisfied with the success in achieving desired foreign policy objectives. He warned, however, that much still had to be done because the Soviets remained a major threat to the United States and its allies. (PP 10)

February 6 *Katyn Witness* A former soldier in the Polish army told a special committee of the House of Representatives that he had witnessed the Soviets execute two hundred Polish army officers in the Katyn Forest in October 1939. The witness testified with a mask over his head to protect his identity. (NYT 2/7/52 4)

February 19 *Foreign Ministers Meeting* Secretary of State Acheson, British Foreign Secretary Anthony Eden, and French Foreign Minister Robert Schuman issued a communiqué based on discussions they had among themselves and with Chancellor Adenauer of West Germany. The Western leaders agreed that West Germany would contribute to the proposed European Defense Community (EDC), but the rearming of Germany would be carefully regulated to prevent the resurgence of militarism. The United Kingdom and the United States, in deference to French fears about a rearmed Germany, agreed to keep their troops in Europe for an extended period. The four-power agreement cleared the way for the establishment of a European army and the completion of the contractual agreements between West Germany and the three Western occupying powers. (DSB 3/3/52 325)

February 25 *Katyn Massacre* The State Department sent a letter to the Soviet Union along with a House of Representatives resolution calling for an investigation to determine who was responsible for the Katyn massacre in Poland in 1939. On February 29 the Soviet Union returned the American note saying it was insulting. The Soviets sent a report allegedly proving the massacre was carried out by Nazi Germany. (NT 3/5/52 NP)

March 2 *Germ Warfare Charge* *Pravda* reported that the People's Republic of China had accused the United States of using bacteriological weapons against the communist forces fighting in Korea. Two days later, *Pravda* reported that North Korea had made a similar accusation. On March 4 Secretary of State Acheson denied the communist allegations, and he· called for an impartial investigation. (CDSP IV:9 12)

March 10   *Soviets on German Unification*   The Soviet Union presented identical notes to France, the United Kingdom, and the United States calling for the convening of a Big Four foreign ministers meeting to discuss German unity. The Soviets appended to their note a proposed peace treaty permitting a reunified Germany to have its own armed forces. The Soviet proposal was in response to the decision agreed to by France, the United Kingdom, and the United States to rearm West Germany within the framework of the proposal. (CDSP IV:7 7)

March 25   *U.S. Note on Germany*   The United States responded to the Soviet note of March 10 calling for a Big Four foreign ministers meeting to discuss a peace treaty for Germany. The American note pointed out that before a peace treaty could be concluded, free elections throughout Germany would have to be held leading to the establishment of an all-German government. The American position was that four-power talks would not be useful until a freely elected all-German government was in place. (DSB 4/7/52 530)

March 26   *Acheson on Germ Warfare*   Secretary of State Acheson commented on a report by a commission alleging it had proven the United States was using bacteriological weapons in Korea and China. He pointed out that the commission was composed of communists or those who were sympathetic to communist causes. He again called for an impartial investigation of the charges by a group such as the International Red Cross. The Soviets rejected his suggestion. (DSB 4/7/52 529)

April 1   *Stalin Responds to Questions*   Josef Stalin answered a number of questions put to him by a group of American newspaper editors. He said he did not think a world war was imminent, and he suggested that a meeting of heads of state might be useful. He thought German unification could be achieved, and he repeated the oft-made Soviet assertion that different social systems could coexist. (DIA 224)

April 19   *Acheson on the Soviet Union*   Secretary of State Acheson, in an address to the American Society of Newspaper Editors, commented on Soviet-American relations. He said the United States had assembled a coalition of free nations determined to prevent the spread of communism. In reaction to that effort, the Soviet Union had launched a "peace offensive" with the aim of dividing the Western allies, particularly regarding the issue of Germany. The secretary was not optimistic about negotiating with the Soviet Union. He cited the many meetings that had taken place since World War II that failed to produce any agreements. (DSB 4/28/52 647)

May 5 Germ Warfare The North Korean government announced that two American pilots had confessed to using germ bombs in the Korean conflict. Secretary of State Acheson refuted the alleged confession and said the pilots were coerced into making the statements. (NYT 5/5/52 1)

May 22 Hate-America Campaign Ambassador Kennan reported to Washington on the hate-America campaign then being carried on by the Soviet government. He characterized the campaign as violent and vicious and said the Soviets were effectively manipulating the charge that the United States was using bacteriological weapons in Korea. (FRUS 1952-1954 VIII 971)

May 24 The Soviets and West Germany The Soviet Union, in response to a note from France, the United Kingdom, and the United States, accused the three Western nations of creating obstacles to prevent a Big Four meeting to conclude a peace treaty for Germany. The Soviets also denounced the proposed contractual agreements, signed the next day, granting West Germany sovereignty and allowing it to join the proposed EDC. (DIA 100)

May 26 German Contractual Agreements France, the United Kingdom, the United States, and West Germany signed a number of agreements collectively labeled the *contractual agreements.* These were based on the agreements signed by the Bonn government and the three Western occupying powers in Paris in May 1951. The Allied High Commission in West Germany was abolished and the occupation was terminated, although the three Western powers retained certain rights pending a peace treaty. Plans were made to create a European Defense Community that would include military units from the Federal Republic of Germany. The agreements were to become operative only when all parts of the package were approved by the signatories. (DIA 105)

May 28 The European Defense Community France, Italy, the Federal Republic of Germany, and the three Benelux nations, Belgium, Luxembourg, and the Netherlands, signed an agreement to establish a European Defense Community (EDC) that would permit West Germany to contribute to the defense of Europe within the framework of a European army. (NYT 5/28/52 1)

June 4 America Accused of Atrocities An article in the Soviet magazine *New Times* entitled "Stop the American Atrocities" accused the United States of torturing and murdering North Korean and Chinese prisoners of war. (NT 6/4/52 19)

June 13 Kennan on Soviet Policy Ambassador Kennan sent Washington an analysis of Soviet policy. He said the major thesis on which Soviet policy rested was the idea that the Western nations were in a period of decline that started in 1917 with the victory of communism in Russia. Kennan suggested that the violence of the hate-America campaign reflected some doubt on the part of Soviet officials that the thesis remained valid. (FRUS 1952-1954 VIII 1000)

June 18   Germ Warfare   Ernest A. Gross, the deputy U.S. representative to the United Nations, refuted the Soviet charge that the United States was using bacteriological weapons in Korea. He introduced a resolution in the Security Council calling on all nations to cooperate with the International Red Cross so it could investigate the allegations. The Soviets refused to cooperate. (DSB 7/7/52 32)

June 19   Kennan Meets Vishinsky   Ambassador Kennan reported to Washington about a meeting he had with Foreign Minister Vishinsky. Kennan told the Soviet minister that the hate-America campaign then being carried out by the Soviet Union did not suggest it was interested in improving superpower relations. Kennan believed that as a result of his conversation with Vishinsky, the tone of the hate-America campaign might be moderated. (FRUS 1952-1954 VIII 1011)

June 26   Forced Labor   The NATO nations issued a report charging that many World War II prisoners of war held in the Soviet Union were dying because they were required to engage in forced labor under cruel conditions. (NYT 6/27/52 3)

July 1   World Peace Council Meets   The World Peace Council, a communist-dominated organization, convened in Berlin. The council, attended by delegates from seventy countries, passed a number of resolutions in support of Soviet foreign policy objectives. The contractual agreements regarding West Germany and the EDC were denounced, and a demand was made to convene a Big Four foreign ministers conference to write a peace treaty for Germany. The council also criticized the Japanese peace treaty and the military defense agreement signed by the United States and Japan. The United States was again charged with using bacteriological weapons in Korea. (DIA 252)

August 23   Soviets and Germany   The Soviet Union, in a note to the United States, accused the Western Big Three of refusing to negotiate a peace treaty for Germany. The Soviets charged that the contractual agreements signed on May 26 would revive German militarism. The Soviets demanded the convening of a Big Four conference to write a peace treaty for Germany and to explore the possibility of conducting free elections. (DSB 10/6/52 519)

September 18 *Forced Labor in the Soviet Union* President Truman, in a statement at a news conference, said the State Department had just published a booklet on forced labor in the Soviet Union. The booklet contained all the information the United States had provided to the United Nations commission created to investigate the issue. (PP 581)

September 19 *Kennan in Berlin* Ambassador Kennan, in response to a question while in Berlin, complained about travel and other restrictions in the Soviet Union limiting his contacts with Soviet citizens. He felt isolated, he said, because Russians were afraid to associate with an American official. He compared his isolation as ambassador to the Soviet Union to his experience when he was interned by Nazi Germany at the outbreak of World War II. (FRUS 1952-1954 VIII 1048)

September 23 *U.S. Note to Soviet Union* The United States responded to the August 23 note from the Soviet Union regarding Germany. The United States rejected the Soviet proposal for a Big Four conference to conclude a German peace treaty. The United States also denied the allegations directed at NATO, the EDC, and the agreements the three Western powers signed with the Bonn government on May 26. (DSB 10/6/52 517)

September 24 *Germ Warfare* The Soviet magazine *New Times* printed the report of the International Scientific Commission for Investigation of the Facts Concerning Bacteriological Warfare in Korea and China, composed of individuals associated with communist organizations or who were communist sympathizers. The report concluded that the United States had resorted to bacteriological warfare in both countries. (NT 9/24/52 NP)

September 25 *Ambassador Zarubin* Georgy Zarubin, the newly appointed Soviet ambassador, presented his credentials to President Truman. Zarubin was replacing Alexander S. Panyushkin, who had been appointed in December 1947. (DSB 10/6/52 515)

October 3 *Kennan Ousted* The Soviet Union, responding to the comments made by Ambassador George Kennan in Berlin on September 19, declared him *persona non grata* and demanded his recall. (FRUS 1952-1954 VIII 1053)

October 5 *Malenkov on Foreign Policy* Georgy Malenkov, the deputy chairman of the Soviet Council of Ministers, in an address to the Nineteenth Party Congress, reaffirmed the Marxist doctrine of the inevitability of wars between capitalist nations. Malenkov's speech was a justification for increased defense spending within the Soviet Union and the need to follow completely the line laid down by the Communist party under Stalin's leadership. (DIA 229)

October 6   Acheson on Foreign Policy   Secretary of State Acheson, in a speech in Pittsburgh, said the Soviets had changed their foreign policy methods. He said they were still trying to drive a wedge between the United States and its allies, but the Soviets were now using more subtle, less aggressive, tactics. He attributed the change to the growing military capabilities of the Western nations. (DSB 10/20/52 595)

October 12   Asian Peace Conference   The communist-dominated Asian and Pacific Region Peace Conference, meeting in Beijing, ended. An appeal was issued containing many ideas associated with the Soviet-sponsored peace offensive. The delegates accused the United States of using bacteriological weapons in Korea, and they supported completing a peace pact among the four permanent members of the United Nations Security Council and the People's Republic of China. (DIA 466)

November 1   U.S. Tests Hydrogen Bomb   The United States tested its first device for a hydrogen bomb. (DSB 11/5/52 710)

December 19   World Council of Peace   At the conclusion of the meeting of the communist-dominated World Council of Peace in Vienna attended by delegates from seventy-two countries, a declaration was issued calling for an end to the Korean conflict and the various military engagements in Southeast Asia, a peace pact to be signed by the four permanent members of the United Nations Security Council and the People's Republic of China, an end to racial discrimination, the conclusion of a peace treaty for Germany, and adherence to the 1925 Geneva protocol on biological warfare. The United States had been accused of using biological weapons against North Korean and Chinese military forces in Korea. (DIA 254)

1953

January 7   *State of the Union*   President Truman, in his last State of the Union address, warned Josef Stalin, in a nonthreatening tone, that if the Soviet Union provoked a war, it would be destroyed because of the destructive capabilities of new nuclear and hydrogen weapons. He also accused the Soviets of exploiting postwar economic and social conditions to advance the cause of communism. (PP 1114)

January 12   *U.S. Note on Austria*   The United States, in a note to the Soviet Union, proposed convening a meeting of deputies to discuss an Austrian peace treaty. The Soviet Union was reminded of the United Nations General Assembly resolution passed on December 20, 1952, encouraging the Big Four to try to complete an Austrian treaty. (DIA 142)

January 15   *Truman on Communism*   President Truman, in his farewell address to the American people, said the communist bloc nations had great resources, but their system was godless and would not permit freedom. In the long run, he said, the values of democracy would prevail over those of communism. (PP 1197)

January 21   *Secretary of State Dulles*   The United States Senate confirmed John Foster Dulles as secretary of state. (DSB 2/2/53 203)

January 27   *Soviet Note on Austria*   The Soviet Union, in response to the American note of January 12, again expressed a willingness to resume negotiations on an Austrian peace treaty, but only if the Western powers withdrew the abbreviated treaty put forward in March 1952. The Soviets also rejected as illegal the December 20, 1952, General Assembly Austrian resolution. (DIA 143)

January 27   *Dulles on Foreign Policy*   Secretary of State Dulles, in an address to the nation, accused the Soviet Union of attempting to spread its power throughout the world while at the same time making efforts to avoid a war with the United States until the Soviets were sufficiently strong to guarantee a victory. The secretary expressed confidence the Soviet strategy would fail. (VS 19:9 264)

January 29   *U.S. Note on Austria*   The United States, in response to the January 27 note from the Soviet Union, rejected Soviet conditions that had to be met before negotiations on an Austrian peace treaty could be resumed. (DIA 145)

February 2 *State of the Union* President Eisenhower, in his first State of the Union address, developed several ideas intended to serve as a guide for American foreign policy. He said the United States needed a clear policy in support of American interests, and he emphasized the need for closer cooperation with the nations of Western Europe to deal more effectively with the threat of communism. (PP 12)

February 20 *Eisenhower on Subjugated People* President Eisenhower sent a proposal to Congress urging the passage of a joint resolution on the Soviet absorption of the Eastern European nations after World War II. The president said Soviet policies violated World War II international agreements. (PP 56)

February 27 *Senate Resolution* The United States Senate passed a resolution condemning the Soviet Union for its persecution of ethnic and religious minorities. The resolution encouraged the president to place the issue before the United Nations General Assembly. (NYT 2/28/53 1)

March 2 *Vishinsky Attacks U.S.* Foreign Minister Vishinsky, in an address to the United Nations General Assembly, accused the United States of blocking a Korean armistice and planning to enlarge the war. (NYT 3/3/53 1)

March 5 *Stalin Dies* The Soviet Union officially announced the death of Josef Stalin. He had been in power since the death of Lenin in 1924. On March 6 Georgy Malenkov became chairman of the Council of Ministers and, for ten days, first secretary of the Communist party. This theoretically made him the leader of the Soviet Union. (CDSP V:6 5)

March 6 *Molotov Appointed Foreign Minister* The Soviet government announced that Viacheslav Molotov was again foreign minister, replacing Andrei Vishinsky. No explanation was given for the change. (NYT 3/7/53 3)

March 16 *Malenkov on Foreign Policy* Premier Malenkov, in an address to the Supreme Soviet, said that all Soviet-American differences could be resolved by negotiations. At the time, the Soviets appeared eager to reduce international tensions following the death of Stalin. (NYT 3/17/53 6)

March 18 *American Protest* The United States protested to the Soviet Union after a Soviet airplane fired on an American airplane that had allegedly violated Soviet airspace. The American plane returned the fire and was not damaged. The United States said it expected disciplinary action to be taken against the personnel responsible for the incident. On March 21 the Soviet Union rejected the American protest and then claimed that a B-29 bomber had violated Soviet airspace and had been forced to flee. The United States denied the Soviet claim. (DSB 4/20/53 577)

March 27 *Ambassador Bohlen* The Senate confirmed Charles Bohlen as ambassador to the Soviet Union. He succeeded George F. Kennan. (DSB 4/6/53 519)

March 31 *Secretary General Approved* The United Nations Security Council, after a long stalemate, agreed to recommend to the General Assembly the selection of Dag Hammarskjöld as secretary general. The United States and the Soviet Union approved the resolution. (NYT 4/1/53 1)

April 9 *Vishinsky at the UN* Andrei Vishinsky, Soviet deputy foreign minister, in an address to the United Nations General Assembly, emphasized the need to avert another world war. He said differences in political systems should not prevent nations from cooperating. His speech was part of a Soviet campaign to improve relations with the United States following the death of Josef Stalin. (CDSP V:15 10)

April 16 *Eisenhower Speech* President Eisenhower, in a speech to the American Society of Newspaper Editors, listed a number of things the Soviets could do that would give hope of a better world in the future. These included releasing prisoners of war still in captivity, concluding a Korean armistice, completing a peace treaty for Austria, cooperating to achieve arms control treaties, and reducing the violence in Southeast Asia. Resolving some of these issues, he said, would lay the foundation for arms control agreements. The president hoped his speech would contribute to better Soviet-American relations. (PP 179)

April 18 *Dulles on Foreign Policy* Secretary of State Dulles, in a speech to the American Society of Newspaper Editors, said the recent statements of Soviet leaders indicating a willingness to reduce international tensions represented a change in tactics, not strategy. (NYT 4/19/53 84)

April 23 *Germ Warfare Investigation* The United Nations General Assembly voted to create a commission to investigate the germ warfare charges directed at the United States by North Korea, the Soviet Union, and the People's Republic of China. But Soviet Deputy Foreign Minister Andrei Vishinsky's comments during the course of the General Assembly debate made it clear the communist nations would not cooperate with the commission. (NYT 4/24/53 1)

April 24 *Changes Since Stalin* Ambassador Bohlen wrote to Secretary of State Dulles on changes taking place in the Soviet Union since the death of Stalin. The ambassador noted that the Soviet government had ceased its hate-America campaign, was emphasizing the need for peace, and seemed preoccupied with China and the nations of Eastern Europe. (FRUS 1952-1954 VIII 1156)

April 24 *Dulles on Changes* Secretary of State Dulles, in an address to the North Atlantic Council, said he did not see any significant change in Soviet policies since the death of Stalin. He said the Soviet Union had a powerful dictatorial government, distrusted states not under its control, and had no scruples about using force to achieve its objectives. (FRUS 1952-1954 V 373)

April 25 *North Atlantic Council* At the conclusion of two days of talks in Paris, the ministers attending the North Atlantic Council meeting issued a communiqué. They did not think the Soviet threat to the West had diminished since the death of Stalin. They called for an increase in military units available to NATO, and they emphasized the need to improve the quality of their forces. (DSB 5/11/53 673)

April 25 *Soviets Respond to Eisenhower* *Pravda* criticized President Eisenhower's April 16 speech. The Soviets blamed the United States for existing international tensions and berated Eisenhower for demanding changes in Soviet policies without altering those American policies offensive to the Soviet Union. Despite the criticism, the Soviets said they were interested in improving relations with the United States. (CDSP V:14 5)

May 4 *Churchill to Eisenhower* President Eisenhower received a letter from Prime Minister Churchill with a copy of a message he intended to send to Foreign Minister Molotov suggesting that Churchill travel to Moscow for talks with the new Soviet leaders and explore the possibility of convening a summit meeting. Churchill wanted to know whether the president approved the idea. On May 5 President Eisenhower replied to Churchill's inquiry. Eisenhower said he did not favor a summit meeting, but if one were convened he did not want it to be in Moscow. (FRUS 1952-1954 VIII 1169)

May 14 *Eisenhower on Summits* President Eisenhower, in response to a question at a news conference, said he would be willing to attend a summit meeting with Soviet leaders provided there was some indication it would be successful. At the time, he saw no evidence to justify a summit. (PP 284)

May 30 *Soviets Renounce Territorial Claims* The Soviet Union, in a note to Turkey, renounced the territorial claims made by Moscow in the past.

The Soviets also said they wanted no special privileges in the Dardanelles. These claims were a major source of tension in Soviet-Turkish
and Soviet-American relations. (DIA 277)

June 15 *The World Peace Council* The World Peace Council met in
Budapest for a five-day conference. Among other things, the communist-dominated council called for an end to the Korean War, German
unification, the closing of foreign military bases, and an end to the arms
race. The council took positions on international issues in conformity
with Soviet policies and in opposition to those of the United States.
(CDSP V:25 23)

June 16 *Unrest in Germany* Three months after the death of Stalin, there
was widespread labor unrest in East Berlin that quickly spread to East
Germany. In some areas where violence erupted, demands were made
for economic and political reforms. The East German government,
assisted by Soviet troops, brought the rioting under control. (FRUS
1952-1954 VII 1584)

June 17 *Berlin Uprising* The Allied military authorities in West Berlin
denied Soviet charges that Western agents were responsible for causing
disturbances in East Berlin. (DSB 7/6/53 8)

June 18 *Western Notes to Soviets* France, the United Kingdom, and the
United States, in notes to the Soviet Union, protested its policies in East
Germany and Berlin. The Western nations condemned "the irresponsi-
ble recourse to military force which had as its result the killing or
serious wounding of a considerable number of citizens of Berlin. . . ."
(DSB 6/29/53 897)

June 20 *Berlin Uprising* The Soviet commandant in Berlin responded to
the June 18 protest by the three Western nations. The Soviets justified
the use of force against demonstrators in East Berlin because the
disturbances were allegedly the result of Western agents fomenting
disorder. The Western nations denied the charge. (DSB 7/6/53 8)

June 26 *Eisenhower Message to Adenauer* President Eisenhower sent a
message to Chancellor Adenauer on the uprising in East Berlin and East
Germany. The president said the aspirations of the German people for
more freedom could only be achieved through German unity based on
free elections. He predicted that the events in Berlin would have
repercussions "throughout the Soviet satellite empire." (PP 457)

June 30 *Dulles on Berlin* Secretary of State Dulles, in a statement at a news
conference, said he was not surprised by the uprising in East Berlin and
East Germany because the Soviets had overextended their power. He

said that as long as free nations existed, the hopes of people subjugated by communism would be kept alive. (DSB 7/13/53 40)

July 10 *Beria Removed* The Soviet Union announced that Lavrenty Beria, head of the Ministry of Internal Affairs, had been removed from office because of alleged criminal activities. Soviet officials feared Beria could become another Stalin. (DIA 18)

July 10 *U.S. Food Offer* The United States, in response to the East German uprising the previous month, offered to provide food to East Germany. The offer was made to the Soviet Union because the United States had no official ties with East Germany. On July 11 the Soviet Union informed the United States that the people in East Germany did not need food from foreign nations. Foreign Minister Molotov said the Soviets could provide their ally with whatever was needed. He accused the United States of being responsible for the disorders in East Germany that brought about the food shortage. (DSB 7/20/53 68)

July 14 *Washington Meeting* The French foreign minister, the acting British foreign secretary, and Secretary of State Dulles issued a communiqué after their meeting in Washington that began July 9. They reviewed East-West relations and problems in Asia. The British wanted to convene a summit meeting with the new Soviet leaders, but the United States would only consent to a preliminary meeting to determine whether a summit would be useful. (DSB 7/27/53 104)

July 15 *Proposed Four-Power Meeting* The foreign ministers of France, the United Kingdom, and the United States sent an invitation to the Soviet Union proposing a Big Four meeting of foreign ministers to discuss peace treaties for Germany and Austria. (DSB 7/27/53 107)

July 27 *The Korean Armistice Signed* An armistice was signed ending the Korean War. The willingness of China and North Korea to end the fighting was in part attributable to the death of Stalin in March. The new Soviet leaders were attempting to improve relations with the United States. (DSB 8/3/53 132)

July 28 *Germ Warfare Charges* President Vijaya Lakshmi Pandit of the United Nations General Assembly reported that the commission created to investigate germ warfare charges in Korea was unable to do so because North Korea and the People's Republic of China refused to cooperate. (AFP 1950-1955 II 2670)

August 4 *Soviet Note to U.S.* The Soviet Union, in response to the July 15 note from France, the United Kingdom, and the United States, rejected the proposed agenda for a foreign ministers meeting, insisting that it be expanded to include questions regarding foreign military bases and armaments. The Soviets also suggested that the People's Republic of China be invited to the proposed meeting. (DAFR 220)

August 8 *Malenkov Speech* Premier Malenkov, in an address to the Supreme Soviet, suggested the possibility of a thaw in the cold war. He said differences in social-economic systems should not prevent nations from cooperating, and he reiterated the Soviet view of being committed to a policy of peaceful relations with other nations. (DIA 22)

August 15 *Soviet Note on Germany* The Soviet Union sent another note to the United States on the proposed four-power meeting of foreign ministers regarding the question of peace treaties for Germany and Austria. The Soviets proposed establishing a provisional German government that would then decide how to conduct national elections. The provisional government would have to agree not to join any military alliances directed against those nations that participated in the war against Nazi Germany. The United States took the position that a peace treaty could be negotiated only after free elections to create an all-German government. (DSB 9/14/53 354)

August 20 *Soviets Explode Hydrogen Bomb* The Soviet Union announced it had exploded a hydrogen bomb. This was a boosted fission bomb, not a true fusion or hydrogen bomb, something American officials did not know at the time. (CDSP V:30 3)

September 2 *Foreign Ministers Meeting* The United States invited the Soviet Union to attend a Big Four foreign ministers meeting to be convened in Lugano, Switzerland on October 15. The United States wanted to limit the agenda to peace treaties for Germany and Austria. The note to the Soviet Union was sent after the United States consulted with France and the United Kingdom. (DSB 10/14/53 351)

September 2 *Dulles Warns China* Secretary of State Dulles, in a speech to the American Legion in Los Angeles, warned the People's Republic of China not to send military units into Indochina. He said if China did so, the American response would not necessarily be confined to Indochina. (DSB 9/14/53 342)

September 9 *Soviets on Dulles Speech* *Pravda* criticized Secretary of State Dulles for his September 2 speech. The secretary was accused of threatening China with renewed aggression and with preparing the American people for a war in Southeast Asia. (CDSP V:36 15)

September 13 *First Secretary Khrushchev* Nikita Khrushchev became first secretary of the Communist party. This made him the most powerful leader in the Soviet Union. (NYT 9/13/53 1)

September 17 *Dulles Addresses the UN* Secretary of State Dulles, in an address to the United Nations General Assembly, discussed a number of international problems, including arms control, the division of Korea, peace treaties for Austria and Germany, the fighting in Indochina, and revising the United Nations Charter. He said since 1939, 600 million people had been brought under Soviet control, none of them voluntarily. He said the Soviets allegedly supported peaceful coexistence, but their words were not backed by deeds. (DSB 9/28/53 403)

September 20 *Soviets Criticize Dulles* *Pravda* criticized Secretary of State Dulles for his September 17 speech to the United Nations General Assembly. He was accused of continuing to rely on a policy of strength when dealing with the communist nations despite their growing power since the end of World War II. (CDSP V:38 15)

September 28 *Soviet Note on Meeting* The Soviet Union, in response to the September 2 note from the Western Big Three, again called for a foreign ministers meeting to discuss Germany and other international problems. The Western nations were warned not to ratify the Paris agreements permitting West Germany to rearm within the framework of the EDC. (DIA 91)

September 30 *Religious Persecution* The State Department issued a statement on religious persecution in Poland. The Polish government was denounced for arresting the primate of Poland, Stefan Cardinal Wyszynski. (DSB 10/19/53 528)

October 18 *London Foreign Ministers Meeting* The foreign ministers of France, the United Kingdom, and the United States issued a communiqué after their three-day meeting in London. The ministers discussed a number of issues, including the Indochina war, a conference regarding Korean issues, and the West German contribution to a European army. They also agreed to invite the Soviet Union to a Big Four foreign ministers meeting to discuss peace treaties for Austria and Germany. (DIA 97)

October 25 *Soviets and London Conference* An article in *Pravda* said the London meeting attended by the Western foreign ministers failed to resolve differences between the United States and its European allies regarding the contribution of West Germany to a European army. The Soviets claimed there was growing opposition in France to the rearming of West Germany. (CDSP V:43 18)

November 3 *Germ Warfare* Henry Ford II, an American representative at the United Nations, issued an announcement regarding the air force personnel who, after capture by North Korea during the Korean War, allegedly confessed to using germ warfare. The airmen had returned to the United States and said they were coerced into making the confessions. (DSB 11/30/53 758)

November 3 *Foreign Ministers Meeting* The Soviet Union, in a note to the United States, accused it of ignoring issues the Soviets had raised in various communications. The Soviets wanted to know if a German peace treaty were going to be considered at a Big Four foreign ministers meeting or if the Western powers were going to proceed with the ratification of the Paris agreements signed in November 1951. The Soviets said they would not attend a foreign ministers conference if the agreements to restore German sovereignty and to create the EDC were ratified. A major Soviet effort at this time was to delay or prevent the ratification of the Paris agreements. (DIA 100)

November 16 *Western Notes to the Soviet Union* France, the United Kingdom, and the United States, in notes to the Soviet Union, rejected its suggestion that the People's Republic of China be invited to participate in the proposed foreign ministers meeting. The Western powers also accused the Soviet Union of establishing conditions that had to be satisfied before it would agree to attend a foreign ministers meeting. (DIA 106)

December 3 *Atrocities in Korea* The United Nations General Assembly passed a resolution, supported by the United States and opposed by the Soviet Union, condemning North Korea and the People's Republic of China for atrocities committed during the Korean War. (DAFR 438)

December 7 *Forced Labor* The United Nations General Assembly passed a resolution, supported by the United States and opposed by the Soviet Union, requesting the secretary general to obtain information about the use of forced labor from those governments that had thus far refused to cooperate with the United Nations. The Soviet Union was one of the nations accused of not cooperating. (DAFR 441)

December 8 *Atoms for Peace* President Eisenhower, in an address to the United Nations General Assembly, proposed a plan whereby those nations with atomic resources would contribute to an international agency that would design programs for the peaceful uses of atomic energy. He believed his plan would assist the economically underdeveloped nations in their efforts to improve living standards. He advocated the establishment of an International Atomic Energy Agency (IAEA) to promote and monitor the peaceful uses of atomic energy. The president also emphasized the terrible destruction that would result from a nuclear war and the need to negotiate arms control agreements. (PP 813)

December 26 *Four-Power Meeting* The Soviet Union, in a note to the United States, suggested that the foreign ministers of the Big Four meet in Berlin on January 25 to discuss ways to reduce tensions in Europe. The Soviets also suggested convening a five-power conference, with the People's Republic of China, to discuss Asian problems. France, the United Kingdom, and the United States accepted the invitation. (DIA 112)

1954

January 7 *State of the Union* President Eisenhower, in his State of the Union address, said that American freedom would be endangered until the world communist conspiracy ceased to exist. His prescription for defeating communism without a war was to promote the unity of the free world. He also urged the Congress to approve legislation to enable the United States to share its knowledge of tactical nuclear weapons with allied nations. (PP 8)

January 12 *Massive Retaliation* Secretary of State John Foster Dulles, in a speech in New York City, outlined a new nuclear strategy for the United States. The current policy, Dulles said, of being prepared to meet a communist challenge wherever the Soviet leaders decided to apply pressure would cause the United States "grave budgetary, economic and social consequences." As an alternative, he suggested a policy that would allow the United States "to retaliate instantly and at places of our own choosing." This policy came to be known as *massive retaliation* and was a part of President Eisenhower's strategic program entitled the *New Look*. (DSB 1/25/54 107)

January 25 *The Berlin Conference* The foreign ministers of France, the United Kingdom, the Soviet Union, and the United States met in Berlin. Topics on the agenda included peace treaties for Austria and Germany, European security, and arms control. (DAFR 200)

January 26 *Dulles at Berlin* Secretary of State Dulles, at the Berlin foreign ministers meeting, accused the Soviet Union of supporting policies to prevent German unification. The secretary also made clear that the United States would not accept the People's Republic of China as one of the five great powers having responsibility for the establishment of a more peaceful world. He said China had committed aggression in Korea and was supporting aggression in Indochina. (DSB 2/8/54 179)

January 30 *Soviets on Nuclear Weapons* Foreign Minister Molotov, at the Berlin foreign ministers meeting, presented the three Western leaders with a draft declaration that would require the five permanent members of the United Nations Security Council to renounce the use of weapons of mass destruction such as atomic and hydrogen weapons. The Western powers rejected the Soviet proposal. (DAFR 468)

February 1 *Soviet Peace Treaty* Foreign Minister Molotov, at the Berlin foreign ministers meeting, introduced a draft of a peace treaty for

Germany. The main provisions of the treaty called for German unification, the withdrawal of all occupation forces, and a prohibition on Germany joining any military alliance directed against any of the World War II Allies. France, the United Kingdom, and the United States rejected the Soviet proposal. (DOG 1944-1985 411)

February 10 *Soviets Propose European Treaty* Foreign Minister Molotov, at the Berlin foreign ministers meeting, introduced a draft of a European collective security treaty. Any European nation could join the proposed treaty, and signatories would have to agree not to attack any other members or to threaten the use of force. The United States, as a non-European power, was not eligible for membership. The proposed Soviet fifty-year treaty would have required abolishing NATO and would have precluded completing the European Defense Community treaty. The Western nations rejected the Soviet proposal. (DIA 37)

February 10 *A Neutral Germany* Foreign Minister Molotov, at the Berlin foreign ministers meeting, presented a proposal for the withdrawal of all occupation forces from Germany and the neutralization of the country pending the completion of a peace treaty. The Western nations rejected the Soviet proposal. (DOG 1944-1985 414)

February 13 *Soviet Aide-Mémoire* The Soviet Union presented an aide-mémoire to Secretary of State Dulles at the Berlin foreign ministers meeting. Among other things, it suggested that the permanent members of the United Nations Security Council plus a few other nations, including the People's Republic of China, meet to discuss problems related to the peaceful uses of atomic energy. The United States rejected the Soviet proposal. (DAFR 468)

February 18 *Four-Power Communiqué* The Big Four foreign ministers at the conclusion of their meeting in Berlin issued a communiqué. The four powers failed to complete peace treaties for Austria or Germany, but they did agree to convene a conference in Geneva in April to discuss problems regarding Korea and Indochina. (DAFR 218)

February 19 *Tripartite Statement* France, the United Kingdom, and the United States, at the conclusion of the Berlin foreign ministers meeting, issued a statement blaming the Soviet Union for the failure to complete peace treaties for Austria and Germany. (DAFR 219)

February 24 *Dulles on Berlin Conference* Secretary of State Dulles addressed the American people on the recently concluded Berlin conference. He said the Soviets' determination to keep their troops in Germany and Austria was the obstacle preventing the completion of peace treaties for the two countries. (DAFR 221)

March 11 *Molotov on Foreign Policy* Foreign Minister Molotov, in an election speech in Moscow, accused the United States of using NATO as an instrument to dominate the European members of the alliance. He again proposed a European security system as a substitute for military blocs within Europe that he said threatened the peace. (CDSP VI:10 13)

March 12 *Malenkov on Foreign Policy* Premier Malenkov, in a speech in Moscow, called for an end to the cold war, and he deviated from the party line by stating that a nuclear war would mean "the destruction of world civilization." His theme was similar to that of President Eisenhower's address to the United Nations General Assembly in December 1953. Some members of the Soviet ruling elite did not share Malenkov's views. (CDSP VI:11 6)

March 25 *Sovereignty for the GDR* The Soviet Union announced that the German Democratic Republic was now a sovereign state. The Soviets hoped the alleged change in the GDR's status would give it more legitimacy, as the Bonn government claimed to speak for all of Germany. (NYT 3/26/54 1)

March 31 *A Collective Security Pact* The Soviet Union, in a note to the United States, again proposed establishing a European collective security pact. This time, however, Moscow invited the United States to participate in the European security arrangements, but in return the Soviets wanted to join NATO. (DSB 5/17/54 757)

April 8 *The West Reacts to East Germany* France, the United Kingdom, and the United States responded to the March 25 announcement by the Soviet Union allegedly granting sovereignty to East Germany. The three Western nations said they did not recognize East Germany as a sovereign nation, and they continued to hold the Soviet Union responsible for controlling events in its zone in Germany. (DAFR 228)

May 7 *U.S. Reacts to Soviets in NATO* The United States, in a note to the Soviet Union, rejected the Soviet suggestion that it be allowed to join NATO. The United States pointed out that NATO was founded on "the principle of individual liberty and the rule of law." The United States also rejected the Soviet proposal for a European security treaty. (DAFR 232)

May 8 *Geneva Conference on Indochina* The Geneva Conference on Indochina opened, attended by France, the three Associated States of Indochina (Cambodia, Laos, and South Vietnam), the Democratic Republic of Vietnam (North Vietnam), the People's Republic of China, the Soviet Union, the United Kingdom, and the United States. On July 20 France, Cambodia, and the Democratic Republic of Vietnam signed cease-fire agreements bringing the first Indochina war to an end. (NYT 5/9/54 1)

May 31 *Eisenhower on Foreign Policy* President Eisenhower, in an address at Columbia University, analyzed the need to understand the struggle between the communist bloc and the free world. He accused the Soviet Union of seeking to dominate the world in a "campaign of deceit, subversion, and terrorism." (PP 517)

June 7 *Soviet Capabilities* The National Intelligence Estimate group assessing Soviet capabilities through mid-1959 concluded that the Soviet Union would avoid situations, at least for a couple of years, that might lead to a general war. The assessment also stated that as the Soviet nuclear arsenal grew, the leaders in Moscow might be tempted to exploit the fear of a nuclear war to advance their foreign policy goals. (FRUS 1952-1954 VIII 1235)

June 10 *Dulles on Foreign Policy* Secretary of State Dulles, in a speech in Seattle, accused communists of relying on force to suppress differences and promote conformity. He said the spiritual and natural forces that create diversity in democratic nations would eventually prevail over communism. (VS 20:18 552)

July 24 *Soviets Propose a Conference* The Soviet Union responded to the May 7 note from the United States. The Soviets once more proposed convening a European security conference to be attended by all the European nations, the United States, and an observer from the People's Republic of China. The purpose of the conference would be to conclude a European security treaty that would prevent the remilitarization of Germany. Such a treaty, said the Soviets, would contribute to reunifying Germany and solving the Austrian problem. The United States rejected the Soviet proposal. (DAFR 235)

August 30 *France Rejects EDC* The French National Assembly rejected the EDC. The rejection compelled the Western allies to find a new method for rearming the Federal Republic of Germany. (NYT 8/31/54 1)

September 9 *Soviets React to EDC Failure* The Soviet Foreign Ministry issued a statement welcoming the French rejection of the European Defense Community on August 30. The Soviets again called for the convening of an all-European conference to negotiate a European collective security agreement. The United States rejected the Soviet proposal. (DIA 51)

September 28 *The London Conference* Representatives from nine nations, Belgium, Canada, France, the United Kingdom, Italy, Luxembourg, the

Netherlands, the United States, and West Germany, met in London to find an alternative to the European Defense Community the French had just rejected. The task of the diplomats was to restore German sovereignty and permit it to rearm within a framework satisfactory to the French and the Bonn governments. (NYT 9/29/54 1)

October 3 *Agreement on Germany* The foreign ministers of the nine nations that met in London concluded their meeting on September 28. Among the matters the ministers agreed to were an end to the occupation of West Germany and the restoration of its sovereignty, the creation of a Western European Union, and an invitation to West Germany and Italy to join the Brussels Treaty Organization and NATO. The delegates scheduled another meeting to be convened in Paris on October 20 to complete the London agreements. (FRUS 1952-1954 V 1329)

October 19 *The Paris Agreements* Representatives of the nine nations seeking an alternative to the failed EDC met in Paris and reached a number of agreements, collectively known as the Paris agreements, based on the negotiations at the London nine-power conference. The Paris agreements dealt with the Brussels Treaty Organization, a Western European Union, the rearmament of West Germany, an invitation to West Germany and Italy to join NATO, and an end to the occupation of West Germany. These agreements replaced the Paris agreements negotiated in November 1951. (NYT 10/20/54 1)

October 21 *The Western European Union* Belgium, Canada, France, the Federal Republic of Germany, Italy, Luxembourg, the Netherlands, the United Kingdom, and the United States issued a communiqué on an agreement to enlarge the Brussels Treaty Organization by admitting Italy and the Federal Republic of Germany as members. A Western European Union was established to regulate the rearmament of the Federal Republic of Germany. (DAFR 145)

October 22 *NATO Communiqué* The ministers attending the North Atlantic Council meeting in Paris issued a communiqué at the close of their meeting. The ministers approved linking the Western European Union to NATO, and they agreed to a protocol inviting Italy and the Federal Republic of Germany to join the NATO alliance. (DSB 11/15/54 732)

October 23 *Occupation Ended* France, the United Kingdom, the United States, and the Federal Republic of Germany signed an agreement ending the occupation of West Germany. This was one of a number of agreements, known as the Paris agreements, that had to be accepted as a package. (DAFR 134)

October 23   *Foreign Ministers Meeting* The Soviet Union, in notes to France, the United Kingdom, and the United States, again proposed a Big Four foreign ministers meeting to discuss holding free elections in Germany. The Soviets said there was no progress at the January foreign ministers meeting because of the proposed EDC plan. Now that it had been rejected by France, the Soviet Union said it was willing to again take up the issue of German elections. At the time of the Soviet note, the Western powers were meeting in Paris to complete plans for ending the occupation of Germany. (DSB 12/13/54 902)

November 8   *Bohlen and Malenkov* Ambassador Bohlen, in a memorandum to the Department of State, reported on a conversation he had with Georgy Malenkov, the chairman of the Council of Ministers. The ambassador reported that Malenkov seemed to have a genuine desire to improve relations with the United States. Bohlen suggested this might have something to do with the Paris agreements, which granted sovereignty to West Germany and allowed it to join NATO. (FRUS 1952-1954 VIII 1257)

November 13   *The Paris Agreements* The Soviet Union, in notes to twenty-five nations, including the United States, alleged that the October 23 Paris agreements would allow West Germany to rearm under the authority of German generals associated with the Nazi regime. The Soviets warned that the creation of military blocs in Europe could lead to another war. To avoid war, the Soviets again suggested the immediate convening of a conference to create an all-European collective security alliance. The Western nations rejected the Soviet invitation. (DSB 12/13/54 905)

November 29   *Foreign Ministers Meeting* The United States responded to the Soviet call to convene a foreign ministers meeting to discuss European security issues. The United States charged the Soviet Union with attempting to prevent or delay the ratification of the Paris agreements. (DSB 12/13/54 901)

December 2   *Eight-Power Conference* The foreign ministers of eight communist nations attending a conference in Moscow issued a declaration condemning the Paris agreements permitting the rearming of West Germany. They again proposed creating an all-European security system that would include the two German states. The ministers warned that ratification of the Paris agreements would block efforts to unify Germany and would threaten the peace. (DAFR 253)

1955

January 1 *Malenkov on Foreign Policy* Premier Malenkov, in response to a question from a correspondent, said the Soviet Union wanted to have peaceful relations with the United States but that American policies regarding Germany made that difficult. He also criticized American overseas military bases, alleging they were a source of international tension. (NYT 1/1/55 1)

January 6 *State of the Union* President Eisenhower, in his State of the Union address, said the United States must deter Soviet aggression and must also prevent the communists from achieving their goals through acts of subversion. (PP 9)

January 15 *The Paris Agreements* The Soviet Union issued a statement criticizing the Paris agreements restoring sovereignty to West Germany and permitting it to join NATO. The Soviets said ratification of the Paris agreements would lead to the remilitarization of West Germany and would threaten world peace. The Soviets made it clear Germany would remain divided if the Paris agreements were implemented. (CDSP VII:3 23)

February 8 *Molotov on Foreign Policy* Foreign Minister Molotov, in a speech to the Supreme Soviet, said the communist bloc nations were getting stronger under the leadership of the Soviet Union and the People's Republic of China. He said the Soviet Union had a nuclear arsenal comparable to that of the United States and predicted the end of capitalism if the Western nations engaged in another war. (NYT 2/9/55 1)

February 8 *Malenkov Ousted* Premier Malenkov was ousted from power and was succeeded by Nikolai Bulganin. (NYT 2/9/55 1)

March 8 *Dulles on Nuclear Weapons* Secretary of State Dulles, in a speech to the nation, said the United States had the ability, because of new, powerful weapons, to destroy enemy targets while keeping civilian casualties to a minimum. The secretary was alluding to tactical nuclear weapons. (DSB 3/21/55 459)

March 16 *Eisenhower on Nuclear Weapons* President Eisenhower, in response to a question at a news conference, said tactical nuclear weapons could be used "just exactly as you would use a bullet or anything else." (PP 332)

April 22 *Note to the Soviet Union* The United States accepted the Soviet proposal for completing an Austrian peace treaty. The United States suggested having the British, French, and American ambassadors to Austria meet with Soviet and Austrian representatives to complete the treaty. The foreign ministers could then meet to sign the treaty. (DSB 5/2/55 733)

May 5 *Paris Agreements* The October 1954 Paris agreements entered into force, and the Occupation Statute that governed relations between West Germany and the three Western occupying powers was officially terminated. The Federal Republic of Germany became sovereign. (NYT 5/6/55 1)

May 6 *Germany Joins NATO* The Federal Republic of Germany joined NATO. (NYT 5/7/55 1)

May 10 *Soviets Invited to a Summit* France, the United Kingdom, and the United States, in a note to the Soviet Union, proposed convening a four-power summit meeting to discuss outstanding issues. The invitation was extended after France, the United Kingdom, and the United States had ratified the Paris agreements restoring sovereignty to West Germany. The Soviets accepted the invitation. (DSB 5/23/55 832)

May 14 *The Warsaw Treaty* Albania, Bulgaria, Czechoslovakia, Hungary, the German Democratic Republic, Poland, Romania, and the Soviet Union signed a treaty establishing the Warsaw Treaty Organization (WTO). The signatories pledged to come to the assistance of any WTO member that was the victim of aggression. (NT 5/21/55 63)

May 15 *Austrian Treaty Signed* France, the United Kingdom, the Soviet Union, and the United States signed a treaty ending the occupation of Austria and prohibiting it from completing any type of economic or political union with Germany. Austria was required to follow a policy of neutrality, to refrain from joining any military alliances, and to prohibit the establishment of any military bases on its territory. (DAFR 127)

June 25 *Soviets Apologize* The Soviet Union apologized for shooting down an American airplane on June 22 that had allegedly violated Soviet airspace. The Soviets said the plane might have been shot down in error. This was the first time the Soviets had apologized for such an incident, and they also offered partial compensation for the destruction of the plane. (NYT 6/26/55 1)

June 29 *Eisenhower and Eastern Europe* President Eisenhower, in response to a question at a news conference regarding Eastern Europe, said he did not think there could be "real peace in the world" until all states have the right to determine their own form of government. On July 2 *Pravda* criticized President Eisenhower for his June 29 comments, accusing him of seeking to interfere in the internal affairs of the Eastern European nations. Soviet leaders repeatedly claimed that the nations of Eastern Europe were free and independent and that the communist governments in those nations were supported by the people. (PP 648)

July 18   Geneva Summit Meeting   The Big Four Geneva summit meeting convened on a relatively optimistic note attributable to the end of the Korean and Indochina wars and the completion of an Austrian peace treaty. But West Germany's entry into NATO and the creation of the WTO made clear that the division of Europe could not be easily changed. The major topics at the summit were German unity, European security problems, disarmament, and East-West contacts. This was the first meeting of Soviet-American leaders since the 1945 Potsdam conference and the only Big Four summit in the cold war era. (NYT 7/19/55 1)

July 18   Eisenhower at the Summit   President Eisenhower, at the Geneva summit meeting, outlined the topics he thought should be discussed, including German unity, arms control, and Soviet control over Eastern Europe. He said he hoped the conference would do more than simply catalog differences among the conference participants. (DAFR 182)

July 20   A Collective Security System   Premier Bulganin, at the Geneva summit meeting, proposed a collective security system for Europe that would include the United States. The system he proposed required the eventual dismantling of NATO and the WTO. (NYT 7/21/55 4)

July 21   The Open-Sky Proposal   President Eisenhower made the most dramatic proposal at the Big Four summit meeting. He suggested that the United States and the Soviet Union should exchange blueprints of their military establishments, and both nations should be allowed to conduct reconnaissance flights over each other's territory. (PP 713)

July 21   A Collective Security Treaty   Premier Bulganin, at the Geneva summit meeting, suggested that the NATO and WTO nations sign an agreement pledging not to attack each other. The agreement was to remain in effect until a European security treaty was negotiated. The Western nations rejected the Soviet proposal. (DAFR 212)

July 22   East-West Contacts   President Eisenhower, at the Geneva summit meeting, addressed the issue of East-West contacts. He said he hoped that an East-West exchange agreement would reduce some of the barriers to mutual understanding. (PP 716)

July 23 *Summit Follow-Up*   The leaders of the Big Four, on the last day of the Geneva summit meeting, issued a directive to their foreign ministers on issues they were to examine at a follow-up conference. These included German unification, a European security system, disarmament, and East-West contacts. The ministers were scheduled to meet in October. (DAFR 225)

July 25 *Eisenhower on Summit Results*   President Eisenhower addressed the nation on the results of the Geneva summit meeting. He gave a generally optimistic assessment of the meeting, although he said success would be determined by the work of the foreign ministers when they met in October. The president said that one of the important developments of the conference was that all four countries recognized the disastrous consequences of a thermonuclear war. (DAFR 227)

August 13 *Soviet Troop Reductions*   Tass, the Soviet news agency, issued a statement announcing the decision of the Soviet government to reduce its armed forces by 640,000 personnel before December 15, 1955. The following day Secretary of State Dulles, at a news conference, said he welcomed the Soviets' decision to reduce their armed forces but, he added, verification measures were necessary to ensure the accuracy of the data. (CDSP VII:32 13)

August 24 *Eisenhower on Foreign Policy*   President Eisenhower, in a speech to the American Bar Association, said the most important problem in the world was the contest between two competing ideologies, communism and democracy. He was optimistic that in the long run democracy would prevail. He called for the unification of Germany and an end to Soviet domination of the Eastern European nations. (PP 802)

September 19 *Bulganin to Eisenhower*   Premier Bulganin wrote to President Eisenhower on the subject of aerial inspections and the exchange of military blueprints. Bulganin gave a conditional acceptance to Eisenhower's proposal for exchanging military blueprints, but he said an aerial reconnaissance agreement had to be part of a comprehensive arms control package. (DAFR 441)

September 20 *Soviet-GDR Treaty*   The Soviet Union and the German Democratic Republic signed a treaty allegedly giving the East German government control over traffic between West Germany and West Berlin. (NYT 9/21/55 1)

October 3 *Note to Soviet Union*   France, the United Kingdom, and the United States, in identical notes to the Soviet Union, insisted, despite the Soviet-East German treaty signed on September 20, that the Soviet

Union remained responsible for carrying out the wartime agreements pertaining to Germany and Berlin. (DAFR 113)

October 10 *Dulles on Foreign Policy* Secretary of State Dulles, in a speech to the American Legion, said the Soviet Union was now pursuing a more friendly policy toward the Western nations in part because it had failed to prevent growing European unity. He warned, however, that the Soviets were capable of changing their policy at any time. (DSB 10/24/55 639)

October 27 *Foreign Ministers Meeting* The foreign ministers of France, the United Kingdom, the United States, and the Soviet Union met in Geneva to continue the negotiations that began at the July summit meeting. The purpose of the meeting was to explore solutions to problems identified at the summit. (DSB 11/7/55 727)

October 28 *Proposal on Germany* The foreign ministers of France, the United Kingdom, and the United States introduced a resolution regarding German unification at the Big Four foreign ministers meeting in Geneva. The Soviets rejected the Western proposal. (DSB 11/7/55 729)

October 28 *Soviet Proposal on Security* Foreign Minister Molotov introduced a draft treaty at the Big Four foreign ministers meeting in Geneva regarding European security. The United States and its allies rejected the Soviet proposal. (DSB 11/7/55 732)

October 31 *East-West Contacts* France, the United Kingdom, and the United States submitted a treaty on East-West contacts to the Big Four foreign ministers meeting in Geneva. The Soviets submitted a separate treaty on the same subject. (DSB 11/14/55 778)

November 4 *Elections in Germany* France, the United Kingdom, and the United States, at the foreign ministers meeting in Geneva, introduced a proposal for conducting free elections in Germany leading to reunification. The Soviets rejected the proposal. (DSB 11/21/55 828)

November 16 *Foreign Ministers End Meeting* The foreign ministers of France, the United Kingdom, the United States, and the Soviet Union ended their meeting that began on October 27. A four-power communiqué was issued stating that the foreign ministers would report the results of their meeting to their respective governments. Little progress was made in resolving outstanding issues. (DAFR 288)

November 16 *Tripartite Declaration* The foreign ministers of France, the United Kingdom, and the United States issued a communiqué at the close of the Geneva four-power meeting. The three Western ministers blamed the Soviet Union for the lack of progress at Geneva. They said the Soviets opposed the unification of Germany based on free elections. (DAFR 288)

November 18   *Dulles Reports to the Nation*   Secretary of State Dulles reported to the American people on the Geneva foreign ministers meeting. He said no agreements were reached because of the opposition of the Soviet Union but, he said, the United States would continue to negotiate with the Soviets to find solutions to international problems. On November 20 *Pravda* criticized Secretary of State Dulles for his November 18 evaluation of the Geneva foreign ministers meeting and accused him of distorting Soviet policies. *Pravda* blamed the Western powers for the lack of progress at Geneva. (DAFR 289)

December 8   *Dulles on Foreign Policy*   Secretary of State Dulles, in a speech in Illinois, analyzed international communism and its challenge to the United States. The secretary said the United States and its allies had a variety of tools to cope with international communism and they had to be used flexibly. He said the communists had changed their tactics and were now relying on less violent methods because of American policies. He also accused the Soviets of exploiting the aspirations of people living in the Third World for a better life. (DAFR 12)

December 25   *Eisenhower and Eastern Europe*   President Eisenhower sent a Christmas message to the Soviet satellite countries through Radio Free Europe. The president said he supported efforts on their part to regain their freedom. (NYT 12/30/55 1)

December 29   *Khrushchev and Eisenhower*   First Secretary Khrushchev, in a major foreign policy address, denounced the United States and the policies of President Eisenhower. The Soviet leader said Eisenhower's Christmas message to the nations of Eastern Europe constituted interference in their internal affairs, and he rejected Eisenhower's plan for aerial inspections. Khrushchev's speech seemed to dispel the generally optimistic spirit of the July Geneva summit conference. (NYT 12/30/55 4)

December 30   *Liberating Eastern Europe*   James Hagerty, President Eisenhower's press secretary, issued a statement reaffirming that "a major goal of United States foreign policy" was the peaceful liberation of the Eastern European nations. (DSB 1/16/56 84)

1956

January 5 *State of the Union* President Eisenhower, in his State of the Union address, commented on what he thought to be the new tactics used by the Soviet Union. He said the communist nations now relied on "division, enticement, and duplicity" to create disunity among the Western nations rather than relying on violence. (PP 4)

January 10 *The Satellites* A study by the National Intelligence Estimate concluded that the Soviet Union would continue to dominate the nations of Eastern Europe through a variety of instruments, including the military. The study covered the period 1956 through 1960. (FRUS 1955-1957 XXV 115)

January 23 *Bulganin Letter to Eisenhower* Premier Bulganin, in a letter to President Eisenhower, said the Soviet Union was eager to improve relations with the United States by signing a treaty of friendship and cooperation. A draft treaty was included with the letter. On January 28 President Eisenhower rejected the proposal for a friendship treaty. He said both nations were members of the United Nations, and if they abided by the principles of the UN Charter, a friendship treaty would be unnecessary. (DIA 575)

February 1 *Eden-Eisenhower Talks* President Eisenhower and British prime minister Eden, after three days of talks in Washington, issued a declaration in support of democratic values. The two leaders criticized the Soviet Union for its record on human rights and the occupation of Eastern Europe. They rejected the use of force to settle international disputes, and they reaffirmed their determination to protect the integrity of West Berlin. (DAFR 150)

February 1 *Bulganin Letter to Eisenhower* Premier Bulganin, in a letter to President Eisenhower, again proposed negotiating a friendship treaty. The Soviet premier said a treaty would be useful in regulating relations between the two countries and would complement the United Nations Charter. (DIA 584)

February 10 *Protest to the Soviet Union* France, the United Kingdom, and the United States, in identical notes to the Soviet Union, protested the arming of civilians and the creation of paramilitary units in East Germany. (DOG 1944-1959 487)

February 14 *Khrushchev on Foreign Policy* First Secretary Nikita Khrushchev, in an address to the Twentieth Congress of the Communist party, rejected the Leninist idea of the inevitability of war because, he said, the communist and the nonaligned nations were capable of preventing the outbreak of war. He favored negotiating a friendship treaty with the United States, and he supported a policy of "peaceful coexistence." He called for a European collective security system and the renunciation of the Paris agreements permitting the Federal Republic of Germany to join NATO. (CDSP VIII:4 1)

February 14 *Peaceful Coexistence* First Secretary Khrushchev, in an address to the Twentieth Congress of the Soviet Communist party, modified traditional Soviet foreign policy doctrine by elevating the idea of peaceful coexistence to party doctrine. Peaceful coexistence resulted from the development of weapons of mass destruction and the need to find a basis for the long-term competition between communism and capitalism. Peaceful coexistence was based on the assumptions that war had to be avoided and that communism could come to power in a variety of ways, including parliamentary means. (CDSP VIII:4 10)

February 14 *Soviets on Middle East* The Soviet Foreign Ministry issued a statement on Anglo-American policies in the Middle East. The Soviets warned the Western nations not to dispatch troops to the region without the consent of the concerned governments or without the approval of the United Nations Security Council. (DIA 53)

February 25 *Khrushchev on Stalin* First Secretary Khrushchev, in a "secret speech" to the Twentieth Party Congress, denounced Stalin for his crimes and misdeeds. Following his surprising speech, a de-Stalinization program was carried out in the Soviet Union and in the nations of Eastern Europe. (FRUS 1955-1957 XXIV 72)

February 26 *Dulles on the Soviet Union* Secretary of State Dulles, in a speech in Philadelphia, commented on some of the changes in Soviet foreign policy announced at the Twentieth Party Congress. He said the Soviet Union no longer relied on hatred and violence as much as in the past because such tactics were counterproductive. Western policies, he said, such as the collective security pacts and bilateral treaties the United States had with other nations, were sufficiently successful to force the Soviets to change their policies. The secretary did not think that Soviet goals had changed, only the tactics. (DAFR 196)

February 29 *Dulles Criticized* *Pravda* criticized Secretary of State Dulles for claiming the United States was in part responsible for changes in Soviet foreign policies. According to *Pravda*, the policies of Secretary Dulles had been failures. (CDSP VIII:9 36)

March 1 *Eisenhower Letter to Bulganin*   President Eisenhower, in a letter to Premier Bulganin, proposed a number of arms control measures that could be studied by the United Nations. The president favored reducing armaments rather than manpower, and he further elaborated on his open skies proposal first put forward at the 1955 Geneva summit meeting. (PP 283)

April 3 *Dulles on Stalinism*   Secretary of State Dulles, in a statement at a news conference, said although the Soviet Union remained a threat, the United States welcomed the de-Stalinization program provided it meant fundamental changes in the way the Soviets were governed. (DAFR 201)

April 18 *Cominform Dissolved*   The Soviet Union announced the dissolution of the Cominform, established in 1947. The dissolution was intended as a gesture toward President Tito. Yugoslavia had been expelled from the Cominform in 1948, but now the Soviets were trying to improve relations. The Cominform had also been an instrument for Soviet propaganda and subversion. (DIA 377)

April 21 *Eisenhower on Foreign Policy*   President Eisenhower, in a major foreign policy address to the American Society of Newspaper Editors, said he thought a new, more peaceful era was developing because more nations were supporting freedom. He also said that the new leaders in the Soviet Union had not made any substantial changes in the foreign policies formulated by Josef Stalin and that most of the postwar issues were still on the superpower agenda. He added that the Soviets had moderated their violence and hostility and now placed more emphasis on economic and political means to achieve their foreign policy objectives. (PP 411)

April 23 *Khrushchev and Missiles*   First Secretary Khrushchev, during a visit to the United Kingdom, said he had no doubt the Soviet Union would develop a missile with a nuclear warhead capable of reaching targets anywhere in the world. (DSB 9/10/56 428)

April 25 *Soviets Evaluate Eisenhower*   An article in *Pravda* evaluated President Eisenhower's April 21 speech. The Soviets believed a struggle was going on in the United States between those individuals who wanted to change the cold war policies and those who wanted them continued. (CDSP VIII:17 23)

April 25 *Eisenhower on Another Summit*   President Eisenhower, in response to a question at a news conference, said he did not favor attending another summit conference with Soviet leaders unless there were some progress solving problems dealt with at the 1955 Geneva summit. (PP 430)

April 27 *The Middle East* First Secretary Khrushchev, at a news conference, commented on arms shipments to the Middle East. He said the Soviet Union would be willing to cooperate in implementing an arms embargo in the region provided other nations followed the Soviet example. (DOD 1945-1956 I 615)

May 3 *U.S. Arms Control Memorandum* The United States issued a memorandum to the subcommittee of the United Nations Disarmament Commission containing eight principles to serve as a framework for America's arms control policies. Effective verification measures and on-site inspections were two of the major principles, both of which were opposed by the Soviet Union. (DAFR 456)

May 5 *North Atlantic Council* At the conclusion of two days of talks in Paris, the ministers attending the North Atlantic Council meeting issued a communiqué. They agreed the success of the alliance compelled the Soviet Union to accept the policy of coexistence, and they hoped the Soviets would now be more willing to abide by the principles of the United Nations Charter. (DAFR 106)

May 14 *Soviet Troop Reduction* The Soviet Union issued a statement critical of the United States and its allies for failing to agree to various arms control proposals put forward by the Soviets. They again rejected President Eisenhower's aerial reconnaissance proposal, claiming there was no relationship between it and genuine arms control measures. The Soviets said their military forces, within one year, would be reduced by 1.2 million troops. A number of divisions and brigades were to be demobilized and the military budget reduced. The Soviets suggested the United States should also make troop reductions. (DSB 8/20/56 301)

May 15 *Dulles on Troop Reductions* Secretary of State Dulles, in response to a question at a news conference, said he welcomed the Soviet announcement on troop reductions made the previous day, but, he pointed out, there was no way to verify the reductions. (DSB 5/28/56 881)

May 25 *Eisenhower on Communism* President Eisenhower, in an address at Baylor University, said communism was a failure and cited as evidence the desire for greater freedom in many parts of the communist world. He said an ideology denying people freedom would ultimately perish. (PP 526)

June 1 Molotov Replaced Dmitry Shepilov replaced Viacheslav Molotov as foreign minister. Marshal Tito was to visit the Soviet Union, and Molotov had been foreign minister when Yugoslavia was expelled from the Cominform in 1948. (NYT 6/2/56 1)

June 21 Dulles on Foreign Policy Secretary of State Dulles, in a speech in San Francisco, commented on Khrushchev's "secret speech" at the Twentieth Party Congress the previous February. The crimes of Stalin, said Dulles, were not just the result of one individual but were a reflection of the communist system itself. Dulles noted that Mao Zedong was an admirer of Stalin and wanted to emulate him. (DSB 7/2/56 3)

June 28 Khrushchev Evaluated Secretary of State Dulles, at a meeting of the National Security Council, said First Secretary Khrushchev was the most dangerous leader since the October 1917 revolution. The secretary characterized Khrushchev as emotionally unstable and a heavy drinker. (FRUS 1955-1957 XXIV 119)

June 29 U.S. Reacts to Polish Uprising The State Department issued a statement condemning the Polish government for using force against individuals and groups in Poznan who were demonstrating for greater freedom and national autonomy. The demonstrations resulted in many government reforms and brought back to power Wladyslaw Gomulka, who had been jailed by Stalin. (DIA 393)

July 4 Kennan on Soviet Behavior The CIA presented a memorandum to the deputy under secretary of state for political affairs containing the views of former ambassador Kennan on the de-Stalinization program in the Soviet Union. Kennan did not believe the policies of the new leaders were different from those of the past. He said the new leaders used different tactics than did Stalin but had basically the same goals. He also thought the de-Stalinization program launched by Khrushchev would have a devastating effect on the communist leaders in Eastern Europe. (FRUS XXIV 125)

July 6 The Satellites A study by the National Security Council analyzed the relationship between the satellite nations and the Soviet Union. The report concluded that although the Soviets dominated the satellite nations by military force, the United States must continue to support a greater degree of autonomy for the Eastern European nations. (FRUS 1955-1957 XXV 198)

July 11 Dulles and Stalin Secretary of State Dulles, in a statement at a news conference, said Stalin not only brutalized the Russian people but also many individuals and groups in the satellite countries. Dulles suggested that if the Soviet leaders wanted to disassociate themselves from Stalin, they could do so by granting the satellite nations their independence. (DSB 7/23/56 145)

July 16 *Soviets Accuse U.S.* *Pravda* accused the United States of launching a propaganda campaign to promote the independence of nationalist communist parties and thus weaken the international communist movement. (CDSP VIII:29 3)

August 4 *Eisenhower Letter to Bulganin* President Eisenhower, in response to a letter from Premier Bulganin, said the United States welcomed unilateral reductions in the size of the Soviet military forces but that international controls were necessary to guarantee the effectiveness of arms control measures. The president expressed regret that the Soviet Union had not carried out the agreement made at the 1955 Geneva summit meeting regarding elections in Germany. (PP 651)

September 1 *Soviets Resume Testing* Tass, the Soviet news agency, announced that the Soviet Union had carried out nuclear tests on August 24 and August 30. The announcement said testing was resumed because the United States refused to agree to a nuclear test ban treaty. This was the first Soviet test since March. (CDSP VIII:35 17)

September 11 *Bulganin Letter to Eisenhower* Premier Bulganin, in response to the August 4 letter from President Eisenhower, again suggested that the superpowers take unilateral measures to promote disarmament such as the Soviets were doing. Bulganin once more asserted there was no relationship between aerial inspections favored by President Eisenhower and arms control. (DIA 595)

October 4 *Dulles in Berlin* Secretary of State Dulles, in a speech at the Free University in West Berlin, analyzed changes in Soviet foreign policy tactics. He said the new leadership did not want to have a nuclear war with the West and rejected the tactics relied on by Stalin. According to the secretary, the Soviets were confronted with difficult economic problems, but Moscow did not appear eager to seek a "final settlement" with the United States and its allies. (DSB 10/29/56 671)

October 17 *Bulganin and Eisenhower* President Eisenhower received a letter from Premier Bulganin in which he accused the United States of failing to cooperate in efforts to prohibit the use of atomic weapons. The Soviet leader, implicitly, supported the position taken by Adlai Stevenson, the Democratic presidential candidate, in support of a nuclear test ban. (DSB 10/29/56 662)

October 21 *Eisenhower and Bulganin* President Eisenhower, in response to the October 17 letter from Premier Bulganin, objected to the Soviets writing that letter during a presidential campaign and releasing it to the press before delivering it to him. (DSB 10/29/56 662)

October 23 *Demonstrations in Hungary* Anticommunist demonstrations began in Budapest. Among other things, the demonstrators wanted Soviet troops withdrawn from Hungary. (NYT 10/24/56 1)

October 24 *Call for Soviet Troops* An announcement read over the Budapest Radio said the Hungarian government had requested the assistance of the WTO nations to help suppress the counterrevolutionary effort to overthrow the government. No source, authority, or name was cited for making the announcement. (DIA 447)

October 25 *Eisenhower on Hungarian Events* President Eisenhower issued a statement on the Hungarian uprising. The Hungarian people, he said, were demanding respect for those human rights guaranteed in the United Nations Charter and the 1946 Treaty of Peace. He deplored the use of Soviet troops to suppress the quest for freedom. (PP 1018)

October 28 *U.S. Accused* Radio Moscow and Soviet newspapers began a propaganda campaign accusing the United States and its allies of being responsible for the uprising in Hungary. (NYT 10/28/56 1)

October 30 *Soviets and Eastern Europe* The Soviet leaders issued a "Declaration on the Basis of the Development and Further Strengthening of Friendship and Cooperation Between the Soviet Union and Other Socialist States." The declaration, issued at the end of the WTO meeting in Bratislava, admitted the Soviets had made mistakes in the past in Eastern Europe but were now correcting them. The declaration seemed to support the idea of national communism, a policy identified with the Tito regime in Yugoslavia. The declaration conveyed the impression that the WTO nations would not intervene in Hungary to suppress the rebellion. (DSB 11/12/56 745)

October 30 *Soviets on Hungary* Ambassador Bohlen notified the State Department that Defense Minister Georgy Zhukov said that Soviet forces had been ordered to leave Budapest. At this time, the Soviet leaders seemed uncertain about how to deal with the situation in Hungary. (FRUS 1955-1957 XXV 346)

November 1 *Hungarian Neutrality* Premier Imre Nagy announced that Hungary had adopted a policy of neutrality, and he requested the Soviets to begin negotiations on the withdrawal of their troops from Hungary. The following day he announced that Hungary would leave the WTO, would adopt a policy of neutrality, and would request assistance from the United Nations. At the time of Nagy's announcement, Soviet troops had surrounded Budapest. (DIA 474)

November 4 *Soviet Troops Attack Hungary* Soviet troops attacked Budapest, occupied the parliament building, and took control of the Hungarian government. In response, the United States introduced a resolution in the United Nations Security Council calling on the Soviet Union to cease its military actions in Hungary. The Soviet Union vetoed the resolution. (NYT 11/4/56 1)

November 4 *Eisenhower and Bulganin* President Eisenhower, in a letter to Premier Bulganin, noted that the Soviet government on October 30 had issued a statement affirming it would not interfere in the internal affairs of other states, then massively intervened in Hungary to overthrow the government. The president requested the immediate withdrawal of Soviet troops from Hungary. (PP 1080)

November 5 *New Government in Hungary* The Soviet Union installed a new government in Hungary under the leadership of Janos Kadar. (NYT 11/5/56 1)

November 14 *Eisenhower on Hungary* President Eisenhower, in a statement issued at a news conference, said the United States had never encouraged the people of Eastern Europe to rebel against the overwhelming military power of the Soviet Union. Some critics accused the president of wanting to roll back the iron curtain, thus encouraging the uprising in Poland and Hungary. (PP 1096)

November 17 *Soviet Declaration* Premier Bulganin, in a letter to President Eisenhower, informed him of a declaration issued by the Soviet Union blaming "imperialists" for the war in the Middle East and the uprising in Hungary. Bulganin said the Suez War, involving Egypt on the one hand and France, Israel, and the United Kingdom on the other, had weakened NATO. As a result, the Soviets could attack Western Europe and be victorious without using nuclear weapons. (DSB 1/21/57 89)

November 21 *Nagy Leaves Embassy* Imre Nagy, Hungary's former premier, left the Yugoslav embassy after being assured that he would be safe. He had sought asylum in the embassy after his government was overthrown by Soviet troops on November 4. On November 23 the Yugoslav press reported that Nagy was taken into custody by Soviet security police and taken to Romania. (NYT 11/23/56 1)

December 4 *Resolution on Hungary* The United Nations General Assembly passed a resolution calling on the Soviet Union to desist from its intervention in Hungary and to permit United Nations observers to enter the country so they could report on conditions there. Tass, the Soviet news agency, announced the refusal of the Hungarian government to permit observers to enter Hungary to investigate the causes of the October uprising. (DSB 12/17/56 963)

1957

January 2 *Eisenhower to Bulganin* The White House released the text of a letter from President Eisenhower to Premier Bulganin. The president rejected Bulganin's assertion on November 17 that the Suez War had weakened NATO, and he criticized the Soviet Union for ignoring the resolutions of the United Nations regarding the Soviet intervention in Hungary. (PP 3)

January 5 *The Eisenhower Doctrine* President Eisenhower appeared before a joint session of Congress to ask its support for what came to be known as the Eisenhower Doctrine. He analyzed events in the Middle East and said that much of the unrest in the region was the result of Soviet policies. He proposed offering certain countries in the region military and economic aid, and he suggested the possibility of using American military forces to assist nations endangered by communism. (PP 6)

January 10 *UN on Hungary* The United Nations General Assembly adopted a resolution, supported by the United States, to establish a special committee to observe and report on conditions in Hungary. The resolution called on the Soviet Union to cooperate with the committee and to allow it to travel throughout Hungary so its mission could be accomplished. The Soviet Union voted against the resolution, and the Hungarian government refused to cooperate with the United Nations. (DSB 1/28/57 140)

January 10 *State of the Union* President Eisenhower, in his State of the Union address, emphasized the continuing threat posed by the Soviet Union and the need for the United States to remain militarily strong in concert with its allies. (PP 25)

January 12 *Soviets React to Eisenhower Doctrine* Tass, the Soviet news agency, charged that the Eisenhower Doctrine was nothing more than a vehicle for American intervention in the Middle East that would allow the United States to replace British and French colonial power. (DIA 242)

February 11 *Middle East Proposal* The Soviet Union, in a note to the United States, suggested that France, the United Kingdom, the United States, and the Soviet Union agree to a set of principles to prevent any of the four powers from interfering in the internal affairs of the Middle Eastern nations. The Soviet proposal was a reaction to the Eisenhower Doctrine. On March 11 the United States rejected the Soviet proposal. (DSB 4/1/57 524)

February 13 *Peaceful Coexistence* *Pravda* published a speech by Foreign Minister Shepilov in which he accused the United States of spending enormous sums of money for espionage and sabotage in the Soviet Union and the nations of Eastern Europe. He blamed American activities for the 1956 uprising in Hungary. (CDSP IX:11 3)

February 15 *Shepilov Ousted* Foreign Minister Shepilov was ousted from power and replaced by Andrei Gromyko. (NYT 2/16/57 1)

March 26 *Soviets Warn Norway* The Soviet Union made public a letter from Premier Bulganin to the government of Norway warning it not to permit NATO bases on its territory. (NYT 3/27/57 4)

April 22 *Dulles on Foreign Policy* Secretary of State Dulles, in a speech in New York, advocated the peaceful liberation of the Soviet satellite states and suggested the United States could serve as a model for those nations desiring freedom. (DAFR 36)

May 6 *Dulles and Soviets* Secretary of State Dulles, at a conference in Paris with American diplomats, reviewed foreign policy issues. He discussed the difficulty of reaching any arms control agreements with the Soviet Union, and he said the NATO nations opposed any reduction in nuclear weapons unless accompanied by an agreement on conventional forces. (FRUS 1955-1957 IV 574)

May 21 *Eisenhower on Foreign Policy* President Eisenhower, in an address to the American people, sought support for his mutual security program. He said the fight against communism required worldwide defense systems and the spread of democracy. He cited Greece and Turkey as examples of the successful outcome of previous mutual security programs. (DSB 6/10/57 915)

June 2 *Khrushchev on Television* First Secretary Khrushchev appeared on the television program "Face the Nation." Among other things, he said the Soviet-imposed Janos Kadar regime in Hungary was supported by the Hungarian people. He justified the jamming of the Voice of America broadcasts, and he accused the United States of preparing for a war with the Soviet Union. (NYT 6/3/57 1)

June 11 *Dulles and Khrushchev* Secretary of State Dulles, in response to a question at a news conference, said he did not favor First Secretary Khrushchev being given the opportunity to address the American people on television while no American was given the same opportunity in the Soviet Union. (DSB 7/1/57 14)

June 24 *Eisenhower on Foreign Policy* President Eisenhower, in a speech in Virginia, criticized the Soviet Union for imposing its will on the Eastern

European nations, and he expressed the belief that the nations of Eastern Europe would inevitably obtain their freedom. (PP 486)

July 16 *Dulles on Soviet Changes* Secretary of State Dulles, in response to a question at a news conference, said in the long run the Russian people would demand more freedom and a better way of life. He called this an "irreversible trend" and said the United States was in part responsible. (DSB 8/5/57 228)

August 27 *Soviets Test ICBM* Tass issued a communiqué claiming the Soviet Union had successfully tested an intercontinental ballistic missile. (CDSP IX:34 15)

September 3 *The ICBM* President Eisenhower, in response to a question at a news conference, said although the Soviet Union had tested an intercontinental ballistic missile, perfecting it would take time. The president noted there was a significant difference between testing weapons and producing them. (PP 639)

September 10 *Gromyko's Press Conference* Foreign Minister Gromyko, at a press conference in Moscow, criticized the Eisenhower Doctrine, and he accused "certain foreign circles" of encouraging Turkey to overthrow the Syrian government. (CDSP IX:37 23)

September 12 *U.S. Responds to Gromyko* The State Department responded to the comments made by Foreign Minister Gromyko on September 10 regarding the Eisenhower Doctrine. A department spokesperson said Soviet opposition to the Eisenhower Doctrine was similar to the criticism directed at the Truman Doctrine, NATO, and other collective security measures adopted in reaction to the threat of communism. (DSB 9/30/57 525)

September 18 *Gromyko on U.S. Policy* Foreign Minister Gromyko, at a news conference in Moscow, denounced American foreign policy in general and the Eisenhower Doctrine in particular. He accused the United States of wanting to overthrow the Syrian government, and he specifically warned Turkey not to intervene militarily in Syria. He said the Soviet government was giving a high priority to a halt in nuclear testing, the withdrawal of foreign troops from Germany, the abolition of foreign military bases, and the establishment of control posts to help verify arms control measures. (CDSP IX:37 23)

October 2 *The Rapacki Plan* Adam Rapacki, Poland's foreign minister, presented a plan to the United Nations General Assembly advocating a nuclear-free zone in central Europe to include the territories of Czecho-slovakia, the German Democratic Republic, the Federal Republic of Germany, and Poland. (DOG 1944-1985 512)

October 4 *Soviets Launch* **Sputnik** The Soviet Union launched *Sputnik*, the first earth satellite. The launching of *Sputnik* proved to be a dramatic event in the cold war, and many people assumed that the Soviet Union had overtaken the United States in science and technology. (NYT 10/5/57 1)

October 7 *Reston Interviews Khrushchev* First Secretary Khrushchev was interviewed by James Reston of the *New York Times*. Khrushchev said despite the Soviets' success in developing an intercontinental ballistic missile, they were still interested in negotiating an arms control agreement with the United States. He blamed the United States for contributing to international tensions, citing as an example America's alleged encouragement of Turkey to invade Syria. (DIA 161)

October 9 *Eisenhower on* **Sputnik** President Eisenhower, in response to a question at a news conference, said he did not think the Soviet Union's launching of *Sputnik* had any immediate bearing on American national security, but he did recognize that *Sputnik* proved the Soviets had rockets with a powerful thrust. (PP 730)

December 3 *Dulles on Negotiations* Secretary of State Dulles, in answer to a question during an interview, said he did not think it was useful to have direct negotiations with the Soviet leaders because they could not be relied on to carry out agreements they signed. He said the 1955 Geneva summit meeting produced an agreement on Germany that the Soviets subsequently disavowed. (DSB 12/23/57 989)

December 10 *Bulganin and Eisenhower* Premier Bulganin, in a note to President Eisenhower in support of the Rapacki Plan, accused the United States of pressuring the NATO nations to accept American tactical nuclear weapons. The Soviet leader suggested that the United Kingdom, the United States, and the Soviet Union agree not to use atomic weapons, to cease testing nuclear weapons, and to refrain from stationing nuclear weapons in East or West Germany. (DSB 1/27/58 127)

December 17 *U.S. Launches ICBM* The United States successfully launched an intercontinental ballistic missile from Cape Canaveral, Florida. (NYT 12/18/57 1)

December 19 *NATO Communiqué* The members of the North Atlantic Council decided to stockpile nuclear warheads for use in case of aggression, and they decided to make intermediate range ballistic missiles available to the NATO command. (DSB 1/6/58 12)

December 19 *Dulles on Soviet Policies* Secretary of State Dulles, in a speech in Paris, delineated the strengths and weaknesses of the Soviet Union. According to the secretary, the strength of the Soviet Union was its ability to mobilize its population in support of state-defined goals. The greatest weakness, he said, was the denial of freedom to its people and those of the satellite states. (DSB 1/13/58 53)

1958

January 8 *Bulganin to Eisenhower* Premier Bulganin, in a note to President Eisenhower, proposed convening a summit meeting with the leaders of the WTO and NATO alliances plus some additional countries to explore means for reducing international tensions. (NYT 1/10/58 6)

January 9 *State of the Union* President Eisenhower, in his State of the Union address, said he believed the United States had an adequate deterrent capability to prevent the outbreak of war. In addition to a military deterrent, he said other factors such as diplomacy and economic development were also important in dealing with the threat of communism. He emphasized the necessity of waging a "total peace" to cope with the "total cold war" conducted by the Soviet Union. (PP 2)

January 10 *Dulles on Summit Meeting* Secretary of State Dulles, in answer to a question at a news conference, said he did not think a summit meeting with Soviet leaders should be scheduled unless there were adequate preparation and some indication that such a conference would be successful. At the time, the Soviet Union favored convening another summit but balked at the preparations required by the United States. (DSB 1/27/58 131)

January 12 *Eisenhower to Bulganin* President Eisenhower responded to the December 10, 1957, letter from Premier Bulganin and refuted his assertion that collective defensive arrangements such as NATO threatened the peace. The president described many of Bulganin's suggestions for improving relations as too vague and therefore not useful as a basis for negotiations. Eisenhower suggested that much of what Bulganin recommended could be achieved simply by respecting the United Nations Charter. (PP 75)

January 22 *Khrushchev on Summit Meeting* First Secretary Khrushchev, in a speech in Minsk, criticized President Eisenhower's insistence that before a summit meeting could be convened, adequate preparations would have to be completed. Khrushchev said those individuals delaying the convening of a summit were not in favor of reducing international tensions. He accused France, the United Kingdom, and the United States of not responding to the many Soviet initiatives to strengthen the peace, and he again insisted that the question of German unity not be on the summit agenda. (AFPCD 730)

January 27 *East-West Exchange Agreement* The United States and the Soviet Union announced an agreement on an exchange program pertaining to culture, science, and education. The agreement stemmed from the 1955 Geneva summit. (DSB 2/17/58 243)

January 27 *Dulles and the Soviets* Secretary of State Dulles, in an address to the ministers representing the Baghdad Pact nations, said the Soviet Union had a long history of seeking to dominate the Middle East. He pledged American support for the Baghdad Pact members attempting to contain the spread of communism. (DSB 2/17/58 250)

February 1 *U.S. Launches Satellite* The United States successfully launched an earth satellite into orbit four months after *Sputnik*. (NYT 2/1/58 1)

February 11 *Negotiating with the Soviets* Secretary of State Dulles, in response to a question at a news conference, commented on the problems encountered when negotiating with the Soviets. He said it was difficult to negotiate agreements that would be equally beneficial to each of the superpowers because of their fundamental differences. (DSB 3/3/58 336)

March 9 *An Asian Peace Zone* Tass, the Soviet news agency, denounced the forthcoming session of the Southeast Asian Treaty Organization, alleging it was called to make plans for another war. The United States was accused of wanting to deploy nuclear weapons in the SEATO countries rather than accepting the Soviet proposal for creating an Asian zone of peace free of nuclear weapons. (CDSP X:10 27)

March 24 *Aide-Mémoire on Germany* The Soviet Union, in an aide-mémoire to the United States, said the two parts of Germany had a right to decide by themselves what form reunification should take. The Soviets did not want the question of German reunification to be a summit agenda item should a summit meeting be convened. (DOG 1944-1985 527)

March 25 *Soviets on Summit Meeting* Secretary of State Dulles, in response to a question at a news conference, said the United States had received a note from the Soviet Union on conditions for convening a Soviet-American summit. The Soviets wanted some Eastern European satellites to be represented at a summit, a termination of Big Four responsibility for the control of Germany, and Soviet-controlled governments to be represented on all United Nations committees in numbers that would equal Western representation. The United States rejected the Soviet conditions. (DSB 4/14/58 602)

March 27 *Khrushchev Replaces Bulganin* Nikita Khrushchev replaced Nikolai Bulganin as premier. Khrushchev retained his position as first secretary of the Communist party, thus making him officially the undisputed leader of the Soviet Union. (NYT 3/28/58 1)

April 4 *Khrushchev to Eisenhower* Premier Khrushchev, in a note to President Eisenhower, proposed that the United States and the United Kingdom agree to suspend nuclear testing as the Soviets had done. On March 31 the Soviets announced they would cease nuclear testing, provided the United Kingdom and the United States also ceased testing. (DSB 4/28/58 680)

April 8 *Eisenhower to Khrushchev* President Eisenhower, in response to the April 4 letter from Premier Khrushchev, noted that the Soviets had just completed a series of nuclear tests before announcing a suspension of further testing. The president remarked that the Soviets said they would again test if the United States did so and, at the time, the Soviets knew the U.S. was about to resume testing. (PP 290)

April 16 *Eisenhower on Soviet Diplomacy* President Eisenhower, in response to a question at a news conference, said he disapproved of the Soviets using diplomacy for propaganda purposes. He lamented their habit of making public the correspondence between heads of state because he thought the exchanges should be treated as confidential. (PP 318)

April 17 *Eisenhower on Foreign Policy* President Eisenhower, in a speech to the American Society of Newspaper Editors, spoke about the relationship between American strength and world peace. He criticized the Soviet Union for enslaving the people of Eastern Europe, but he said the Soviet leaders would eventually realize that freedom would be victorious in the competition with tyranny. Peace in the world, he said, depended on America's military might. (PP 325)

April 22 *Khrushchev to Eisenhower* Premier Khrushchev, in a letter to President Eisenhower, criticized him for the negative tone of his April 8 letter. Khrushchev said his proposals for ending nuclear testing were not made to score propaganda points. (DSB 5/19/58 812)

April 28 *Arctic Inspection Zone* The United States introduced a resolution to the United Nations Security Council calling for the creation of an Arctic zone within which international inspections would be conducted to help prevent a surprise nuclear attack. On May 2 the Soviet Union vetoed the proposal. (DSB 5/19/58 820)

April 28 *Eisenhower to Khrushchev* President Eisenhower, in response to the April 22 note from Premier Khrushchev, suggested that the Soviets support a number of American-sponsored proposals, including measures to help prevent a surprise attack, a cutoff of fissionable material for making nuclear weapons, "open skies," and limited nuclear testing. Eisenhower urged Khrushchev to allow technical experts to examine some of the proposals. (PP 350)

May 2 *Dulles on Foreign Policy* Secretary of State Dulles, in a speech to the Atomic Power Institute, spoke about a strategy of peace. He emphasized the difficulty of reaching agreements with the Soviet Union and implementing them once they have been completed. He said the Soviets wanted the United States to accept things not in America's interests such as the Soviet domination of Eastern Europe, the partition of Germany, the abolition of NATO, or the recognition of the Beijing government. (DSB 5/19/58 799)

May 3 *The U.S. Rejects the Rapacki Plan* The United States, in a note to the Polish government, rejected the Rapacki Plan for a nuclear-free zone in central Europe. The plan was rejected because it would endanger the nations of Western Europe by upsetting the existing balance of power in favor of the Soviet Union. (DIA 134)

May 8 *Dulles on Berlin* Secretary of State Dulles, in a speech in Berlin, said President Eisenhower had instructed him to reassert the Western position on Berlin as stated by the foreign ministers of France, the United Kingdom, and the United States on October 3, 1954. At that time, the ministers announced that an attack on Berlin would be considered an attack on the three Western nations. (DSB 5/26/58 854)

May 9 *Soviet Note on Nuclear Testing* Premier Khrushchev, in a letter to President Eisenhower, agreed to have a group of experts meet to study technical problems related to the cessation of nuclear testing. The United States welcomed the Soviet decision. Khrushchev again advocated an immediate halt to nuclear testing, a position the United States rejected. (DIA 80)

June 2 *Soviets Want Trade* Premier Khrushchev, in a letter to President Eisenhower, suggested a number of ways to expand trade between the United States and the Soviet Union. The Soviets said they were interested in purchasing consumer goods, industrial equipment, and complete plants and factories. They were also seeking long-term credits to make the purchases. (DSB 8/4/58 200)

June 6 *Dulles on Foreign Policy* Secretary of State Dulles, in a statement made before the Senate Foreign Relations Committee, expressed what he considered to be the basic philosophy underlying American foreign policy. He discussed the scope of change in the international political system since World War II, including the increase in the number of nation-states, the end of the Western colonial empires, and the aspirations of people around the globe for a better life. He said the communist nations were seeking to dominate the process of change, and if they succeeded, freedom would be imperiled. (AFPCD 34)

June 16 *Nagy Executed* Radio Moscow announced the execution of Imre Nagy, the leader of Hungary during the October 1956 uprising. General Pal Maleter, a supporter of Nagy, was also executed. On June 18 President Eisenhower, in response to a question at a news conference, said the execution of Nagy was detrimental to negotiations because so many people were repelled by the Soviet action. Radio Moscow gave no indication of where or when the execution took place. (DSB 7/7/58 7)

July 1 *Eisenhower to Khrushchev* President Eisenhower, in a letter to Premier Khrushchev, deplored the Soviet government's practice of releasing to the press, without much warning, diplomatic documents. Eisenhower said such an action indicated the Soviets were not serious about holding a summit meeting. (PP 509)

July 2 *Khrushchev to Eisenhower* Premier Khrushchev, in a letter to President Eisenhower, agreed that a group of experts should be convened to study problems associated with preventing a surprise military attack. (DIA 94)

July 14 *Eisenhower to Khrushchev* President Eisenhower, in response to the June 2 note from Premier Khrushchev, said he favored expanded trade with the Soviet Union but did not promise to grant the Soviets long-term credits. He did say the Department of State would examine Khrushchev's proposals. (PP 538)

July 15 *American Troops to Lebanon* President Eisenhower announced that American military forces had landed in Lebanon to help that country defend its independence and to protect about twenty-five hundred Americans there. On July 16 the Soviet Foreign Ministry issued a statement objecting to the American military intervention in Lebanon, alleging it was intended to allow the Western oil companies to retain their influence in the Middle East. The Soviets called for the withdrawal of the American forces. (PP 549)

July 17 *British Troops to Jordan* The United Kingdom announced that its troops had landed in Jordan to help protect that nation's independence. The landing of British troops was carried out in conjunction with the American action in Lebanon. (DAFR 311)

July 18 *Soviet Statement on Middle East* The Soviet Union issued a statement accusing the United Kingdom of invading Jordan and the United States of invading Lebanon. The Soviets said the actions of the two Western nations violated the United Nations Charter and endangered world peace. (DIA 298)

July 19 *Khrushchev to Eisenhower* Premier Khrushchev, in a letter to President Eisenhower, proposed a conference on the Middle East to be composed of the heads of government of France, the United Kingdom, India, the Soviet Union, and the United States as well as the United Nations General Secretary Dag Hammarskjöld. The alleged purpose of the conference was to avert a Middle Eastern war that might possibly involve the superpowers. Khrushchev criticized American policies in the Middle East, saying they endangered world peace. (NYT 7/20/58 2)

July 22 *Eisenhower to Khrushchev* President Eisenhower rejected the allegations contained in the Soviets' July 19 letter and denied the charge that America's intervention in Lebanon made war in the Middle East more likely. Eisenhower suggested that Middle Eastern problems be dealt with in the United Nations rather than by convening a five-power conference. (PP 560)

July 23 *Soviets Protest* Premier Khrushchev, in a letter to President Eisenhower, accused the United States and the United Kingdom of aggression against Lebanon and Jordan. The Soviets wanted to convene a meeting of the United Nations Security Council, with India as a participant, to discuss problems in the Middle East. On July 25 President Eisenhower, in response to the July 23 letter from Premier Khrushchev, said he would welcome a discussion of the Lebanese crisis in the United Nations Security Council, but he also asserted that Lebanon was only part of a larger problem, namely, the protection of small nation-states. (DSB 8/11/58 234)

July 28 *Khrushchev to Eisenhower* Premier Khrushchev, in a letter to President Eisenhower, accused him of delaying a United Nations Security Council meeting on the Middle East. Khrushchev again raised the issue of convening a five-power meeting to discuss Middle East issues. (DSB 8/18/58 275)

August 1 *Eisenhower to Khrushchev* President Eisenhower, in response to the July 28 letter from Premier Khrushchev, denied the charge that the United States was guilty of aggression in Lebanon. Eisenhower said he would attend a United Nations Security Council debate on Lebanon, and he expressed the hope that Khrushchev would also participate. (PP 577)

August 3 *Khrushchev-Mao Communiqué* Premier Khrushchev and Mao Zedong issued a communiqué at the conclusion of their talks that began on July 31 in Beijing. They condemned the United Kingdom and the United States for their alleged aggression in the Middle East, and the two communist leaders demanded a heads-of-government conference to discuss Middle East problems. (DIA 516)

August 5 *Khrushchev to Eisenhower* Premier Khrushchev, in a letter to President Eisenhower, opposed having the United Nations Security Council discuss the situation in the Middle East because, according to the Soviet leader, the nations supporting aggression in the Middle East would be able to dominate the council meeting. Khrushchev preferred a meeting of the United Nations General Assembly. President Eisenhower issued a statement welcoming the Soviet decision to have the United Nations General Assembly discuss the situation in the Middle East. (DSB 9/1/58 342)

August 13 *Eisenhower at the UN* President Eisenhower, in an address to the United Nations General Assembly on the crisis in the Middle East, presented a six-point peace plan to bring stability to the region. He criticized the Soviet Union for using what he referred to as "ballistic blackmail" to generate a war scare the Soviets could then exploit to advance their own political objectives. (PP 606)

August 18 *Dulles on Foreign Policy* Secretary of State Dulles, in a speech to the Veterans of Foreign Wars in New York, accused the Soviet Union of wanting to dominate the world through a combination of its own military might and the international communist movement. He said the United States was seeking to meet that challenge with a foreign policy based on the principles of democracy. (AFPCD 48)

September 4 *Dulles on Taiwan* Secretary of State Dulles, with the authorization of President Eisenhower, issued a statement reaffirming the American commitment to help defend Taiwan and the offshore islands should they be attacked. The Beijing government had been bombing some of the offshore islands as a possible prelude to an invasion. (PP 687)

September 7 *Khrushchev on Asian Crisis* Premier Khrushchev, in a letter to President Eisenhower, said the United States was the primary cause of the Taiwan crisis. He accused the United States of using atomic blackmail against the Beijing government, and he warned that a military attack on the People's Republic of China would be considered an attack on the Soviet Union. (DIA 182)

September 11 *Eisenhower on Taiwan* President Eisenhower addressed the nation on the Quemoy and Matsu crisis. The two islands under the control of Taiwan were being bombarded by the People's Republic of China, and it was also attempting to prevent the two islands from being resupplied. The president compared the situation in 1958 to the 1930s when the democracies failed to assist Ethiopia, a failure that helped bring about World War II. In his speech, the president warned Beijing and Moscow that the United States would carry out its treaty commitments to Taiwan, and he reminded them that the 1954 congressional resolution on Formosa (Taiwan) was still in effect. (PP 694)

September 12 *Eisenhower to Khrushchev* President Eisenhower, in response to Premier Khrushchev's September 7 letter, rejected his charge that American policies were responsible for the Taiwan crisis. The president said the policies of the Beijing government caused the crisis. (PP 701)

September 18 *Dulles on Foreign Policy* Secretary of State Dulles, in an address to the United Nations General Assembly, expressed the hope that the crisis in the Taiwan Straits could be peacefully resolved. He condemned the Soviet Union for intervening in Hungary in 1956 and for executing Premier Nagy. He also accused the Soviets of abusing the veto power in the Security Council, thus preventing a uniform application of the principles of the United Nations Charter. (AFPCD 122)

September 18 *Gromyko and American Policies* Foreign Minister Gromyko, in an address to the United Nations General Assembly, criticized American policies in the Taiwan Straits, Cuba, and Lebanon. He demanded that the United States close its overseas military bases. (NYT 9/19/58 1)

September 18 *Soviet Note on Germany* The Soviet Union, in a note to the United States, supported the recommendations made by the German Democratic Republic on September 5 for concluding a German peace treaty. The GDR wanted a two-tier conference to complete a peace treaty. The Big Four would conduct one set of negotiations and the two German governments would conduct the second set. At the time, the Western allies did not recognize the GDR government. The United States rejected the Soviet proposal. (DIA 140)

September 20 *Khrushchev to Eisenhower* President Eisenhower received a letter from Premier Khrushchev in which he accused the United States of being responsible for the increase in tensions in the Far East. The letter was returned to the Soviet Union because of its abusive language and factual errors. (DSB 10/6/58 530)

September 30 *Soviets Resume Testing* The State Department reported that the Soviet Union had resumed nuclear testing, which had been suspended since March. The State Department charged that the temporary suspension of nuclear testing by the Soviets was nothing more than a pause between tests. The Soviets were accused of seeking propaganda advantages rather than a genuine test ban agreement. (DSB 10/20/58 617)

September 30 *German Unity* The United States, in a note responding to the September 18 note from the Soviet Union, accused the Soviets of ignoring the proposals made by the Western powers to unify Germany. Eisenhower rejected the Soviet proposal to have representatives from the German Democratic Republic and the Federal Republic of Germany meet to discuss unification. (DIA 143)

October 17 *Dulles on Foreign Policy* Secretary of State Dulles, in response to a question asked by a reporter in London, said the struggle between communism and the free world was primarily a moral struggle transcending power politics. He predicted that if the Soviet Union were denied foreign policy victories, demand for change within the Soviet system would increase. (AFPCD 55)

October 24 *The Soviets Protest* The Soviet Union, in a note to the United States, protested the anti-Soviet demonstrations that had taken place outside the Soviet United Nations mission in New York on October 18 and 23. The Soviets wanted the United States to prevent such demonstrations in the future. (FRUS 1958-1960 II 72)

November 10 *Khrushchev on Berlin* Premier Khrushchev, in a speech in Moscow, said the Soviet Union intended to change the status of Berlin and, as a result, the Western powers would have to deal with the East German government about any questions regarding Berlin. Khrushchev's speech contained numerous threats against West Germany and the United States, and his Berlin policies created an East-West crisis that was not resolved until 1961. (CDSP X:45 7)

November 10 *Discussion of Surprise Attack* On November 10, Soviet and American representatives met in Geneva to discuss reducing the danger of a surprise military attack. The Soviets wanted to link the issue of a surprise military attack to other arms control issues, but the United States rejected the linkage. (NYT 11/11/58 1)

November 26 *Dulles on Berlin* Secretary of State Dulles, in response to a question at a news conference, said the Soviet Union could not transfer to the East German regime responsibility for access to West Berlin. (AFPCD 588)

November 27 *Soviet Ultimatum on Berlin* The Soviet Union, in notes to France, the United Kingdom, and the United States, informed them that the international legal agreements, including the Potsdam agreement, that were the basis for the four-power occupation of Germany after Word War II were no longer valid. The Soviets wanted to make West Berlin a "free city" and thereby undermine the legal basis for the Western presence there. The Soviets threatened to turn control over the access routes to the German Democratic Republic in six months. (DSB 1/9/59 81)

November 27 *Soviet Ultimatum Rejected* The State Department announced that it would not accept the Soviet proposals on West Berlin. The United States was determined to maintain the Western presence in Berlin and to protect its inhabitants. (DSB 12/15/58 948)

December 14 *Foreign Ministers Meeting* The foreign ministers of France, the United Kingdom, West Germany, and the United States met in Paris to discuss a response to the Soviet threat to Berlin. The ministers rejected the Soviet claim that it could unilaterally abrogate the rights of the Western powers in Berlin. They agreed to consult with their NATO allies before answering the November 27 Soviet note. (DIA 372)

December 18 *NATO and Berlin* The ministers of the North Atlantic Council issued a declaration on Berlin in which they expressed NATO's support for the position taken by the three Western powers regarding Premier Khrushchev's November ultimatum. (DSB 1/5/59 3)

December 31 *U.S. Responds to Ultimatum* The United States responded to the Soviet ultimatum on Berlin. Washington reaffirmed the validity of the Potsdam agreement on Germany, charged the Soviet Union with responsibility for creating the Berlin crisis, and vowed to continue the Allied presence in West Berlin. (DSB 1/19/59 79)

1959

January 9 *State of the Union* President Eisenhower, in his State of the Union address, said he wanted to strengthen the United Nations to enable the rule of law to replace reliance on violence. He accused the communists of disregarding international law by their habit of violating international treaties. He said the United States could have no confidence in negotiating treaties with the Soviet Union unless they contained self-enforcing mechanisms. (PP 6)

January 10 *Soviet Note to the U.S.* The Soviet Union, in a note to the United States, called for completing a German peace treaty to help reduce tensions in Europe. The note said the failure to complete a peace treaty for Germany had created an abnormal situation in Europe. A draft treaty was included with the note. One provision of the treaty would prevent either German state from being members of a military alliance aimed at any of the World War II Allies. (CDSP XI:2 36)

January 13 *Dulles on Germany* Secretary of State Dulles, in response to a question at a news conference, explained the philosophical differences between the United States and the Soviet Union regarding German unification. He said the Soviets wanted to isolate and neutralize Germany, but the United States favored a policy of incorporating Germany into the Western European community. (AFPCD 601)

January 14 *Eisenhower on Germany* President Eisenhower, in response to a question at the National Press Club, said the United States and the Soviet Union had different ideas about Germany. The president rejected a policy of neutralism and demilitarization for West Germany because of its power and geographic location. He did not think West Germany was a military threat to anyone because of its close relations with Western European countries and the development, within the Federal Republic, of democratic institutions. At the time, the Soviets were advocating the neutralization and demilitarization of Germany. (PP 27)

January 14 *Dulles on Foreign Policy* Secretary of State Dulles, in an appearance before the Senate Foreign Relations Committee, said that China and the Soviet Union were continuing their efforts to expand their power and influence. He cited the administration's determination to oppose the use of force to bring about change in the international political system and said progress was being made in establishing a world order based on institutions such as the United Nations. (DAFR 15)

January 20 *Nuclear Testing* An article in *Pravda* criticized American scientists for claiming there were new data indicating the difficulty of accurately detecting nuclear tests. The Soviets maintained that tests could be detected with prevailing technologies. (CDSP XI:3 23)

January 22 *Nuclear Testing* The Soviet Union issued a statement accusing the United States and the United Kingdom of opposing a nuclear test ban treaty. On January 24 the United States issued a statement denying the accusation and insisted that a nuclear test ban treaty must have adequate controls to prevent treaty violations. (DAFR 311)

January 27 *Khrushchev on Foreign Policy* Premier Khrushchev, in his address to the Twenty-first Congress of the Communist party, called for a reduction of troops in Germany, a "zone of separation" between WTO and NATO forces, and a nuclear-free zone in central Europe and the Pacific Basin. Khrushchev was particularly critical of American and West German foreign policies. He said the military balance in the world had shifted in favor of the socialist countries, and he predicted a similar shift in economic power. (CDSP XI:4 20)

January 29 *Gromyko on Foreign Policy* Foreign Minister Gromyko, in an address to the Twenty-first Congress of the Communist party meeting in Moscow, criticized the policies of the United States and its allies. He said the Western nations would not sign a nonaggression pact with the WTO nations, rejected the Soviet call for a summit meeting, refused to accept Soviet proposals on Germany and Berlin, and would not sign an agreement banning nuclear weapons. (CDSP XI:8 20)

February 5 *Soviets Exposed* The State Department made public a transcript of a conversation among Soviet fighter pilots as they shot down an unarmed American C-130 airplane on September 2 killing seventeen men. Soviet officials said the plane had crashed and denied it had been shot down. On February 7, Radio Moscow accused the United States of fabricating the tape recording of the conversation. (DSB 2/23/59 262)

February 6 *Eisenhower and Khrushchev* James Hagerty, the president's press secretary, said that President Eisenhower had not received an official invitation to visit the Soviet Union, nor did he have any plans to make such a visit. On February 5 Khrushchev, in a speech, had informally invited the president to visit the Soviet Union. (AFPCD 875)

February 9 *War and Berlin* The *New York Times* reported that Secretary of State Dulles had told a congressional committee that the United States would go to war rather than yield to the demands of the Soviet Union regarding Berlin. (NYT 2/9/59 2)

February 13 *The Soviets and Iran*   *Pravda* accused Iran of agreeing to sign a treaty with the Soviet Union, then reneging because of pressure from the United States and the nations of the Baghdad Pact. The article warned Iran that its policy of cooperating militarily with the United States could have "serious consequences. . . ." (CDSP XI:6 24)

February 24 *Soviets Want German Treaty*   Premier Khrushchev, in an election speech in Moscow, said the two German states, not the Big Four, must assume primary responsibility for bringing about reunification. He rejected the Western proposal to convene a Big Four foreign ministers meeting and instead wanted to convene a summit meeting to reduce world tensions. (AFPCD 614)

February 25 *Eisenhower on Berlin*   President Eisenhower, in response to a question at a news conference, said the Western powers were determined to protect their rights in Berlin. He rejected Khrushchev's call for a summit meeting unless there were evidence that progress could be made in resolving mutual problems. (AFPCD 616)

March 4 *Khrushchev on Germany*   Premier Khrushchev, in a speech in the German Democratic Republic, demanded that the Western powers sign a peace treaty recognizing the existence of two German states. (CDSP XI:9 39)

March 5 *Military Treaties*   Despite threats from the Soviet Union, Iran, Turkey, and Pakistan signed defense pacts with the United States, thus linking the United States to the Baghdad Pact. (NYT 3/6/59 6)

March 9 *Khrushchev and Berlin*   Premier Khrushchev, in a speech in Berlin, again demanded that West Berlin be made a "free city" and that a peace treaty between the two German states be signed. He warned that if the Western powers did not agree to his proposals, the Soviet Union would sign a peace treaty with the German Democratic Republic. (CDSP XI:10 10)

March 16 *Eisenhower on Berlin*   President Eisenhower, in a speech to the American people, talked about the defense of Berlin and America's military capabilities. He reiterated his determination to protect Western rights in Berlin, and he asserted that American military forces were capable of protecting the vital interests of the nation. (PP 273)

March 19 *Khrushchev and Germany*   Premier Khrushchev, during a news conference, said that his November 27, 1958, assertion that the Soviet Union would sign a treaty with the German Democratic Republic in six months if he could not get an agreement with the Western powers was not intended as an ultimatum. He said he believed six months was sufficient time to complete a treaty, but negotiations could go beyond that time. (CDSP XI:12 13)

**March 26 *U.S. Note to the Soviet Union* ** The United States, in a note to the Soviet Union, agreed to attend a four-power foreign ministers meeting to discuss the problem of Germany. The United States said the purpose of the meeting should be to narrow differences between the two sides in preparation for a summit meeting. (DAFR 255)

**April 1 *Four-Power Communiqué* ** The foreign ministers of the Federal Republic of Germany, France, the United Kingdom, and the United States issued a communiqué at the conclusion of their talks that began on March 31 in Washington. The ministers met to discuss issues likely to be brought up at the proposed Big Four summit meeting. They expressed a desire to negotiate with the Soviet Union, but they insisted that Western rights in Berlin had to be protected. They rejected any Soviet renunciation of its obligations in East Germany and Berlin. (DSB 4/20/59 555)

**April 4 *Eisenhower on Foreign Policy* ** President Eisenhower, in a speech in Pennsylvania, accused the communists of using whatever techniques they could to promote world revolution. He said it was in the American national interest to help protect small and weaker nations against the dangers of communism. (PP 309)

**April 10 *Khrushchev and Eisenhower* ** Premier Khrushchev, in response to questions from a *Pravda* reporter regarding American foreign policies, accused President Eisenhower of making false allegations that distorted Soviet policies and led to increased international tensions. Khrushchev also berated Eisenhower's mutual security program, claiming it would permit the United States to intervene in the internal affairs of other countries. (CDSP XI:15 4)

**April 13 *Eisenhower to Khrushchev* ** President Eisenhower wrote to Premier Khrushchev about the resumption of negotiations for a nuclear test ban treaty. Eisenhower insisted there must be verifiable inspections if a treaty were to be completed. If the Soviets would not accept provisions for on-site inspections, the president suggested that the two sides should agree to a treaty banning nuclear tests in the atmosphere. At the time, Khrushchev opposed a limited test ban treaty. (PP 331)

**April 15 *Dulles Resigns* ** President Eisenhower announced that Secretary of State Dulles was resigning for reasons of health. He was succeeded by Christian Herter. (PP 327)

April 21 *Soviet Protest* The Soviet Union, in a note to the United States, said the United States would be violating international treaties if atomic weapons were deployed in the Federal Republic of Germany as part of NATO's modernization program. The Soviets launched a propaganda and diplomatic campaign to keep nuclear weapons out of West Germany. (DSB 5/25/59 741)

April 30 *Foreign Ministers Meeting* The foreign ministers of France, the Federal Republic of Germany, the United Kingdom, and the United States issued a communiqué at the conclusion of their meeting in Paris. The purpose of the meeting was to coordinate policies in preparation for a summit meeting with Premier Khrushchev. (AFPCD 643)

May 5 *Eisenhower to Khrushchev* President Eisenhower wrote to Premier Khrushchev on the Soviet proposal to have a designated number of inspections each year to monitor a nuclear test ban treaty. The president insisted there had to be an adequate number of inspections to detect violations should they occur. (PP 408)

May 5 *Mutual Defense Agreement* The United States and the Federal Republic of Germany signed an agreement that would permit the United States to provide West Germany with classified information regarding atomic weapons. The agreement also enabled the United States to train personnel in the use of atomic weapons. (AFPCD 644)

May 8 *NATO Defenses* The United States responded to the April 21 Soviet note protesting the modernization program carried out by the NATO nations. The United States said the program had been agreed to in 1957 and was not, as charged by the Soviets, designed to influence the forthcoming foreign ministers meeting scheduled to meet in Geneva on May 11. The American note pointed out that the Soviet army was equipped with modern weapons, including nuclear arms. (DSB 5/25/59 740)

May 11 *Foreign Ministers Meeting* The foreign ministers of France, the United Kingdom, the United States, and the Soviet Union met in Geneva to discuss problems pertaining to Germany and Berlin. (DAFR 257)

May 14 *Khrushchev to Eisenhower* Premier Khrushchev, in a note to President Eisenhower, said that if the United Kingdom, the United States, and the Soviet Union could agree on the number of inspections to be carried out to determine if a test ban treaty had been violated, there would be no need for any nation to have a right of veto. (DAFR 329)

May 23 *Soviet Note on NATO* The Soviet Union, in another note to the United States, protested the decision to modernize NATO military units by providing some of them with nuclear weapons. In particular, the Soviets objected to nuclear weapons being deployed in the Federal Republic of Germany. (DAFR 351)

May 26 *Atomic Weapons for Mutual Defense* President Eisenhower sent a special message to Congress on agreements the United States signed with the Federal Republic of Germany, the Netherlands, and Turkey that would allow the United States to train NATO troops in the use of nuclear weapons. (PP 422)

June 3 *Eisenhower on the Summit* President Eisenhower, in response to a question at a news conference, said he did not think the foreign ministers meeting in Geneva had made sufficient progress in resolving issues to justify convening a summit meeting. (PP 425)

June 10 *Herter Reacts to Soviet Proposal* Secretary of State Herter rejected the Soviet proposal regarding Berlin problems. The Soviets proposed conditions that had to be met to permit the Western powers to continue to station military units in Berlin. The Soviets also insisted that all propaganda conducted in Berlin cease, but they failed to distinguish propaganda from legitimate news or news commentary. (DAFR 268)

June 25 *An Atom-Free Zone* The Soviet Union issued a statement proposing the creation of an atom-free zone in the Balkan-Adriatic region. The proposal was in response to an agreement by Italy and Turkey to allow NATO missile bases on their territory. The Soviets warned that if there were no agreement, they would build missile bases in some of the satellite countries. On July 11 the United States rejected the Soviet proposal because the NATO members were vulnerable to a Soviet atomic attack and needed adequate protection. (DAFR 355)

July 17 *Captive Nations Week* President Eisenhower, in response to a congressional joint resolution, designated the week beginning July 19 "Captive Nations Week." On July 23 Premier Khrushchev, in a speech in Moscow, denounced the United States for designating one week of the year "Captive Nations Week." (DAFR 207)

July 21 *Soviet-American Exchange Program* The United States and the Soviet Union announced that on July 9 they had signed a two-year agreement on the exchange of scientists. (AFPCD 951)

July 25 *Nixon's Kitchen Debate* Vice President Nixon and Premier Khrushchev had their famous kitchen debate at the United States National Exhibition in Moscow. During the debate Khrushchev said the Soviet

Union would catch up and surpass the American standard of living. (NYT 7/25/59 1)

July 28 *Khrushchev on Berlin* Premier Khrushchev, in a speech in the Soviet Union, called for the convening of a four-power summit meeting to deal with Berlin issues. He said a solution to the Berlin problem would reduce international tensions and might lead to agreements on other issues. Khrushchev said he told Vice President Nixon that if a war broke out with Germany, the Soviets could "wipe West Germany from the face of the earth." (CDSP XI:30 15)

August 3 *Khrushchev and Eisenhower* President Eisenhower announced that he had invited Premier Khrushchev to visit the United States sometime in September. Khrushchev accepted. (PP 560)

August 5 *Foreign Ministers Meeting* The Big Four foreign ministers meeting in Geneva adjourned after meeting for sixty-five working days. The two sides were unable to reconcile their differences over Berlin and Germany despite the numerous meetings. (DSB 8/24/59 265)

August 25 *Eisenhower and Khrushchev* President Eisenhower, in response to a question at a news conference, delineated what he hoped to achieve in his meeting with Premier Khrushchev beginning September 15. The president said he wanted to impress on the Soviet leader the power of the United States as demonstrated by the way people lived in this country. Another purpose, said Eisenhower, was to determine whether Khrushchev was willing to help reduce international tensions. (PP 592)

September 15 *Khrushchev Arrives in U.S.* Premier Khrushchev arrived in the United States to address the United Nations, to take a tour of the country, and to meet with President Eisenhower. (DSB 10/5/59 476)

September 15 *Khrushchev and Eisenhower* Premier Khrushchev met with President Eisenhower for the first time since the 1955 Geneva summit. The leaders had a rather long agenda for their talks, including issues pertaining to Berlin, Germany, and the convening of a four-power summit meeting with France and the United Kingdom. Khrushchev was the first Soviet leader to visit the United States. (NYT 9/16/59 1)

September 17 *Herter at the UN* Secretary of State Herter, in an address to the United Nations General Assembly, emphasized the importance of bringing about changes in the international political system through peaceful means. He criticized the Soviet Union for imposing a puppet government on the Hungarian people, and he criticized the Kadar government for failing to cooperate with the United Nations investigation of the 1956 Hungarian uprising. (DSB 10/5/59 467)

September 27 *Eisenhower and Khrushchev* Eisenhower and Khrushchev issued a joint statement at the conclusion of their talks at Camp David. The two leaders discussed several issues, including disarmament, Berlin, Germany, and trade. The Soviet leader extended an invitation to President Eisenhower to visit the Soviet Union. Although not mentioned in the communiqué, Premier Khrushchev agreed to remove his six-month ultimatum for resolving the Berlin problem. The United States had refused to negotiate with the Soviet Union while the deadline was in place. (PP 692)

September 28 *Khrushchev on the Summit* Premier Khrushchev, in a speech to the Council of Ministers after his return from the United States, said he was satisfied with the results of his meeting with President Eisenhower. Khrushchev expressed the belief that the president was genuinely interested in ending the cold war. (DAFR 194)

1960

January 7 *State of the Union* President Eisenhower, in his State of the Union address, suggested several ways the United States and the Soviet Union might seek to improve relations. Among other things, he suggested negotiations leading to arms control agreements, more cultural agreements, and an agreement "looking to a controlled ban on the testing of nuclear weapons." (PP 3)

January 14 *Soviet Arms Control Measure* Premier Khrushchev, in a report to the Supreme Soviet, announced a unilateral reduction in the Soviet armed forces by 1.2 million personnel. Other governments were encouraged to follow the Soviet example. The State Department welcomed the Soviet announcement but noted there was no way to verify the reductions. (CDSP XII:2 9)

January 17 *Eisenhower Accepts Invitation* The White House announced that President Eisenhower would visit the Soviet Union from June 10 to June 19, 1960. (DSB 2/1/60 147)

February 3 *Eisenhower and Nuclear Weapons* President Eisenhower, in response to a question at a news conference, said he favored liberalizing American laws to enable the United States to provide the NATO nations with the same types of nuclear weapons possessed by the Soviet Union. (PP 147)

February 8 *Herter on Berlin* Secretary of State Herter, in response to a question at a news conference, said he thought the Soviets were adopting a more uncompromising line regarding Berlin and a German peace treaty. Herter's comments were based on statements by Soviet officials. (DSB 2/29/60 320)

March 24 *Status of Berlin* The State Department released photocopies of the original agreement on the occupation of Germany. The United States maintained that, despite the claims of East German authorities, the original agreement proved that Berlin was not considered a part of East Germany. (DSB 4/11/60 554)

March 25 *Khrushchev on Berlin* Premier Khrushchev, while visiting Paris, renewed his threat to sign a peace treaty with East Germany that would end all Western rights in Berlin. (NYT 3/27/60 1)

April 25 *Khrushchev and Berlin* Premier Khrushchev, in a speech in Baku on Soviet-American relations, revived the idea of making West Berlin a "free city." The tone of his speech suggested there was little likelihood of any major agreements at the Paris summit scheduled to convene in May. (CDSP XII:17 3)

May 5   *U-2 Downed*   Premier Khrushchev announced that an American U-2 plane on an intelligence-gathering mission was shot down over Soviet territory on May 1. The Soviet leader said those responsible for dispatching the U-2 wanted the scheduled summit conference to fail. (NYT 5/6/60 1)

May 6   *U-2 Note to Soviet Union*   The United States, in a note to the Soviet Union, requested that it provide the American government with information about the plane the Soviets said they had shot down on May 1. The American note repeated the assertion that the missing plane was on a weather research mission. (DSB 5/23/60 818)

May 7   *U-2 Pilot Alive*   Premier Khrushchev confirmed that Francis Gary Powers, the pilot of the U-2 plane, had been captured, and Soviet specialists were analyzing the intelligence-gathering devices on the plane. (CDSP XII:19 3)

May 7   *U.S. Announcement on U-2*   The State Department admitted that the U-2 plane shot down on May 1 was not on a weather research mission but was in fact on an intelligence-gathering mission over the Soviet Union. (DSB 5/23/60 818)

May 9   *Herter on U-2 Flight*   Secretary of State Herter issued an announcement justifying the use of U-2 flights because of the nature of the Soviet political system and the hostile quality of its foreign policies since 1945. The United States, he said, had to take unilateral measures, such as the U-2 flights, to prevent a surprise military attack. President Eisenhower, in a statement at a news conference two days later, said the United States, for reasons of national security, had to engage in intelligence-gathering activities regarding the Soviet Union. (DAFR 115)

May 10   *Soviet Note on U-2*   The Soviet Union, in a note to the United States, said Francis Gary Powers, the pilot of the U-2 plane, would be brought to trial. According to the Soviets, the evidence proving the U-2 plane was on a military reconnaissance mission was "incontrovertible." (DAFR 117)

May 11   *Khrushchev on U-2 Flight*   Premier Khrushchev, at a news conference, criticized Secretary of State Herter for his May 9 justification of the U-2 flights. Khrushchev said that such flights were an act of aggression that could lead to war. He suggested that President Eisenhower, because of the U-2 incident, would not be well received if he visited the Soviet Union. The president had been scheduled to visit the Soviet Union in June. (NYT 5/13/60 4)

May 11   *U.S. Note on U-2*   The United States, in a note to the Soviet Union, admitted that the U-2 plane was gathering intelligence information but denied that U.S. policy had an aggressive intent. The note stated that the United States hoped that agreement on various issues could be reached at the Paris summit beginning May 16. (DAFR 123)

May 16   *Khrushchev at Paris Summit*   Premier Khrushchev, in Paris for the scheduled Big Four summit meeting, said the U-2 incident had doomed the summit. He said a number of demands had to be satisfied if the summit were to proceed. He wanted President Eisenhower to apologize for the U-2 incident, promise that the flights would be discontinued, and punish those responsible for the incident. (DAFR 138)

May 16   *Eisenhower at the Summit*   President Eisenhower, in Paris for the scheduled summit meeting, announced that U-2 flights had been discontinued. He said Premier Khrushchev was determined to wreck the summit and used the U-2 incident for that purpose. (DAFR 143)

May 17   *Tripartite Communiqué*   France, the United Kingdom, and the United States issued a communiqué blaming Premier Khrushchev for disrupting the summit and preventing the four powers from discussing major problems. (PP 429)

May 25   *Eisenhower on the Summit*   President Eisenhower addressed the American people on events at the aborted Paris summit. He accepted full responsibility for whatever the government had to do to gather and evaluate military intelligence for reasons of national security. He accused Khrushchev of being responsible for scuttling the summit. (PP 437)

June 27   *Khrushchev to Eisenhower*   Premier Khrushchev, in a note to President Eisenhower, criticized the proposal of the five Western nations, including the United States, on arms control introduced to the Ten-Nation Committee on Disarmament on March 15. Khrushchev accused the Western powers of not being serious about disarmament, and therefore he decided the Soviet Union would no longer participate in the disarmament committee. (DSB 7/18/60 92)

July 9   *Khrushchev's Threats*   Premier Khrushchev, in a speech to the All-Russian Teachers' Congress, warned the United States that if it attacked Cuba, the Soviet Union would come to its assistance. Khrushchev pointed out that the Soviet Union had missiles that could hit targets in the United States. (CDSP XII:28 3)

July 9 *Eisenhower and Khrushchev* President Eisenhower issued a statement in response to Khrushchev's threat to assist Cuba if it were attacked. Eisenhower said that Khrushchev's statement revealed the close ties that existed between the two communist nations. Eisenhower said the United States would do whatever was necessary to oppose communist intervention in Latin America, despite the Soviet threat. (DSB 7/25/60 139)

July 10 *Captive Nations Week* President Eisenhower designated the week beginning July 17 as "Captive Nations Week." (DSB 8/8/60 219)

July 11 *Aircraft Incident* The Soviet Union informed the United States that an American RB-47 warplane had been shot down after allegedly penetrating Soviet airspace. On July 12 the United States, in a note to the Soviet Union, protested the downing of the American aircraft and charged the Soviets with misrepresenting the facts concerning the incident by alleging that the plane was shot down inside the Soviet Union. On July 13 President Eisenhower issued a statement saying the United States was willing to take the issue to the United Nations Security Council. (DAFR 169)

July 12 *The Monroe Doctrine* Premier Khrushchev, at a news conference, accused the United States of using the Monroe Doctrine to plunder the people of Latin America. He said the doctrine was no longer relevant to events in that region. On July 14 the State Department reaffirmed the relevance of the Monroe Doctrine to Latin America and accused the Soviet leader of violating the principles of the UN Charter by resorting to threats of force to settle international disputes. (CDSP XII:28 9)

July 19 *Missiles to West Germany* The Soviet Union, in a note to the United States, protested the decision to provide West Germany with Polaris missiles capable of carrying atomic warheads. On August 8 the United States rejected the Soviet protest because West Germany's defense needs were within the framework of the NATO alliance, which was modernizing its equipment just as the Soviet Union was doing. (DSB 8/29/60 349)

September 22 *Eisenhower at the UN* President Eisenhower, in an address to the United Nations General Assembly, criticized the Soviet Union for failing to agree to verification measures regarding arms control. Eisenhower said that arms control agreements and secrecy were incompatible. (PP 707)

September 23 *Khrushchev at the UN* Premier Khrushchev, in an address to the United Nations General Assembly, demanded the resignation of

Secretary General Dag Hammarskjöld. Khrushchev wanted to reconstitute the United Nations secretariat so it would be composed of three individuals, one representing the Western bloc, one the Soviet bloc, and one the nonaligned bloc, each with the right of veto. He also called for relocating the United Nations outside the United States. The bitter tone of Khrushchev's speech, and the ones he delivered on October 1 and 3, increased Soviet-American tensions. (DAFR 562)

September 26 *Soviet Note to the U.S.* The Soviet Union, in a note to the United States, charged it with interfering in the internal affairs of the German Democratic Republic. The Soviets again alleged that the GDR was a sovereign state with the authority to regulate the flow of traffic into East Berlin. On October 26, the United States, in a note to the Soviet Union, rejected the Soviet claims. (DAFR 178)

October 1 *Khrushchev at the UN* Premier Khrushchev, in an address to the United Nations General Assembly, lashed out at the Western nations in general and the United States in particular. He demanded that the Beijing government be seated in the United Nations. On October 3 Khrushchev again addressed the General Assembly and repeated his demand for a restructuring of the executive office of the United Nations, alleging that Secretary General Hammarskjöld represented Western nations, not the Soviet or nonaligned bloc. (NYT 10/2/60 1)

November 8 *Kennedy Elected President* John F. Kennedy was elected president. He defeated his Republican party rival, Richard Nixon. On November 9 Premier Khrushchev sent President Kennedy a congratulatory message stating that the Soviet Union was eager to seek solutions to Soviet-American problems, including disarmament and a German peace treaty. (NYT 11/9/60 1)

1961

January 6   Wars of National Liberation   Premier Khrushchev, at a meeting of the Communist parties in Moscow, said the Soviet Union supported wars of national liberation because they were the result of Western imperialism and colonialism and were compatible with the policy of peaceful coexistence. Soviet support for these wars alarmed President-elect Kennedy and was a source of tension in Soviet-American relations. (AFPCD 555)

January 23   Rusk on Diplomacy   Dean Rusk, confirmed by the Senate as secretary of state on January 21, released a statement saying that the Kennedy administration preferred to conduct diplomacy through normal diplomatic channels rather than at a summit. The Soviets had indicated a desire to arrange a summit meeting. (NYT 1/24/61 1)

January 25   Soviets Release Pilots   President Kennedy announced that the Soviet Union had released the pilots of the plane that had been shot down in July 1960. Their release was in keeping with Khrushchev's claim that he wanted to improve relations with the United States now that President Eisenhower was no longer in office. (PP 8)

January 30   State of the Union   President Kennedy, in his first State of the Union address, said the Soviet Union had not abandoned its goal of world domination and, as a result, the United States had to use a full array of instruments, political, economic, and military, to meet the communist challenge. He ordered an increase in America's airlift capabilities and an acceleration in the development of the Polaris submarine and other military programs. (PP 22)

March 23   Kennedy on Laos   President Kennedy issued a statement accusing the communist Pathet Lao, supported by the Soviet Union, of using military means to take control of the country. The president said he supported a policy of neutrality for Laos, and he urged the Soviets to do the same. (PP 213)

April 17   Bay of Pigs   The Cuban Revolutionary Council in New York City announced that rebel forces opposed to Fidel Castro had landed in Cuba. This was the beginning of the Bay of Pigs invasion. (AFPCD 292)

April 18   Khrushchev Message to Kennedy   Premier Khrushchev, in a note to President Kennedy, demanded that he halt the aggression taking place in Cuba. He accused the United States of being responsible for the invasion and for financing and supplying the rebel forces. Khrushchev said the Soviet Union would do all it could to aid the Cuban government in repelling the attacks. Kennedy responded to Khrushchev's threat by warning that if an outside power intervened in Cuba, the United States would immediately honor its treaty obligations under the inter-American system. (PP 286)

April 20 *Kennedy and Cuba* President Kennedy, in a speech to the American Society of Newspaper Editors, after the failure of the Bay of Pigs invasion, commented on its consequences. He said that if necessary, the United States would not hesitate to use military force to protect its national interests. He said Cuba was not a threat to the United States but was to other nations in the hemisphere. (DIA 23)

April 22 *The U.S. Accused* Premier Khrushchev, in a note to President Kennedy, accused the United States of directly participating in the Cuban invasion. He charged the United States with wanting to again make Cuba a colony to be exploited by American capitalists. (CDSP XIII:16 7)

May 19 *Kennedy and Khrushchev* The White House announced that President Kennedy had agreed to meet with Premier Khrushchev in Vienna in June. (AFPCD 569)

May 25 *Kennedy's Message to Congress* President Kennedy, in an address to a joint session of Congress, asked it to approve a $1.8 billion budget increase to help finance space exploration, defense, and foreign aid. He also announced that the United States would make an effort to put a man on the moon and return him to earth before the end of the decade. Regarding the scheduled summit meeting with Khrushchev, the president said he would exchange ideas with the Soviet leader when they met in Vienna, but there would be no negotiations. (PP 396)

June 3 *Vienna Summit* President Kennedy met with Premier Khrushchev in Vienna, where they discussed international issues for about four hours. (NYT 6/4/61 1)

June 4 *The Berlin Crisis* Premier Khrushchev, at the Vienna summit, gave President Kennedy an aide-mémoire pertaining to Germany and Berlin. The Soviet Union wanted to conclude a peace treaty with Germany that would terminate Western rights in Berlin. Khrushchev proposed making Berlin a demilitarized "free city," with access to it controlled by the East German government. The United States opposed Khrushchev's recommendations and insisted that the Soviet Union retain responsibility for access routes to the city through East Germany. (DIA 277)

June 4 *Soviet Aide-Mémoire on Testing* Premier Khrushchev, at the Vienna summit, gave President Kennedy an aide-mémoire on nuclear testing. The Soviets allegedly favored a ban on all nuclear testing with no exemptions permitted. To ensure compliance with the ban, the Soviets proposed establishing a commission of one representative each from the socialist, nonaligned, and Western states. Each of the three representatives would have the right of veto. The United States opposed the troika formula. (DSB 7/3/61 22)

June 4 *Kennedy and Khrushchev* President Kennedy and Premier Khrushchev, after two days of talks in Vienna, issued a joint statement. The two leaders discussed a number of topics, including Germany, Laos, wars of national liberation, and nuclear testing. Their discussions made clear that fundamental disagreements existed between the two countries. (PP 438)

June 6 *Kennedy Addresses the Nation* President Kennedy addressed the nation on his recent trip to Europe that included a meeting with Premier Khrushchev. The president said he had a frank exchange of views with the Soviet leader, but little, if any, progress was made on a test ban treaty, German unification, or the Berlin problem. (PP 441)

June 15 *Khrushchev on Vienna* Premier Khrushchev, in an address to the Soviet people on the results of the Vienna summit meeting with President Kennedy, accused the Western nations of opposing arms control agreements and a test ban treaty. He criticized Dag Hammarskjöld, the United Nations secretary general, for siding with the Western nations in the Congo dispute, and he accused France, the United Kingdom, and the United States of refusing to negotiate a peace treaty for Germany. (DIA 286)

June 17 *The U.S. and Nuclear Testing* The United States, in response to the June 4 Soviet aide-mémoire on nuclear testing, accused the Soviets of opposing genuine controls to verify compliance with a test ban treaty. The United States questioned whether the Soviet government wanted a treaty. (DSB 7/3/61 18)

June 21 *Khrushchev on Germany* Premier Khrushchev, in a speech in the Kremlin, announced that the Soviet Union would sign a peace treaty with the German Democratic Republic at the end of the year. The Soviet leader criticized Chancellor Adenauer and demanded that the Federal Republic of Germany accept the new German borders established after World War II. (CDSP XIII:25 6)

June 22 *Rusk on Germany* Secretary of State Rusk, in a statement at a news conference, accused the Soviet leaders of increasing international tensions. He said the Soviets believed the division of Berlin and Germany was normal, something the United States could not accept. The secretary reaffirmed the determination of the Kennedy administration to protect Western rights in Berlin. (DSB 7/10/61 51)

July 5 *The Soviets on Nuclear Testing* The Soviet Union, in response to the June 17 American note, accused the United States of creating obstacles to delay the signing of a nuclear test ban treaty. The Soviets said the verification procedures supported by the United States would be used to gather intelligence in the Soviet Union. (DIA 443)

July 8 *Khrushchev on Foreign Policy* Premier Khrushchev, in a speech in Moscow, again called for making West Berlin a "free city" and completing a peace treaty for Germany. Khrushchev said he had ordered an increase in Soviet military spending by more than three million rubles in response to Kennedy's call for a greater allocation of funds for defense. Khrushchev also suspended the military reductions planned for 1961. (DIA 307)

July 14 *Captive Nations Week* President Kennedy designated the week beginning July 16 "Captive Nations Week." (DSB 8/21/61 325)

July 17 *U.S. Note on Berlin* The United States responded to the June 4 aide-mémoire from the Soviet Union regarding the question of making Berlin a "free city." The United States insisted that Western rights in Berlin could not be unilaterally abrogated nor could access to Berlin be regulated by the German Democratic Republic. (DIA 323)

July 23 *Rusk on Berlin* Secretary of State Rusk, in response to a question on the television program "Editor's Choice," said the United States had to be skeptical about agreements with the Soviets regarding Berlin because they had violated agreements in the past. He warned that a very dangerous situation would exist if the Soviets tried to abrogate Western rights in Berlin. (AFPCD 603)

July 25 *Kennedy and Foreign Policy* President Kennedy, in a radio and television address to the American people, reasserted the determination of the Western nations to protect their rights in Berlin despite Soviet threats. He said the Western nations were prepared to use force if necessary, and if war began, the fault would be in Moscow, not Berlin. The president identified measures to be taken to strengthen America's military capabilities, including a defense budget increase of $3.457 billion and an increase in military personnel of 217,000. (PP 533)

August 5 *Warsaw Pact Communiqué* The ministers attending a WTO meeting in Moscow issued a communiqué. They agreed that if the Western nations did not sign a German peace treaty by the end of the year, the Soviet Union and its allies would sign a peace treaty with the German Democratic Republic, and West Berlin would be made a "free city." (DIA 339)

August 13 *The Berlin Wall* The communists began to erect the Berlin Wall as a means of preventing East Germans from fleeing to West Berlin. On August 15 the American, British, and French commandants in Berlin sent a note to the Soviet commandant protesting the building of the Berlin Wall. (DSB 8/28/61 362)

August 17 *U.S. Note to Soviet Union* France, the United Kingdom, and the United States, in identical notes to the Soviet Union, protested the border restrictions put into place in Berlin on August 13. The United States charged the Soviets with violating several treaties regarding the free flow of traffic between the two parts of Berlin. (DIA 345)

August 23 *Soviet Note on Berlin* The Soviet Union, in a note to the United States, said the Federal Republic of Germany was illegally interfering in the affairs of West Berlin by promoting subversion. The Soviets demanded that the United States stop the Federal Republic from such interference. On August 24 the United States rejected the Soviet charges. (DSB 9/11/61 433)

August 31 *Soviets Resume Testing* The Soviet Union announced it was resuming nuclear testing in the atmosphere because of the aggressive policies of the NATO nations and their preparations for a new war. (CDSP XIII:35 3)

August 31 *Reaction to Soviet Testing* The White House issued a statement on the Soviet decision to resume nuclear testing, accusing the Soviets of "promoting a form of atomic blackmail designed to substitute terror for reason." There was speculation the Soviets would explode a powerful weapon in the 100-megaton range. (PP 584)

September 5 *Nuclear Testing* President Kennedy announced that the United States would resume underground nuclear testing because the Soviet Union was again testing. (DOD 355)

September 8 *Rusk on Soviet Policy* Secretary of State Rusk, in a speech in Washington, criticized the Soviet Union for its policies since World War II. He said the Soviets opposed self-determination, tried to paralyze the United Nations, and pursued policies that caused the cold war. (DSB 9/25/61 507)

September 9 *Arms Control* Premier Khrushchev issued a statement calling on the Western powers to conclude a nuclear test ban treaty, to liquidate all military forces, and to complete a peace treaty for Germany. He accused the United States and its NATO allies of preventing these agreements from being reached. (DOD 384)

September 15 *Nuclear Tests* President Kennedy announced that the United States had conducted an underground nuclear test that did not produce any fallout. He said the United States resumed testing because of the unwillingness of the Soviet Union to sign a nuclear test ban treaty with adequate verification measures. (DOD 438)

September 25 *Kennedy at the UN* President Kennedy, in an address to the United Nations General Assembly, warned of the possibility of war because of the Berlin problem. He said France, the United Kingdom, and the United States would use whatever means were necessary to protect their rights in Berlin. (PP 618)

September 26 *Gromyko at the UN* Foreign Minister Gromyko, in an address to the United Nations General Assembly, said the Berlin issue was one of war or peace. He emphasized the importance of establishing Berlin as a "free city" and of completing a peace treaty for Germany, one that recognized both German states. (NYT 9/27/61 1)

October 17 *Khrushchev Speech* Premier Khrushchev, in a speech to the Twenty-second Congress of the Communist party, removed his December 31 deadline for completing a peace treaty for Germany. The Western powers had refused to negotiate with the Soviet Union on the German issue as long as the deadline was in place. Premier Khrushchev emphasized the importance of his policy of peaceful coexistence, and he recognized the growing importance of Third World countries in international politics as a force for peace, even though they might not be aligned with the Soviet Union. He also announced that the Soviet Union planned to test a fifty-megaton hydrogen bomb, the largest ever tested. (CDSP XIII:43 5)

October 17 *U.S. Reacts to Russian Test* The United States condemned the Soviet decision to test a fifty-megaton bomb. The White House statement said there was no technical justification for testing such a powerful bomb, and therefore the Soviet Union was doing so for political purposes. (PP 674)

October 22 *Rusk on War* Secretary of State Rusk, in response to a question on a television program, said the cold war was basically a conflict between the communist revolutionary movement and those who believed in the principles of the United Nations Charter. (DSB 11/13/61 805)

October 27 *Nuclear Testing* The United Nations General Assembly passed a resolution, supported by the United States, calling on the Soviet Union to refrain from exploding a fifty-megaton bomb. On October 30 the Soviet Union detonated a nuclear device in the fifty-megaton range. (AFPCD 1162)

November 2 *Nuclear Testing* President Kennedy issued a statement on the Soviet Union's nuclear testing program. He criticized the Soviets for breaking off the nuclear test ban negotiations that had been ongoing since October 31, 1958. He accused the Soviets of being contemptuous of world public opinion as evidenced by the decision to detonate a fifty-megaton bomb. He said the United States would conduct nuclear tests, but only when necessary for military, not political reasons. (PP 692)

November 25 *Kennedy Interviewed* President Kennedy was interviewed by an *Izvestia* editor. In response to a question, the president said peace was threatened by the Soviet desire to spread its ideology around the world. If, he said, the Soviet Union concentrated on improving the quality of life of its people, relations between the superpowers could improve. (PP 742)

December 9 *Khrushchev and War* Premier Khrushchev, in a speech to the Fifth World Congress of Trade Unions, said a shift had occurred in the international balance of power that favored the socialist nations. He warned the Western nations that if they unleashed a war, the Soviet Union would retaliate by using its 50- and 100-megaton bombs. (CDSP XIII:49 7)

December 26 *Dobrynin Appointed Ambassador* The *New York Times* reported that Anatoly Dobrynin had been named ambassador to the United States, succeeding Mikhail Menshikov. (NYT 12/27/61 5)

December 30 *Rusk on Foreign Policy* Secretary of State Rusk, in a speech to the American Historical Association, declared that the United States would do whatever was necessary to protect its rights in Berlin. He said the United States was eager to peacefully resolve the crisis, but it was necessary to back diplomacy with military might. (DSB 1/15/62 83)

1962

January 3 *The U.S. and Cuba* The State Department announced the release of a document detailing the ties the Castro government had with the Sino-Soviet bloc. (DSB 1/22/62 129)

January 11 *State of the Union* President Kennedy, in his State of the Union address, called on the Soviet Union to recognize Western rights in Berlin, and he underscored the determination of the Western powers to maintain their presence there. Despite Soviet-American differences, the president said he would continue efforts to reach arms control agreements with the Soviet Union, including a ban on nuclear testing. (PP 9)

January 12 *Thompson-Gromyko Talks* Ambassador Llewellyn Thompson met with Foreign Minister Gromyko in Moscow to discuss the Berlin situation. The purpose of this and other meetings between the two was to find a basis for resolving the Berlin crisis that began with Khrushchev's ultimatum in November 1958. (DSB 2/12/62 243)

January 12 *The Berlin Wall* Secretary of State Rusk, in response to a question during an interview, referred to the Berlin Wall as a symbol for a concentration camp. He said the wall was erected because the people of East Berlin wanted to be free. (DSB 1/29/62 166)

January 15 *Soviets Criticize Kennedy* *Pravda* criticized President Kennedy's January 11 State of the Union address for his failure to recognize the government of the German Democratic Republic. He was accused of seeking to destabilize the Cuban government and he was taken to task for wanting to build America's military might to enable the United States to deal with the Soviet Union from a position of strength. (CDSP XIV:2 27)

February 2 *Soviets Issue Warning* *Pravda* published the responses of Admiral Sergei Gorshkov, commander in chief of the Soviet navy, to questions from a *Pravda* reporter. Gorshkov said if war broke out in Europe, those nations with American military bases, such as Turkey, would be attacked. (CDSP XIV:5 28)

February 7 *Nuclear Testing* President Kennedy announced that the United States was prepared to resume nuclear atmospheric testing if necessary. He said preparations to resume testing did not contradict the American goal of negotiating a test ban treaty with the Soviet Union. The Soviets had just completed a round of nuclear testing, which, the president said, necessitated the American resumption. (DOD 26)

February 7 *Message to Khrushchev* President Kennedy and British Prime Minister Harold Macmillan sent a joint message to Premier Khrushchev asking for his views on how the three nations could go about bringing a halt to the arms race. (PP 128)

February 10 *Khrushchev and Arms Control* Premier Khrushchev responded to the letter sent by President Kennedy and Prime Minister Macmillan on February 7. The Soviet leader suggested that the disarmament negotiations scheduled to begin in Geneva in March should be opened by the heads of government rather than the foreign ministers. (DSB 3/5/62 356)

February 10 *Powers Pardoned* The Soviet Union announced that Francis Gary Powers had been pardoned and would be allowed to return to the United States. He was the pilot of the U-2 plane shot down over the Soviet Union on May 1, 1960. In exchange for the release of Powers, the United States returned Rudolph Abel, a Soviet spy held by the United States. (CDSP XIV:6 22)

February 12 *Rusk on Berlin* Secretary of State Rusk, in reply to a question on the radio program "Washington Viewpoint," said he could see no basis for an agreement with the Soviet Union on the Berlin issue. (DSB 3/5/62 360)

February 14 *Kennedy to Khrushchev* President Kennedy rejected Premier Khrushchev's request that the heads of government open the Eighteen-Nation Disarmament Committee scheduled to meet in Geneva. The president favored preliminary negotiations to determine areas of agreement and disagreement with the possibility that the heads of government would eventually attend the conference. (PP 132)

February 14 *Kennedy on Summits* President Kennedy, in response to a question at a news conference, said he did not think summit meetings were useful for negotiating the details of an agreement. He said summits should be convened to sign agreements previously negotiated. Premier Khrushchev often called for convening summit meetings to try to resolve Soviet-American differences. (PP 136)

February 14 *Kennedy to Khrushchev* President Kennedy, in response to the February 10 letter from Premier Khrushchev, said he did not approve of having the heads of government open the Geneva discussions, although he did not rule out their attendance at a later date. The president favored preliminary negotiations to determine areas of agreement and disagreement. (PP 132)

February 15 *U.S. Note on Berlin* The United States, in a note to the Soviet Union, protested Soviet harassment of traffic in the Berlin air corridors. (DSB 3/5/62 370)

February 18 *Soviets Support Castro* The Soviet government expressed its support for the Castro government in Cuba. According to the Soviet statement, Cuba was expelled from the Organization of American States on January 31 because of American pressure. (DIA 174)

February 20 *John Glenn* Colonel John Glenn became the first American astronaut to orbit the earth, doing so three times. (NYT 2/21/62 1)

February 21 *Khrushchev to Kennedy* Premier Khrushchev wrote to President Kennedy congratulating the United States on Colonel Glenn's successful space flight on February 20. Khrushchev said the two nations should cooperate in exploring outer space. (DSB 3/12/62 411)

February 21 *Khrushchev to Kennedy* Premier Khrushchev, in a letter to President Kennedy, criticized his refusal to attend the Eighteen-Nation Disarmament Committee meeting in Geneva. Khrushchev said Kennedy's reaction to the Soviet proposal indicated he expected the negotiations to fail. The Soviet leader also condemned the American decision to prepare for the resumption of nuclear testing as announced by President Kennedy on February 7. (DSB 3/19/62 466)

February 21 *Kennedy to Khrushchev* President Kennedy responded to the note from Premier Khrushchev received that same day. The president thanked the Soviet leader for his comments about Colonel Glenn's space flight and welcomed the Soviet suggestion that the two nations should cooperate in the exploration of space. (DSB 3/12/62 411)

March 2 *Nuclear Testing* President Kennedy, in a radio and television address to the American people, announced that the United States would resume atmospheric nuclear testing sometime in April. (DOD 66)

March 3 *Khrushchev to Kennedy* Premier Khrushchev wrote to President Kennedy consenting to have the foreign ministers, rather than the heads of government, open the Geneva disarmament talks. In his note, Khrushchev accused the Kennedy administration of wanting to build nuclear weapons because of the influence of "monopolistic capital." (DSB 3/26/62 494)

March 5 *Kennedy to Khrushchev* President Kennedy, in response to the March 3 note from the Soviet Union, said he was pleased the Soviets had agreed to have the foreign ministers open the Geneva disarmament negotiations scheduled to begin on March 14. The president said he rejected, but would not respond to, the various allegations in Khrushchev's message. (PP 193)

March 7 *Kennedy to Khrushchev* President Kennedy, in a letter to Premier Khrushchev, proposed several projects for joint cooperation in the exploration of outer space. Among other things, the president suggested establishing a weather satellite system and mapping the earth's magnetic field. (PP 244)

March 8 *Cultural Agreement* The United States and the Soviet Union signed an agreement for cultural, technical, and educational exchange programs. (AFPCD 1962 726)

March 16 *Khrushchev on Foreign Policy* Premier Khrushchev, in an address at the Kremlin, called upon the Western nations to recognize the German Democratic Republic and to complete a peace treaty for Germany. He said the Soviets could not wait indefinitely for a peace treaty to be completed. Khrushchev criticized President Kennedy for ordering the resumption of nuclear atmospheric testing, but the Soviet leader insisted he still wanted to complete a disarmament treaty with the Western nations. Khrushchev also said the United States could not defend itself against a Soviet missile attack. (CDSP XIV:13 5)

March 17 *Soviets and Vietnam* The Soviet government issued a statement calling on the United States to withdraw its military forces from Vietnam. The Soviets defended the efforts of the communist forces seeking to overthrow the South Vietnamese government. (NYT 3/18/62 1)

March 23 *Kennedy on World Order* President Kennedy, in a speech at the University of California (Berkeley), said the emerging world order, based on freedom and self-determination, was incompatible with the Soviet concept of a world order. He said more nations were moving away from communism and embracing independence and freedom. He expressed support for a pluralist international political system where independent nations can cope with their problems within the framework of their traditions. He accused the communists of preferring a monolithic world with little diversity. (PP 263)

March 27 *Aid to Castro* The State Department issued a report detailing the substantial military aid the Castro government received from the communist bloc for approximately the last eighteen months. (AFPCD 357)

March 27 *Rusk-Gromyko Talks* Secretary of State Rusk and Foreign Minister Gromyko, at the conclusion of their talks in Geneva, said they had discussed "German problems and related questions." They agreed to meet again for further discussions. (DSB 4/16/62 625)

March 29 *Kennedy on Nuclear Test Ban* President Kennedy, in a statement issued at a news conference, commented on the arms control negotiations taking place in Geneva. He said a major problem in completing a test ban treaty was Soviet opposition to verification measures. (PP 271)

March 29 *Kennedy on Nuclear Weapons* President Kennedy, in response to a question at a news conference, said there might be circumstances, such as a Soviet attack on Western Europe, that would require the president to order the use of whatever means were available to halt the aggressor. (PP 276)

March 29 *Kennedy on Nuclear Testing* President Kennedy issued a statement on the need to have on-site inspections to verify compliance with a nuclear test ban treaty. He said the United States could detect many underground eruptions but could not identify what caused the eruption. Detection could not, he said, differentiate between an earthquake and a nuclear test. The Soviets continued to insist that on-site inspections would be used for espionage purposes and were unnecessary for detecting a nuclear explosion. (PP 278)

April 10 *Nuclear Testing* The United States and the United Kingdom, in a joint statement to Premier Khrushchev, said they planned to go forward with their schedule for nuclear testing unless the Soviet Union changed its policy and accepted adequate verification measures to be included in a test ban treaty. (DIA 61)

April 12 *Soviets on Nuclear Testing* The Soviet Union proposed putting into effect an uninspected moratorium on nuclear testing to last for the duration of the Eighteen-Nation Disarmament Committee meeting. The United States rejected the Soviet proposal. (DSB 4/30/62 708)

April 20 *Khrushchev on Summits* Premier Khrushchev, in response to a question during an interview with the publishers of *Look Magazine*, said he would like to again meet with President Kennedy but only if such a meeting would produce significant agreements. (AFPCD 1962 693)

April 24 *Gromyko on Foreign Policy* Foreign Minister Gromyko reported to the Supreme Soviet on his talks with Secretary of State Rusk regarding Berlin. He said the talks helped clarify their respective positions, although major differences remained. Gromyko criticized the Western nations for the inadequate proposals put forward at the Geneva arms control talks. He said the Western nations wanted to regulate the arms race rather than disarm. (CDSP XIV:18 10)

April 26 *Rusk News Conference*   Secretary of State Rusk, in response to a question at a news conference, commented on the discussions he had with Foreign Minister Gromyko the previous month. The secretary told Gromyko that the Western presence in Berlin was not a negotiable issue and that the Western powers were determined to remain in Berlin. (DSB 5/14/62 798)

May 17 *Rusk on Foreign Policy*   Secretary of State Rusk, in a speech at the University of Tennessee, analyzed American leadership in building a community of free and independent nations. The secretary said while communist governments appeared to be in control of nations they dominated, the peoples of these nations desired freedom. This desire, he said, would not be diminished by the Berlin Wall or the iron curtain. (DSB 6/4/62 895)

May 18 *Khrushchev on Foreign Policy*   Premier Khrushchev, in a speech in Bulgaria, said the Soviet Union favored peace but also supported the class struggle, wars of national liberation, and the fight against colonialism. He criticized President Kennedy for resuming nuclear testing in April and sending American military forces to Thailand in May. (CDSP XIV:20 5)

May 25 *Rusk on Foreign Policy*   Secretary of State Rusk, in a speech in Seattle, said the United States and the Soviet Union had different ideas about how the international political system should be organized. He accused Premier Khrushchev of defending peaceful coexistence as a means for extending communism around the world short of war. (DSB 6/11/62 931)

June 7 *Soviet Note on Berlin*   The Soviet Union, in a note to the United States, alleged that forces in West Berlin were guilty of engaging in acts of violence against the German Democratic Republic along the border between East and West Berlin. The Soviets said they would use force if necessary to end the acts of violence. (DSB 7/16/62 98)

June 8 *Space Agreement*   The United States and the Soviet Union signed an agreement on cooperation in the peaceful uses of outer space. (DSB 12/24/62 963)

June 12 *Khrushchev to Kennedy*   Premier Khrushchev, in a letter to President Kennedy, expressed satisfaction that the three major factions in Laos had agreed to establish a coalition government the previous day. When Khrushchev and Kennedy met in Vienna in June 1961 they expressed support for a neutral Laos governed by a coalition. (DSB 7/2/62 12)

June 16 *U.S. Nuclear Strategy* Defense Secretary Robert McNamara, in a speech in Ann Arbor, Michigan, outlined what he thought should be America's nuclear strategy. He said the United States needed enough power to deter a nuclear attack, but if war did break out, the American nuclear arsenal would be used initially to destroy military, not civilian targets. He reassured the American people that the United States had a sufficient second-strike capability to destroy the enemy if it launched a nuclear attack. (DOD 622)

June 25 *U.S. Note to the Soviet Union* The United States, in a note to the Soviet Union, protested the many acts of violence in Berlin because of the Berlin Wall. A number of individuals had been killed attempting to escape from East Berlin. The United States suggested that representatives of the four occupying powers meet to discuss "means to facilitate the movement of persons and goods within Berlin." On July 14 the Soviet Union rejected the American request. (DSB 7/16/62 97)

July 5 *Ambassador to the Soviet Union* President Kennedy named Foy Kohler to be ambassador to the Soviet Union, replacing Llewellyn Thompson. (PP 541)

July 10 *Khrushchev on Berlin* Premier Khrushchev, in a speech to the World Congress for General Disarmament, proposed that France, the United Kingdom, and the United States remove their troops from Berlin and have them replaced by military units of the smaller nations in the WTO and NATO alliances. (NYT 7/11/62 1)

July 12 *Rusk on Foreign Policy* Secretary of State Rusk, in response to a question at a news conference, said the Soviets were only interested in discussing issues vital to the United States. As an example, he cited Soviet willingness to discuss the status of West Berlin but not a permanent peace settlement for a united Germany. (DSB 7/30/62 172)

July 13 *Captive Nations Week* President Kennedy designated the week of July 15 "Captive Nations Week" in compliance with a congressional resolution passed in 1959. (DSB 8/6/62 222)

July 13 *Laotian Neutrality* The United States, the Soviet Union, and the other participants at the Geneva conference on Laos signed an agreement formally designating Laos a neutral nation. The agreement was never fully implemented, in part because of the importance of the Ho Chi Minh trail linking North Vietnam with South Vietnam. (DSB 8/13/62 259)

August 10 *Soviet Note on Berlin* The Soviet Union, in a note to the United States, accused the government of the Federal Republic of Germany of being responsible for bomb explosions along the dividing line between East and West Berlin. The Soviets also charged the West German government with distributing leaflets inciting the population of East Berlin to engage in subversive activities. On August 11 the State Department rejected the Soviet charges and said they were the result of misinformation or a desire on the part of the Soviet government to deceive world opinion. (DSB 8/27/62 320)

August 22 Soviet Berlin Commandant The Soviet Union announced it was abolishing the post of Soviet commandant in Berlin, cutting another link with the three Western powers in Berlin. (DOG 1944-1985 823)

August 24 Soviet Note on Berlin The Soviet Union, in a note to the United States, accused it of being responsible for acts of violence directed at Soviet troops in Berlin. The Soviets said the United States should cease its activities and punish those individuals engaging in the provocative actions. (DSB 9/17/62 418)

August 27 Tensions in Berlin The United States, in a note to the Soviet Union, condemned it for the violence that had erupted because of the Berlin Wall. The violence included the shooting of people attempting to escape from East Berlin. The United States again suggested that representatives of the Big Four meet to discuss the situation. (DSB 9/17/62 417)

August 29 Kennedy and Cuba President Kennedy, in response to a question at a news conference, said he did not support invading Cuba to overthrow the Castro government. (PP 652)

August 29 Kennedy on a Test Ban Treaty President Kennedy, in response to a question at a news conference, said he would be willing to sign a test ban treaty prohibiting only atmospheric testing if a total ban could not be negotiated owing to Soviet opposition to verification measures. (PP 650)

September 4 The U.S. and Cuba The White House issued a statement by President Kennedy expressing concern about recent Soviet policies to bolster the military power of the Castro government in Cuba. He said the United States would do whatever was necessary to prevent the Castro government from committing aggression. Kennedy noted there was no evidence of offensive missiles in Cuba "or of other significant offensive capabilities," but "were it to be otherwise, the gravest issues will arise." (DSB 9/24/62 450)

September 5 Soviet Note on Berlin The Soviet Union, in a note to the United States, accused it, France, and the United Kingdom of being responsible for the tense situation in Berlin. The Soviets called on the three Western governments to do whatever was necessary to prevent attacks against Soviet and East German forces in Berlin. (DSB 10/15/62 558)

September 6 *U.S. Comments on Soviet Note* The State Department issued a statement rejecting the unsubstantiated charges in the September 5 Soviet note regarding violence in Berlin. The United States accused the Soviet Union of being unresponsive to Western proposals pertaining to the increase in tensions in Berlin since the building of the Berlin Wall. (DSB 9/24/62 448)

September 11 *Arms to Cuba* The Soviet government issued a statement declaring that the arms and military equipment sent to Cuba were for defensive purposes only. The Soviets said they would come to the assistance of Cuba should it be attacked. (AFPCD 370)

September 13 *Kennedy on Cuba* President Kennedy, in a statement at a news conference, said should Cuba "become an offensive military base of any significant capacity for the Soviet Union," then the United States would do whatever was necessary to protect its national interest and allied nations. (DSB 10/1/62 481)

September 21 *Gromyko on Cuba* Foreign Minister Gromyko, in an address to the United Nations General Assembly, accused the United States of committing aggression against Cuba. He insisted that the United States must refrain from interfering in Cuba's internal affairs, and warned that an American attack on Cuba would mean war with the Soviet Union. (NYT 9/22/62 1)

September 25 *U.S. Note on Berlin* The United States, in a note to the Soviet Union, accused it of being responsible for the building of the Berlin Wall and the brutality of the East German government. The Soviets were again charged with refusing to engage in consultations to reduce tensions in Berlin. (DSB 10/15/62 558)

September 30 *Rusk on Cuba* Secretary of State Rusk, in response to a question on the television program "News and Comment," said the United States was carefully observing events in Cuba to determine whether the Cuban government was developing an offensive military capability. (DSB 10/15/62 595)

October 14 *Kennedy on Eastern Europe* President Kennedy, in a speech in Buffalo, said Soviet domination of Eastern Europe was only "temporary," and the United States must never do anything to suggest that Soviet control was permanent. (PP 782)

October 22 *Kennedy and Cuba* President Kennedy, in an address to the American people, said evidence was now available proving that offensive missile sites were being built in Cuba. He said Soviet officials, including Foreign Minister Gromyko, had repeatedly lied about the type of weapons the Soviet Union was sending to Cuba. The president ordered a quarantine on all offensive weapons going to Cuba and said if any missiles were launched from Cuba, the United States would retaliate by attacking the Soviet Union. (PP 806)

October 22 *Kennedy to Khrushchev* President Kennedy sent a message to Premier Khrushchev warning the Soviet Union that the United States was determined to have the Soviet missiles in Cuba removed. (DSB 11/19/73 635)

October 23 *Khrushchev to Kennedy* Premier Khrushchev, in a message to President Kennedy, accused the United States of interfering in Cuba's internal affairs and those of the Soviet Union. He said the Soviet Union rejected the idea that the United States had the right to control armaments the Soviets shipped to Cuba. (DSB 11/19/73 636)

October 23 *The Soviets on Cuba* The Soviet government issued a statement alleging that President Kennedy's decision to quarantine Cuba violated international law. (AFPCD 406)

October 23 *Soviet Military Measures* The Soviet Union announced it was taking certain measures to raise the combat readiness of its military forces because of the Cuban missile crisis. (AFPCD 407)

October 23 *Kennedy to Khrushchev* President Kennedy, in a message to Premier Khrushchev, asked him to issue instructions to have Soviet ships observe the terms of the quarantine. (DSB 11/19/73 637)

October 24 *Khrushchev to Kennedy* Premier Khrushchev, in a letter to President Kennedy, angrily rejected the American demands regarding the missiles in Cuba and the quarantine. Khrushchev accused the United States of violating international law and said the Soviets would do what was necessary to protect the rights of the Soviet Union. (DSB 11/19/73 637)

October 25 *Kennedy to Khrushchev* President Kennedy, in a message to Premier Khrushchev, said the Soviets had deceived the United States by asserting in September that no offensive weapons were being shipped to Cuba. He again called on the Soviets to "take the necessary action to permit a restoration of the earlier situation." (DSB 11/19/73 639)

October 26 *Kennedy on Cuba* The White House issued a statement declaring that the building of offensive ballistic missile sites in Cuba was continuing at a rapid pace. (DSB 11/12/62 740)

October 27 *Khrushchev to Kennedy* Premier Khrushchev, in a message to President Kennedy, declared that the sole purpose of Soviet aid to Cuba was to strengthen its defensive capabilities. Khrushchev said he would agree to remove Soviet missiles from Cuba if the United States promised not to invade Cuba and to remove American missiles in Turkey. (DSB 11/12/62 741)

October 27 *U.S. and Cuba* President Kennedy, in a message to Premier Khrushchev, insisted that the Soviet Union must cease work on the missile sites in Cuba and undertake measures to render the missiles inoperable. Kennedy pledged that the United States would not invade Cuba if Khrushchev removed the missiles. (DSB 11/19/73 649)

October 28 *Khrushchev to Kennedy* Premier Khrushchev wrote to President Kennedy to inform him that the Soviet missiles would be removed from Cuba. (DSB 11/19/73 650)

October 28 *Kennedy and Khrushchev* President Kennedy issued a statement welcoming the decision to remove the missiles from Cuba. Khrushchev's decision defused one of the most dangerous cold war confrontations. (AFPCD 444)

November 18 *Adenauer Criticized* An article in *Izvestia* criticized Chancellor Adenauer because of his two-day visit to the United States earlier in the month. Adenauer was accused of promoting Soviet-American tensions as a means to enable the Bonn government to join the nuclear club. (CDSP XIV:46 18)

December 12 *Khrushchev on World Affairs* Premier Khrushchev, in a report to the Supreme Soviet, blamed the United States for the Cuban missile crisis but, he said, the Soviet Union succeeded in getting the United States to declare that it would not invade Cuba. (CDSP XIV:52 3)

December 13 *Gromyko on Foreign Policy* Foreign Minister Gromyko, in a speech to the Supreme Soviet, said the Soviet Union was eager to improve relations with the United States. He supported completing a peace treaty for Germany, but he criticized the Bonn government for allegedly making reckless statements that exacerbated international tensions. The Soviets wanted to improve relations with the United States following the Cuban missile crisis. (CDSP XV:1 11)

December 17 *Kennedy and Foreign Policy* President Kennedy, in response to a question during an interview, said the United States nuclear arsenal had sufficient second-strike capability to destroy the Soviet Union if it launched a nuclear attack against the United States. He said the differences the United States had with the Soviet Union were the result of the latter's desire to extend its power and influence around the world. (PP 897)

December 19 *Khrushchev to Kennedy* Premier Khrushchev, in a letter to President Kennedy, said the Soviet Union would be willing to permit two or three inspections a year in support of a nuclear test ban treaty. Khrushchev mistakenly believed that President Kennedy would accept a limited number of inspections. (CDSP XV:3 9)

December 21 *Polaris Missiles* President Kennedy and Prime Minister Macmillan issued a statement on nuclear defense systems. The president decided to make Polaris missiles, without warheads, available to the United Kingdom, and both countries agreed to make some of their nuclear weapons available to NATO as part of a potential NATO multilateral nuclear force. The Soviet Union opposed the creation of such a force. (DIA 483)

December 28 *Kennedy to Khrushchev* President Kennedy, in a letter to Premier Khrushchev, welcomed the Soviet decision to accept two or three on-site inspections in support of a nuclear test ban treaty. The president, however, said the United States required a minimum of eight to ten inspections. (AFPCD 1310)

1963

January 7 *Khrushchev to Kennedy* Premier Khrushchev, in a letter to President Kennedy, repeated his offer to allow three inspections a year to monitor a test ban treaty, although he continued to insist that such inspections were unnecessary. (DSB 2/11/63 201)

January 14 *State of the Union* President Kennedy, in his State of the Union address, said the Sino-Soviet dispute was over means to be used to spread communism rather than the goals of the communist movement. He predicted that nationalism and the inefficiencies of command economies would lead to the collapse of communism. (PP 15)

January 15 *Soviets Criticize Kennedy* *Izvestia* criticized President Kennedy for his comments in the State of the Union address on January 14. He was berated for calling for an increase in defense spending and for failing to accept the Soviet policy of peaceful coexistence. (CDSP XV:3 25)

January 16 *Khrushchev on Foreign Policy* Premier Khrushchev, in a speech in the German Democratic Republic, said Soviet-American differences regarding Germany and Berlin made it difficult to negotiate arms control agreements. He insisted that the German Democratic Republic should have control over its borders and a German peace treaty should be concluded. He again advocated making West Berlin a "free city." (CDSP XV:3 6)

January 24 *Kennedy and Foreign Policy* President Kennedy, in response to a question at a news conference, said some missile sites in Italy and Turkey were no longer needed because the United States was deploying Polaris submarines in the Mediterranean region. He did not expect any Soviet concessions in return for the site reductions. (PP 98)

January 27 *Soviet Troops in Cuba* Secretary of State Rusk, in response to a question on the television program "Meet the Press," said the United States did not consider a Soviet military presence in Cuba "as a normal condition." He expressed the hope that at least some Soviet troops would be withdrawn. (DSB 2/18/63 245)

February 8 *Nuclear Testing* The United States resumed underground nuclear testing. On February 12 Tass, the Soviet news agency, criticized the American decision and said it would complicate the process of trying to complete a nuclear test ban treaty. President Kennedy was unmoved by the Soviet criticism. (NYT 2/9/63 1)

February 13 *Rusk on Foreign Policy* Secretary of State Rusk, in a speech in Los Angeles, reviewed Soviet-American relations. He said the Soviets were now convinced that the independence of West Berlin remained a vital American national interest. He said the United States opposed the stationing of Soviet troops in Cuba and would oppose efforts by the Cuban government to spread communism in the hemisphere. (DAFR 16)

February 26 *Rusk on Foreign Policy* Secretary of State Rusk, in a speech in Texas, said the United States was willing to develop a NATO multilateral nuclear force, provided the NATO nations wanted such a force. He said the United States, in addition to strengthening NATO, was trying to find points of common interest with the Soviet Union. He vowed, despite the hurdles, to continue efforts to negotiate agreements with the Soviets. (DSB 3/18/63 383)

March 4 *Chemical Weapons Charge* *Pravda* accused the United States of using chemical weapons against the people of Vietnam from January 13 to January 24. (CDSP XV:9 21)

March 27 *Poison Gas Charge* *Pravda* carried an article again alleging that the United States was using poison gas in Vietnam. (CDSP XV:13 20)

April 8 *Soviet Note on NATO* The Soviet Union, in a note to the United States, protested plans for creating a NATO multilateral nuclear force. The NATO nations were accused of seeking a military superiority that would enable them to achieve their foreign policy goals by force. The Soviets said that should war break out, bases with nuclear weapons, wherever they might be, would be subject to attack. The Soviets also charged that the multilateral force would permit West Germany to have nuclear weapons. (DIA 190)

May 8 *Nuclear Testing* President Kennedy, in response to a question at a news conference, said he was not hopeful the United States and the Soviet Union would agree on the terms of a nuclear test ban treaty. As a result, he said, the United States would probably engage in another round of underground nuclear testing. (PP 377)

May 18 *U.S. Note on NATO Force* The United States responded to the April 8 note from the Soviet Union. The United States rejected all the Soviet charges regarding a NATO nuclear force and said the NATO nations were only interested in self-defense. (DIA 197)

May 20 *Soviets Protest Nuclear Force* The Soviet Union, in a note to the United States, protested the creation of a NATO nuclear force and the deployment of Polaris missiles on submarines in the Mediterranean.

Khrushchev suggested that the Mediterranean be made a nuclear-free zone. (CDSP XV:21 22)

May 23 *Khrushchev on Foreign Policy* While Fidel Castro, the Cuban prime minister, was visiting the Soviet Union, Premier Khrushchev warned the United States not to attack Cuba. He expressed support for wars of national liberation and declared that communism would ultimately be victorious throughout the world. (DIA 218)

May 24 *North Atlantic Council* The ministers attending the North Atlantic Council meeting in Ottawa issued a communiqué. They approved arrangements for organizing NATO's nuclear forces, and they agreed that some of them should be placed under the control of the supreme commander of the NATO forces in Europe. (DAFR 199)

May 29 *Soviets Criticize NATO* *Pravda* criticized the NATO ministers for their decision at the Ottawa North Atlantic Council meeting to place nuclear weapons under the control of the NATO supreme commander. The NATO nations were accused of planning to permit the Bonn government to have access to nuclear weapons. (CDSP XV:22 19)

June 10 *Kennedy on Soviet-American Relations* President Kennedy, in a speech at American University in Washington, spoke about the prospects for peace. He said the United States and the Soviet Union had an interest in developing a lasting peace and ending the arms race. The president said the United States would cease testing when negotiations for a test ban treaty resumed, provided the Soviet Union did not test. Kennedy's speech was considered a major effort to improve Soviet-American relations. (DIA 14)

June 15 *Khrushchev Interviewed* *Pravda* published the answers given by Premier Khrushchev to reporters from *Pravda* and *Izvestia*. Khrushchev said he supported many of the ideas expressed by President Kennedy on June 10, but Khrushchev reiterated a desire to solve the West Berlin problem by making it a "free city." (CDSP XV:24 21)

June 20 *Hot-Line Agreement* The United States and the Soviet Union agreed to install a hot line that would enable the leaders of the two countries to communicate with each other during a crisis. President Kennedy was unhappy about delays in communicating with Premier Khrushchev during the Cuban missile crisis. (DIA 164)

June 24 *Kennedy and Adenauer* President Kennedy and Chancellor Adenauer, after two days of talks in Bonn, issued a communiqué. The two leaders pledged to strengthen NATO, to continue their close collaboration on world problems, and to do all that was necessary to protect West

Berlin. They also discussed the proposed multilateral nuclear force for NATO, including a seaborne medium-range ballistic missile force. The Soviets opposed the proposed multilateral nuclear force. (DIA 33)

June 24 *U.S. Note on Nuclear Arms* The United States responded to the May 20 note from the Soviet Union regarding the creation of a NATO nuclear force and the establishment of a nuclear-free zone in the Mediterranean. The United States said strengthening NATO was essential because of Soviet policies and rejected the Soviet proposal for creating a nuclear-free zone in the Mediterranean because of its unfavorable impact on the balance of power in Europe. (DIA 166)

June 26 *Kennedy in Berlin* President Kennedy, in a speech in Berlin, called the Berlin Wall "an offense against humanity." The president received an enthusiastic response when he told his Berlin audience "Ich bin ein Berliner." (PP 524)

July 2 *Kennedy on Communism* President Kennedy, in a speech at the NATO headquarters in Brussels, said communism was "outmoded and doomed to failure." The advantages of freedom, he said, could be seen by comparing East Berlin with West Berlin, East Germany with West Germany, and Eastern Europe with Western Europe. (DAFR 216)

July 2 *Khrushchev on Foreign Policy* Premier Khrushchev, in a speech in East Berlin, criticized President Kennedy for his anticommunist comments in West Berlin and the Federal Republic of Germany. Khrushchev also berated Chancellor Adenauer and the leader of the Social Democrats, Willy Brandt. (CDSP XV:27 6)

July 5 *Captive Nations Week* President Kennedy designated the week of July 14 "Captive Nations Week." (DSB 7/29/63 161)

July 17 *Kennedy and Cuba* President Kennedy, in response to a question at a news conference, said Cuban-American relations could not improve while Cuba remained a Soviet satellite and permitted Soviet troops to be stationed on its territory. (PP 571)

July 26 *Kennedy and the Test Ban Treaty* President Kennedy, in a speech to the nation, explained the importance of the nuclear test ban treaty that had been agreed to but not yet signed. He said it would reduce radioactive fallout, could serve as a foundation for additional agreements, and could contribute to improved Soviet-American relations. (DAFR 132)

August 5 *Test Ban Treaty* Great Britain, the Soviet Union, and the United States signed the partial nuclear test ban treaty prohibiting testing in the atmosphere, outer space, and under water. Underground testing was not prohibited because the United States and the Soviet Union could not agree on verification measures. (DOD 291)

September 6   *Soviets Accuse the U.S.*   Tass, the Soviet news agency, accused the United States of violating the 1962 Geneva accords on Laos by illegally introducing aircraft into the country. The United States denied the Soviet allegation. (DSB 9/30/63 500)

September 20   *Kennedy at the UN*   President Kennedy, in an address to the United Nations General Assembly, spoke about the major differences that separated the United States and the Soviet Union. He said people, including the people of Eastern Europe, should have the right to choose their own government. Despite Soviet-American differences, the president pledged he would continue to try to reach agreements with the Soviet Union to reduce international tensions. (DSB 10/7/63 530)

October 9   *Wheat Sale to Soviet Union*   President Kennedy announced that private organizations would sell $250 million worth of wheat to the Soviet Union, the largest commercial transaction ever between the two countries. The president also approved the sale of wheat to the nations of Eastern Europe. (DAFR 160)

October 10   *Khrushchev and Kennedy*   Premier Khrushchev, in a letter to President Kennedy, expressed the hope that the signing of the nuclear test ban treaty would lead to other Soviet-American agreements and better relations between the two nations. He again suggested that the NATO and WTO countries sign a nonaggression pact. (DAFR 148)

October 12   *Rusk on Foreign Policy*   Secretary of State Rusk, in a speech in Ohio, said the nations of Eastern Europe were acquiring more autonomy and were reaching out to have more frequent contacts with the West. He said there was even pressure in the Soviet Union to grant the people a little more freedom, a trend the United States wanted to encourage. (DSB 10/28/63 654)

October 19   *Kennedy on Foreign Policy*   President Kennedy, in a speech in Maine, reviewed Soviet-American relations since the October 1962 Cuban missile crisis. He applauded the improved relations between the superpowers, but he noted that significant differences remained. According to the president, the Soviets had not abandoned their global ambitions, but the United States would continue to try to improve relations. (DAFR 162)

October 27   *Rusk on Foreign Policy*   Secretary of State Rusk, in a speech in the Federal Republic of Germany, said the agreements the United

States had signed with the Soviet Union, such as the test ban treaty and the hot-line agreement, did not add up to a policy of détente. He said a policy of détente could be achieved only if issues such as Berlin, Germany, Vietnam, Laos, and Cuba were resolved. (DSB 11/11/63 726)

November 12 Barghoorn Arrested The Soviet Union announced that Frederick Barghoorn, a professor at Yale University and an expert on Soviet affairs, had been arrested on October 31 and charged with espionage. (NYT 11/13/63 P 1)

November 14 Kennedy and Barghoorn President Kennedy, in response to a question at a news conference, said the arrest of Professor Barghoorn endangered cultural exchange programs between the United States and the Soviet Union. Two days later, the Soviets, supposedly owing to President Kennedy's concerns, released Barghoorn. (PP 845)

November 18 McNamara on U.S. Power Secretary of Defense McNamara, in a speech in New York, compared the military might of the United States and the Soviet Union. He said there was no doubt that if the Soviet Union launched a first strike, the United States had sufficient power to launch a second strike that would completely destroy the Soviet Union. (DIA 20)

November 22 Kennedy Assassinated President Kennedy was assassinated in Dallas. He was succeeded in office by Vice President Lyndon Johnson. (NYT 11/23/63 1)

December 13 Arms Control Premier Khrushchev, in an address to the Central Committee of the Communist party, accused the NATO nations of opposing measures to reduce military forces in Europe, including Germany. He did not think force reductions would upset the European balance of power. (CDSP XV:49 3)

December 18 Rusk on Foreign Policy Secretary of State Rusk, in response to a question on "CBS Reports," said the United States and the Soviet Union had the responsibility to conduct their relations in a way that prevented the outbreak of war. He also said the nations of Eastern Europe were trying to improve relations with the nations of Western Europe. (DSB 1/6/64 5)

December 18 Soviets and NATO Izvestia criticized the ministers at the recently concluded North Atlantic Council meeting in Paris for failing to endorse a nonaggression pact to be signed by the NATO and WTO nations. (CDSP XV:51 31)

December 31 *Khrushchev to Johnson*   Premier Khrushchev, in a letter to President Johnson and most other world leaders, said that force should not be used to settle territorial disputes. The Soviets were particularly sensitive to protect the borders established in Europe after World War II. Khrushchev suggested that a treaty should be signed whereby states renounced the use of force to bring about territorial changes. (DSB 2/3/64 158)

1964

January 10 *Rusk on Foreign Policy* Secretary of State Rusk, in a speech at Columbia University read by Harlan Cleveland, assistant secretary for international organization affairs, said the United Nations had not performed as expected when it was organized because Stalin's policies violated the principles of the UN Charter. Rusk expressed the hope the Soviet Union would cooperate with the United States to strengthen the United Nations because he considered it an important instrument in building a peaceful international community. (DSB 1/27/64 112)

January 18 *Johnson and Khrushchev* President Johnson, in response to the December 31, 1963, letter from Premier Khrushchev, said he supported many of the ideas in the letter, and he went on to list areas where the superpowers could cooperate, including arms control. Johnson also called for more cooperation by the permanent members of the United Nations Security Council to help resolve matters such as territorial disputes. (DSB 2/3/64 157)

January 22 *Rusk on Foreign Policy* Secretary of State Rusk, in a speech in New York, declared that the cause of freedom was the major issue in the conflict between the United States and the Soviet Union. He said the Soviet leaders had demonstrated a better understanding of nuclear war than the Chinese leaders, but the Soviets were still willing to resort to violence to achieve their foreign policy goals. (DSB 2/10/64 190)

January 23 *Castro Visits the Soviet Union* *Pravda* published a communiqué issued by Khrushchev and Castro at the close of Castro's visit to the Soviet Union. Khrushchev warned that if the United States attacked Cuba, "the Soviet Union will fulfill its international duty and will render the necessary help, with all the means at its disposal, to defend the freedom and independence of the fraternal Republic of Cuba." (CDSP XVI:4 26)

February 7 *Rusk on Foreign Policy* Secretary of State Rusk, in response to a question at a news conference, declared that the use of the word *détente* to describe Soviet-American relations was inaccurate. He said the Soviets seemed less militant in pursuing some of their goals, but major differences between the superpowers remained. (DSB 2/24/64 281)

February 25 *Rusk on Foreign Policy* Secretary of State Rusk, in a speech in Washington, said that although Moscow and Beijing were committed to world revolution, the United States had to deal with each of the communist nations individually rather than treating them alike. He said the United States would do all it could to contain communism, to reduce the danger of war, and to encourage greater autonomy for the nations of Eastern Europe. (DSB 3/16/64 390)

March 6 *Rusk on Foreign Policy* Secretary of State Rusk, in a speech at the University of Wisconsin, said the United States, although it maintained a large military arsenal to deter aggression, continually endeavored to find areas of agreement with the Soviet Union. He said American policy toward the communist nations had three components: to prevent aggression, to reduce the risk of a general war, and to encourage the communist nations to move in the direction of freedom. (DSB 3/23/64 434)

March 6 *Rusk on Foreign Policy* Secretary of State Rusk, in response to a question at a news conference, said he was not optimistic about a Soviet-American agreement on arms control, but the United States would not abandon the effort. He expected talks on arms control to continue for a long time. (DSB 4/23/64 445)

March 19 *Rusk on Foreign Policy* Secretary of State Rusk, in a speech in Salt Lake City, explained how the United States formulated its foreign policies regarding the communist nations. He said the United States had to remain militarily strong to deter aggression, while at the same time encouraging trends among the Eastern European countries for greater autonomy vis-à-vis the Soviet Union. (DSB 4/6/64 530)

April 20 *Johnson on Foreign Policy* President Johnson, in a speech to the Associated Press in New York, reviewed some basic principles of American foreign policy, including the need to check the expansion of communism. He hoped for a gradual improvement in Soviet-American relations and expressed confidence that, in the long run, freedom would prevail over communism. (DSB 5/11/64 726)

April 25 *Violating Cuba's Airspace* *Izvestia* criticized the United States for allegedly planning to send reconnaissance planes over Cuba. The article said that Premier Khrushchev wanted to improve relations with the United States but not at the expense of Cuba. (CDSP XVI:17 31)

May 10 *Rusk on Foreign Policy* Secretary of State Rusk, in an interview on British television, said changes were beginning to occur in the communist bloc nations because of their citizens' desires for more freedom and better economic conditions. (DSB 5/25/64 817)

May 14 *North Atlantic Council* The ministers attending the North Atlantic Council meeting in The Hague issued a communiqué. They accused the communist nations of adopting policies that resulted in increased international tensions, and they berated the Soviet Union for failing to resolve the Berlin and German problems. (DAFR 76)

May 23 *Bridge-Building in Europe* President Johnson, in a speech in Virginia, said he wanted to build "bridges of increased trade, of ideas, of visitors and humanitarian aid" to help bring freedom to all of Europe. The Soviets considered President Johnson's bridge-building policies interference in the internal affairs of the Eastern European nations. (NYT 5/24/64 1)

June 12 *Soviet-East German Treaty* The Soviet Union and the German Democratic Republic signed a Treaty of Friendship, Mutual Assistance and Cooperation. The two nations reaffirmed the integrity of the German frontiers and said that German unity could come about only as a result of negotiations between the two "sovereign" governments in East and West Germany. The United States refused to recognize the German Democratic Republic as a sovereign nation. (CDSP XVI:24 3)

June 18 *Nuclear Agreement with NATO* The United States signed a new agreement with the NATO nations to provide them with additional information about nuclear weapons. A previous agreement was signed in 1955. (DSB 7/20/64 93)

June 26 *Tripartite Declaration* France, the United Kingdom, and the United States issued a declaration on the Soviet-East German treaty signed on June 12. The three Western allies said the Soviet Union continued to be responsible for control over the access routes to West Berlin. (DAFR 95)

July 4 *Kohler on Moscow Television* Ambassador Kohler was allowed to go on Moscow television to address the Russian people on the meaning of the American July 4 holiday. In his brief message, he spoke about civil rights in America and he emphasized the need for both countries to work to improve relations. (DSB 7/27/64 108)

July 9 *Rusk on Foreign Policy* Secretary of State Rusk, during an interview with a reporter from a West German television station, said there had been some improvement in Soviet-American relations but that fundamental differences remained in relation to Cuba, Berlin, and Southeast Asia. (DSB 7/27/64 106)

July 11 *Soviet Protest to U.S.* In a protest note to the United States, the Soviet Union alleged that the development of a NATO multilateral nuclear force was designed to supply the Federal Republic of Germany with nuclear weapons. The Soviets charged that this would eventually lead to a European nuclear force dominated by the FRG. (AFPCD 476)

July 11 *Captive Nations Week* President Johnson designated the week beginning July 12 "Captive Nations Week." (DSB 7/13/64 63)

July 15 *Captive Nations Week* *Izvestia* criticized the United States for its "Captive Nations Week." The article said that designating one week of each year as "Captive Nations Week" was a "yearly crime against honesty." (CDSP XVI:28 18)

July 25 *Soviets and NATO* Tass, the Soviet news agency, issued a statement criticizing the United States for its June 18 decision to share information about atomic weapons with its NATO allies. Tass said this policy would lead to more nations acquiring atomic weapons. (CDSP XVI:30 21)

July 26 *Soviet Statement on Laos* The Soviet Union issued a statement accusing the United States of militarily intervening in Laos, thus violating the 1962 neutrality agreement. The Soviets wanted to convene another international conference to deal with the Laotian crisis, but the United States opposed the Soviet proposal. (DSB 8/17/64 220)

August 3 *Soviet Protest* The Soviet Union, in a note to the United States, charged that American warplanes and naval vessels were carrying out maneuvers that endangered Soviet shipping en route to Cuba. (DSB 10/5/64 484)

August 28 *Note to Soviet Union* The United States, in response to the July 11 note from the Soviet Union, said the proposed NATO multilateral nuclear force was a defensive force intended to provide the alliance with a capability for dealing with the Soviet nuclear arsenal. (DSB 9/14/64 367)

September 14 *Rusk on Foreign Policy* Secretary of State Rusk, in a speech in Detroit, expressed confidence that freedom would eventually be victorious over communism. He said the United States wanted to contain communism, strengthen the forces of freedom, and explore with the communist nations means for reducing international tensions. He said there were trends in Eastern Europe toward more national independence and freedom. (DSB 10/5/64 463)

October 14 *Khrushchev Removed* Premier Khrushchev was removed from power in a bloodless coup. He was replaced by Aleksei Kosygin as premier and by Leonid Brezhnev as first secretary of the Communist party. (CDSP XVI: 40 3)

November 6 *Brezhnev on Foreign Policy* First Secretary Brezhnev, in a speech in Moscow, called for improved relations between communist and capitalist nations. He urged the Western nations to recognize the two German states and said he opposed the creation of a NATO multilateral nuclear force. (CDSP XVI:43 7)

December 2 *Johnson on Eastern Europe* President Johnson, in a speech at a luncheon for supporters of Radio Free Europe, said the United States was eager to build bridges to Eastern Europe regarding such things as trade, education, and technical and cultural exchanges. (DSB 1/1/65 151)

December 7 *Gromyko at the UN* Foreign Minister Gromyko, in an address to the United Nations General Assembly, warned against establishing a NATO multilateral nuclear force. He said that such a force would make a nonproliferation treaty impossible and would make the problem of German reunification more difficult. (DOG 1944-1985 884)

December 8 *Arms Control* *Pravda* printed an eleven-point memorandum on arms control. Among other things, the Soviets favored establishing nuclear-free zones, banning underground nuclear tests, and negotiating a nonaggression pact between the NATO and WTO nations. (CDSP XVI:50 9)

December 19 *Atomic Mine Barrier* *Pravda* accused some NATO nations, including the United States, of planning to install an atomic mine field along the border of the German Democratic Republic and Czechoslovakia. (CDSP XVI:51 20)

December 23 *Rusk on Foreign Policy* Secretary of State Rusk, in a statement at a news conference, said resolving the problem of a divided Germany based on free elections would contribute to the peace and stability of all of Europe. The Soviets opposed uniting Germany on the basis of free elections. (DSB 1/11/65 34)

1965

January 3 *Rusk on Foreign Policy* Secretary of State Rusk, in response to a question during an interview, said the new Soviet leaders had expressed a desire to improve relations with the United States, but Soviet support for North Vietnam and the communist rebellion in the Congo were obstacles. He did not think the policies of the new Soviet leaders differed from those of the deposed Nikita Khrushchev. (DSB 1/18/65 68)

January 4 *State of the Union* President Johnson, in his State of the Union address, said he would welcome a visit by the Soviet leaders to the United States and that he favored increasing trade with the communist bloc nations. (PP 2)

January 15 *Soviets Object* The Soviet Union, in a note to the United States, objected to plans being made for anti-Soviet demonstrations in New York and the erection of a plaque on a synagogue across the street from the Soviet United Nations mission denouncing the Soviet Union for its treatment of Jews. (DSB 7/12/65 85)

January 18 *Atomic Mine Belt* The Soviet Union again accused the United States of planning to install an "atomic mine belt" on the territory of the Federal Republic of Germany. The Soviets said such an act would increase tensions in Europe and would violate the Potsdam agreement. (DOG 1944-1985 890)

January 20 *WTO Communiqué* The ministers representing the WTO nations issued a communiqué opposing the establishment of a multilateral nuclear force within NATO, in part because the Federal Republic of Germany would allegedly then be provided with nuclear weapons. (AFPCD 417)

January 30 *Cultural Exchange Agreement* The State Department announced that the United States and the Soviet Union had agreed on a cultural exchange program for 1965. (AFPCD 553)

January 31 *Soviets React to Johnson* *Pravda* welcomed the comments of President Johnson in his January 4 State of the Union address. The article specifically mentioned his desire to have Soviet leaders visit the United States, his call for more trade, and a desire to increase contacts between the American and Soviet people. (CDSP XVII:5 3)

February 3 *Johnson on Visiting the Soviet Union* President Johnson, in a speech in Washington, again expressed the hope that the new leaders of the Soviet Union would visit the United States and that he would visit the Soviet Union. (PP 126)

February 7   *Attacks Against North Vietnam*   The White House announced that President Johnson had ordered United States air units to launch attacks against North Vietnam. The air attacks, the first against North Vietnam since the Gulf of Tonkin incident in August 1964, were in response to Vietcong attacks on a number of American military installations. Air attacks against North Vietnam continued until the end of the war, although they were at times suspended to encourage the Hanoi government to negotiate an end to the war. (DAFR 129)

February 7   *Kosygin in Hanoi*   Soviet Premier Kosygin, in a speech in North Vietnam, assured Vietnamese leaders that the Soviet Union would provide the Hanoi government with whatever aid it needed to cope with attacks launched by the United States. (CDSP XVII:6 4)

February 9   *American Embassy Attacked*   More than two thousand Asian and Russian students attacked the American embassy in Moscow in retaliation for the American air strikes against North Vietnam. This was the first of several anti-American demonstrations in the Soviet Union. On February 10 the White House issued a statement charging the Soviet Union with failing to provide adequate police protection at the American embassy. (PP 170)

February 22   *Soviet Shipping*   Tass, the Soviet news agency, made public a note to the United States accusing it of interfering with Soviet shipping in Indochina. On April 5 the United States rejected the Soviet charge. (NYT 2/23/65 8)

February 24   *U.S. Rejects Soviet Protest*   The United States rejected the Soviet protest of January 15, pointing out that placing a plaque on a building near the Soviet mission was a private act the government could not control. The Soviets were also told the American people had a right to demonstrate and protest, provided they broke no laws. (DSB 7/12/65 84)

March 6   *Rusk on Foreign Policy*   Secretary of State Rusk, in an address to the Cleveland Council of Foreign Affairs, supported the right of the German people to self-determination and said a lasting peace could not be achieved if Germany remained divided. He noted that the United States and its allies were seeking closer contacts with the Soviet Union to try and resolve central European problems. (DSB 3/22/65 427)

March 24   *Chemical Weapons*   The Soviet Union, in a note to the United States, accused it of using chemical weapons in Vietnam, thus violating the 1925 Geneva agreement outlawing such weapons. (CDSP XVII:13 26)

April 2 U.S. Protests Harassment The United States, in a note to the Soviet Union, protested the harassment of United States ships by Soviet naval vessels. The American note cited six incidents in which the Soviets allegedly violated the International Rules of the Road. (DSB 5/3/65 655)

April 7 Berlin Harassment The United States, in a note to the Soviet Union, protested the harassment of vehicles on access routes to Berlin. The Soviets were accused of using tactics that violated international agreements signed by the Soviet Union. (DSB 5/3/65 658)

April 12 Nuclear Capabilities Secretary of Defense McNamara, in an interview with the editors of *U.S. News & World Report*, said the American nuclear arsenal was superior to that of the Soviet Union. (AFPCD 558)

April 18 Moscow-Hanoi Communiqué The Soviet Union and North Vietnam issued a joint communiqué in which the Soviet Union threatened to send military volunteers to Vietnam if the United States continued its aggression. (CDSP XVII:16 13)

April 23 Rusk on Foreign Policy Secretary of State Rusk, in an address to the American Society of International Law, criticized the Soviet Union for its commitment to support wars of national liberation. The secretary said that such wars violated the United Nations Charter and international law. (DSB 5/10/65 694)

April 23 Atomic Mine Belt The United States, in a note to the Soviet Union, denied the Soviet allegation that an "atomic mine belt" was being installed on the territory of the Federal Republic of Germany. The Soviets were reminded that the nuclear warheads in the NATO nations were under the control of the United States. (DOG 1944-1985 894)

April 26 Soviet Arms Proposal Nikolai Fedorenko, the Soviet representative to the United Nations Disarmament Commission, suggested that certain partial arms control measures be considered to help reduce international tensions. Among other things, he suggested dismantling military bases on foreign soil, withdrawing troops from foreign countries, reducing military forces in central Europe, and prohibiting the creation of a NATO multilateral nuclear force. (AFPCD 269)

April 28 Troops to the Dominican Republic President Johnson ordered American troops to the Dominican Republic, allegedly to protect American citizens endangered because of military clashes between different groups, including communists and anticommunists. (PP 461)

April 30 Pravda on Dominican Republic *Pravda* said President Johnson's decision to send military forces to the Dominican Republic was nothing more than armed intervention in support of reactionary political forces opposed to former president Juan Bosch. (CDSP XVII:17 30)

May 2 Johnson and the Dominican Republic President Johnson, in an address to the American people, said he ordered additional troops to the Dominican Republic because the rebels attempting to overthrow the government were now under the control of communists. The president said another communist government in the western hemisphere must not be tolerated. (PP 469)

May 7 Johnson on Foreign Policy President Johnson, in remarks on the twentieth anniversary of V-E day, said the Western nations must continue to try to erode the iron curtain by building bridges to the nations of Eastern Europe and must continue to work for German unification. (AFPCD 436)

May 13 Announcement on Germany The foreign ministers of France, the United Kingdom, and the United States, at the conclusion of their talks with the West German foreign minister, announced they were discussing ways of approaching the Soviet Union to study the problem of German unification. (DSB 6/7/65 927)

May 26 Rusk on Foreign Policy Secretary of State Rusk, in response to a question at a news conference, said the Soviet Union had installed surface-to-air missiles in the Hanoi area. (AFPCD 871)

June 1 Communists in the Dominican Republic President Johnson, in response to a question at a news conference, said the communists did not begin the revolution in the Dominican Republic, but they joined it and in some areas were leading it. He said the threat of communists taking over the government had diminished since the arrival of American military forces. (PP 613)

June 3 Johnson on Foreign Policy President Johnson, in a speech in Chicago, appealed to the Soviet Union to join the United States in the search for peace. He emphasized the need for the superpowers to cooperate, and he added that Soviet interests would not be advanced by supporting aggression or subversion. (PP 630)

June 4 Soviets and NATO Meeting *Pravda* criticized the meeting of NATO defense ministers in Paris that convened on May 31. The ministers were accused of preparing for another war, intensifying the arms race, and raising international tensions. (CDSP XVII:22 16)

June 4 *Erhard Meets Johnson* President Johnson and West German Chancellor Ludwig Erhard, at the conclusion of their meeting in Washington, issued a joint communiqué. They expressed a desire to improve relations with the nations of Eastern Europe, to improve European unity, and to explore ways to end the division of Germany. (DAFR 99)

July 2 *Captive Nations Week* President Johnson designated the week of July 18 "Captive Nations Week." (DSB 7/26/65 171)

July 3 *Soviet Nuclear Capabilities* First Secretary Brezhnev, in response to the April 12 comments made by Secretary of Defense McNamara, declared that the Soviet nuclear arsenal was capable of defeating any nation or group of nations that attacked the Soviet Union. (AFPCD 560)

July 13 *Johnson on Relations with the Soviets* President Johnson, in response to a question at a news conference, said Soviet-American relations were strained because of America's involvement in the Indochina conflict. The president said the nation's honor required the United States to protect South Vietnam. (PP 739)

July 15 *Information on War Criminals* The United States, in a note to the Soviet Union, requested that the Soviets provide information to the West German government on Nazi war crimes committed by officials in East Germany. The United States had made a similar request on March 15. (DSB 8/2/65 191)

August 2 *Rusk on Foreign Policy* Secretary of State Rusk, in response to a question at a news conference, said he saw no conflict between developing a multilateral nuclear force within the framework of NATO and the need to conclude a nuclear nonproliferation treaty. (AFPCD 441)

August 9 *Rusk on Foreign Policy* Secretary of State Rusk, in response to a question on a television program, said the United States wanted to improve relations with the Soviet Union but not at the expense of abandoning South Vietnam. (AFPCD 565)

August 17 *Nuclear Weapons* The United States presented a draft treaty to the Eighteen-Nation Disarmament Committee to prevent the spread of nuclear weapons. (PP 890)

August 31 *Nuclear Weapons* The Soviet Union responded to the draft treaty presented to the Eighteen-Nation Disarmament Committee on August 17 by the United States. The Soviets rejected the idea of a nonproliferation treaty permitting the NATO nations to share nuclear secrets. (DSB 9/20/65 470)

October 11 *Soviets Accuse West Germany* An editorial in *Pravda* accused the Federal Republic of Germany of attempting to acquire nuclear weapons through the NATO alliance and warned of grave consequences if the Federal Republic succeeded. The Bonn government was accused of being the chief ally "of the aggressive imperialist circles of the U.S.A." (CDSP XVII:41 21)

November 5 *Soviet-American Relations* Secretary of State Rusk, in response to a question at a news conference, said the United States was willing to reach agreements with the Soviets on issues outside Southeast Asia, but they were unwilling to cooperate. (DSB 11/29/65 861)

November 17 *China at the UN* The United Nations General Assembly rejected a resolution to seat the Beijing government and to expel the government of Chiang Kai-shek. The United States opposed the resolution; the Soviet Union supported it. (DSB 12/13/65 952)

November 22 *Nuclear Warheads* The White House announced that the United States had made nuclear warheads available to NATO nations, but the warheads could not be used without the authorization of the American president. The Soviets had consistently opposed any American plan to have nuclear weapons in Europe. (DOD 534)

November 29 *Arms Control* The United Nations General Assembly approved a resolution, supported by the United States and the Soviet Union, to convene a preparatory committee to discuss the possibility of organizing a disarmament conference to which all nations would be invited. (DSB 12/27/65 1033)

December 3 *A Nuclear-Free Zone* The United Nations General Assembly passed a resolution recognizing Africa as a nuclear-free zone. The Soviet Union and the United States supported the resolution. (DAFR 77)

December 6 *Soviet-American Relations* Premier Kosygin, in an interview with James Reston of the *New York Times*, blamed the United States for the tensions in Soviet-American relations. He said there was no contradiction between favoring peace and supporting wars of national liberation. He cited support for the National Liberation Front in Vietnam as an example. (AFPCD 580)

December 9 *Soviets Warn West Germany* Foreign Minister Gromyko, in an address to the Supreme Soviet, warned the Federal Republic of Germany that the territorial lines drawn in Europe after World War II were permanent and not subject to further negotiation. He said any effort by

the Federal Republic to change the borders with Poland, Czechoslovakia, or any other Eastern European nation would bring about Soviet
retaliation. (AFPCD 494)

December 9 *Supreme Soviet on Vietnam* The Supreme Soviet passed a
resolution condemning the United States for its intervention in Vietnam. (CDSP XVII:51 7)

December 16 *North Atlantic Council* The ministers attending a meeting of
the North Atlantic Council in Paris issued a communiqué. They
expressed regret that the Soviet Union was uninterested in resolving
European problems such as the division of Germany. (DSB 1/3/66 7)

December 21 *Johnson-Erhard Talks* President Johnson and Chancellor
Erhard issued a joint communiqué at the conclusion of their meeting
that began on December 19 in Washington. Both leaders agreed that a
reduction of tensions in Europe was predicated on progress made
toward peacefully unifying Germany. They also discussed ways of
strengthening the NATO alliance. (PP 1165)

December 24 *Johnson-Erhard Talks* *Izvestia* criticized the recent Johnson-
Erhard meeting in Washington. The West German government was
accused of wanting to obtain nuclear weapons in return for supporting
America's policies in Vietnam. The article alleged that Johnson and
Erhard negotiated secret agreements pertaining to nuclear weapons.
(CDSP XVII:51 18)

1966

January 12 *State of the Union* President Johnson, in his State of the Union address, said the United States would remain in Vietnam until communist aggression was defeated. (PP 9)

January 17 *Plane Crashes* An American B-52 bomber carrying nuclear weapons crashed off the coast of Spain. On February 16 the Soviet Union sent a protest note to the United States. (NYT 1/20/66 1)

January 21 *Rusk on Foreign Policy* Secretary of State Rusk, in response to a question at a news conference, said Soviet-American relations had become more difficult because of the Vietnam War. He was, however, generally optimistic about the chances of a lasting peace. (DSB 2/7/66 193)

January 25 *U.S. Nuclear Might* Secretary of Defense McNamara, in testimony before a House subcommittee, said the United States could absorb a nuclear first strike launched by the Soviet Union and still inflict an unacceptable amount of damage in a retaliatory strike. (AFPCD 456)

January 31 *Resumption of Bombing* President Johnson ordered the renewed bombing of North Vietnam. For thirty-seven days the United States did not bomb North Vietnam, but still the Hanoi government gave no indication it was willing to seek a negotiated settlement. (PP 114)

February 1 *Soviets React to Bombing* *Pravda* published a statement denouncing the American decision to resume bombing North Vietnam. The bombing was described as barbaric and evidence the United States did not want the war to end. (CDSP XVIII:5 19)

February 12 *Honolulu Declaration* *Pravda* criticized the Honolulu Declaration issued by President Johnson and South Vietnamese President Nguyen Van Thieu at the conclusion of their talks on February 12. They were accused of planning to enlarge the scope of the Vietnam War. (CDSP XVIII:6 22)

February 16 *Soviets React to Plane Crash* The Soviet Union, in a note to the United States, said the crash of the B-52 bomber on January 17 endangered the people of the Mediterranean region because of radioactive fallout. The Soviets called on the United States to keep nuclear weapons off airplanes that flew outside national borders. (CDSP XVIII:7 19)

February 23 *Rusk on Foreign Policy* Secretary of State Rusk told the Joint Committee on Atomic Energy that the Soviets were wrong in charging that NATO's nuclear policies were contributing to nuclear proliferation. The Soviets were referring to the multilateral nuclear force the NATO nations were trying to develop at the time. (DSB 3/14/66 406)

March 19 *Soviet-American Agreement* The United States and the Soviet Union signed an exchange agreement on scientific, technical, educational, cultural, and other matters. (DSB 4/4/66 543)

March 25 *Soviet-American Collusion* Secretary of State Rusk, in response to a question at a news conference, denied the Chinese claim that the Soviet Union and the United States were cooperating to encircle the People's Republic of China. (DSB 4/11/66 558)

March 25 *West German Peace Initiative* The Federal Republic of Germany proposed reducing British, French, and Soviet nuclear arsenals in Europe. The Bonn government also expressed a willingness to sign nonaggression treaties with the Soviet Union and the nations of Eastern Europe. The Bonn initiative was supported by the United States. (AFPCD 391)

March 29 *Brezhnev on Foreign Policy* General Secretary Brezhnev, in a speech to the Twenty-third Party Congress, said Soviet-American relations had deteriorated because of American policies. He expressed support for a policy of peaceful coexistence, wars of national liberation, and military aid to enable the North Vietnamese government to defeat the United States. (CDSP XVIII:12 9)

April 2 *Gromyko on Foreign Policy* Foreign Minister Gromyko, in a report to the Twenty-third Party Congress in Moscow, said the European nations had not responded to Soviet suggestions for improving security in Europe because of America's influence. He charged the United States with abrogating President Roosevelt's commitment to withdraw American forces from Europe two years after World War II. (AFPCD 327)

April 15 *Poison Gas* *Izvestia* accused the United States of using poison gas in Vietnam. (CDSP XVIII:15 26)

May 17 *Soviet Note to West Germany* The Soviet government responded to the March 25 proposals made by the Federal Republic of Germany. The Soviets criticized the proposals and rejected the idea that the West German government represented all the German people. Moscow warned West Germany not to acquire nuclear weapons nor seek to change the borders established after World War II. (AFPCD 395)

May 24 *Rusk on Foreign Policy* Secretary of State Rusk, in a speech in New York, said the communist bloc was no longer monolithic but China and the Soviet Union were still committed to world revolution. He said the two communist nations disagreed about tactics, not goals. (DSB 6/13/66 926)

June 9 *North Atlantic Council* At the conclusion of the Brussels meeting of the North Atlantic Council, the ministers issued a communiqué. They emphasized the need to deal with the question of German unity as part of a process for reducing East-West tensions. The ministers called for an end to the division of Europe, and they announced their support for East-West cultural exchange programs. (DSB 6/27/66 1001)

June 13 *World Peace Council* The World Peace Council, a communist-dominated peace organization, met in Moscow for four days of talks. At the conclusion of the meeting, the council issued a number of resolutions pertaining to American threats to Cuba, the Vietnam War, and European security issues. The council criticized the United States for not supporting many of the proposals put forward by the Soviet Union, including creating nuclear-free zones, pledging not to be the first to use nuclear weapons, and preventing West Germany from acquiring access to nuclear weapons. (NT 7/13/66 SUPPLEMENT)

June 14 *East-West Relations* Secretary of State Rusk, in a speech in Denver, said there were signs of evolutionary change taking place in Eastern Europe. He said trends suggested that the Eastern European nations were becoming more autonomous and were seeking better relations with the nations of the West. (DSB 7/11/66 44)

June 15 *Johnson on Eastern Europe* President Johnson, in comments at the White House to a goodwill delegation from Austria, said he thought the division of Europe into competing political blocs was beginning to change, and he urged the Western nations to continue their efforts to improve relations with the Eastern European countries. (DSB 7/11/66 56)

June 25 *Disinformation* *Pravda* accused the United States of using disinformation tactics to mask the real reasons for its intervention in Vietnam and the Dominican Republic and of using the same tactics to discredit the National Liberation Front in South Vietnam. (CDSP XVIII:25 28)

July 1 *Widening the Vietnam War* *Pravda* said the American bombing raids on the outskirts of Hanoi and Haiphong proved the United States intended to widen the Vietnam conflict. (CDSP XVIII:26 17)

July 5 *European Security* The ministers of the WTO nations issued a declaration accusing the United States of using the Western European nations as an instrument of America's policies. The declaration called for the dissolution of NATO and the WTO, the withdrawal of foreign troops, guarantees that the Federal Republic of Germany would not have access to nuclear weapons, and the convening of an all-European conference to discuss security issues and measures to be taken to improve relations among all the European states. (CDSP XVIII:27 3)

July 8 *Captive Nations Week* President Johnson designated the week of July 17 "Captive Nations Week." (WCPD 907)

July 9 *Soviets Protest Bombing* The Soviet Union, in a protest note to the United States, said Soviet ships and seamen were endangered because of the American bombing of Haiphong on July 7. (CDSP XVIII:28 18)

July 12 *Rusk on Foreign Policy* Secretary of State Rusk, in response to a question at a news conference, said he hoped the Soviet Union would make some effort to help end the fighting in Vietnam. (AFPCD 835)

July 23 *Soviet Protest Rejected* The United States responded to the Soviet protest on July 9. The American note blamed the North Vietnamese for widening the Vietnam War and for failing to seek a negotiated settlement. The Soviets were criticized for supplying North Vietnam with petroleum products to aid in its aggression against South Vietnam. (DSB 8/8/66 213)

July 24 *West Germans in Vietnam* *Pravda* said that West Germans were producing and using chemical weapons in South Vietnam. (CDSP XVIII:30 23)

July 29 *West Germans in Vietnam* *Pravda* claimed that soldiers from the Federal Republic of Germany were fighting in Vietnam in American units. (CDSP XVIII:30 24)

August 5 *Rusk on Soviet Policy* Secretary of State Rusk, in response to a question at a news conference, said that improving relations with the Soviet Union was difficult because of the Vietnam War. He blamed the Soviets for being unwilling to reconvene the Geneva Indochina conference to help bring about a resolution of the conflict. (DSB 8/22/66 260)

August 7 *Indians Poisoned* *Pravda* claimed that many people in India were poisoned after eating American food. The article alleged that Indian children died and others became paralyzed because of the American food. (CDSP XVIII:32 15)

August 22 *Rusk on Foreign Policy* Secretary of State Rusk, in a speech in New York, said the Soviet leaders would have to change their policies if the division of Europe were to end. He said the United States would continue to work to bring about European unity. (DSB 9/12/66 362)

August 26 *Johnson on Soviet-American Relations* President Johnson, in a speech in Idaho Falls, said the United States was determined to halt the spread of communism, while avoiding war with the Soviet Union. He promised, despite Soviet-American differences, to continue the search for areas of agreement between the superpowers. (PP 900)

September 1 *Johnson Criticized* An editorial in *Pravda* criticized President Johnson's August 26 speech. The editorial claimed that while he talked about improving Soviet-American relations, sections of his speech were anti-Soviet, anticommunist, and anti-Vietnam. The editorial accused the United States of playing the role of a global policeman and of being guilty of acts of aggression against Vietnam. (CDSP XVIII:35 21)

September 5 *Johnson on Foreign Policy* President Johnson, in a speech in Ohio, said the United States was attempting to build "bridges of friendship" to the nations of Eastern Europe. The Soviet Union viewed Johnson's "bridge-building" policies as an attempt to interfere in the internal affairs of the nations of Eastern Europe. (DSB 9/26/66 453)

September 13 *All-European Conference* *Izvestia* called for the convening of an all-European conference to discuss questions of national security, economic and cultural ties, trade, and science. The newspaper accused the United States of opposing a European conference because it would interfere with American plans to dominate Europe. (CDSP XVIII:37 15)

September 21 *Rusk on Foreign Policy* On September 21, Secretary of State Rusk, in a speech in New York, said a desire for more freedom and better living conditions would bring about evolutionary change in the Soviet Union and the nations of Eastern Europe. (DSB 10/17/66 586)

September 23 *Gromyko on Foreign Policy* Foreign Minister Gromyko, in an address to the United Nations General Assembly, said the Soviet Union would provide the Democratic Republic of Vietnam with all the assistance it needed to carry out its struggle against the United States and South Vietnam. (AFPCD 859)

October 6 *Thompson New Ambassador* Llewellyn E. Thompson was again named ambassador to the Soviet Union replacing Foy Kohler. (NYT 10/7/66 1)

October 7 *Johnson on Foreign Policy* President Johnson, in a speech in New York City, said that peace in Europe could never be secure as long as it remained divided. He said ending the division of Europe required strengthening NATO and the Western European community and improving relations between East and West. He said the United States wanted to move from peaceful coexistence with the Soviet Union to a policy of peaceful engagement. (DSB 11/24/66 622)

October 9   Soviets and Johnson   *Pravda* accused President Johnson of increasing international tensions both in Asia and Europe because of his Vietnam policies. He was criticized for claiming to want to improve relations with the socialist nations while ordering the bombing of one of them. (CDSP XVIII:41 19)

October 15   Brezhnev on Foreign Policy   General Secretary Brezhnev, in a speech in the Kremlin, said that if the United States wanted to improve relations with the Soviet Union, the air attacks against North Vietnam would have to cease. He also criticized efforts made by the United States to strengthen NATO. (CDSP XVIII:42 4)

November 4   Soviet-American Agreement   The United States and the Soviet Union signed an agreement for direct air service between Moscow and New York. (DSB 11/21/66 791)

November 18   Rusk on Foreign Policy   Secretary of State Rusk, in response to a question at a news conference, said the United States did not give détente with the Soviet Union a higher priority than German reunification. He said that a divided Germany would remain a cause of international tensions. (DSB 12/5/66 848)

December 7   Soviets Attack Peace Corps   *Pravda* said the Peace Corps was created for purposes of espionage. (CDSP XVIII:49 20)

December 16   NATO Nuclear Planning Group   The ministers of the North Atlantic Council at the close of their two-day meeting in Paris issued a communiqué. They agreed to establish a seven-nation NATO Nuclear Planning Group and a Nuclear Defense Affairs Committee to allow all the members an opportunity to share in the decision-making process pertaining to nuclear strategy. The two groups were in part a substitute for the multilateral nuclear force that was proposed but never created. The ministers supported efforts to increase contacts with the nations of Eastern Europe, and they agreed on the need to continue efforts to bring about German unification. (DSB 1/9/67 49)

1967

January 10 *State of the Union* President Johnson, in his State of the Union address, proposed a treaty banning defensive systems for ballistic missiles. He called on the Soviets to suspend work on the antiballistic missile defense system they had started to deploy. (PP 2)

January 13 *Brezhnev and Vietnam* General Secretary Brezhnev, in a speech in Gorky, said the war in Vietnam was "the most acute problem of world politics in our day." He condemned the United States for the bombing of Hanoi and labeled the American intervention in Vietnam "disgraceful." (CDSP XIX:2 3)

January 14 *Pravda Criticizes Johnson* *Pravda* criticized President Johnson's January 10 State of the Union address. He was accused of supporting policies in Vietnam that contradicted his alleged desire to improve relations with the Soviet Union. (CDSP XIX:2 9)

January 27 *Outer Space Treaty* Great Britain, the Soviet Union, the United States, and fifty-seven other countries signed a treaty governing the exploration and use of outer space. (DSB 2/20/67 266)

January 28 *Soviets and West Germany* The Soviet Union, in a note to the United States, alleged that Nazism and militarism were on the rise in West Germany. The Soviets again warned against any efforts to alter the boundary between the two German states. (AFPCD: 338)

February 24 *The Soviets and Europe* *Pravda* said the WTO nations were eager to do what they could to improve relations with the nations of Western Europe, excluding the Federal Republic of Germany. The Bonn government was accused of being the instrument of American policy to disunify the Eastern bloc. France was praised for its withdrawal from the NATO integrated command structure. (CDSP XIX:8 16)

March 2 *Arms Control Talks* President Johnson announced that the Soviet Union had agreed to begin discussions to limit offensive and defensive weapons systems. No date was given for the beginning of the talks. (PP 259)

March 16 *Consular Convention Treaty* The Senate approved the Consular Convention treaty with the Soviet Union that was signed in 1964. (PP 356)

April 6 *Nuclear Planning Group* The first meeting of the NATO Nuclear Planning Group convened in Washington. The purpose of the group was to allow the nuclear and nonnuclear powers in NATO to exchange ideas concerning nuclear weapons. The ministers discussed changes in the nuclear threat confronting the NATO allies, ballistic missile defense, tactical nuclear weapons, and nuclear planning. (AFPCD 285)

April 18 *Brezhnev on Foreign Policy* General Secretary Brezhnev, in a speech in East Germany, called for the convening of a European conference to discuss security issues. He criticized the United States for its Vietnam policies, and he accused the Federal Republic of Germany of opposing a nuclear nonproliferation treaty. (CDSP XIX:16 5)

April 24 *Brezhnev on Alliances* General Secretary Brezhnev, in a report to a conference of party workers, accused the United States of supporting the imperialist policies of West Germany. He said security in Europe required a recognition of the two German states, and he also called for the dissolution of NATO and the WTO alliances. A considerable portion of the report was devoted to condemning American policies in Vietnam. (AFPCD 290)

April 24 *Soviets Accuse U.S.* Foreign Minister Gromyko issued a statement accusing the United States of violating the 1962 Laotian neutrality agreement by providing Laos with military and other types of aid. (CDSP XIX:17 22)

April 26 *European Communists* The representatives attending the European Communist and Workers' parties meeting in the Soviet Union issued a communiqué at the conclusion of their two-day meeting. The representatives criticized the policies of the United States and the Federal Republic of Germany. They called for the convening of a European security conference to establish a European security system based on the principles of peaceful coexistence. The Soviets favored a European security alliance as a substitute for NATO and the WTO. (CDSP XIX:17 12)

May 1 *Rusk on Foreign Policy* Secretary of State Rusk, in a speech to the Chamber of Commerce in Washington, said despite Soviet-American differences, the United States must continue to negotiate with the Soviets to reduce international tensions. He said Soviet-American differences did not prevent the completion of the test ban treaty, the civil air and consular agreements, and the outer space treaty. (DSB 5/22/67 770)

May 13 *Soviets Protest* The Soviet Union, in a note to the United States, claimed that an American warship, engaged in a naval exercise in the Sea of Japan, collided with a Soviet ship. The actions of the American vessel were described as dangerous, unlawful, and provocative. (CDSP XIX:19 23)

June 6 *UN Cease-Fire* The United States and the Soviet Union supported a United Nations Security Council resolution calling for a cease-fire in the Middle East. Fighting between Israel and the Arabs began the previous day. (DSB 6/26/67 947)

June 9 *Meeting of Communist Leaders* The leaders of Bulgaria, Czechoslovakia, the German Democratic Republic, Hungary, Poland, the Soviet Union, and Yugoslavia met in Moscow and pledged their support to the Arab nations fighting Israel. They accused the United States of being in collusion with Israel. (CDSP XIX:23 3)

June 13 *The Hot Line* President Johnson, in response to a question at a news conference, said he had used the hot line to communicate with Soviet leaders about the fighting in the Middle East. (PP 615)

June 19 *Johnson on Foreign Policy* President Johnson, at a foreign policy conference for educators, said he hoped to narrow differences with the Soviet Union by negotiating agreements on arms control and cultural exchanges. (PP 630)

June 21 *Soviets and the Middle East* The Central Committee of the Communist party in the Soviet Union approved a resolution condemning Israel for the outbreak of war in the Middle East. The United States was accused of encouraging and assisting the Israeli aggression. (CDSP XIX:25 11)

June 23 *Glassboro Meeting* President Johnson met with Premier Kosygin in Glassboro, New Jersey. The two leaders discussed Indochina, arms control, and a nonproliferation treaty, but most of their discussions dealt with Middle East issues. The two sides remained far apart on most issues, but they did agree to begin arms control negotiations. (AFPCD 428)

June 25 *Glassboro Meeting* President Johnson and Premier Kosygin, following their discussions in Glassboro, issued statements. The two leaders agreed that, because of their meetings, they had a better understanding of each other's foreign policies, but they made little progress in resolving their differences. (AFPCD 431)

July 6 *Rusk on Foreign Policy* Secretary of State Rusk, in a speech in Illinois, said that despite the war in Vietnam, the United States and the Soviet Union were still trying to improve their relations. The secretary supported the effort to reduce tensions with the Soviet Union but, he said, the first requirement of peace is collective action to deter or repel acts of aggression. (DSB 7/24/67 87)

July 9   Soviets and Flexible Response   *Izvestia* criticized the NATO nations for their willingness to accept the American military doctrine of flexible response. The United States was accused of wanting to involve the NATO nations in local wars and of using the NATO alliance to dominate the nations of Europe. (CDSP XIX:27 18)

July 12   Captive Nations Week   President Johnson designated the week of July 16 "Captive Nations Week." (WCPD 1003)

July 19   Rusk on Foreign Policy   Secretary of State Rusk, in response to a question at a news conference, was critical of the Soviet Union for supplying arms to the nations of the Middle East. He said the weapons not only endangered Israel, but might also contribute to one Arab nation attacking another. (DSB 8/7/67 160)

September 18   Missile Defense   Secretary of Defense McNamara, in a speech in San Francisco, said the antiballistic missile system the Soviet Union was constructing would not limit America's ability to retaliate in response to a nuclear attack. He announced that the United States was going to build an ABM system, the Sentinel, to protect against a Chinese nuclear attack or an accidental launch. (AFPCD 16)

September 22   Gromyko at the UN   Foreign Minister Gromyko, in an address to the United Nations General Assembly, denounced American policies in Vietnam. His polemical speech indicated that Soviet-American relations would remain tense as long as the United States was involved in Vietnam. (NYT 9/23/67 1)

September 29   MIRVed Weapons   Secretary of Defense McNamara, in an interview published by *Life* magazine, announced that the United States would rely on MIRVed missiles to penetrate Soviet defensive capabilities. (AFPCD 461)

October 12   Rusk on Foreign Policy   Secretary of State Rusk, in response to a question at a news conference, criticized the militancy of China's foreign policy in attempting to spread its ideological beliefs. The secretary said the United States was interested in a secure peace but that did not necessitate eliminating communism in any particular country. He pointed out that, despite their differences, the United States and the Soviet Union had managed to live in peace with one another since the communists came to power in 1917. (DAFR 275)

November 3   Brezhnev on Foreign Policy   General Secretary Brezhnev, in a report on Soviet foreign policy to the Central Committee of the Communist party, said the United States and other imperialist nations were a threat to world peace. He charged the United States with committing crimes in South Vietnam similar to the atrocities committed by the fascists in the past. (CDSP XIX:44 3)

November 22 *The Middle East* The United Nations Security Council unanimously passed Resolution 242. It called for Israel to return the territory it captured in 1967 in exchange for a general, comprehensive peace. The resolution also endorsed free navigation through international waterways. (DSB 12/18/67 843)

December 8 *The Soviets and West Germany* The Soviet Union, in a note to the United States, alleged that neo-Nazism was growing in the Federal Republic of Germany, which could lead to another war. The Soviets called on the United States to abide by the Potsdam agreement. (CDSP XIX:49 23)

December 13 *The Harmel Report* The North Atlantic Council accepted the Harmel Report prepared by a committee led by Pierre Harmel, the Belgium foreign minister. The report contained two basic recommendations. One was that NATO had to maintain sufficient military strength to protect its members, and the other was that NATO should do all it could to promote negotiations between East and West. The report concluded that "military security and a policy of détente are not contradictory but complementary." (DSB 1/8/68 50)

December 14 *North Atlantic Council* The ministers of the North Atlantic Council issued a communiqué at the conclusion of their talks on December 12 in Brussels. Among other things, they officially approved the policy of flexible response first proposed by Secretary of Defense McNamara. Flexible response required the NATO alliance to have an array of weapons to enable it to respond appropriately to any military aggression by the Soviet Union. (DSB 1/8/68 49)

December 29 *U.S. Responds to Soviets* The United States rejected the allegations in the December 8 note from the Soviet Union regarding the alleged rise of neo-Nazism and militarism in West Germany. (AFPCD 354)

1968

January 4 *Soviets Claim Ship Attacked* The Soviet Union, in a note to the United States, alleged that a Soviet vessel in the port of Haiphong was attacked by American aircraft. On January 5 the United States sought to reassure the Soviets that if their allegations proved to be true, the United States would attempt to avoid such incidents in the future. (CDSP XX:1 21)

January 17 *State of the Union* President Johnson, in his State of the Union address, said despite Soviet-American differences, the superpowers were making progress in increasing cooperation between them. He said he hoped a nuclear nonproliferation treaty could be completed by the end of the year. (PP 25)

January 19 *Protest to U.S.* *Pravda* printed the text of a protest the Soviet Union sent to the United States alleging that it was violating the neutrality of Laos and Cambodia. The Soviets denied the frequently made American charge that North Vietnam was using the territory of Laos and Cambodia to launch attacks against South Vietnam. (CDSP XX:3 16)

January 25 *Johnson Criticized* *Izvestia* criticized President Johnson for his assertion on January 17 that Soviet-American relations were improving. The Soviets did not think relations could improve owing to the conflict in Southeast Asia. (CDSP XX:4 17)

February 10 *Soviets Protest to U.S.* The Soviet Union delivered an aide-mémoire to the United States on the crash of an American B-52 bomber on January 21 off the coast of Greenland. The plane was carrying four hydrogen bombs, and the Soviets alleged that the crash produced radioactive contamination that could endanger regions of the Atlantic Ocean for years to come. (CDSP XX:6 20)

February 21 *Soviets Protest to U.S.* A bomb exploded in the Soviet embassy in Washington, D.C. No one was injured. The Soviet Union, in a note to the United States, protested the bombing and demanded that those responsible be severely punished. (CDSP XX:8 20)

March 23 *WTO Summit* The leaders of the WTO nations, excluding President Nicolae Ceausescu of Romania, met in Dresden to discuss the changes taking place in Czechoslovakia. President Alexander Dubcek was present to reassure the bloc leaders that his reforms in Czechoslovakia would not endanger communism. (NYT 3/24/68 7)

April 1 *Democracy in Czechoslovakia* Alexander Dubcek, in a speech to the Central Committee of the Czech Communist party, said he was determined to bring democracy to Czechoslovakia. (NYT 4/2/68 7)

April 16 *Masaryk Murdered* *Rudo Pravo,* a Czech newspaper, reported that Soviet agents may have been responsible for the death of Foreign Minister Jan Masaryk in 1948. At the time, the communists claimed that he had committed suicide. (NYT 4/17/68 1)

May 3 *Vietnam Talks* President Johnson announced that representatives of the United States and North Vietnam would meet in Paris to begin preliminary negotiations on ending the Vietnam War. The talks began on May 13. (DSB 5/20/68 629)

June 4 *Johnson on Foreign Policy* President Johnson, in an optimistic speech at Glassboro State College, said U.S.-Soviet relations were more productive than at any time in the past. He said the United States and the Soviet Union were cooperating to find an agreement on a nuclear nonproliferation treaty and he suggested that the two sides should begin negotiations to reduce their nuclear stockpiles. Soviet leaders, however, did not share President Johnson's optimistic assessment of Soviet-American relations. (PP 679)

June 12 *Nonproliferation Treaty* The United Nations General Assembly approved a nonproliferation treaty that was supported by the United States and the Soviet Union. President Johnson, in an address to the assembly, welcomed the signing of the treaty and expressed the hope it would lead to other arms control agreements. (DSB 7/1/68 8)

June 13 *Soviets React to Johnson* *Izvestia* criticized President Johnson for his assertion on June 4 that Soviet-American relations were improving. The article pointed out that relations could not improve while the war in Southeast Asia continued. (CDSP XX:24 19)

June 25 *The Reykjavik Meeting* The ministers attending the North Atlantic Council meeting at Reykjavik issued a communiqué. They announced their intention to continue efforts to promote détente with the Soviet Union, but they were critical of Soviet policies pertaining to Berlin. In a separate document, the ministers agreed to begin preparations for negotiating mutual and balanced force reductions in central Europe with the Soviet Union. (DSB 7/15/68 75)

June 27 *Gromyko on Foreign Policy* Foreign Minister Gromyko, in a report to the Supreme Soviet, said the United States was responsible for existing international tensions, for continuing the Vietnam War, for lack of progress in arms control negotiations, and for opposing changes in the international status quo. He called on President Johnson to sign a treaty banning the use of nuclear weapons. He said the Soviet Union was ready to enter into negotiations with the United States to limit the deployment of antimissile defense systems. (CDSP XX:28 11)

July 1 *Nonproliferation Treaty* Great Britain, the United States, and the Soviet Union signed the nuclear nonproliferation treaty. The signatories agreed not to transfer nuclear weapons to other nations or to assist or encourage them to develop their own. Since the signing of the treaty, the United States and the Soviet Union have cooperated on developing a nonproliferation regime in support of the treaty. It went into effect on March 5, 1970. (PP 763)

July 1 *Arms Control* President Johnson announced that the United States and the Soviet Union had agreed to begin talks on limiting and reducing nuclear arms. No date was given for the start of the talks. (PP 765)

July 3 *Note on Berlin* The United States, in a note to the Soviet Union, protested the restrictions the East German authorities had placed on travel to West Berlin. The Soviets were asked to fulfill their international obligations to guarantee access to Berlin. (DSB 7/22/68 90)

July 5 *Soviets Threaten Germany* The Soviet Union, in a note to the Federal Republic of Germany, suggested that Soviet troops might have to intervene in West Germany to halt neo-Nazi activity and renewed militarization measures. (NYT 9/19/68 1)

July 10 *Captive Nations Week* President Johnson designated the week of July 14 "Captive Nations Week." (WCPD 1094)

July 15 *Exchange Agreement Signed* The United States and the Soviet Union signed an exchange agreement on culture, science, technology, and education. (DSB 8/5/68 154)

August 3 *Bratislava Communiqué* Communist leaders from Bulgaria, Czechoslovakia, Hungary, the German Democratic Republic, Poland, and the Soviet Union met in Bratislava, Czechoslovakia, to review events associated with the Prague Spring, the code word for reforms initiated by President Dubcek. The ministers emphasized the importance of maintaining the unity of the communist bloc because of the aggressive intentions of countries such as the United States and the Federal Republic of Germany. The Czech government incorrectly assumed that the Soviet Union, as a result of the declaration made at Bratislava, would not intervene in Czechoslovakia to reverse the reforms implemented by President Dubcek. (CDSP XX:31 4)

August 21 *Intervention in Czechoslovakia* Soviet and WTO troops invaded Czechoslovakia, allegedly at the request of "party and government leaders," because the country was threatened by "counterrevolutionary forces." (CDSP XX:34 3)

August 21 *Johnson and Czechoslovakia* President Johnson issued a statement calling on the Soviet Union and the WTO nations to withdraw their troops from Czechoslovakia. (PP 905)

August 22 *Rusk on Soviet Policy* Secretary of State Rusk, in response to a question at a news conference, said the Soviet invasion of Czechoslovakia would damage Soviet-American relations, but he did not think the Senate would refuse to ratify the nonproliferation treaty because of the Soviet actions. (DSB 9/9/68 262)

August 23 *Soviets Veto Resolution* The Soviet Union vetoed a United Nations Security Council resolution condemning the Soviet Union for its invasion of Czechoslovakia. (DSB 9/9/68 274)

August 30 *Johnson on Soviet Policy* President Johnson, in a speech in Texas, said the invasion of Czechoslovakia demonstrated Soviet unwillingness to tolerate even a moderate amount of autonomy and freedom for the nations of Eastern Europe. (DSB 9/23/68 311)

September 10 *Johnson on Foreign Policy* President Johnson, in a speech in Washington, said that events in Eastern Europe and the Middle East threatened world peace. He called upon the Soviet Union to change its policies in Eastern Europe, and he called on the Israelis and the Arabs to resolve their differences. (DSB 10/7/68 345)

September 12 *Rusk on Foreign Policy* Secretary of State Rusk, in a speech in Connecticut, rejected the idea that Eastern Europe was in the Soviet sphere of influence and, therefore, the Soviet invasion of Czechoslovakia was acceptable. He emphatically denied any similarity between Soviet policy in Czechoslovakia and American policies in Vietnam. (DSB 10/7/68 350)

September 17 *Bonn Reassured* A spokesperson for the State Department said the Bonn government had been reassured that the NATO nations would respond to any Soviet military attack on the Federal Republic of Germany. On July 5 the Soviet Union had threatened to militarily intervene in the Federal Republic. (DSB 10/7/68 365)

September 18 *Soviets Threaten West Germany* *Pravda* repeated the threat made in July that Soviet troops might have to intervene in West Germany to halt neo-Nazi activities and renewed militarization measures. (CDSP XX:38 15)

October 2 *Rusk at the UN* Secretary of State Rusk, in an address to the United Nations General Assembly, criticized the Soviet Union for its invasion of Czechoslovakia. He said the invasion violated the United Nations Charter, and he denied that the Czech uprising was the result of a plot by Western nations. (DSB 10/21/68 405)

October 16 *Soviet-Czech Treaty* The Soviet Union and Czechoslovakia signed a treaty for the temporary stationing of Soviet troops in Czechoslovakia. The treaty was similar to the one signed in 1956 after the Soviets suppressed the Hungarian uprising. (CDSP XX:42 3)

November 6 *Nixon Elected* Richard Nixon, the Republican party nominee, defeated Hubert Humphrey, his Democratic party opponent, in the presidential election. (NYT 11/7/68 1)

November 13 *The Brezhnev Doctrine* General Secretary Brezhnev, at the Fifth Congress of the Polish United Workers' party, presented what came in the West to be known as the "Brezhnev Doctrine" (also referred to as the Doctrine of Limited Sovereignty). The doctrine justified the Soviet intervention in Czechoslovakia and limited the sovereignty of the Eastern European countries; it asserted that the Soviets had the right and the obligation to use military force to protect a "socialist system" in danger of collapse. (CDSP XX:46 3)

November 16 *North Atlantic Council* The ministers attending the North Atlantic Council meeting in Brussels issued a communiqué criticizing the Brezhnev Doctrine and the Soviet invasion of Czechoslovakia. The ministers reaffirmed their determination to protect West Berlin and West Germany. (DSB 12/9/68 595)

November 19 *China at the UN* The United Nations General Assembly defeated an Albanian-sponsored resolution to seat the Beijing government and to expel the government of Chiang Kai-shek. The United States opposed the resolution; the Soviet Union supported it. (DSB 12/9/68 613)

November 24 *Soviets Respond to NATO* *Pravda* accused the NATO nations of pursuing policies that endangered world peace. The Soviets were particularly critical of the NATO ministers' decision, taken at the North Atlantic Council meeting in Brussels earlier in the month, to establish a naval strike group for the North Atlantic area similar to the Sixth Fleet operating in the Mediterranean. (CDSP XX:47 5)

December 2 *Kissinger and Rogers* President-elect Nixon selected Henry Kissinger as his national security assistant. On December 11 Nixon appointed William Rogers secretary of state; Nixon thought himself expert in foreign policy and personally knew many world leaders. (NYT 12/3/68 1)

1969

January 14 *State of the Union* President Johnson, in his State of the Union address, supported negotiations with the Soviet Union to reduce nuclear arsenals and promised to seek agreements where the superpowers had common interests. (PP 1268)

January 20 *Arms Control* The Soviet Foreign Ministry issued a statement calling for arms control measures that should be adopted. The statement criticized the United States and the NATO nations for allegedly opposing arms control measures. (CDSP XXI:3 6)

January 27 *Nixon on Linkage* President Nixon, in response to a question at a news conference, implicitly linked arms control agreements with the resolution of political issues. The question of "linkage" became an important issue in Soviet-American relations up to the end of 1991, when the Soviet Union ceased to exist. (PP 17)

January 28 *Gromyko on Laos* *Pravda* published the text of a statement by Foreign Minister Gromyko accusing the United States of militarily intervening in Laos in violation of the 1962 neutrality agreement. (CDSP XXI:5 15)

February 6 *Nixon on Summits* President Nixon, in response to a question at a news conference, said he thought a summit meeting with Soviet leaders required careful preparation and prior consultation with the NATO allies. He said he expected to meet with Soviet leaders sometime in the future. (PP 67)

February 24 *Nixon at the North Atlantic Council* President Nixon, in an address to the North Atlantic Council meeting in Brussels, called for greater cooperation between the United States and the nations of the alliance. He also emphasized the need for the United States and the Soviet Union to move from an era of confrontation to an era of negotiations. (PP 134)

March 4 *The Soviet Union and Vietnam* President Nixon, in response to a question at a news conference, said he believed the Soviet Union could be helpful in efforts to end the fighting in Vietnam, but he was not sure what role the Soviets would play. (PP 187)

March 13 *The Nonproliferation Treaty* The United States Senate voted its consent to ratification of the nonproliferation treaty initially approved by the United Nations General Assembly in June 1968. The Senate delayed ratification because of the Soviet invasion of Czechoslovakia. (NYT 3/14/69 1)

March 13 *Beam Confirmed* Jacob D. Beam was confirmed by the Senate to be ambassador to the Soviet Union. (DSB 4/7/69 304)

March 14 *The ABM System* President Nixon announced his decision to have the United States deploy a modified Sentinel antiballistic missile system designed to protect missile sites. The president said the Safeguard system, the new name for the Sentinel system, would help protect the United States from an attack by China but would not protect the American people if the Soviet Union were to launch a nuclear attack. (PP 216)

March 17 *WTO Meeting* The ministers attending a WTO meeting issued a call for a meeting of all the European nations to discuss security issues and to reaffirm the legitimacy of the boundaries established after World War II. (NT 1)

March 25 *Nixon and Arms Control* President Nixon, in a speech in Washington, said the United States had to be militarily strong if it were to seriously engage in arms control negotiations with the Soviet Union. If the United States did not maintain its military might, he did not think the Soviet Union would have any incentive to negotiate. (PP 246)

April 10 *Soviets Denounce NATO* *Pravda* published a statement by the Soviet government proposing a number of measures to strengthen peace and security in Europe, including abolishing NATO, recognizing the existence of two German states, accepting postwar territorial boundaries, and preventing the Federal Republic of Germany from obtaining nuclear weapons. (CDSP XXI:15 14)

April 11 *North Atlantic Council* At the conclusion of two days of talks in Washington, the ministers attending the North Atlantic Council meeting issued a communiqué. They accused the Soviet Union of hindering traffic to West Berlin, and they called for measures to bring about the unification of Germany. They also agreed to draw up a list of topics for possible negotiation with the Soviet Union. (DSB 4/28/69 354)

April 18 *Soviet Military Might* President Nixon, in response to a question at a news conference, said the Soviet Union would achieve nuclear superiority over the United States if steps were not taken to counterbalance the Soviet nuclear buildup. He thought parity could be achieved either by matching the Soviet buildup or by negotiating arms control agreements. (PP 303)

April 23 *Soviets Fault NATO* *Izvestia* criticized the NATO nations for their failure to respond to the Soviet call for a European security conference. (CDSP XXI:17 17)

April 26 *Soviets and Student Protests* *Pravda* reported on the antiwar demonstrations at Harvard and Cornell universities. The article said students were protesting ties between the universities and the CIA. (CDSP XXI:17 21)

May 27 *MBFR Talks* The ministers attending the North Atlantic Council meeting in Rome issued a declaration calling for exploratory talks with the Soviet Union on mutual and balanced force reductions. (DSB 6/22/69 775)

June 4 *Nixon on Foreign Policy* President Nixon, in a speech at the Air Force Academy, said the United States had to rethink its foreign policy priorities. He rejected a policy of isolationism, which had again become popular because of the Vietnam War. He said the United States had to remain militarily strong if it were to exert leadership in resolving international problems. (PP 432)

June 7 *Brezhnev on Foreign Policy* General Secretary Brezhnev, in a speech at a meeting of Communist parties in Moscow, accused the United States of unleashing wars, wanting to revise territorial boundaries in Europe, and engaging in subversive activities in socialist states. He expressed support for the policy of peaceful coexistence and the waging of ideological war, and he did not think the two were incompatible. (CDSP XXI:23 3)

June 7 *Nixon Criticized* *Pravda* reported there was widespread criticism in the United States of President Nixon because of his June 4 speech in which he criticized isolationists and those who wanted to sharply reduce the American military budget. The article quoted criticisms of President Nixon made by senators J. William Fulbright and Albert Gore and *New York Times* correspondent John Finney. (CDSP XXI:23 29)

June 10 *Safeguard Criticized* *Pravda* said there was growing opposition to President Nixon's plan to build the Safeguard antiballistic missile system. The Pentagon was accused of employing cold war tactics and anti-Soviet propaganda in an effort to win support for the program. (CDSP XXI:23 29)

June 17 *International Conference Ends* The International Conference of Communist and Workers Parties ended, and the delegates approved a document that called for an end to the Vietnam conflict, support for the Arabs in their struggle with Israel, and greater unity within the communist bloc. The United States was accused of committing aggression in Vietnam and subversion in Cuba. The delegates agreed that socialism was emerging victorious in the conflict with imperialism. They cited the inability of the United States to defeat the forces of socialism in Vietnam as an example. (CDSP XXI:28 14)

June 28   Nixon to Romania   The White House announced that President Nixon would visit Romania in August. Romania and the Soviet Union were often at odds on foreign policy issues, and this influenced President Nixon's decision to make the visit. (DSB 7/21/69 49)

July 10   Gromyko on Foreign Policy   Foreign Minister Gromyko, in an address to the Supreme Soviet, emphasized the powerful influence the Soviet Union had become in defending the values of socialism throughout the world. He promised continued aid to the communist forces fighting in South Vietnam, and he accused the United States of committing aggression there. Gromyko said the Soviet government welcomed President Nixon's proposal for an era of negotiations rather than confrontation, but the Soviet minister insisted that American forces be withdrawn from Vietnam. (CDSP XXI:28 4)

July 14   Captive Nations Week   President Nixon designated the week of July 13 "Captive Nations Week." (WCPD 994)

August 2   Nixon Visits Romania   President Nixon visited Romania, the first American president to do so. The Romanian government demonstrated its independence from the Soviet Union by welcoming Nixon warmly. (DSB 8/25/69 167)

August 8   Rogers on Foreign Policy   Secretary of State Rogers, in an address in Australia, said the United States was eager to bring about an improvement in Sino-American relations but the United States did not intend to take sides in the Sino-Soviet dispute. President Nixon wanted to improve relations with both countries. (DSB 9/1/69 178)

August 20   Rogers on Soviet Policy   Secretary of State Rogers, in response to a question at a news conference, said he did not think the Soviets were playing a constructive role in searching for ways to end the Vietnam War. (DSB 9/8/69 203)

September 18   Nixon at the UN   President Nixon, in an address to the United Nations General Assembly, said he hoped relations between the United States and the Soviet Union would improve despite their differences. He wanted the two countries to negotiate on a broad range of issues, and he also wanted to engage the People's Republic of China in a diplomatic exchange. The president called on the Soviet Union to set a date for the beginning of strategic arms control negotiations, and he called on the United Nations to help bring the Vietnam War to an end. (PP 724)

September 19 *Arms Control* Foreign Minister Gromyko, in an address at the United Nations General Assembly, advocated a number of measures to limit the arms race. Some of these included a cessation in the production of nuclear weapons, the creation of nuclear-free zones, and the elimination of nuclear weapons. Gromyko also called for the United States to withdraw its forces from Vietnam. He did not respond to President Nixon's call for setting a date to begin strategic arms negotiations. (DOD 457)

September 20 *Soviets Evaluate Nixon* *Izvestia* said President Nixon had nothing new to say in his September 18 address to the United Nations General Assembly and described his address as a "notable disappointment." (CDSP XXI:38 18)

October 12 *European Conference* *Pravda* alleged that more and more Europeans now favored convening a European security conference and attributed this to the growing influence of the socialist commonwealth. (CDSP XXI:41 11)

October 15 *Soviet Aid to Vietnam* Premier Kosygin, in a speech in Moscow, said the Soviet Union "will give all possible support and aid" to North Vietnam until it was victorious in its military conflict with the United States. (CDSP XXI:42 6)

October 18 *Vietnamization Criticized* *Izvestia* criticized President Nixon's policy of Vietnamization. The article charged that the consequence of Nixon's policy would be Asians killing Asians. (CDSP XXI:42 14)

October 25 *SALT Talks* A White House press release said the United States and the Soviet Union agreed to begin strategic arms limitation talks (the SALT talks) in Helsinki on November 17. (DSB 11/10/69 390)

November 3 *Gromyko Accuses the U.S.* *Pravda* reported that Foreign Minister Gromyko had sent notes to all the governments that had participated in the 1962 Geneva conference on Laos accusing the United States of militarily intervening in Laos in violation of the 1962 neutrality agreement. (CDSP XXI:44 20)

November 3 *The Nixon Doctrine* President Nixon, in an address to the American people, elaborated on what came to be known as the Nixon Doctrine. It consisted of three basic principles. First, the United States would continue to play a major role in Asia and honor all treaty commitments. Second, Washington would provide its allies with a nuclear shield. "Nuclear power," he said, "is the element of security that our friends either cannot provide or could provide only with great and disruptive efforts." His last point was that the United States would furnish economic and military assistance to Asian allies, but they would be primarily responsible for manpower requirements to meet any internal communist threat. The Nixon Doctrine, in effect, meant the United States would not again commit ground troops to combat in situations such as that in Vietnam. (PP 905)

November 6 *Soviets Criticize Nixon* *Izvestia* criticized President Nixon's November 3 speech, accusing him of failing to produce any new initiatives to bring the Vietnam War to an end. His Vietnamization program was criticized because it aimed at continuing, rather than ending, the war. The Soviets advocated the immediate withdrawal of American forces from Vietnam. (CDSP XXI:45 22)

November 13 *Rogers on Arms Control* Secretary of State Rogers, in a speech in Washington, said the United States had three foreign policy goals. First was to enhance international security by developing a more stable strategic relationship between the superpowers. Second was to halt the arms race and thereby reduce its attendant costs. And third was to reduce the risk of nuclear war by engaging the Soviets in a dialogue on strategic issues. (DSB 12/1/69 465)

November 14 *Solzhenitsyn Expelled* Alexander Solzhenitsyn was expelled from the Russian Republic Writers' Union. He was charged with "antisocial" behavior and allowing his writings and statements to be used in a campaign of slander against the Soviet Union. (CDSP XXI:46 3)

November 17 *SALT Talks* Phase one of the SALT talks began in Helsinki, Finland. These talks eventually led to the signing of the SALT I treaty in May 1972. (PP 938)

November 20 *European Security Conference* *Izvestia* claimed that more and more Europeans approved the convening of a European security conference. The article suggested that the meeting could be convened in Helsinki during the first half of 1970. The United States and its NATO allies had not yet agreed to attend such a conference. (CDSP XXI:47 16)

November 21 *Nixon and Sato* President Nixon and Prime Minister Eisaku Sato of Japan issued a joint statement at the conclusion of their talks in Washington that commenced on November 19. Among other things,

the two leaders agreed to keep in force the Treaty of Mutual Cooperation and Security and to begin negotiations leading to the return of
Okinawa to Japan. The two leaders expressed the hope that the
negotiations would be completed sometime in 1972. The Soviets opposed the American-Japanese security treaty, and they feared that the
return of Okinawa would increase Japanese demands for a return of the
islands taken by the Soviets after World War II. (PP 953)

December 5 *North Atlantic Council* At the conclusion of two days of talks
in Brussels, the ministers attending the North Atlantic Council meeting
issued a communiqué and a declaration. They said they would not
participate in any European conference intended to ratify the division
of Europe, but they did support negotiations with the Soviet Union and
the nations of Eastern Europe to try to resolve outstanding issues. (DSB
12/29/69 627)

December 5 *Soviets and NATO* *Pravda* criticized the NATO ministers for
the policies they adopted at their recently concluded meeting in
Brussels. The newspaper accused the ministers of wanting to strengthen
their conventional military capabilities and for accepting a plan
whereby tactical nuclear weapons would be used at an early stage in a
conflict. (CDSP XXI:49 22)

December 16 *Soviets Criticize Japan* An editorial in *Pravda* criticized the
United States and Japan for their decision to keep in force the Japanese-
American security treaty signed in 1960. (CDSP XXI:50 3)

December 19 *The U.S. and China* A spokesman for the State Department
said the United States had implemented measures to ease restrictions on
trade with the People's Republic of China. This was one of the first
measures taken by the Nixon administration in an effort to improve
relations with the Beijing government. (DSB 1/12/70 31)

December 20 *Arab Summit Conference* *Izvestia* expressed support for the
Arab summit meeting scheduled to meet that same day in Rabat,
Morocco. The article expressed the hope that the summit would result
in greater Arab unity to enable those countries to deal more effectively
with the imperialism of the United States and Israel. (CDSP XXI:51 23)

December 22 *SALT Talks Recess* The SALT talks in Helsinki recessed. The
United States and the Soviet Union agreed to resume negotiations in
Vienna on April 16, 1970. (DAFR 126)

December 23 *Rogers on Foreign Policy* Secretary of State Rogers, in
response to a question at a news conference, reviewed foreign policy
events of the past year. He said that America's standing in the

international community had risen as a result of President Nixon's Vietnam policies, improved relations with the nations of NATO, and the strategic arms control negotiations with the Soviet Union. (DSB 1/12/70 25)

December 24 *SALT Talks* *Pravda* praised the results of the recently concluded preliminary SALT talks. (CDSP XXI:52 22)

1970

January 2 *European Security Conference* *Pravda* accused some NATO nations of creating artificial obstacles to prevent the convening of a European security conference. The article said the socialist countries would continue to press for such a conference. (CDSP XXII:1 20)

January 18 *The U.S. and China* Secretary of State Rogers, in response to a question at a news conference, said he did not think that talking to the Chinese would alienate the Soviet Union. The secretary said the United States desired to have good relations with both communist countries. (DSB 2/9/70 153)

January 20 *Exchange Agreement* The State Department announced that the United States and the Soviet Union would begin negotiations on January 29 to conclude exchange agreements in the technical, educational, and cultural fields. (DSB 2/16/70 178)

January 20 *Sino-American Talks* Representatives of the United States and the People's Republic of China met in Warsaw to discuss common concerns. On January 25 *Pravda* suggested that the Sino-American talks might have been intended to promote cooperation between the two countries at the expense of the Soviet Union. (NYT 1/21/70 1)

January 22 *State of the Union* President Nixon, in his State of the Union address, called for the development of a new relationship with the Soviet Union to ensure the peace. He again expressed the desire to move from "an era of confrontation to an era of negotiations." (PP 9)

February 2 *European Security Conference* *Pravda* accused the United States of seeking to strengthen NATO rather than convene a European security conference. The article said the British were following the American lead in opposing a conference. (CDSP XXII:5 16)

February 10 *Exchange Agreement Signed* The United States and the Soviet Union signed an agreement on an exchange program pertaining to scientific, technical, educational, cultural, and other subjects. (DSB 3/2/70 260)

February 13 *Soviets and the Middle East* *Pravda* said that Premier Kosygin sent a letter to President Nixon and British Prime Minister Harold Wilson on the dangerous situation in the Middle East caused by aggressive Israeli policies. The article accused the president of defending Israel and its policies rather than seeking to restrain its aggression. (CDSP XXII:7 10)

February 18 *Nixon and Foreign Policy* President Nixon, in his "First Annual Report to the Congress on United States Foreign Policy," warned the Soviet Union against seeking predominance in the Middle East. The United States, according to the report, would view such an effort with "grave concern." The president again emphasized a willingness to negotiate with the Soviet Union to reduce international tensions. (NYT 2/19/70 1)

February 18 *Soviets Respond to Nixon* Tass, the Soviet news agency, issued a commentary that was critical of President Nixon's "annual report," particularly those sections dealing with the Middle East and Vietnam. The commentary gave no indication of Soviet willingness to respond to the president's desire to begin an era of negotiations. (CDSP XXII:7 12)

February 20 *Soviet-American Communiqué* The United States and the Soviet Union issued a joint communiqué on Soviet-American talks dealing with nuclear explosions for peaceful purposes. They discussed the peaceful application of nuclear energy and agreed to hold more talks and to exchange research and engineering data. (DSB 3/16/70 343)

March 1 *The Soviets and Laos* Tass, the Soviet news agency, issued a statement condemning the United States for allegedly expanding the war in Laos and violating its neutrality. (CDSP XXII:9 12)

March 6 *Nixon and Laos* President Nixon issued a statement on the deteriorating situation in Laos owing to the large number of troops North Vietnam was sending there. The president said he had written to the British and the Soviets asking their aid to help restore Laotian neutrality. (PP 244)

March 18 *MIRV and Safeguard* *Izvestia* said the American decision to deploy MIRVed missiles, scheduled to begin in three months, and to proceed with the second stage of the Safeguard system demonstrated the increased influence of the Pentagon in the Nixon administration. The article questioned the sincerity of Nixon in pursuing arms control agreements with the Soviet Union. (CDSP XXII:11 18)

March 21 *Nixon and the Soviets* President Nixon, in a statement at a news conference, said the United States had received reports that the Soviet Union was delivering SA-3 missiles to the United Arab Republic. The president said he would reevaluate American policies if the Soviets brought about a change in the balance of power in the Middle East. (PP 288)

March 23 *Rogers on Foreign Policy* Secretary of State Rogers, in a statement at a news conference, announced that there was evidence the

Soviet Union was providing SA-3 missiles to Egypt to improve its air defense system. He said the United States was monitoring events in the Middle East to determine whether Israel should be provided with additional military equipment. (DAFR 129)

March 26 *Talks on Berlin* France, the United Kingdom, the Soviet Union, and the United States began discussions on problems pertaining to Berlin. (DOG 1944-1985 1081)

April 14 *Vietnamization Criticized* General Secretary Brezhnev, in a speech in Kharkov, criticized America's policy of Vietnamization. He said the policy would not work because the government in Hanoi was supported by all the Vietnamese people and the Soviet Union. According to Brezhnev, the Vietnam conflict demonstrated that revolutionary forces supported by the socialist countries could defeat any imperialist power. (CDSP XXII:15 1)

April 15 *European Security Conference* Secretary of State Rogers, in an interview for a German television show, said he was not opposed to the Soviet desire to convene a European security conference, provided it were not used for propaganda purposes. (DSB 5/4/70 567)

April 16 *SALT Talks Resume* The United States and the Soviet Union resumed negotiations on strategic arms reductions in Vienna. (DSB 5/4/70 572)

April 18 *Rogers and the Soviets* Secretary of State Rogers, in a speech in New York, said he thought the best way to achieve a balance of power with the Soviet Union was to conclude a strategic arms limitation treaty. He said the Soviets seemed serious in their desire to complete a treaty. (DSB 5/11/70 605)

April 26 *Soviets Criticize Nixon* *Pravda* criticized President Nixon for his April 20 decision to withdraw 150,000 more troops from Vietnam. He was accused of planning to slow the rate of withdrawal of American troops in the future, thus enabling the United States to continue the war. (CDSP XXII:17 17)

April 29 *Soviet Pilots in Egypt* The State Department announced there was no reason to doubt the Israeli assertion that Soviet pilots were flying combat missions for the Egyptian air force. (DSB 6/1/70 675)

April 30 *Nixon and Cambodia* President Nixon, in a radio and television address to the nation, announced that American military units were sent into Cambodia to stop the communist military forces from using portions of that country as a sanctuary to launch attacks against South Vietnam. (DAFR 156)

May 4 *The Soviets and Cambodia* Premier Kosygin, at a news conference in Moscow, denounced the United States for its intervention in Cambodia. He accused the United States of pursuing an aggressive foreign policy, violating Cambodia's neutrality, and enlarging the war. (CDSP XXII:18 1)

May 8 *Nixon and the Soviet Union* President Nixon, in response to a question at a news conference, said that despite major policy differences between the United States and the Soviet Union, he hoped the two countries could conclude a strategic arms control agreement. (DSB 5/25/70 644)

May 13 *Soviets in Egypt* American sources alleged that 100 Soviet pilots were in Egypt to fly jet interceptors. (NYT 5/14/70 1)

May 22 *European Security Conference* *Pravda* accused the United States of opposing the convening of a European security conference because American officials wanted to keep U.S. troops in Europe. (CDSP XXII:21 16)

May 27 *North Atlantic Council* The ministers attending the North Atlantic Council meeting in Rome issued a communiqué. They expressed support for the negotiations undertaken by the Federal Republic of Germany with the German Democratic Republic, Poland, and the Soviet Union. The ministers also endorsed the four-power negotiations on Berlin and the Soviet-American arms control negotiations. The council declared its willingness to discuss the convening of a conference on European security with the Soviet-bloc nations. (DAFR 84)

June 7 *Rogers and the Soviet Union* Secretary of State Rogers, in response to a question on the television program "Face the Nation," said the United States was disturbed by the Soviet military presence in Egypt and had asked the Soviet Union to discontinue the policy of having its pilots fly combat missions in the Middle East. (DSB 6/29/70 790)

June 12 *European Borders* General Secretary Brezhnev, in a speech in Moscow, said the most important factor determining the peace in Europe "is the question of the inviolability of the frontiers established following the second world war." His initiative for convening an all-European security conference was to legitimate the existing borders. (CDSP XXII:25 7)

June 25 *Rogers on Soviet Policy* Secretary of State Rogers, in response to a question at a news conference, said the Soviet presence in the Middle East was a new factor that had to be considered when formulating American policy. He cited the Soviet deployment of SA-3 missiles in

Egypt, Soviet pilots flying planes in Egypt, and the large number of Soviet technicians in that country. (DSB 7/13/70 27)

June 27 *European Security Conference* *Izvestia* printed a memorandum by the Hungarian government, on behalf of the WTO nations, on modifications they had agreed to in order to convene an all-European security conference. The memorandum said that both East and West Germany could attend the conference as equals and invited the United States and Canada to attend. The memorandum also included a tentative agenda for the conference. (CDSP XXII:26 27)

July 7 *Captive Nations Week* President Nixon designated the week of July 12 "Captive Nations Week." (WCPD 892)

July 30 *Jewish Defense League* *Pravda* accused the United States of permitting members of the Jewish Defense League to damage Soviet diplomatic property and harass Soviet officials, in violation of international agreements. (CDSP XXII:30 15)

August 12 *West German-Soviet Treaty* The Federal Republic of Germany and the Soviet Union signed a treaty whereby both sides renounced the use of force and the Federal Republic agreed to recognize the European boundaries that resulted from World War II. (DAFR 105)

August 12 *West German-Soviet Treaty* Secretary of State Rogers issued a statement in support of the treaty signed by the Federal Republic of Germany and the Soviet Union. He said that the West German government kept France, the United Kingdom, and the United States informed during the course of the negotiations. (DSB 9/7/70 275)

August 14 *SALT Talks* The second phase of the SALT talks in Vienna concluded. (DSB 8/31/70 245)

September 25 *Cienfuegos* A Department of Defense briefing described the construction of a submarine base at Cienfuegos, a port on the southern coast of Cuba. A flotilla of Soviet ships had been spotted bringing equipment to Cuba that could be used to service nuclear submarines. (NYT 9/26/70 1)

October 7 *Nixon Peace Initiative* President Nixon, in an address to the nation, presented a new initiative for peace in Indochina. He called for a cease-fire in place throughout Indochina to be supervised by international observers. (DSB 10/26/70 465)

October 8 *Solzhenitsyn Wins Nobel Prize* Alexander Solzhenitsyn won the Nobel Prize for literature. The Soviets alleged the award was granted for political reasons. (CDSP XXII:41 1)

October 9 *Rogers and the Soviet Union* Secretary of State Rogers, in response to a question at a news conference, said there was conclusive evidence that the Soviet Union had moved SA-3 missiles into the Suez Canal cease-fire zone, a violation of the August 7 cease-fire agreement. The Soviets denied the allegation. (DSB 10/26/70 474)

October 13 *Nixon's Peace Initiative* *Izvestia* dismissed President Nixon's October 7 Indochina peace initiative, claiming that it would not bring peace. His proposal for a cease-fire and the convening of an international conference to help negotiate an end to the war was also rejected. (CDSP XXII:41 12)

October 23 *Nixon at the UN* President Nixon, in an address to the United Nations General Assembly, said there were several reasons the United States and the Soviet Union had to cooperate. Both nations wanted to avoid a nuclear war, and both were aware of the enormous costs of armaments. If the superpowers cooperated, he said, they could increase their trade, and both would be better able to cope with global economic and social problems. (PP 926)

October 29 *Soviet-American Space Effort* The United States and the Soviet Union signed an agreement to cooperate in a joint rendezvous and docking mission in space. (NYT 10/30/70 1)

November 2 *SALT Talks* The United States and the Soviet Union began the third phase of the SALT talks in Helsinki, Finland. (DAFR 63)

December 2 *WTO Conference* The ministers representing the WTO nations issued a communiqué at the close of their meeting in Berlin. Among other things, they expressed support for convening an all-European conference on security and cooperation. At the time this was a major priority of General Secretary Brezhnev. The ministers criticized American policies pertaining to Berlin, the Middle East, and Indochina. (CDSP XXII:49 1)

December 4 *North Atlantic Council* The ministers attending the North Atlantic Council meeting in Brussels issued a communiqué. They pointed out that the Soviet Union and the nations of Eastern Europe had not yet responded to a request to commence negotiations on mutual and balanced force reductions in Europe. The ministers reaffirmed the NATO policy of strengthening the alliance, while at the same time seeking to pursue a policy of détente with the Soviet Union. (DAFR 92)

December 10 *SALT Talks* The United States and the Soviet Union completed the third phase of the SALT negotiations and agreed to resume negotiations in Vienna on March 15, 1971. (DAFR 65)

1971

January 4 *Nixon and the Soviet Union* President Nixon, in response to a question during an interview, said although there were major differences between the United States and the Soviet Union, the two sides were at least talking to each other, and both nations had scaled down their cold war rhetoric. (PP 15)

January 4 *Cuba and the Soviet Union* President Nixon, in response to a question during an interview, said if the Soviet Union had a nuclear submarine serviced in Cuba, that would be a violation of the 1962 Soviet-American understanding between President Kennedy and Premier Khrushchev that helped end the Cuban missile crisis. (PP 17)

January 6 *Soviets Denounce Zionists* Tass, the Soviet news agency, announced that a protest had been sent to Washington because of the anti-Soviet activities of Zionist groups. Soviet officials and artist groups were being harassed in the United States in part because of the trial of Jews in the Soviet Union, two of whom had been sentenced to death. (CDSP XXIII:1 18)

January 11 *Violence Against the Soviets* President Nixon sent a message to American Jewish leaders deploring the bombing of a Soviet-occupied building in Washington, allegedly by a Zionist group. These groups were engaged in frequent demonstrations against the Soviet Union to protest the trial in Leningrad of eleven people, nine of whom were Jews, for attempting to hijack an airplane to flee the Soviet Union. (PP 28)

January 21 *Cooperation in Outer Space* A joint communiqué was issued at the close of a meeting attended by representatives of the Academy of Sciences of the USSR and NASA. The representatives agreed to increase cooperation in outer space. (DSB 2/15/71 202)

February 7 *SALT Talks* *Izvestia* criticized Gerard Smith, the American ambassador to the SALT talks, for his opposition to a treaty with the Soviet Union limiting only defensive arms. The article pointed out that a number of U.S. senators favored completing such a treaty. The United States insisted that a SALT agreement would have to cover both offensive and defensive weapons. (CDSP XXIII:6 27)

February 11 *The Seabed Treaty* President Nixon signed the Treaty on the Prohibition of the Emplacement of Nuclear Weapons and Other Weapons of Mass Destruction on the Seabed and the Ocean Floor and in the

Subsoil Thereof. Altogether, sixty-two nations, including the Soviet Union, signed the treaty. (PP 150)

February 19   WTO Communiqué   The foreign ministers from the WTO nations issued a communiqué at the conclusion of a two-day meeting. They called for the convening of a European security conference, and they criticized efforts to establish preconditions for holding such a conference. (CDSP XXIII:8 19)

February 25   Nixon on Foreign Policy   President Nixon spoke to the American people on the foreign policy report he was submitting to Congress. In the portion of his report regarding Soviet-American affairs, he said relations were getting better but there was a need for more cooperation in areas such as the Middle East. He emphasized the importance of the SALT talks and the need for both countries to continue the search for a stable peace. (PP 212)

February 25   Nixon and China   President Nixon, in his second "Annual State of the World" report to Congress, said the United States would not exploit Sino-Soviet differences. The president wanted better relations with the People's Republic of China, but he was not optimistic relations would soon improve. (PP 276)

March 4   SALT I   President Nixon, in response to a question at a news conference, said he expected the United States and the Soviet Union to complete a SALT I agreement involving offensive and defensive weapons. He said that because the superpowers now had nuclear parity, they would eventually conclude a treaty. (PP 394)

March 9   Rogers on China   Secretary of State Rogers, in an interview with Elizabeth Drew of the Public Broadcasting Service, said the United States would like to improve relations with the People's Republic of China. He said as a result of the Sino-Soviet split, the Beijing government appeared to be moving toward the West. (DSB 3/29/71 445)

March 10   Nixon Doctrine   Tass, the Soviet news agency, issued a statement condemning the Nixon Doctrine. The Soviets said it would allow the United States to continue to follow its aggressive policies throughout the world. Tass also claimed the doctrine would require America's allies to engage in an arms race. (CDSP XXIII:10 29)

March 15   Travel to China   The State Department announced it had lifted restrictions on travel to the People's Republic of China. (DSB 4/12/71 510)

March 17   U.S. Protest to Soviets   The United States, in a note to the Soviet Union, protested the unauthorized entry by Soviet policemen into the

American embassy in Moscow on March 16. They entered to arrest four Soviet citizens seeking information on emigration to the United States. (DSB 4/12/71 509)

March 18 *Soviets Protest to U.S.* Soviet ambassador Anatoly Dobrynin protested the harassment of Soviet officials in Washington by members of the Jewish Defense League. Members of the league would often demonstrate outside Soviet-occupied buildings, making entry and exit difficult. He demanded that the United States take whatever measures were necessary to protect Soviet diplomats. (CDSP XXIII:11 24)

March 26 *Rogers on Foreign Policy* Secretary of State Rogers, in a report on foreign policy submitted to Congress, said the United States and its NATO allies were making a collective effort to improve relations with the Soviet Union and the nations of Eastern Europe. (DSB 4/5/71 467)

March 30 *Brezhnev Addresses Party Congress* General Secretary Brezhnev, in his address to the Twenty-fourth Party Congress, reiterated many of the foreign policy goals he articulated at the Twenty-third Party Congress in 1966. He pledged to give "undeviating support" to national liberation movements, many of which were anti-Western. He called for the dissolution of NATO and the WTO and the convening of a five-power meeting, including the People's Republic of China, to discuss arms control. He accused the United States of pursuing aggressive policies all over the world. (NYT 3/31/71 14)

April 7 *Ping Pong Diplomacy* The United States Table Tennis Association accepted an invitation to send a table tennis team to the People's Republic of China for a ten-day tour. The invitation was an important step in the process of improving Sino-American relations. (NYT 4/8/71 1)

April 14 *Nixon and China* The White House released a statement by President Nixon dealing with trade and travel with the People's Republic of China. He said the United States would expedite the granting of visas for visitors from China, and he also agreed on certain measures to facilitate trade between the two countries. (DSB 5/3/71 567)

April 16 *Nixon and Allende* President Nixon, in response to a question at the Annual Convention of Newspaper Editors, said that if the Soviet-supported Allende government in Chile implemented a foreign policy endangering American interests, the United States would have to respond. (PP 544)

April 21 *Soviets Criticize Nixon* *Pravda* criticized President Nixon for comments he made about Chile on April 16. The article asserted that

President Nixon's implied threat to intervene in Chile's internal affairs violated the United Nations Charter. (CDSP XXIII:16 38)

April 23   Rogers on China   Secretary of State Rogers, in response to a question at a news conference, said the United States wanted to improve relations with the People's Republic of China because it was in America's national interest to do so. He denied the effort was intended to antagonize the Soviet Union. (DSB 5/10/71 593)

April 28   Rogers on Soviet Policy   Secretary of State Rogers, in response to a question during an interview in London, said he did not think the Soviets wanted to start a war but, he added, they wanted to expand their influence and promote communism wherever they could. (DSB 5/31/71 688)

April 29   Nixon and China   President Nixon, in response to a question at a news conference, said he would like to visit the People's Republic of China. (PP 594)

April 30   Soviet Invitation Declined   The State Department issued a press release announcing the refusal of the United States to accept an invitation to send a delegation to the Moscow Film Festival. According to the press release, previous film festivals emphasized political films considered to be offensive to the United States. (DSB 5/31/71 705)

May 3   Ulbricht Replaced   Erick Honecker succeeded Walter Ulbricht as leader of the German Democratic Republic. Ulbricht had been an opponent of Brezhnev's policy of détente. (CDSP XXIII:18 31)

May 17   Force Reductions   The State Department announced that the Soviet Union had expressed a desire to begin negotiations to reduce military forces in Europe. The announcement said the NATO nations would be informed of the Soviet interest. (DSB 6/7/71 741)

May 20   Nixon on Arms Control   President Nixon announced that the United States and the Soviet Union would concentrate on reaching an agreement to limit the deployment of antiballistic missile systems and offensive nuclear weapons. The arms control talks had been deadlocked over limits on offensive weapons. The Soviet Union wanted to proceed with an initial agreement limiting only defensive weapons, but the United States insisted that both defensive and offensive weapons be covered. (PP 648)

May 25   SALT Talks   President Nixon, in a meeting with a group of editors, spoke of the importance of the May 20 agreement pertaining to SALT. He said the agreement could help in concluding a SALT agreement, which could have a significant impact in improving the superpower relationship. (DSB 6/14/71 758)

May 28 *SALT Talks* The fourth session of the SALT talks recessed, and the United States and the Soviet Union issued a joint communiqué. The ministers agreed to resume negotiations on July 8 in Helsinki based on the May 20 agreement to link offensive and defensive systems. (AFRADR 102)

May 30 *Rogers on Foreign Policy* Secretary of State Rogers, in a speech at Colgate University, analyzed creativity and realism in American diplomacy. As an example, he mentioned the favorable American response to the desire on the part of the nations of Eastern Europe to have more contacts with the nations of the West. He said the United States was going to deal with the Eastern European nations as individual entities, not as a bloc. (DSB 6/21/71 795)

June 1 *Nixon on Foreign Policy* President Nixon, in response to a question at a news conference, said he hoped the Soviet-Egyptian treaty, signed on May 27, would not lead to an arms race in the Middle East. He said that would happen if the Soviets provided Egypt with more weapons. (PP 691)

June 4 *North Atlantic Council* The ministers attending the North Atlantic Council meeting in Lisbon issued a communiqué. They agreed to engage in exploratory discussions with the Soviet Union to set the framework for negotiating a military force reduction agreement in central Europe. (DSB 6/28/71 819)

June 10 *Trade with China* The White House announced that controls on trade with the People's Republic of China were being further reduced. This was one of several steps to demonstrate to the Beijing government the American desire to improve relations. (DSB 6/28/71 815)

June 17 *Okinawa to Be Returned* The United States agreed to return the island of Okinawa to Japan. The Japanese welcomed the agreement and hoped it might serve as a precedent to encourage the Soviet Union to return islands it took as a result of World War II. (DSB 7/12/71 33)

July 6 *Nixon and the Soviets* President Nixon, in a meeting with news media executives, said he hoped to bring about a fundamental change in Soviet-American relations, and he again said he wanted negotiations to replace confrontation. He pointed out that the United States and the Soviet Union were negotiating on various issues and that some progress was being made. (DSB 7/26/71 94)

July 8 *SALT Talks* The fifth phase of the SALT talks began in Helsinki. Ambassador Gerard C. Smith said he hoped that as a result of the May 20 agreement between the United States and the Soviet Union, greater progress could be made in completing a treaty. (DSB 7/26/71 ⁹8)

July 9 *Kissinger Visits China* Henry Kissinger, President Nixon's assistant for national security affairs, made a two-day secret visit to the People's Republic of China. During his stay, the Beijing government issued an invitation to President Nixon to visit China. (DSB 8/2/71 121)

July 9 *Captive Nations Week* President Nixon designated the week of July 18 "Captive Nations Week." (WCPD 1045)

July 15 *Nixon to China* President Nixon announced he had received and accepted an invitation to visit the People's Republic of China sometime before May 1972. The invitation was the result of a secret trip to China made by Henry Kissinger from July 9 to 11. (PP 819)

July 25 *Soviets on Nixon to China* *Pravda* said President Nixon's planned visit to the People's Republic of China was a continuation of America's aggressive policies in such places as Southeast Asia and the Middle East. (CDSP XXIII:30 1)

August 2 *China at the UN* Secretary of State Rogers announced that the United States would support the seating of the People's Republic of China in the United Nations but would oppose efforts to expel the Republic of China. (DSB 8/23/71 193)

August 4 *Nixon and the Soviet Union* President Nixon, in response to a question at a news conference, said he would not go to Moscow before visiting Beijing. He said negotiations with the Soviets were going forward regarding arms control, Berlin, and the Middle East. He said he expected to meet with Soviet leaders sometime in the future. (PP 852)

August 10 *Sino-American Relations* Georgy Arbatov, the leading Soviet authority on American foreign policy, suggested that some officials in Washington wanted better relations with China because of its hostility toward the Soviet Union. He said the Soviets would carefully observe the results of President Nixon's visit to China. (CDSP XXIII:32 1)

August 31 *Rogers on Foreign Policy* Secretary of State Rogers, in a speech in Texas, said the United States wanted to improve relations with both the People's Republic of China and the Soviet Union. He emphasized the need to improve relations with the Soviet Union given its superpower status. (DSB 9/20/71 300)

September 3 *Berlin Agreement* The ambassadors from France, Great Britain, the United States, and the Soviet Union signed a Berlin Quadripartite Agreement establishing the right of civilians to travel freely in and out of West Berlin. The agreement required the approval of the four governments and would not become operative until a final protocol was completed. This was done in June 1972. (AFRADR 162)

September 24 *SALT Talks* The fifth phase of the SALT talks in Helsinki concluded. The two sides agreed to resume the talks on November 15 in Vienna. (DSB 10/18/71 403)

September 25 *Nixon on Arms* President Nixon, at a question-and-answer session in Portland, Oregon, said the superpowers had rough parity in their nuclear arsenals; therefore, neither country could gain any advantage by launching a first strike. He said progress was being made in the SALT negotiations. (PP 993)

September 30 *Hot-Line Agreement* The United States and the Soviet Union signed an agreement to improve the direct communication link between Moscow and Washington. The original hot-line agreement had been signed in June 1963. (AFRADR 113)

September 30 *Nuclear War Treaty* The United States and the Soviet Union signed a Nuclear Accidents Measures agreement that was designed to prevent the accidental outbreak of nuclear war. (DSB 10/18/71 399)

October 12 *Nixon to Soviet Union* President Nixon announced he would visit the Soviet Union sometime in May 1972. (PP 1030)

October 12 *Nixon on Summits* President Nixon, in response to a question at a news conference, said his planned visits to China and the Soviet Union would not be for ceremonial purposes. He said he expected serious negotiations to occur in both countries. (PP 1035)

October 20 *Soviet Mission Attacked* Four shots were fired into a building housing the Soviet United Nations mission in New York. The next day George Bush, the American ambassador to the United Nations, issued a statement condemning the violent act. (DSB 11/22/71 598)

October 25 *China at the UN* The United Nations General Assembly voted to seat the Beijing government as the representative of China and to expel the Republic of China. The United States favored seating the Beijing government but opposed expelling the Republic of China. The Soviet Union voted with the majority, the United States with the minority. (DSB 11/15/71 556)

November 9 *Nixon on Foreign Policy* President Nixon, at a "Salute the President" dinner, said his planned trips to Beijing and Moscow would not resolve differences between the United States and the communist world but the trips would create an opportunity to develop a lasting peace. (PP 1086)

December 1 *European Conference* Secretary of State Rogers, in a speech in New York, outlined the American approach to a European security conference to be held in the future. He thought such a conference should deal with security issues in a substantive, not a cosmetic way, and he also wanted it to develop principles that would govern the behavior of states based on sovereign equality. Finally, he said the conference should do whatever it could to promote greater cooperation among the nations attending the conference. (DSB 12/20/71 693)

1972

January 20 *State of the Union* President Nixon, in his State of the Union address, said he would visit the People's Republic of China and the Soviet Union to explore the possibility of negotiating differences and thereby lower international tensions. (PP 36)

January 26 *Warsaw Pact Declaration* The nations attending a WTO meeting in Prague issued a declaration at the close of their meeting condemning the United States for its policies in Indochina. The WTO nations called for an end to the bombing of Vietnam and the withdrawal of American combat forces. (CDSP XXIV:4 8)

February 21 *Nixon to China* President Nixon arrived in China for a summit meeting with Chinese leaders. He met with Mao Zedong for an hour, and in the evening the president attended a banquet in his honor given by Premier Chou Enlai. (PP 365)

February 22 *Nixon Meets with Chou* President Nixon met with Premier Chou Enlai for four hours of discussions. (PP 365)

February 25 *Nixon and Chou* President Nixon met with Premier Chou Enlai for an hour, and in the evening Chou attended a banquet given in his honor by President Nixon. (PP 366)

February 27 *Shanghai Communiqué* The United States and the People's Republic of China issued a joint communiqué at the conclusion of President Nixon's visit. The two sides departed from conventional diplomatic procedure in that they decided to delineate not only areas of agreement, but also their disagreements regarding Japan, Korea, Indochina, and, the most contentious issue of all, Taiwan. (DSB 3/20/72 435)

February 29 *Soviets on Nixon in China* *Pravda* emphasized the fact that President Nixon and Premier Chou Enlai refused to make public the details of their talks. The article speculated that China would probably support the Nixon Doctrine and America's Vietnamization program. Readers were reminded that while Nixon was in China, the American air force carried out bombing raids against North Vietnam. (CDSP XXIV:8 10)

March 24 *Nixon on Soviet Summit* President Nixon, in response to a question at a news conference, said he hoped to negotiate substantive agreements with the Soviet leaders at their scheduled May meeting, but he was not optimistic that a SALT treaty could be completed in time for the summit. (PP 498)

March 28 *China and the U.S.* *Pravda* criticized the foreign policies of the United States and the People's Republic of China. Both nations were accused of favoring military blocs and opposing Soviet efforts to organize an Asian collective security system. (CDSP XXIV:13 22)

April 11 *Soviet-American Agreement* The United States and the Soviet Union signed a new Agreement on Exchanges and Cooperation in Scientific, Technical, Educational, Cultural and Other Fields for 1972-1973. (DSB 5/15/72 707)

May 22 *Moscow Summit* President Nixon arrived in Moscow to begin a summit meeting with Chairman Brezhnev. That evening President Podgorny, in a toast at a dinner honoring President Nixon, said the Soviet Union favored a "radical turn toward relaxation of existing tensions in all continents. . . ." In response, President Nixon said he hoped an era of negotiations between the United States and the Soviet Union had begun. The president wanted negotiations to replace confrontations. (PP 619)

May 23 *Accord on Health* The United States and the Soviet Union signed an Accord on Medicine and Health. (CDSP XXIV:22 19)

May 24 *Soviet-American Agreement* The United States and the Soviet Union signed two agreements, one regarding space exploration and a second on cooperation in science and technology. The following day they signed an agreement intended as a guide to prevent naval ships from colliding. (CDSP XXIV:22 17-18)

May 26 *SALT I Agreement* The United States and the Soviet Union signed the Interim Agreement on the Limitation of Strategic Offensive Weapons placing limits and controls on both submarine-launched and intercontinental ballistic missiles. The agreement also prohibited the conversion of older missiles to newer models. (PP 674)

May 26 *ABM Treaty* The United States and the Soviet Union signed the Anti-Ballistic Missile treaty. The two countries agreed to limit the deployment of ABM systems to two areas, one for the defense of each nation's capital and the other for the defense of an ICBM site. Each country was limited to one hundred ABM launchers and one hundred interceptor missiles for each of the two sites. (PP 674)

May 28 *Nixon on Soviet Television* President Nixon, in a radio and television address to the Soviet people, emphasized the need for the superpowers to cooperate to preserve the peace. (PP 629)

May 29 *Basic Principles Agreement* President Nixon and General Secretary Brezhnev signed a Basic Principles Agreement containing twelve principles intended to serve as a political framework for relations between the two superpowers. Among other things, they agreed to avoid military confrontations and to respect each other's legitimate security interests. (PP 633)

May 29 *Summit Progress* Leonid Zamyatin, the director of the Soviet press center, said the Soviet leaders believe "the Moscow talks [between Brezhnev and Nixon] and the documents signed will be of great importance in changing the political climate in the world for the better and in creating a lasting peace." (CDSP XXIV:21 5)

May 31 *Joint Communiqué* The United States and the Soviet Union issued a joint communiqué at the close of the Moscow summit meeting. The communiqué listed topics that were discussed and agreements that had been concluded. General Secretary Brezhnev accepted an invitation to visit the United States. (CDSP XXIV:22 23)

June 2 *Brezhnev and the Summit* *Pravda* reported that General Secretary Brezhnev had appeared before the Central Committee of the Communist party to report on the results of his meetings with President Nixon. The Soviet leader considered the summit a success and hoped it would contribute to better Soviet-American relations. (CDSP XXIV:22 25)

June 3 *Berlin Agreement* France, the United Kingdom, the Soviet Union, and the United States signed a protocol to bring into force the September 1971 quadripartite agreement on Berlin. The Soviets agreed that traffic into West Berlin "would be unimpeded and would receive preferential treatment." The agreement contributed to better Soviet-American relations. (DOG 1944-1985 1204)

June 15 *Basic Principles Agreement* *Pravda* analyzed the importance of the Basic Principles Agreement signed at the Moscow summit meeting in May. The article said the BPA document established a legal basis for Soviet-American relations predicated on the principle of peaceful coexistence. (CDSP XXIV:24 1)

June 22 *Summit Evaluated* *Izvestia* published a report by Georgy Arbatov, the leading Soviet authority on American foreign policy, on the results of the May summit. He said the success of the summit was in part attributable to a change in the correlation of forces in favor of the socialist states. He said international tensions increased when the correlation of forces favored the imperialists but decreased when it favored the socialists. (CDSP XXIV:25 4)

July 5 *Castro in Moscow*   The Soviet Union and Cuba issued a joint communiqué at the close of a visit to Moscow by Fidel Castro. The communiqué condemned American policies in Indochina, Korea, and the Caribbean and praised Cuba for the role it was playing "in deepening the liberation process in Latin America." (CDSP XXIV:27 14)

July 15 *Captive Nations Week*   President Nixon designated the week of July 16 "Captive Nations Week." (WCPD 1160)

August 3 *Soviet Exit Tax*   The Soviet Union imposed an "exit tax" on anyone wanting to emigrate. People who wanted to leave the Soviet Union had to compensate the government for such things as the cost of their education. The tax quickly became an irritant in Soviet-American relations because the tax was a barrier preventing many Jews from emigrating. (CDSP XXV:3 3)

August 16 *Rogers on Foreign Policy*   Secretary of State Rogers, during an interview with James McCartney of Knight Newspapers, said he thought much progress had been made in improving Soviet-American relations and he hoped relations would continue to improve. He thought they would. (DSB 9/11/72 268)

September 5 *China and the U.S.*   *Pravda* condemned the People's Republic of China for supporting the presence of American military troops in Asia and Europe, building a more powerful nuclear arsenal, and advocating policies that would weaken the Soviet bloc. (CDSP XXIV:36 1)

September 16 *Kissinger in Moscow*   Henry Kissinger, President Nixon's national security advisor, at a news conference in Washington discussed the talks he had with Soviet leaders during his trip to Moscow earlier in the month. Kissinger said the second set of SALT negotiations would probably begin before the end of the year. One problem he identified was that of reaching an agreement with the Soviet Union on the meaning of *equality*, because the security needs of the superpowers were dissimilar. Kissinger said progress was made on the lend-lease problem, trade, a maritime agreement, mutual and balanced force reductions, and the proposed Conference on Security and Cooperation in Europe. (DSB 10/9/72 389)

September 28 *Rogers on Foreign Policy*   Secretary of State Rogers, in a speech in New York, said President Nixon had brought about a fundamental transformation in American foreign policy. He said the United States and the Soviet Union were moving away from a world of containment to one of engagement. (DSB 10/23/72 470)

October 18 *Soviet-American Trade* The United States and the Soviet Union signed a three-year trade agreement that granted the Soviet Union most-favored-nation (MFN) status, subject to U.S. Senate approval. The agreement was one aspect of President Nixon's desire to create a web of interlocking relations between the United States and the Soviet Union. (DSB 11/20/72 581)

October 26 *Nixon and Foreign Policy* President Nixon, in a speech in Kentucky, said that as a result of his policies and meetings with leaders in Moscow and Beijing, more progress had been made in achieving a lasting peace than in any year since 1945. (PP 1038)

November 2 *Nixon on Foreign Policy* President Nixon, in a radio address to the American people, said the United States had signed more agreements with the Soviet Union since he came to power than were negotiated in all the years since 1945. He also claimed a basis had been established for a new relationship with the People's Republic of China. (PP 1086)

November 23 *European Security Conference* Preparatory talks began for convening an all-European security conference. The question of convening a European security conference had been the subject of Soviet-American talks for many years. The Soviets were enthusiastic about such a conference, the United States much less so. (NYT 11/24/72 11)

December 20 *Soviets Condemn Bombing* *Pravda* condemned the United States for the large-scale bombing of Hanoi and Haiphong on December 18. The Soviets demanded a halt to the bombing. (CDSP XXIV:51 28)

December 21 *Brezhnev and Vietnam* General Secretary Brezhnev, in a speech in Moscow, said future relations with the United States would depend on bringing the war in Vietnam to an end. (CDSP XXIV:51 14)

December 21 *Consultative Commission* The United States and the Soviet Union established the Standing Consultative Commission to help implement the SALT I agreements. A major function of the commission was to resolve any differences that might arise in interpreting the agreements. (AFRADR 110)

1973

January 27 *Vietnam War Agreement* North Vietnam, South Vietnam, the United States, and the Viet Cong signed an Agreement on Ending and Restoring Peace in Vietnam. A cease-fire was to be established and all American troops would be withdrawn from South Vietnam in sixty days. During that time all American prisoners of war were to be returned to the United States. The North Vietnamese troops were not required to leave South Vietnam, but they could not be resupplied or reinforced. (AFRADR 39)

February 22 *Kissinger to China* The United States and the People's Republic of China issued a communiqué at the conclusion of a visit by Henry Kissinger, President Nixon's national security advisor, that began on February 15. The leaders of both countries pledged to expedite the process of normalizing their relations, and they agreed to establish a liaison office in the capital of each country. On February 25 *Pravda*, commenting on Kissinger's visit to China, pointed out that China opposed détente, the convening of an all-European security conference, and arms control agreements. (AFRADR 82)

April 16 *Nixon on Foreign Policy* President Nixon, in a speech in Washington, insisted that the United States had to remain militarily strong if negotiations with the communist nations were to be successful. He said the Soviet Union and the WTO nations would have no incentive to negotiate in good faith with the United States if Congress were to reduce defense spending and the number of American troops in Europe. (PP 293)

April 19 *Soviet Exit Tax* President Nixon, in a talk to a group of Jewish leaders, said he had received a communication from the Soviet Union informing him that the exit tax imposed on individuals wanting to emigrate had been suspended. The Soviets had announced the imposition of the tax in August 1972. (NYT 4/20/73 1)

May 3 *Nixon's Annual Report* President Nixon, in an address to the American people, discussed his "Fourth Annual Report to Congress on United States Foreign Policy." This long and detailed report expressed Nixon's foreign policy philosophy, reviewed events of the past year, and suggested things yet to be done. He asserted that Soviet-American relations were no longer as confrontational as they had been in the past. (PP 345)

May 9 *Kissinger Ends Talks* Henry Kissinger, President Nixon's national security advisor, ended his talks in Moscow that began on May 4. He consulted with General Secretary Brezhnev and Foreign Minister Gromyko about mutual concerns, including laying the groundwork for the Nixon-Brezhnev summit meeting scheduled for June in the United States. (CDSP XXV:19 20)

June 8 *Nixon on Foreign Policy* President Nixon, in a speech in Florida, warned that if the United States unilaterally reduced its military forces, it would then be difficult to negotiate troop reductions with the Soviet Union. He said the United States had to remain militarily strong if a structure of peace were to develop. (PP 580)

June 16 *Washington Summit* General Secretary Brezhnev arrived in the United States for a ten-day summit meeting with President Nixon. (DSB 7/23/73 113)

June 18 *Nixon Toasts Brezhnev* President Nixon toasted General Secretary Brezhnev at a state dinner and sounded an optimistic note on the outcome of the superpower summit. In response, General Secretary Brezhnev said the United States and the Soviet Union were "on the right track" in their efforts to improve the superpower relationship. (PP 595)

June 21 *Nixon to Moscow* President Nixon, at a state dinner for the Soviet leaders, announced he had accepted an invitation to visit the Soviet Union in 1974. The president said he supported regularly scheduled summit meetings. (PP 603)

June 22 *Prevention of Nuclear War* President Nixon and General Secretary Brezhnev signed an Agreement on the Prevention of Nuclear War. It was, in effect, a declaration of intentions by the United States and the Soviet Union to avoid creating situations conducive to conflict between the superpowers. They agreed "that each party will refrain from the threat or use of force against the other party. . ." and pledged to conduct their relations with third parties in ways that would help prevent local disagreements from escalating to more dangerous levels. (DSB 7/23/73 160)

June 24 *Brezhnev Addresses America* General Secretary Brezhnev, in a televised address to the American people, discussed the improvement in Soviet-American relations and the importance of détente. (CDSP XXV:25 7)

June 25 *Summit Communiqué* President Nixon and General Secretary Brezhnev, at the conclusion of their summit meeting, issued a joint communiqué listing the issues the leaders discussed and the agreements they had reached. (PP 611)

June 25 **Kissinger on the Summit** Henry Kissinger, at a news conference, said he considered the summit a success in bringing about a further improvement in Soviet-American relations. Kissinger believed the superpowers would be able to complete the SALT II agreement in 1974. (AFRADR 269)

July 13 **Captive Nations Week** President Nixon designated the week of July 15 "Captive Nations Week." (WCPD 901)

July 22 **Peaceful Coexistence** *Pravda* published an analysis of Soviet-American relations by Georgy Arbatov, the leading Soviet authority on American foreign policy. He said President Nixon accepted the idea of peaceful coexistence because the power alignment in the world was shifting in favor of the socialist states. He noted changes in the Soviet-American relationship that were contributing to a more stable international political system. (CDSP XXV:29 1)

August 22 **Kissinger Nominated Secretary of State** President Nixon, at a news conference, announced that Henry Kissinger would be nominated secretary of state replacing William Rogers. (PP 710)

September 8 **Pravda Assails U.S. Senate** *Pravda* assailed the United States Senate for approving a bill to continue the financing of Radio Liberty and Radio Free Europe. The radio stations were accused of conducting "licentious provocational propaganda against the Soviet Union." (CDSP XXV:36 11)

September 11 **Coup in Chile** The military in Chile carried out a coup d'état and seized control of the government. President Salvador Allende, a Marxist supported by Cuba and the Soviet Union, was allegedly killed opposing the coup, but others maintain he committed suicide. Supporters of Allende accused the Central Intelligence Agency of being responsible for the coup and Allende's death. (NYT 9/12/73 1)

September 14 **Soviets Protest Allende** *Pravda* carried a statement issued by the Central Committee of the Communist party in the Soviet Union condemning the overthrow of the Allende government in Chile. The Soviets claimed the coup was carried out by reactionary forces backed by foreign imperialists. (CDSP XXV:37 18)

September 28 **Nixon-Gromyko Talks** Foreign Minister Gromyko met with President Nixon in Washington. Among other things, the two leaders discussed trade and the SALT II negotiations. President Nixon pledged to carry out his promise to have the Soviet Union granted most-favored-nation status. (NYT 9/29/73 1)

October 6 *Yom Kippur War* The Yom Kippur War between allied Egyptian and Syrian forces and Israeli forces exacerbated Soviet-American relations. The Soviet Union was supporting Egypt's military while the United States supported Israel's. (DSB 11/12/73 585)

October 8 *Kissinger on Foreign Policy* Secretary of State Kissinger, in an address before the Third Pacem in Terris Conference sponsored by the Center for the Study of Domestic Institutions, discussed the complexity of Soviet-American relations. He said there were certain principles underlying American foreign policy the Soviets could not disregard without endangering the policy of détente. He said the United States opposed hegemony, would not allow détente with the Soviet Union to weaken America's relations with its allies, and would oppose efforts to exploit volatile areas around the world. (DSB 10/29/73 525)

October 20 *Kissinger to Moscow* The White House announced that Secretary of State Kissinger was leaving for Moscow to confer with General Secretary Brezhnev regarding problems that arose as a result of the Yom Kippur War. (PP 897)

October 23 *Cease-Fire Resolution* The United Nations Security Council approved a resolution confirming the resolution passed the previous day calling for a cease-fire in the Yom Kippur War. The United States and the Soviet Union supported both resolutions. (DSB 11/12/73 604)

October 24 *Sadat Calls for Troops* Egypt's president Anwar Sadat requested the United States and the Soviet Union to send troops to the Middle East to supervise the cease-fire authorized by the United Nations Security Council. Israel was not abiding by the cease-fire resolution. (NYT 10/25/73 1)

October 24 *Soviet Threat to Intervene* The Soviet Union, in a note to President Nixon, called for a Soviet-American force to intervene in the Middle East to police the United Nations-sponsored cease-fire resolution. The Soviets warned they would consider unilaterally intervening if the United States did not support the Brezhnev proposal. (NYT 10/25/73 1)

October 25 *Military Alert* President Nixon, in part to dissuade the Soviet Union from militarily intervening in the Middle East, issued a worldwide military alert of American forces. The Soviets did not intervene. (PP 896)

October 25 *Kissinger on Foreign Policy* Secretary of State Kissinger, in a statement at a news conference, said the United States and the Soviet Union have a special responsibility, because of their nuclear arsenals, to make certain that conflicts do not expand to the point that endangers humanity. He was referring to Soviet-American differences regarding the Yom Kippur War. In response to a question, he said he was not yet prepared to say that Soviet policies endangered détente. He said the military alert ordered by President Nixon earlier in the day was to make certain the Soviets did not go beyond prudent limits regarding the Middle East crisis. (DSB 11/12/73 585)

October 26 *Military Alert* President Nixon, in a statement at a news conference, said he had ordered U.S. military forces worldwide on alert in response to a Soviet threat to unilaterally intervene in the Yom Kippur War. The purpose of the alert was to send a signal to the Soviet Union that neither of the superpowers should intervene in the Arab-Israeli dispute. (AFRADR 470)

October 26 *Nixon on Foreign Policy* President Nixon, in response to a question at a news conference, said the United States and the Soviet Union could not afford to allow their conflicting interests in the Middle East to jeopardize détente in Europe, where their national interests were much more important. He said the policy of détente pursued by the superpowers helped avert a general war in the Middle East. (PP 901)

October 26 *Brezhnev and World Congress* General Secretary Brezhnev, in an address to the World Congress of Peace Forces meeting in Moscow, said international peace was necessary to enable nations to deal with problems such as the environment, hunger, and disease. He accused Israel of refusing to abide by the cease-fire resolutions passed by the United Nations, and he expressed support for dispatching American and Soviet military units to police the cease-fire. He criticized China's foreign policies for attempting to weaken the cause of socialism, and he condemned the coup in Chile that ousted the Allende government. He said the Soviet Union would continue to support revolutionary movements around the world. (CDSP XXV:43 1)

October 28 *Soviets and Military Alert* Tass, the Soviet news agency, issued a statement critical of President Nixon's October 25 decision to put America's military forces on alert. Tass alluded to a *New York Times* article by James Reston, who asserted that some people thought the alert was intended to divert attention from the Watergate scandal and the resignation of Vice President Agnew. (CDSP XXV:43 7)

October 30 *Military Force Reductions* Negotiations began in Vienna on mutual and balanced reductions of forces in central Europe. The United States and the Soviet Union had agreed to the talks at the May 1972 summit. (DSB 11/26/73 657)

November 15 *Soviets on American Policy* *Pravda* said that more people were demanding a change in America's policies toward the Soviet Union because of its growing might and prestige. According to the article, public opinion in America favored negotiations with the Soviet Union and opposed any more military involvements such as Vietnam. The article went on to warn that the demand for better Soviet-American relations was endangered by "Zionists and ultrarightists." (CDSP XXV:46 4)

November 21 *Soviet-American Relations* Secretary of State Kissinger, in response to a question at a news conference, said the relationship that had developed between President Nixon and General Secretary Brezhnev did not prevent the Arab-Israeli war but did help end it. (DSB 12/10/73 706)

December 11 *Trade Bill Passed* The House of Representatives passed the foreign trade bill that included the Jackson-Vanik amendment. It tied MFN status to the emigration policies of the communist nations. (NYT 12/12/73 1)

December 21 *Geneva Peace Conference* A Middle East peace conference opened in Geneva. Secretary General Kurt Waldheim of the United Nations and representatives from Egypt, Israel, Jordan, the Soviet Union, and the United States attended. (AFRADR 603)

December 21 *Kissinger at Geneva* Secretary of State Kissinger addressed the Geneva conference dealing with Middle Eastern problems. He said the Arab-Israeli cease-fire had to be strengthened and an agreement on the disengagement of forces had to be negotiated before work could begin on finding solutions to the many Arab-Israeli problems. The United States favored a step-by-step effort to find solutions to the Arab-Israeli disagreements, but the Soviet Union favored a comprehensive approach. (AFRADR 608)

December 21 *Gromyko at Geneva* Foreign Minister Gromyko addressed the Geneva conference on Middle Eastern issues. He said a settlement of Arab-Israeli problems would be aided by the policy of détente now favored by nations throughout the world. He said resolving Arab-Israeli problems would not be easy, but, he said, other difficult problems had been resolved. He cited as examples ending the Vietnam War and the improved relations between the superpowers. (CDSP XXV:51 1)

December 27 *Kissinger on Foreign Policy* Secretary of State Kissinger, at a news conference, reviewed the major events of the year and suggested things yet to be done. He said the major task was to construct an international system based on justice and balanced power. He reiterated that détente did not imply American agreement with the values of the Soviet Union but that both countries recognized the need to have better communication and more cooperation to resolve international problems. (AFRADR 618)

1974

January 3 *Kissinger and the Soviets* Secretary of State Kissinger, in response to a question at a news conference, said the policy of détente was the result of a desire to avoid a nuclear war and was never based on America's approval of the Soviet political system. (DSB 1/28/74 850)

January 30 *State of the Union* President Nixon, in his State of the Union address, said he would continue negotiations with the Soviet Union and the nations of Eastern Europe to achieve nuclear and conventional arms control agreements. The president declared that building a structure of peace remained his top priority. (PP 53)

February 3 *Gromyko in Washington* Foreign Minister Gromyko began two days of talks with President Nixon and Secretary of State Kissinger. They discussed a SALT II treaty, trade, problems in the Middle East, and the CSCE process. (CDSP XXVI:6 15)

February 4 *NATO Criticized* *Pravda* criticized the NATO nations for planning to introduce smaller nuclear arms, claiming that such an action would violate the 1973 nuclear war prevention agreement. (NYT 2/5/74 3)

February 14 *Solzhenitsyn Deported* Tass, the Soviet news agency, announced that Alexander Solzhenitsyn had been stripped of his citizenship and deported to the Federal Republic of Germany. The Soviet action was a response to the publication in the West of his award-winning book, *The Gulug Archipelago, 1918-1956.* (CDSP XXVI:7 1)

February 25 *Nixon and Solzhenitsyn* President Nixon, in response to a question at a news conference, said although he was an admirer of Alexander Solzhenitsyn, his expulsion from the Soviet Union would not influence Nixon's desire to pursue a policy of détente with the Soviet Union. (PP 206)

March 15 *Nixon and Détente* President Nixon, in response to a question at a news conference, defended his policy of détente. He said it helped bring the Vietnam War to an end, contributed to better relations with the People's Republic of China and the Soviet Union, kept Soviet-American relations within proper bounds during the Arab-Israeli conflict, and helped bring about arms control agreements. (PP 271)

March 28 *Soviet-American Communiqué* The United States and the Soviet Union issued a joint communiqué at the conclusion of Secretary of State Kissinger's visit to the Soviet Union. The two sides discussed a broad range of issues in preparation for the Brezhnev-Nixon summit scheduled for the end of June. (DSB 4/22/74 417)

April 12   Gromyko in Washington   Foreign Minister Gromyko met with President Nixon and Secretary of State Kissinger at the White House. They discussed a number of problems, including the SALT II negotiations, the scheduled summit meeting, and problems in the Middle East. (DSB 4/29/74 457)

April 18   WTO Meeting   The representatives of the WTO nations, after meeting in Warsaw for two days, issued a communiqué. The ministers supported the development of détente and the reduction of international tensions. They called on the CSCE negotiators to complete a final document with the expectation that the heads of state of the participating nations would attend the signing ceremony. (CDSP XXVI:16 7)

April 28   Kissinger and Gromyko   Secretary of State Kissinger met with Foreign Minister Gromyko for two days of talks in Geneva. Kissinger raised the issue of Soviet emigration policies, which had become a major source of friction in Soviet-American relations. The two leaders also discussed issues regarding the SALT II treaty. (NYT 4/29/74 1)

June 5   Nixon on Foreign Policy   President Nixon, in a speech at the U.S. Naval Academy, said a blend of idealism and pragmatism was needed when formulating policies for the Soviet Union. He said despite the different principles of the superpowers, there was a need to search for areas of agreement, and he thought much had been accomplished in the last five years to better Soviet-American relations. (DSB 7/1/74 1)

June 14   Arms Control   General Secretary Brezhnev, in a speech in Moscow, said the Soviet Union was willing to reach an agreement with the United States to eliminate underground nuclear testing. He also thought there could be some force reductions in central Europe before the completion of an MBFR treaty. He said Soviet-American relations were improving because of a shift in the world balance of power in favor of the socialist states. (CDSP XXVI:24 1)

June 19   North Atlantic Council   At the conclusion of a two-day meeting of the North Atlantic Council in Ottawa, the ministers issued a communiqué and a declaration. They welcomed the improved relations between the WTO and the NATO nations, but the ministers took note of the continuing buildup of Soviet military capabilities. The ministers declared that progress in détente was linked to the question of Western access to Berlin. (DSB 7/8/74 41)

June 21 *Soviets Criticize NATO* *Pravda* criticized those ministers who had opposed the policy of détente at the recently concluded North Atlantic Council meeting in Ottawa. The Soviet leaders believed that détente was becoming more popular throughout Europe. (CDSP XXVI:25 31)

June 25 *Nixon to Moscow* President Nixon, before leaving for Moscow, said he wanted to achieve three objectives in his meetings with General Secretary Brezhnev: strengthen Soviet-American relations, develop further areas of superpower cooperation, and make progress completing the SALT II talks. (PP 546)

June 26 *Nuclear Weapons* Secretary of State Kissinger, at a news conference in Brussels, said the United States was guided by three principles in negotiating with the Soviet Union on arms control measures. He said neither side should gain an advantage, neither side should be able to perceive that it has an advantage over the other, and third parties should not perceive an advantage because of a superpower agreement. (DSB 7/29/74 196)

June 27 *Nixon and Brezhnev* President Nixon and General Secretary Brezhnev exchanged toasts at a state dinner in Moscow hosted by the Soviet government. (PP 553)

June 28 *Energy Cooperation* The United States and the Soviet Union completed three agreements: an Agreement on Cooperation in the Field of Energy, an Agreement on Cooperation in Housing and Other Construction, and an Agreement on Cooperation in Artificial Heart Research and Development. (DSB 7/29/74 219, 221, 222)

June 29 *Economic Agreement* President Nixon and General Secretary Brezhnev signed a Long-Term Agreement on Economic, Industrial, and Technical Cooperation. (DSB 7/29/74 219)

July 2 *Nixon Addresses the Russian People* President Nixon, in a radio and television address to the Russian people, said despite Soviet-American differences, the two nations were learning to cooperate on behalf of world peace. (PP 559)

July 2 *Nixon and Brezhnev* President Nixon hosted a state dinner for General Secretary Brezhnev and other Soviet leaders. (PP 564)

July 3 *ABM Agreement* The United States and the Soviet Union signed an agreement limiting each nation to one ABM site, rather than the two agreed to in 1972. (DAFR 226)

July 3 *Threshold Test Ban Treaty* The United States and the Soviet Union signed a Threshold Test Ban treaty (TTB) prohibiting underground nuclear explosions in excess of 150 kilotons. (DAFR 229)

July 3 *Soviet-American Communiqué* President Nixon and General Secretary Brezhnev issued a communiqué at the close of their summit meeting. The leaders said they were satisfied with the improved relations between the superpowers since 1972; they planned to continue to improve relations and said that they hoped recent improvements would prove "irreversible." The summit produced modest results, in part because it took place during the Watergate scandal. (PP 567)

July 3 *Kissinger on Summits* Secretary of State Kissinger, in a statement at a news conference, said the Soviet-American summit meetings had three purposes. One was to exchange ideas, second was to prevent a nuclear arms race, and third was to identify common interests. (DSB 7/29/74 205)

July 3 *Nixon Returns* President Nixon, addressing America after returning from the Moscow summit, said he hoped his trip would help improve relations between the superpowers. (PP 578)

July 12 *Captive Nations Week* President Nixon designated the week of July 14 "Captive Nations Week." (WCPD 801)

August 6 *Soviets Praise Nixon* *Pravda* praised the results of the Nixon visit to the Soviet Union. The article said that because of improved Soviet-American relations, the political climate of Europe was much less tense than in the past. (CDSP XXVI:31 1)

August 8 *Nixon Resigns* President Nixon, in an address to the American people, announced he was resigning from office effective at noon the next day. His resignation was the result of the Watergate scandal. Nixon was succeeded by Vice President Gerald Ford. (DAFR 279)

August 12 *Ford Addresses Congress* President Ford addressed a joint session of Congress. In his address, the president promised to continue Nixon's policies of trying to improve relations with the Soviet Union and the People's Republic of China. Ford was anxious to demonstrate continuity in American foreign policy despite President Nixon's resignation. (DSB 9/2/74 333)

August 20 *Kissinger on Foreign Policy* Secretary of State Kissinger, in an address in Miami, analyzed America's strengths and purposes. He said the United States would maintain a nuclear balance with the Soviet Union either by negotiation or by unilateral action. He declared that after reaching a particular level, the acquisition of additional nuclear weapons by the superpowers would have no military or political value. He pledged that the Ford administration would do whatever was necessary to develop the new spirit of cooperation with the Soviet Union and the People's Republic of China. (DSB 9/16/74 373)

September 6   SALT Talks Resume   President Ford announced that the SALT II talks would resume on September 18 in Geneva. The previous negotiations had ended on March 19. At the time of the resumption of the talks, the United States and the Soviet Union held significantly different positions on the provisions of a SALT II agreement. (DSB 9/30/74 461)

September 15   U.S. and Chile   *Pravda* stated there was new evidence implicating the Central Intelligence Agency in preparing the coup d'état in Chile that ousted the Allende government in September 1973. Allende had been a supporter of Fidel Castro. (CDSP XXVI:37 15)

September 18   Ford at the UN   President Ford, in an address to the United Nations General Assembly, pledged to continue efforts to improve Soviet-American relations and to continue to normalize relations with the People's Republic of China. (DSB 10/7/74 465)

September 19   Kissinger on Foreign Policy   Secretary of State Kissinger, in an appearance before the Senate Committee on Foreign Relations, analyzed Soviet-American relations. He characterized the relationship as one of cooperation and competition. Cooperation, he said, was necessary to avoid a nuclear conflict, and conflict was the result of the different value systems of the superpowers. He said Soviet policy was influenced by the reality of the balance of power and by the Soviets' perception of the balance of power. (DSB 10/14/74 505)

September 21   Gromyko in Washington   *Pravda* reported on a meeting Foreign Minister Gromyko had with President Ford and Secretary of State Kissinger at the White House. They discussed the Middle East, arms control, and bilateral issues. (CDSP XXVI:38 17)

September 23   Kissinger at the UN   Secretary of State Kissinger, in an address to the United Nations General Assembly, discussed the need to remedy and not just manage international problems. He said many issues threatened the structure of world stability, and ideologies developed in the nineteenth century were not helpful in resolving those issues. He said the United States wanted to move from a policy of détente with the Soviet Union to one of cooperation. (DSB 10/14/74 498)

September 24 *Gromyko on Foreign Policy* Foreign Minister Gromyko, in an address to the United Nations General Assembly, called for the successful completion of the CSCE negotiations, and he praised the results that had already been achieved. He also called for additional arms control agreements between the United States and the Soviet Union. The major theme of his address was the benefits of détente, and he praised President Ford for announcing that he hoped to do more to improve Soviet-American relations. At the time, more critics were questioning the wisdom of détente for the United States. (VS XXXXI:2 34)

October 5 *Sino-Soviet Relations* Secretary of State Kissinger, in answer to a question during an interview with James Reston of the *New York Times,* said the United States would not support policies that increased Sino-Soviet tensions. He favored improving relations with both countries. (DSB 11/11/74 637)

October 15 *Soviet-American Trade* General Secretary Brezhnev, in an address to the American-Soviet Trade and Economic Council in Moscow, said trade was the foundation for building better Soviet-American relations. He complained about American laws that discriminated against the Soviet Union, particularly those creating barriers to Soviet trade and the financing of trade. The Soviet leader rejected any link between trade and internal Soviet policies. (CDSP XXVI:42 1)

October 24 *Kissinger in Moscow* Secretary of State Kissinger met in Moscow with Foreign Minister Gromyko and General Secretary Brezhnev. Their discussions included arms control, the Middle East, and the Conference on Security and Cooperation in Europe. (CDSP XXVI:43 12)

October 24 *PLO at the UN* The United Nations General Assembly approved a resolution, opposed by the United States and supported by the Soviet Union, inviting the Palestine Liberation Organization to participate in the General Assembly debate on the Middle East. The Soviet Union consistently supported the policies of the PLO. (AFRADR 409)

October 26 *Gromyko and Kissinger* Foreign Minister Gromyko, in a letter to Secretary of State Kissinger, insisted the Soviet Union would not permit the linkage of trade with its emigration policies. (AFRADR 386)

October 27 *Gromyko and Kissinger* Secretary of State Kissinger and Foreign Minister Gromyko issued a communiqué at the conclusion of their talks that began on October 24. They agreed that relations between the United States and the Soviet Union continued to improve, and they pledged to do all they could to resolve outstanding differences. (DSB 11/25/74 703)

November 6 *Soviet Peace Program* Foreign Minister Gromyko, in a speech in the Kremlin, said the improvement in Soviet-American relations was the result of Brezhnev's Peace Program adopted at the Twenty-fourth Congress of the Communist party in March 1971. (CDSP XXVI:45 1)

November 23 *Ford and Brezhnev* President Ford traveled to the Soviet Union to meet with General Secretary Brezhnev in Vladivostok. (AFRADR 501)

November 24 *Vladivostok Communiqué* President Ford and General Secretary Brezhnev issued a communiqué at the close of their meeting in Vladivostok. The two leaders discussed arms control, underground nuclear explosions for peaceful purposes, the CSCE negotiations, Cyprus, and the Middle East. Brezhnev accepted an invitation to visit the United States in 1975. (DSB 12/23/74 879)

November 24 *Vladivostok Arms Agreement* The United States and the Soviet Union, at the close of the Vladivostok meeting, issued a joint statement containing a number of principles to be incorporated in a SALT II agreement. Each side agreed to limit its arsenal to twenty-four hundred bombers and offensive missiles, thirteen hundred of which could have multiple warheads. (DSB 12/23/74 879)

November 24 *Kissinger on Vladivostok* Secretary of State Kissinger briefed the press on the discussions President Ford was having with General Secretary Brezhnev. The two leaders discussed the world situation, but they spent most of their time trying to resolve differences regarding the SALT II treaty. Kissinger said progress was being made. He said the Ford-Brezhnev meeting made a SALT II agreement in 1975 a possibility. (DSB 12/23/74 893)

November 26 *Palestinian Resolution* The United Nations General Assembly approved a resolution inviting the Palestine Liberation Organization to participate, as an observer, in the work of the General Assembly. The Soviet Union supported the resolution; the United States opposed it. (DSB 12/16/74 859)

November 29 *Soviets Praise Vladivostok* *Pravda* reported that Soviet leaders praised the agreements reached by General Secretary Brezhnev and President Ford at Vladivostok, particularly the agreement on the SALT II negotiations. (CDSP XXVI:47 5)

December 3 *Emigration and Trade* Secretary of State Kissinger appeared before the Senate Committee on Finance. He said the United States persistently encouraged the Soviet Union to allow a greater number of people to emigrate. The committee was considering a bill to grant most-favored-nation status to the Soviet Union, but some congressmen wanted to link MFN to Soviet emigration policies. (DSB 12/30/74 935)

December 7 *Kissinger on Vladivostok* Secretary of State Kissinger, in response to a question at a news conference, defended the Vladivostok arms agreement. He said the important thing about the agreement was the willingness of the two sides to accept equal numbers for strategic nuclear forces. He admitted that a SALT II agreement would not prevent a qualitative arms race. (AFRADR 514)

December 13 *North Atlantic Council* At the conclusion of a North Atlantic Council meeting in Brussels, the ministers issued a communiqué. They expressed support for the policy of détente, provided an adequate defensive military posture were maintained. They said the success of détente in Europe was linked to the implementation of the 1972 Quadripartite Agreement on Berlin. (DSB 1/6/75 5)

December 18 *Soviets on Trade* Tass, the Soviet news agency, issued a statement denying there could be any link between trade with the United States and Soviet emigration policies. (AFRADR 568)

1975

January 3 *The Trade Act* President Ford signed the Trade Act, which, among other things, granted the Soviet Union MFN status. The act, however, contained the Jackson-Vanik amendment denying MFN status to any communist country restricting emigration; the amendment was aimed at the Soviet Union. (AFRADR 25)

January 14 *Soviets Reject Trade Act* Secretary of State Kissinger announced that the Soviet Union had rejected the 1972 trade agreement with the United States because of the Jackson-Vanik amendment linking MFN status to emigration policies. (AFRADR 26)

January 15 *State of the Union* President Ford, in his State of the Union address, warned against America turning inward and abandoning international obligations. He supported a policy of peaceful coexistence vis-à-vis the Soviet Union and said both countries had to practice restraint if the world were to be made safe. (PP 44)

January 15 *Kissinger and Détente* Secretary of State Kissinger, during an interview on television, said that because of détente international tensions in Europe had been reduced and there was now greater Soviet-American cooperation than in the past. (DSB 2/10/75 174)

January 19 *Protests in New York* Members of the Jewish Defense League blocked traffic in New York on their march to the Soviet United Nations mission. That same day shots were fired into the Soviet mission. (NYT 1/20/75 25)

January 21 *Ford on Détente* President Ford, in response to a question at a news conference, said he thought the policy of détente with the Soviet Union would be expanded despite the Soviet rejection of the 1972 trade agreement. (PP 67)

January 22 *Soviets Protest to U.S.* The Soviet Union, in a note to the United States, protested the January 19 incident in which two bullets hit the building in New York used by the Soviet delegates at the United Nations mission. The Soviets also protested the demonstrations by the Jewish Defense League and reminded the United States that it was responsible for protecting Soviet diplomats and property. (CDSP XXVII:4 22)

January 24 *Kissinger on Foreign Policy* Secretary of State Kissinger, in an address to the Los Angeles World Affairs Council, discussed some principles guiding American foreign policy. Among other things, he mentioned the need to cooperate with allied nations and to resolve differences with adversaries without going to war. He said without some Soviet-American cooperation, a stable international political system could not develop. (DSB 2/17/75 197)

February 6 *Soviets Warn U.S.* *Izvestia* warned the United States not to use force against the Arab nations should they institute another oil embargo. (CDSP XXVII:6 11)

February 16 *Kissinger Meets with Gromyko* Secretary of State Kissinger concluded two days of talks with Foreign Minister Gromyko in Geneva. They discussed a number of issues, including those pertaining to Cyprus, the CSCE, and the Middle East. They were unable to resolve their differences concerning the Middle East. (NYT 2/17/75 1)

April 10 *Ford on Foreign Policy* President Ford addressed a joint session of Congress and announced he had sent notes to the People's Republic of China and the Soviet Union requesting them to use their influence to halt the fighting that had resumed in South Vietnam and Cambodia. The president endorsed the policies of détente but said he would not permit it "to become a license to fish in troubled waters." He expressed the hope that the SALT II agreement could be concluded in 1975, and he asked Congress to remove restrictions on trade with the Soviet Union. (AFRADR 93)

April 13 *Ford Criticized* *Pravda* criticized President Ford's April 10 speech. The article said the president had been encouraged to change America's foreign policies by individuals such as Senator Mike Mansfield but had refused to do so. Mansfield favored reducing the number of American troops in Europe, and he opposed any military intervention abroad except for national security reasons. (CDSP XXVII:15 19)

April 15 *Ford and Foreign Policy* President Ford, in a speech to the Daughters of the American Revolution, said the United States had to remain militarily strong if the policy of détente were to succeed. He said reducing tensions with the Soviet Union is possible only because of American strength. (PP 483)

April 17 *Kissinger on Foreign Policy* Secretary of State Kissinger, in an address to the American Society of Newspaper Editors, expressed disappointment that none of the signatories to the Paris accords allegedly ending the Vietnam fighting did anything to halt the North Vietnamese invasion of South Vietnam. He said the United States would not forget who it was that supplied North Vietnam with its weapons.

On April 29 North Vietnamese troops entered Saigon, and the South Vietnamese government surrendered. (DSB 5/5/75 562)

April 29 *Kissinger on Foreign Policy* Secretary of State Kissinger, at a news conference, said if the People's Republic of China and the Soviet Union adopted policies leading to international conflict, détente would be endangered. The secretary spoke after the fall of South Vietnam. China and the Soviet Union had signed an agreement allegedly guaranteeing the 1973 treaty ending the Vietnam War. (AFRADR 138)

May 5 *Victory in Vietnam* *Izvestia* congratulated the communists on their victory in South Vietnam. The article quoted from an editorial in the *New York Times* that said "the American people in overwhelming number, and Congress with them, have learned the lessons of folly." (CDSP XXVII:18 12)

May 20 *Gromyko and Kissinger* Secretary of State Kissinger met with Foreign Minister Gromyko for two days of talks in Vienna. They discussed arms control issues and problems in the Middle East. They described the talks as constructive. (CDSP XXVII:20 23)

May 30 *Nonproliferation Treaty* The ministers attending the Nonproliferation Treaty Conference in Geneva issued a communiqué at the close of their meeting that began on May 5. The delegates were critical of the United States and the Soviet Union for their failure to reduce nuclear arsenals as called for in the 1968 treaty. (DSB 6/30/75 924)

June 9 *Ford and the Soviet Union* President Ford, in response to a question at a news conference, said progress was being made on the SALT II treaty and compromises were being made to bring the Conference on Security and Cooperation in Europe to a conclusion. He said General Secretary Brezhnev might visit the United States sometime in the fall of 1975. (PP 795)

June 23 *Kissinger and SALT* Secretary of State Kissinger, in response to a question at a news conference, said General Secretary Brezhnev would probably come to the United States in the fall for a summit meeting with President Ford, provided the SALT II treaty were completed. Kissinger did not think Brezhnev would visit if a treaty were not completed. (DSB 7/7/75 18)

June 27 *Captive Nations Week* President Ford designated the week of July 13 "Captive Nations Week." (WCPD 688)

June 30 *Solzhenitsyn on Détente* Alexander Solzhenitsyn, in a speech in Washington, criticized the policy of détente and warned against making concessions to the Soviet Union in the hope its behavior would be modified. (NYT 7/1/75 6)

July 17 Apollo-Soyuz *Mission* The *Apollo* and *Soyuz* spacecraft docked in space. The Soviet-American space project had been agreed to by President Nixon and General Secretary Brezhnev in 1970 as a means to help improve relations between the superpowers. (NYT 7/18/75 1)

July 25 *Ford and Helsinki* President Ford, at a meeting with representatives of Americans of Eastern European Background, said the Helsinki Final Act that he would sign on August 1 would not legitimize the division of Europe nor would it change the American policy of refusing to recognize the Baltic states as a part of the Soviet Union. He said he believed the Final Act would contribute to a lessening of tensions in Europe. (PP 1030)

July 30 *The Helsinki Conference* The final phase of the Conference on Security and Cooperation in Europe opened in Helsinki. Leaders from thirty-five nations, including the United States and the Soviet Union, attended the meeting. (AFRADR 283)

July 30 *Ford and Brezhnev* President Ford, in response to a question at a news conference in Helsinki, said he had met with General Secretary Brezhnev, and the two leaders discussed the SALT II treaty. (PP 1071)

July 31 *Brezhnev at Helsinki* General Secretary Brezhnev, in a speech in Helsinki to the nations attending the Conference on Security and Cooperation in Europe, said the most important result of the Helsinki summit meeting was the strengthening of détente, which, he said, might "prove useful outside of Europe as well." (CDSP XXVII:31 12)

August 1 *The Final Act* The participants at the Helsinki conference signed the Final Act, which contained four "baskets" or categories. Basket I dealt with security issues, along with some human rights provisions; Basket II with economics and related issues; Basket III with humanitarian issues, including human rights; and Basket IV with follow-up conferences to review the implementation of the provisions of the Final Act. (AFRADR 293)

August 1 *Ford at Helsinki* President Ford, in an address to the nations attending the Conference on Security and Cooperation in Europe, said the Final Act was another step "in the process of détente and reconciliation," but its value would be judged by the future policies of the signatories. (PP 1074)

August 7 *Ford and Détente* President Ford, in a television interview, said he believed détente made the SALT I agreement possible and would make it easier to reach a SALT II agreement. He also believed more progress would be made in the MBFR negotiations as a result of the signing of the Helsinki Final Act. (PP 1133)

August 14 *Kissinger on Foreign Policy* Secretary of State Kissinger, in a speech in Birmingham, Alabama, warned the Soviet Union not to interfere in the internal affairs of Portugal. At the time the Portuguese Communist party was attempting to seize power. (DSB 9/15/75 393)

August 28 *Détente Outside Europe* *Izvestia* said because of the Helsinki meeting, détente was spreading outside Europe to the rest of the world. The article recommended negotiating a collective security pact for Asia that would contribute to peace and security for the nations of the region. The United States and the People's Republic of China opposed such a pact. (CDSP XXVII:35 1)

September 18 *Ford Meets with Gromyko* President Ford and Secretary of State Kissinger met with Foreign Minister Gromyko at the White House to discuss arms control issues. In a statement following the meeting, Kissinger said about 85 percent of the SALT II treaty was completed, and he intended to meet with Gromyko again the following day to continue the negotiations. (NYT 9/20/75 8)

September 22 *Kissinger on Foreign Policy* Secretary of State Kissinger, in an address to the United Nations General Assembly, said there had been an improvement in Soviet-American relations over the last decade, and he praised the 1972 Basic Principles Agreement, saying the principles were useful as standards for judging national behavior. (AFRADR 462)

September 22 *Ford and the Helsinki Final Act* President Ford, in response to a question at a news conference, said he thought the Helsinki Final Act was a good document because of the principles it embodied. He pointed out there would be a review conference in 1977 to evaluate how the Final Act was being implemented. Critics of President Ford believed the Soviet Union derived more advantages from the 1975 Helsinki Final Act than did the United States. (PP 1505)

October 1 *Arms Control* President Ford, in response to a question at a news conference in Omaha, Nebraska, said the United States and the Soviet Union were roughly equal in nuclear arms. He said he preferred to achieve a balance within the framework of a SALT II agreement, but if that were not possible, the United States would increase its nuclear arsenal. (PP 1558)

October 9 *Sakharov Wins Nobel Prize* Soviet physicist Andrei Sakharov won the Nobel Peace Prize. The committee of the Norwegian parliament awarding the prize praised Sakharov for recognizing the importance of linking world peace to respect for human rights. (NYT 10/10/75 1)

November 10 *The UN and Israel* The United Nations General Assembly approved a resolution declaring "Zionism is a form of racism and racial discrimination." The United States opposed the resolution; the Soviet Union supported it. (AFRADR 507)

December 12 *North Atlantic Council* At the conclusion of a two-day meeting in Brussels, the ministers of the North Atlantic Council issued a communiqué. They expressed their concern that the balance of power in Europe might be shifting in favor of the Soviet bloc because of the continuing Soviet military buildup. (DSB 1/12/76 57)

December 12 *Kissinger and Angola* Secretary of State Kissinger, in response to a question at a news conference in Brussels, said the United States became concerned about Angola only after massive intervention on the part of the Soviet Union and Cuba. The secretary wanted the superpowers to refrain from interfering in African affairs. (DSB 1/12/76 54)

December 23 *Kissinger and Angola* Secretary of State Kissinger, in response to a question at a news conference, said the decision of Congress to prohibit any aid to the anticommunist forces in Angola would make it more difficult to influence Soviet policies in Africa. The Senate had voted to prevent the Ford administration from using covert funds to aid the rebels fighting the communist-backed government in Angola. He added that Soviet intervention in Angola was incompatible with efforts to reduce Soviet-American tensions. (DSB 1/19/76 69)

1976

January 14 *Kissinger and the Soviets* Secretary of State Kissinger, in a statement at a news conference, said the superpowers must not seek to achieve advantages by militarily intervening in other nations. He said that military intervention would bring forth a reaction, a chain he wanted to see broken. Kissinger was critical of the Soviet Union and Cuba for their intervention in Angola. (DSB 2/2/76 125)

January 19 *State of the Union* President Ford, in his State of the Union address, said it was important for the United States to have a variety of instruments to achieve foreign policy goals. He specifically mentioned the need to aid forces in Angola fighting the communists, a policy opposed by many members of Congress. (PP 41)

January 20 *Kissinger and Nuclear Parity* Secretary of State Kissinger, in response to a question at a news conference, said the United States would never concede nuclear superiority to the Soviet Union. He did say, however, that once a nuclear arsenal reached a certain level, having additional weapons would be of little value. (DSB 2/16/76 163)

January 23 *Kissinger to Soviet Union* Secretary of State Kissinger and Foreign Minister Gromyko issued a joint statement at the close of their talks in Moscow that began on January 20. Topics discussed included SALT II, reduction of military forces in Europe, and Soviet-American relations. Both leaders agreed the talks were useful. (DSB 2/16/76 165)

January 29 *Kissinger on Angola* Secretary of State Kissinger, in an appearance before a subcommittee of the Senate Foreign Relations Committee, discussed the civil war in Angola. He spoke about the massive Soviet intervention there, including military equipment and the presence of approximately eleven thousand Cuban combat troops. The secretary thought it was important for the United States to check communist influence in Angola, but the Congress was reluctant to support the administration. (DSB 2/16/76 174)

January 30 *Ford and Angola* President Ford, at a question-and-answer session with members of the media, said the Soviet Union had spent about $200 million in Angola, and Cuba had more than ten thousand troops there. He scored Congress for not allowing him to aid troops fighting the Soviet-backed government. (PP 122)

February 1 *Soviets Criticize Kissinger* *Pravda* accused Secretary of State Kissinger of distorting Soviet and Cuban assistance to the Angolan government. The article said the Soviet assistance to Angola was in support of its independence and freedom. (CDSP XXVIII:5 22)

February 3 *Kissinger on Foreign Policy* Secretary of State Kissinger, in a speech in San Francisco, analyzed Soviet-American relations. He emphasized the necessity of improving relations with the Soviet Union because of the threat of nuclear war, but he criticized the Soviets for intervening in Africa. He declared that coping with the Soviet Union as a superpower was a major American concern. (DSB 2/23/76 201)

February 4 *Kissinger on Foreign Policy* Secretary of State Kissinger, in a speech at the University of Wyoming, said the United States had done more for peace since World War II than any nation in history. He said the United States was committed to improving relations with the Soviet Union, but he also emphasized the necessity of maintaining American military strength. He warned that should the Soviet Union continue to expand its power and influence, as it was doing in Africa, global security could be threatened. (DSB 3/1/76 249)

February 10 *No Aid to Angola* President Ford signed into law the Defense Department appropriation bill that contained the Tunney amendment prohibiting the president from aiding groups in Angola seeking to oust the Soviet-backed government. (PP 241)

February 24 *Brezhnev and Foreign Policy* General Secretary Brezhnev, in a speech to the delegates of the Twenty-fifth Congress of the Communist party, said Soviet-American relations had improved, but he criticized the Jackson-Vanik amendment as an American effort to intervene in Soviet internal affairs. Brezhnev supported the policy of détente and said it would help promote communist objectives. (CDSP XXVIII:8 3)

March 22 *Foreign Policy and Security* Secretary of State Kissinger, in a speech in Dallas, said the United States and the Soviet Union had different military force structures because they had different security needs. Therefore, comparing the Soviet and American nuclear arsenals was not very useful. He did not think the United States would be able to again acquire nuclear superiority over the Soviet Union. (DSB 4/12/76 460)

April 13 *Ford on Eastern Europe* President Ford, at a question-and-answer session with the American Society of Newspaper Editors, said he opposed the Soviet domination of the nations of Eastern Europe. He wanted the Eastern European countries to have a greater degree of autonomy. (PP 1125)

May 13 *Kissinger on Foreign Policy* Secretary of State Kissinger, in testimony before the Senate Committee on Foreign Relations, said the Soviet and Cuban intervention in Africa had created a dangerous situation. He feared that if the United States failed to counter the Soviet threat, African politics would become increasingly radical. (AFRADR 294)

May 28 *Peaceful Nuclear Explosion Treaty* The United States and the Soviet Union signed the Peaceful Nuclear Explosion treaty (PNE). It prohibited underground nuclear explosions for peaceful purposes from exceeding 150 kilotons. It complemented the July 3, 1974, Threshold Test Ban treaty prohibiting underground nuclear explosions in excess of 150 kilotons. (AFRADR 181)

June 25 *Kissinger on Foreign Policy* Secretary of State Kissinger, in a speech in London, emphasized the necessity for the democratic nations to work together to create a new era in international politics. He said that, measured by performance, the democratic states had already won the contest between communism and democracy. He again endorsed the two major recommendations of the 1967 Harmel Report to the NATO nations: the need to contain the Soviet Union and at the same time seek to foster political cooperation in such areas as arms control. (DSB 7/26/76 105)

July 2 *Captive Nations Week* President Ford designated the week of July 18 "Captive Nations Week." (WCPD 1111)

September 30 *Kissinger on Foreign Policy* Secretary of State Kissinger, in an address to the United Nations General Assembly, discussed the problem of peace. He said the United States had to maintain a balance of strategic forces with the Soviet Union, preferably through agreements rather than an arms race. He said the United States would not permit the Soviet Union to seek unilateral advantages, and he pointed out that arms control agreements required a proper political environment to generate trust and confidence. (DSB 10/25/76 497)

October 24 *The Sino-Soviet Conflict* Secretary of State Kissinger, in response to a question on the television program "Face the Nation," said the United States would be concerned if the People's Republic of China were the victim of a "massive assault." The secretary was referring to a Soviet attack on China. (DSB 11/15/76 608)

October 27 *Kissinger Criticized* *Pravda* criticized Secretary of State Kissinger for his October 24 comments on a possible Soviet attack on China. *Pravda* said Kissinger's comments were designed to bring about better

Sino-American relations at the expense of the Soviet Union. (CDSP XXVIII:43 8)

November 2 Carter Elected Jimmy Carter was elected president. He defeated the Republican incumbent, Gerald Ford. (NYT 11/3/76 1)

November 16 Arms Control Secretary of State Kissinger, at a question-and-answer session with NATO parliamentarians said the United States must remain militarily strong, while at the same time seeking to negotiate arms reduction agreements with the Soviet Union. He said there must be parity between the United States and the Soviet Union at both the nuclear and conventional levels of armaments. (DSB 12/13/76 710)

November 26 WTO Proposal The ministers attending a meeting of WTO nations in Bucharest adopted a proposal calling on all the signatories of the 1975 Helsinki Final Act to sign an agreement pledging not to be the first nation to use nuclear weapons. The Soviets claimed such a pledge would reduce the threat of nuclear war and would improve the political climate to negotiate additional agreements. (CDSP XXVIII:48 9)

November 30 Brezhnev and Foreign Policy General Secretary Brezhnev, in a speech to the American-Soviet Trade and Economic Council, said the Soviet Union wanted to have good relations with the United States. He pointed out, however, that during the recently concluded American presidential election campaign, some individuals incorrectly accused the Soviet Union of seeking military superiority over the United States. He rejected the allegation as untrue. (CDSP XXVIII:48 1)

December 25 Soviet Military Might The *New York Times* reported that President-elect Carter would receive a report from the CIA concluding there was much evidence to support the claim that the Soviet Union was seeking military superiority over the United States. Formerly, CIA officials believed the Soviets were only seeking parity, not preponderance. (NYT 12/26/76 1)

December 26 Bukovsky Expelled *Izvestia* declared that Vladimir Bukovsky, a Soviet dissident, had been expelled from the Soviet Union. (CDSP XXVIII:52 3)

1977

January 12 *State of the Union* President Ford, in his State of the Union address, emphasized the need to remain militarily strong to meet the Soviet challenge. He supported the development of the Trident submarine, the B-1 bomber, and survivable ICBMs. (PP 2918)

January 18 *Brezhnev on Arms Control* General Secretary Brezhnev, in a speech in Tula, called for new arms control measures that he hoped would be considered by President-elect Carter. Brezhnev called for completing a SALT II treaty, adopting measures to prevent a nuclear war, reducing military forces in central Europe, and implementing the 1975 Helsinki Final Act. (CDSP XXIX:3 1)

January 21 *Andrei Sakharov* Andrei Sakharov, the Soviet dissident, wrote to President Carter thanking him for speaking out on behalf of human rights activists in the Soviet Union and elsewhere. (NYT 1/29/77 1)

January 21 *Vance Confirmed* The Senate confirmed Cyrus Vance as secretary of state. (NYT 1/22/77 1)

January 26 *Czech Rights Violations* The State Department issued a statement criticizing Czechoslovakia for its harassment of individuals that had signed Charter 77. The statement noted that the Helsinki Final Act required the signatory states to abide by international agreements on the protection of human rights. Charter 77 was made up of a group of individuals, including Vaclav Havel, who monitored Czech compliance with the 1975 Helsinki Final Act. (DSB 2/21/77 154)

January 27 *Andrei Sakharov* The State Department issued a statement in defense of Andrei Sakharov. It said Soviet efforts to intimidate him would be a human rights violation. (DSB 2/21/77 138)

February 3 *Vance and Linkage* Secretary of State Vance, in response to a question during an interview, said the Carter administration did not plan to link an arms control agreement with the Soviet Union to its human rights violations. (DSB 2/21/77 148)

February 4 *Krimsky Expelled* George A. Krimsky, a correspondent for the Associated Press, was ordered to leave the Soviet Union. He had many contacts with dissidents, and at the time the Soviets were attempting to break the communication link between dissidents and Westerners. In retaliation, the United States, on February 5, expelled Vladimir Alekseyev, a correspondent for Tass. (NYT 2/5/77 3)

February 4 *Ginzburg Arrested* Soviet authorities arrested Alexander Ginzburg, a prominent Soviet dissident. (NYT 2/5/77 3)

February 5 *Carter and Sakharov* President Carter wrote to Andrei Sakharov assuring him that the United States would continue to support human rights at home and abroad and would continue to work for the release of prisoners of conscience. (NYT 2/18/77 3)

February 5 *Nuclear Arms Race* Georgy Arbatov, the senior Soviet analyst of American foreign affairs, said the military-industrial complex in the United States was trying to convince President Carter that the Soviet Union was attempting to gain nuclear superiority over the United States. Arbatov denied the charge and said the Soviets only wanted nuclear parity. (CDSP XXIX:5 1)

February 8 *Carter on Foreign Policy* President Carter, in response to a question at a news conference, said he believed he could speak out on human rights and continue to work with the Soviet Union to achieve arms control agreements. Carter said he had sent a letter to General Secretary Brezhnev explaining the president's concern for human rights and arms control. The president said he wanted to negotiate, as soon as possible, an arms control agreement with the Soviet Union by deferring a resolution of the contentious issues of cruise missiles and Backfire bombers. (PP 99)

February 10 *Orlov Arrested* Yuri Orlov, a prominent Soviet dissident, was arrested by Soviet officials for his activities as a member of a group monitoring Soviet compliance with the Helsinki Final Act. (NYT 2/11/77 1)

February 12 *Soviets on Dissidents* *Pravda* defended the arrests of various dissidents because they allegedly opposed communism and détente and received support from Western nations. The Soviets said they were slandered by opponents in the West, and they charged that the human rights campaign was "a carefully thought-out and coordinated act of sabotage." (CDSP XXIX:6 1)

March 1 *Bukovsky at the White House* President Carter met with Vladimir Bukovsky, a dissident who had been expelled from the Soviet Union. On March 3 a number of articles in *Pravda* criticized President Carter for meeting with Bukovsky. (NYT 3/2/77 1)

March 13 *Carter Criticized* *Pravda* criticized President Carter's policies on human rights, accusing him of interfering in the internal affairs of the Soviet Union and of endangering détente. (CDSP XXIX:10 1)

March 15 *Shcharansky Arrested* Soviet authorities arrested Anatoly Shcharansky, a prominent dissident. Among other things, he was accused of working for the CIA. (NYT 3/16/77 10)

March 15 *Intourist Office Attacked* Tass, the Soviet news agency, reported that the Soviet Intourist office in New York had been attacked by "Zionists from the fascist Jewish Defense League." Tass said U.S. officials knew who the terrorists were but did nothing about them. (CDSP XXIX:11 17)

March 16 *Arms Control* Georgy Arbatov, the senior Soviet analyst of American foreign affairs, said President Carter's support for dissidents in the Soviet Union could imperil the arms control negotiations. (NYT 3/17/77 2)

March 17 *Carter at the UN* President Carter, in an address to the United Nations General Assembly, said the United States was determined to support the ideals associated with the United Nations Charter. The major theme of his address was the need for the United Nations to pay greater attention to human rights, but he also expressed a desire to improve cooperation with the Soviet Union and to complete arms control agreements. (PP 444)

March 21 *Brezhnev Criticizes Carter* General Secretary Brezhnev, in a speech in the Kremlin, criticized the United States for supporting and encouraging dissidents in the Soviet Union. He accused the United States of interfering in Soviet internal affairs, and he berated those individuals who charged that the Soviet Union was seeking military superiority or posed some type of military threat to the United States. He said United States-Soviet relations could not develop normally because of U.S. interference in Soviet internal affairs. (CDSP XXIX:12 4)

March 24 *Carter on Arms Control* President Carter, in a statement made at a news conference, listed some topics Secretary of State Vance would discuss with General Secretary Brezhnev in Moscow, including the SALT II treaty, arms sales, balanced force reductions talks in Europe, and nuclear testing. (PP 496)

March 30 *Vance and Arms Control* Secretary of State Vance, at a news conference in Moscow, announced that the Soviet Union had rejected the two new proposals of President Carter pertaining to the SALT II treaty. The first proposal was to defer a solution pertaining to cruise missiles and the Backfire bomber until all other problems were re-solved. The second proposal called for a substantial reduction in strategic weapons below the level agreed to at Vladivostok by President Ford and General Secretary Brezhnev. (DSB 4/25/77 400)

March 31 *Gromyko on Arms Control* Foreign Minister Gromyko held a news conference to give the Soviet version for the lack of agreement with Secretary of State Vance. Gromyko accused the United States of presenting one-sided arms control proposals that deviated from the agreements reached at Vladivostok. Gromyko also chided President Carter for engaging in public diplomacy pertaining to human rights. (CDSP XXIX:13 5)

April 22 *The Helsinki Final Act* *Pravda* accused the United States of launching propaganda attacks against the Soviet Union and the nations of Eastern Europe, alleging that they were violating the 1975 Helsinki Final Act. The attacks, according to the *Pravda* article, were intended to divert attention from America's failure to implement the Final Act. The Soviets intended to make these alleged failures public at the Belgrade CSCE review conference scheduled to convene later in the year. (CDSP XXIX:16 22)

April 26 *SALT II Talks* The United States and the Soviet Union announced that the SALT II talks would resume in Geneva on May 11. (DSB 5/23/77 512)

April 30 *Vance on Human Rights* Secretary of State Vance, in a speech at the University of Georgia Law School, said the Carter administration was determined to make human rights a central part of America's foreign policies. Nations concerned about human rights, he said, could not be accused of interfering in the internal affairs of other countries, particularly when they had signed international agreements protecting human rights. The secretary said the United States would not engage in polemical attacks against other countries. (DSB 5/23/77 505)

May 2 *Carter on Ideology* President Carter, in reply to a question at a news conference, said he did not mind engaging the Soviet Union in an ideological contest. He said the Soviets always assumed the ideological struggle between the superpowers would continue during a period of détente, and the president said he could accept that. (PP 767)

May 21 *Vance on SALT II* Secretary of State Vance, in a statement at a news conference following his talks with Foreign Minister Gromyko in Geneva, said they agreed on a common framework for the SALT II treaty. The framework consisted of three parts: one was the treaty itself, the second was a protocol to the treaty, and the third was a statement of principles that would apply to a SALT III treaty. However, there was little agreement on what would go into each of the three parts. (DSB 6/13/77 628)

May 22 *Carter at Notre Dame* President Carter delivered the commencement address at the University of Notre Dame, and he used the occasion to explain his foreign policy program. He reaffirmed the American commitment to human rights and said America was "now free of that inordinate fear of communism" that he thought had characterized American policy in the past. In the 1976 presidential campaign, Carter was critical of détente, but now he firmly endorsed it. (PP 954)

June 9 *Missiles Deployed* Joseph Luns, the Secretary General of NATO, announced that the Soviet Union had been deploying intermediate, mobile SS-20 missiles, each with three warheads. The deployment of SS-20s became a contentious issue in Soviet-American relations. (NYT 6/10/77 4)

June 30 *Carter Cancels B-1* President Carter announced at a news conference his decision to cancel the B-1 bomber program. He said he did not anticipate a deterioration in Soviet-American relations, but if that did occur, he might reverse his policy on the B-1. He said the United States would rely on cruise missiles to strengthen America's nuclear arsenal. (DSB 8/1/77 146)

July 4 *Toon Speech Cancelled* Soviet authorities would not permit Ambassador Malcolm Toon to deliver a scheduled July 4 speech on Soviet television because they objected to comments he intended to make about human rights. (NYT 7/5/77 1)

July 5 *Brezhnev to Carter* General Secretary Brezhnev presented Ambassador Toon with a letter for President Carter that was critical of his human rights policies. The United States was accused of interfering in the internal affairs of the Soviet Union under the pretense of protecting human rights. (CDSP XXIX:27 17)

July 10 *Carter Criticized* *Pravda* criticized President Carter for his June 30 announcement that he planned to strengthen America's military capabilities by relying on cruise missiles rather than the B-1 bomber. The president's decision, according to the article, was not conducive to détente. (CDSP XXIX:28 6)

July 12 *Carter on Soviet-American Relations* President Carter, in response to a question at a news conference, said he thought the hostile Soviet rhetoric was not a response to his human rights policies but rather was the result of the United States and the Soviet Union dealing with complex, contentious issues. He did not think there had been a deterioration in Soviet-American relations. (PP 1238)

July 20 *Captive Nations Week* President Carter designated the week of July 17 "Captive Nations Week." (WCPD 1046)

July 21 *Soviet-American Relations* President Carter, in a speech in South Carolina, reviewed Soviet-American relations. He said despite major differences between the two countries, they also had many shared interests, including arms control, banning nuclear tests, expanding trade, and creating a more stable international political system. (DSB 8/15/77 193)

July 30 *Neutron Bomb* Tass, the Soviet news agency, criticized President Carter for attempting to devise a plan to deploy neutron bombs in Europe. Tass said that Carter's decision brought the world closer to a nuclear war. On July 21 President Carter, in response to a question at a news conference, said he had not yet decided whether to deploy the neutron bomb. (CDSP XXIX:30 4)

July 31 *The Soviets and Helsinki* *Izvestia* said the Soviet Union was pursuing numerous policies to help implement the provisions of the 1975 Helsinki Final Act. The article charged some countries with violating the Helsinki Final Act by attempting to interfere in the internal affairs of the communist nations. President Carter was criticized for allegedly deciding to build neutron bombs, for increasing the production of cruise missiles, and for interfering in the domestic affairs of nations. The Soviets said these were all violations of the Final Act. (CDSP XXIX:31 6)

August 3 *Carter Evaluated* Georgy Arbatov, the leading Soviet authority on American foreign policy, in an article in *Pravda* entitled "A Six Month Report Card for Carter," gave the president a *D*. Arbatov accused Carter of launching anti-Soviet propaganda campaigns and placing obstacles in the way of better trade relations. (CDSP XXIX:31 1)

August 5 *Human Rights* The Congressional Committee on Security and Cooperation in Europe issued a report critical of the Soviet Union and the nations of Eastern Europe for their human rights violations. (NYT 8/6/77 1)

August 25 *Vance and China* Secretary of State Vance, in response to a question at a news conference while visiting Beijing, said America's relations with the People's Republic of China were not based on opposition to any third country, meaning the Soviet Union. (AFRADR 404)

September 9 *Andropov's Speech* Yuri Andropov, a member of the Politburo, in a speech in Moscow, criticized the human rights policies of

President Carter, although he was not mentioned by name. Andropov referred to the Soviet dissidents as criminals who disrupted society. He said the propaganda campaigns directed against the Soviet Union violated the principles of détente and those of the 1975 Helsinki Final Act. (CDSP XXIX:35 1)

September 22   *The Interim SALT Agreement* Secretary of State Vance, in a letter to the Senate Foreign Relations Committee, announced that the United States would continue to abide by the SALT I Interim Agreement on the Limitation of Strategic Offensive Weapons, due to expire on October 3, as long as the Soviet Union did. (NYT 9/23/77 1)

October 4   *Carter at the UN* President Carter, in an address to the United Nations General Assembly, said the superpowers were close to completing a SALT II treaty. He expressed support for a fifty-percent reduction in nuclear weapons and a comprehensive test ban treaty. (DSB 10/24/77 547)

October 4   *Belgrade CSCE Meeting* A conference convened in Belgrade to evaluate the implementation of the Helsinki Final Act. At Belgrade, the United States and its NATO allies were determined to completely review each of the three baskets on the assumption that all three were equally important. The Soviet Union was more selective and attempted to place emphasis on certain portions of the Final Act while minimizing the significance of other sections, particularly those pertaining to human rights. (DSB 11/14/77 674)

November 21   *ABM Treaty* The U.S.-U.S.S.R. Consultative Commission issued a communiqué after carrying out a review of the 1972 ABM treaty. The commission concluded that the treaty was working well. (AFPBD 1977-1980 183)

December 15   *Carter on Human Rights* President Carter said he thought the 1948 Universal Declaration of Human Rights permitted nations to criticize human rights abuses in other nations. The criticism, said the president, did not mean these nations were enemies. (AFPBD 1977-1980 418)

December 30   *Tactical Nuclear Weapons* President Carter, at a news conference in Poland, said there had never been any arms control discussions about tactical nuclear weapons in Europe. He thought such talks should be held to analyze the question of deploying the neutron bomb and the Soviet SS-20 missiles. (AFPBD 1977-1980 531)

1978

January 12   *Carter and the Soviet Union* President Carter, in response to a question at a news conference, said, unlike the Soviet Union, the United States would not send arms to any of the nations involved in the conflict in the Horn of Africa. He stated that the United States would do whatever it could to help resolve the conflict between Somalia and Ethiopia, and he called on the Soviet Union and Cuba to stop sending arms and personnel to the region. (PP 56)

January 19   *State of the Union* President Carter, in his State of the Union address, reaffirmed his commitment to human rights, claiming that America had regained a moral basis for its foreign policy. He expected the SALT II treaty to be completed in 1978, and he expressed the wish to negotiate a comprehensive nuclear test ban treaty with the Soviet Union. (PP 95)

February 11   *Arms Control* *Pravda* said there were forces in the United States opposed to negotiating arms control agreements with the Soviet Union. The article criticized those groups in the United States that alleged the Soviet Union presented a military threat to the West requiring a stronger American military arsenal. (CDSP XXX:6 1)

February 24   *Soviets in Ethiopia* Zbigniew Brzezinski, President Carter's national security advisor, at a news briefing at the White House, said a Soviet general was leading Ethiopian troops in an effort to expel Somalian forces from the Ogaden region. (NYT 2/25/78 1)

March 2   *Carter on Soviet Policy in Africa* President Carter, in response to a question at a news conference, said Soviet activities in the Horn of Africa would not be linked to negotiations for a SALT II treaty. The president said he had been assured by Foreign Minister Gromyko that Ethiopian troops, supplied by the Soviet Union, would not cross the border to fight in Somalia. (PP 442)

March 3   *Carter and the CSCE* The White House, a week before the Belgrade CSCE conference ended, issued a statement blaming Soviet policies for the failure to produce a "concluding document." The statement indicated the United States would continue to press the Soviet Union to meet its human rights obligations. (DSB 4/78 41)

March 5   *Soviets Reject Linkage* *Pravda* rejected the idea of linking the SALT II treaty to other foreign policy issues. The article accused Zbigniew Brzezinski, President Carter's national security advisor, of wanting to link the SALT II treaty to Soviet policies in the Horn of Africa. (CDSP XXX:9 22)

March 8 *Belgrade Conference Ends* The Belgrade CSCE follow-up conference ended. The conferees agreed to convene another review conference in Madrid in 1980, but because of Soviet-American differences about the question of human rights, the Belgrade conference ended without new agreements. (DSB 4/78 43)

March 12 *The Neutron Bomb* *Pravda* said the Soviet Union favored a ban on the building of neutron bombs, but if the United States decided to produce the bomb, the Soviets would make an appropriate response. (CDSP XXX:10 10)

March 17 *Carter on Foreign Policy* President Carter, in a speech at Wake Forest University, said there had been a substantial growth in Soviet military power and a willingness on the part of Moscow to use military force to achieve political goals. He said the United States would continue to seek arms control agreements with the Soviet Union, but at the same time he promised that America's military might would remain sufficient to protect the United States and its allies. (PP 529)

March 19 *Carter Criticized* *Pravda* criticized President Carter for his comments at Wake Forest University. He was accused of endangering détente, starting an arms race, and falsely alleging there was some type of military threat from the Soviet Union. The article warned that if the United States created obstacles to completing the SALT II treaty, Soviet-American relations would suffer. (CDSP XXX:11 2)

April 7 *Brezhnev Answers Carter* General Secretary Brezhnev responded to President Carter's March 17 speech. Brezhnev accused the United States of creating obstacles that prevented the conclusion of the SALT II treaty. Brezhnev was particularly critical of plans to build the neutron bomb, which he labeled an offensive nuclear weapon. The Soviet leader expressed support for a military détente and disarmament. (NT 4/78 4)

April 10 *Vance on Arms Control* Secretary of State Vance, in a speech in Washington, listed some American goals vis-à-vis the Soviet Union. The United States, he said, wanted to reduce nuclear weapons and conventional forces and complete a comprehensive test ban treaty. He said a strong defense and arms control agreements were not incompatible, but complementary. (DSB 5/78 20)

April 10 *Soviet Diplomat Defects* The State Department announced that Arkady Shevchenko, the highest ranking Soviet diplomat at the United Nations, decided to defect and remain in America. (NYT 4/11/78 1)

April 22 *Soviet-American Communiqué* The United States and the Soviet Union issued a joint communiqué at the conclusion of talks conducted by Secretary of State Vance and Soviet leaders in Moscow. Among the issues discussed were the SALT II treaty, force reductions in central Europe, and the forthcoming United Nations General Assembly Special Session on Disarmament. (DSB 6/78 26)

April 25 *Carter and the Neutron Bomb* President Carter, in response to a question at a news conference, said the decision of General Secretary Brezhnev not to build a neutron bomb had no value because the Soviets did not need such a weapon. The neutron bomb is basically an antitank weapon, and the WTO nations had many more tanks than did the NATO nations. (PP 776)

May 5 *Carter Critical of Soviets* President Carter, in answer to a question following his speech in Washington State, accused the Soviet Union of interfering in the internal affairs of the African nations. He was particularly critical of Soviet willingness to ship arms to African nations involved in internal or external conflicts. (PP 871)

May 9 *Soviets Criticize Carter* Pravda criticized President Carter and accused him of distorting Soviet policies in Africa. The article said that contrary to what President Carter said in his May 5 talk in Washington State, the Soviets were seeking no privileges or advantages in Africa. (CDSP XXX:19 16)

May 18 *Yuri Orlov Sentenced* Pravda reported that Yuri Orlov, founder of the Moscow Helsinki Watch Group, was sentenced to seven years in prison and five years of internal exile. (CDSP XXX:20 1)

May 20 *Carter and Orlov* President Carter, during a question-and-answer session at the White House, said he was "deeply disturbed" by the trial and sentencing of Yuri Orlov, a Soviet dissident. The president said he conveyed his concerns to Soviet leaders. (PP 938)

May 20 *Relations with China* Zbigniew Brzezinski, President Carter's national security advisor, at a dinner in Beijing, said that Sino-American relations were based on shared strategic concerns and that both countries would oppose any nation with hegemonic ambitions. The Chinese used the term *hegemonic* as a code word for Soviet imperialism. (AFPBD 1977-1980 965)

May 25 *Carter and the Soviet Union* President Carter, in response to a question at a news conference in Chicago, said he opposed linking the SALT II treaty to Soviet human rights policies or interventionist policies in Africa. (PP 974)

May 28 *Soviets and Détente* Zbigniew Brzezinski, President Carter's national security advisor, in a television interview, accused the Soviet Union of violating the "code of détente" by militarily intervening in Africa. (NYT 5/29/78 1)

May 30 *Carter to NATO* President Carter, in a speech to the heads of state attending the North Atlantic Council meeting in Washington, said the Soviet Union and its WTO allies were continuing to expand their military might beyond their legitimate security requirements. He said the United States would use whatever force was necessary, including nuclear weapons, to defend the NATO nations. (PP 1011)

May 31 *Brzezinski Criticized* *Pravda* criticized Zbigniew Brzezinski, President Carter's national security advisor, for his anti-Soviet comments on May 28. The article rejected Brzezinski's criticism of Soviet-Cuban policies in Africa. (CDSP XXX:22 6)

June 1 *Slepak Arrested* Vladimir Slepak, a Soviet dissident, was arrested by Soviet authorities because of his efforts to publicize his failure to receive permission to emigrate. He was brought to trial, convicted, and sentenced to five years of internal exile. (DSB 8/78 10)

June 7 *Carter on Relations with the Soviets* President Carter, in a commencement address at the United States Naval Academy, discussed Soviet-American relations and the need for a policy of détente. He said the Soviets defined *détente* in a manner that exacerbated relations between the superpowers. He said the "Soviet Union can choose either confrontation or cooperation. The United States is adequately prepared to meet either choice." The pessimistic tone of Carter's speech was in sharp contrast to his optimistic assessment of Soviet-American relations when he spoke to students at the University of Notre Dame on May 22, 1977. (PP 1052)

June 17 *Soviets Accuse Carter* *Pravda* criticized President Carter's June 7 speech. The article said he was influenced by Zbigniew Brzezinski, his national security advisor, and other opponents of détente. (CDSP XXX:24 1)

June 25 *Carter Criticized* General Secretary Brezhnev, in a speech in Minsk, criticized the United States and its NATO allies for the lack of progress in concluding arms control agreements. The Soviet leader also warned the United States not to exploit the "China card." (CDSP XXX:26 1)

June 26 *Carter on Relations with the Soviets* President Carter, in response to a question at a news conference, said despite the tensions between the

United States and the Soviet Union, the superpower relationship was stable and, he said, General Secretary Brezhnev wanted to have improved relations with the United States. (PP 1180)

July 8 *Vance on Trial of Dissidents* Secretary of State Vance issued a statement criticizing the Soviets for their decision to try Anatoly Shcharansky and Alexander Ginzburg, prominent dissidents. The trial was scheduled to begin while Vance was in Geneva to confer with Foreign Minister Gromyko. The secretary said he deplored the Soviet actions but would not cancel his meeting with Gromyko. (DSB 8/78 28)

July 10 *Dissidents on Trial* Anatoly Shcharansky and Alexander Ginzburg, prominent Soviet dissidents, were put on trial. Shcharansky, a monitor of the 1975 Helsinki Final Act, was charged with treason. Ginzburg was charged with "anti-Soviet agitation and propaganda." On July 13 Ginzburg was sentenced to eight years in a labor camp. On July 14 Shcharansky, who had been accused of spying for the CIA, was convicted of treason and sentenced to thirteen years in prison, although President Carter had written to General Secretary Brezhnev assuring him that Shcharansky did not work for the CIA. (DSB 8/78 29)

July 11 *Captive Nations Week* President Carter designated the week of July 16 "Captive Nations Week." (WCPD 1251)

July 14 *Political Prisoners in America* *Izvestia* reported on the charge made by Andrew Young, the American ambassador to the United Nations, that there were hundreds or perhaps thousands of political prisoners in American jails. The article said that Young's comments were an official admission of "widespread political persecutions in the United States." (CDSP XXX:28 4)

July 20 *Computer Sale Cancelled* *Pravda* reported that the United States had cancelled the sale of Sperry-Univac computers to the Soviet Union. The cancellation was a response to the jail terms given to Ginzburg and Shcharansky. The article said the cancellation contradicted the many assertions of President Carter that he wanted to improve relations with the Soviet Union. (CDSP XXX:29 4)

July 24 *Brzezinski Criticized* *Pravda* criticized Zbigniew Brzezinski, President Carter's national security advisor, for his foreign policy views. He was accused of opposing détente, favoring confrontation with the Soviet Union, and supporting the anti-Soviet policies of the People's Republic of China. (CDSP XXX:31 6)

September 17 *Camp David Agreement* Egypt, Israel, and the United States signed the Camp David agreement consisting of two documents: a

"Framework for Peace in the Middle East" and a "Framework for the Conclusion of a Peace Treaty between Egypt and Israel." Most Arab nations condemned the Camp David agreement. (AFPBD 1977-1980 653)

September 17 *Soviets and Camp David* *Pravda* criticized the Camp David agreement that the United States negotiated with Israel and Egypt. Egyptian president Sadat was accused of capitulating to Israel and the United States, thus betraying the Arab cause. (CDSP XXX:37 1)

September 22 *Brezhnev on Foreign Policy* General Secretary Brezhnev, in a speech in Baku, criticized the Camp David agreement, alleging it was intended to split the Arab world. He accused the NATO nations of an arms buildup, and he rejected criticism of the way Soviet dissidents were treated. (CDSP XXX:38 1)

October 21 *Vance to Moscow* Secretary of State Vance met with Soviet Foreign Minister Gromyko and Secretary General Brezhnev in Moscow for further discussions on the SALT II treaty. (DSB 12/78 37)

November 19 *Brezhnev Warns the U.S.* General Secretary Brezhnev, in response to a question from a *Pravda* reporter, warned the United States not to intervene in Iran. The Soviet leader said that any military intervention would impinge on the security interests of the Soviet Union. At the time, there was considerable antigovernment unrest in Iran. (CDSP XXX:46 7)

November 24 *WTO Declaration* *Pravda* published a declaration issued by the WTO nations whose representatives had met in Moscow. The ministers criticized the NATO nations for increasing their defense budgets and military arsenals and pursuing policies contrary to the principles contained in the 1975 Helsinki Final Act. The ministers expressed support for disarmament and a military détente in Europe, better implementation of the Helsinki Final Act, and the abolition of military pacts. (CDSP XXX:47 7)

December 11 *Unrest in Iran* Major antigovernment demonstrations erupted throughout Iran. In the following days, the demonstrations turned violent and eventually led to the ouster of the government of Shah Reza Pahlavi, an ally of the United States. (NYT 12/12/78 1)

December 14 *Carter Warns Soviets* President Carter, at a question-and-answer session, said he sent the Soviet Union a warning not to intervene in Iran. The president said he had exchanged letters with General Secretary Brezhnev about conditions in Iran. (PP 2255)

December 15 *U.S.-China Recognition* President Carter announced that the United States and the People's Republic of China had agreed to establish diplomatic relations effective January 1, 1979. (PP 2264)

December 19 *Soviets on China Recognition* *Pravda* said there was a link between the decision of the United States to extend diplomatic recognition to the People's Republic of China and Beijing's hostility to the Soviet Union. (CDSP XXX:51 1)

December 21 *Vance and Gromyko* Secretary of State Vance and Foreign Minister Gromyko met in Geneva to discuss the SALT II treaty. (NYT 12/22/78 1)

1979

January 15 *Global Order* Zbigniew Brzezinski, President Carter's national security advisor, in a special briefing for various American officials, said the United States rejected the idea of a Soviet-American condominium. He said the American decision to extend diplomatic recognition to China was part of President Carter's plan to help develop a pluralistic international political system. He said the Soviets had to decide to be a part of a global system of independent states or remain outside it. (AFPBD 1977-1980 979)

January 17 *Carter on Triangular Diplomacy* President Carter, in response to a question at a news conference, said he did not plan to use improved relations with the People's Republic of China against the Soviet Union. He added that if Soviet-American relations improved, he would not use that against China. (PP 57)

January 23 *State of the Union* President Carter, in his State of the Union address, opined that America's military might helped to strengthen world peace. He said he supported modernizing NATO's military forces and reaffirmed the American commitment to the SALT process, which, he did not think, would weaken America's nuclear capabilities. The president said he would like General Secretary Brezhnev to visit America. (PP 106)

February 1 *Joint Communiqué* Deng Xiaoping and President Carter issued a joint communiqué at the close of their summit meeting in Washington that began on January 29. The two sides signed a number of agreements pertaining to science, technology, and culture. President Carter accepted an invitation to visit the People's Republic of China. (PP 212)

February 1 *Soviets and Deng's Visit* *Pravda* said the purpose of Deng Xiaoping's visit to the United States was to forge a Sino-American alliance directed at the Soviet Union. (CDSP XXXI:5 1)

March 2 *Brezhnev on Foreign Policy* General Secretary Brezhnev, in a speech in the Kremlin, said the SALT II agreement should lead to additional arms control agreements in the future. He was generally optimistic in assessing East-West relations, but he accused the NATO nations of failing to negotiate in good faith in the MBFR talks. (DOD 67)

April 25 *Carter and SALT* President Carter, in a speech to the American Newspaper Publishers Association, said the Senate's rejection of the

SALT II treaty could increase Soviet-American tensions and might cause the Soviet Union to adopt a more aggressive foreign policy. At the time of the president's speech, the SALT II treaty was nearing completion, and evidence was mounting that opponents would try to prevent ratification. (PP 693)

May 9 SALT Treaty Completed Secretary of State Vance and Secretary of Defense Harold Brown announced that the United States and the Soviet Union had completed the SALT II treaty. (DSB 6/79 23)

June 8 MX Missile The White House announced that President Carter had approved the production of the MX missile, although he had not yet decided what type of basing mode would be used to house it. (DOD 188)

June 10 Carter Criticized for MX *Pravda* said President Carter's decision to approve the production of the MX missile was an effort to satisfy members of the military-industrial complex opposed to the SALT II treaty. (CDSP XXXI:23 16)

June 14 Vienna Summit President Carter arrived in Vienna to meet with General Secretary Brezhnev. The primary purpose of the meeting was to sign the SALT II agreement. (PP 1047)

June 18 Joint Communiqué President Carter and General Secretary Brezhnev issued a joint communiqué at the conclusion of their summit meeting in Vienna. The two leaders had discussed a number of international problems, including a comprehensive test ban treaty, nonproliferation of nuclear weapons, the MBFR talks, and chemical weapons. They agreed that neither side should strive for strategic nuclear superiority. (DSB 7/79 54)

June 22 Captive Nations Week President Carter designated the week of July 15 "Captive Nations Week." (PP 1141)

June 25 Gromyko Press Conference Foreign Minister Gromyko, at a news conference, reviewed events at the Vienna summit meeting. He said although the two sides signed the SALT II agreement, they disagreed on a number of issues, including the Camp David agreement, problems in Africa, and bilateral relations. The Soviet foreign minister said there was no possibility of renegotiating the SALT II treaty to satisfy its critics. (CDSP XXXI:26 1)

July 19 Nicaragua The government of Anastasio Somoza in Nicaragua was overthrown by the Sandinistas, who then organized a government similar to the one in Cuba. Although the Sandinistas had promised to establish a democratic government when they came to power, they in fact organized a government based on Marxist principles. The policies of the Marxist government in Nicaragua became a major source of tension in Soviet-American relations. (NYT 7/20/79 1)

August 31 Soviet Troops in Cuba The Department of State issued a statement confirming the presence of a Soviet combat unit in Cuba. There were between two thousand and three thousand Soviet troops in Cuba, but they had been there since 1962—a fact not mentioned in the official statement. (DSB 10/79 63)

September 7 Soviet Troops in Cuba President Carter, in remarks to reporters, confirmed the presence of a Soviet combat unit in Cuba and termed its presence unacceptable. The president did say the Soviet troops might have been in Cuba "for quite a few years." (PP 1602)

October 1 Carter on Troops in Cuba President Carter, in an address to the nation, declared that the presence of Soviet troops in Cuba was not going to lead to a war or to a major superpower confrontation. He said the United States would assist any nation threatened by Soviet or Cuban troops. (DSB 11/79 7)

October 3 Soviets and Carter's Speech Pravda accused President Carter of creating myths in his October 1 speech about the Soviet brigade in Cuba that would be used to justify interfering in the internal affairs of Caribbean countries. (CDSP XXXI:40 15)

October 6 Brezhnev and Arms Control General Secretary Brezhnev, in a speech in the German Democratic Republic, said the Soviet Union was not seeking military superiority vis-à-vis the West. He said the Soviets would be willing to consider reducing the number of SS-20 intermediate-range missiles provided the Western nations did not deploy similar weapons. Finally, he said the Soviet Union would reduce its troops in central Europe by twenty thousand within the next twelve months. (CDSP XXXI:40 2)

November 14 Peace Threatened Pravda accused the United States and the People's Republic of China of working together to implement policies that threatened the security of the Indochina states. The Soviets alleged that China and the United States were coordinating their policies. (CDSP XXXI:46 17)

November 16 Soviets Criticize Kissinger Izvestia criticized former secretary of state Kissinger for material contained in his memoirs, the White House Years. He was charged with distorting facts and promoting anticommunism as a means for making money. (CDSP XXXI:46 8)

November 24 Gromyko Warns FRG Soviet Foreign Minister Gromyko, at a news conference in Bonn, warned the West German government that there would be dangerous consequences if it cooperated with the United States in deploying intermediate-range missiles in Europe. (CDSP XXXI:47 1)

December 12 *Carter on Foreign Policy* President Carter, in remarks to members of the Business Council, said that, in real terms, Soviet defense spending had been going up for twenty years while that of the United States declined from 1968 to 1976. The president said the United States was now embarking on a program to meet the Soviet military challenge, and he listed specific policies such as building cruise missiles, producing the MX missile, and modernizing the strategic submarine force. (DSB 2/80 58)

December 12 *NATO Communiqué* NATO foreign and defense ministers issued a communiqué after a special meeting in Brussels. They expressed concern that Soviet superiority in theater nuclear weapons could undermine NATO's deterrent capabilities. To meet the Soviet challenge, the ministers decided to deploy 108 Pershing II launchers and 464 ground-launched cruise missiles. The ministers concluded that any reduction in the proposed new deployments should only be the result of an agreement with the Soviet Union to reduce its weapons. This dual-track decision became a contentious issue in Soviet-American relations. (DSB 2/80 16)

December 15 *Carter Criticized* *Pravda* said the policies advocated by President Carter in his December 12 remarks would only lead to an arms race. The president's attitude toward the Soviet Union was compared to that of former secretary of state Dulles. (CDSP XXXI:50 4)

December 16 *Soviets Refuse to Negotiate* *Pravda* said the decision of the NATO nations to deploy Pershing II and cruise missiles in Europe negated the possibility of negotiating additional arms control treaties. (CDSP XXXI:50 3)

December 25 *Soviets Invade Afghanistan* The Soviet Union began its invasion of Afghanistan. The State Department called on the international community to condemn the Soviet aggression. (DSB 2/80 65)

December 28 *Carter and Afghanistan* President Carter issued a statement condemning the Soviet Union for its "gross interference" in Afghanistan's internal affairs. He labeled the Soviet intervention a "blatant violation" of international standards. (DSB 2/80 56)

1980

January 1 *Afghan Statement* Tass, the Soviet news agency, issued a statement by the Afghan government claiming it requested military aid from the Soviet Union because imperialist forces were jeopardizing the gains of the Afghan revolution. (CDSP XXXII:1 1)

January 3 *SALT II* The White House announced that President Carter had asked Senate leaders to delay discussions on the ratification of the SALT II treaty because of the Soviet invasion of Afghanistan. (PP 12)

January 4 *Carter on Foreign Policy* President Carter, in an address to the nation, condemned the Soviet Union for its invasion of Afghanistan and the resulting threat to other nations in southwest Asia. The president listed a number of steps he planned to take in retaliation for the Soviet invasion. (PP 21)

January 7 *Agricultural Trade* President Carter directed Secretary of Commerce Philip M. Klutznik to terminate shipments of agricultural products to the Soviet Union, including wheat and corn. The embargo was the result of the Soviet invasion of Afghanistan. (PP 32)

January 8 *Carter and Afghanistan* President Carter, in comments to members of Congress, said the Soviet invasion of Afghanistan was the greatest threat to peace since World War II. (PP 40)

January 12 *Brezhnev Answers Questions* General Secretary Brezhnev, in answer to questions from a *Pravda* reporter, said American policies were responsible for the increase in international tensions. He accused the United States of establishing military bases in the Middle East and the Indian Ocean, supporting the deployment of Pershing II and cruise missiles in Europe, not ratifying the SALT II treaty, and arming rebels in Afghanistan seeking to overthrow the government. (CDSP XXXII:2 1)

January 13 *The UN and Iran* The Soviet Union vetoed a United Nations Security Council resolution calling for economic sanctions against Iran for taking American hostages in 1979. (DSB 3/80 61)

January 14 *The UN and Afghanistan* The United Nations General Assembly passed a resolution demanding that Soviet troops be withdrawn from Afghanistan. On January 15 Tass, the Soviet news agency, said the resolution was an effort to intervene in the internal affairs of Afghanistan. (NYT 1/15/80 1)

January 20 *Carter and the Olympics* President Carter, in a letter to Robert Kane, president of the U.S. Olympic Committee, suggested that the Olympics scheduled to take place in Moscow should, if Soviets troops remained in Afghanistan, be moved to another site or be cancelled. (DSB 3/80 50)

January 23 *Carter and Sakharov* The White House issued a statement denouncing the decision of the Soviet government on January 22 to send Andrei Sakharov and his wife into internal exile. The action was taken after Sakharov criticized the Soviet invasion of Afghanistan. The president said the United States would be happy to welcome Dr. Sakharov. (PP 194)

January 23 *Carter Doctrine* President Carter, in his State of the Union address, enunciated what came to be known as the Carter Doctrine. He said the United States would regard any effort by an outside power to gain control of the Persian Gulf region "as an assault on the vital interests of the United States, and such an assault will be repelled by any means necessary, including military force." The warning was directed at the Soviet Union. (PP 197)

January 29 *Soviets Criticize Carter* An article in *Pravda* criticized President Carter's State of the Union address, accusing him of pursuing policies "permeated with a cold war spirit." The article charged the president with attempting to upset the balance of power between the superpowers by supporting policies to strengthen America's military capabilities. (CDSP XXXII:4 1)

February 4 *Brezhnev on Foreign Policy* General Secretary Brezhnev, in a speech at the Kremlin, said he favored a policy of détente and wanted to build on the advances brought about by détente in the 1970s. He said he favored arms control agreements and the settlement of conflicts in the Middle East and Southeast Asia. (CDSP XXXII:5 19)

February 13 *Carter on Foreign Policy* President Carter, in response to a question at a news conference, said the Soviet invasion of Afghanistan created a dangerous situation because the country was located in an area vital to the transportation of oil. The president was confident that America's military capabilities were sufficient to deal with any Soviet military threat. (PP 308)

February 14 *Tass Criticizes Carter* Tass, the Soviet news agency, said that President Carter, at his February 13 news conference, had slandered the Soviet Union and Afghanistan. The United States was accused of engaging in an arms race to achieve military superiority over the Soviet Union. (CDSP XXXII:7 17)

February 19 *Carter on Foreign Policy* President Carter, in an address to the American Legion, reviewed steps he had taken to improve America's military might. He called for an increase in defense spending, accelerated development of cruise missiles, the building of the MX missile, the building of the Trident submarine, and the strengthening of NATO. Some of these policies were in response to the Soviet invasion of Afghanistan. (PP 344)

February 23 *Brezhnev and Afghanistan* General Secretary Brezhnev, in a speech in Moscow, said the Soviet Union would withdraw all its forces from Afghanistan once it was no longer endangered by outside forces. He accused the United States of using the Afghan crisis to develop a string of military bases around the world to further America's hegemonic ambitions. (CDSP XXXII:8 1)

February 23 *Brezhnev and Soviet Policy* General Secretary Brezhnev, in a report to the Twenty-sixth Congress of the Communist party of the Soviet Union, proposed a long list of measures to help reduce international tensions. He recommended a series of arms control proposals, and he called on all nuclear powers to pledge not to be the first to use nuclear weapons. He favored establishing more nuclear-free zones, negotiating additional confidence-building measures, and initiating a moratorium on deploying INF weapons in Europe. Brezhnev expressed the belief that a balance of power existed between the WTO and NATO. (DOD 64)

February 26 *Carter on Foreign Policy* President Carter, in response to a question at a news conference, said the United States was prepared to help Turkey, Iran, and Pakistan if they were attacked by the Soviet Union. (PP 390)

March 5 *Carter and Schmidt* President Carter and Chancellor Helmut Schmidt of the Federal Republic of Germany, at the conclusion of their meeting in Washington, issued a joint statement condemning the Soviet Union for its invasion of Afghanistan. They agreed that participation in the Moscow summer Olympics would be unacceptable while Soviet forces were in Afghanistan. (PP 438)

March 18 *Soviets Criticize Carter* *Pravda* criticized President Carter for his efforts to either cancel or have the Olympics moved outside the Soviet Union. (CDSP XXXII:11 7)

March 28 *Carter and the Olympics* President Carter announced that, because of the Soviet invasion of Afghanistan, the United States would not participate in the 1980 summer Olympic games in Moscow. (PP 559)

April 10 *Carter on Foreign Policy* President Carter, in an address to the American Society of Newspaper Editors, said the Soviet invasion of Afghanistan demonstrated the unwillingness of the Soviet Union to be influenced by international law, world public opinion, or accepted standards of international behavior. (PP 634)

April 13 *Carter and Afghanistan* President Carter, in response to a question at a news conference, said he decided to react to the Soviet invasion of Afghanistan in economic and political terms because those actions, as well as those of other nations, would eventually result in a Soviet withdrawal from Afghanistan. (PP 672)

April 28 *Vance Resigns* President Carter accepted the resignation of Secretary of State Vance. He resigned, in part, because he opposed the president's decision to try and rescue the hostages being held in Iran. Vance was succeeded by Senator Edmund Muskie. (PP 781)

May 9 *Carter on Foreign Policy* President Carter, in a speech at the Philadelphia World Affairs Council, declared that the United States had several foreign policy objectives. One was to enhance the economic and political unity of the industrialized democracies. Second was to develop better relations with Third World countries. And third was to pursue arms control agreements with the Soviet Union while maintaining a balance of power. In his speech, he vowed to protect America's strategic interests in the Middle East and southwest Asia. (PP 867)

May 10 *Soviets Criticize Carter* Tass, the Soviet news agency, criticized President Carter for his May 9 speech. He was accused of pursuing hegemonic policies throughout the world and of carrying out an undeclared war against the people of Afghanistan. (CDSP XXXII:19 18)

May 14 *Defense Planning Committee* The ministers of the Defense Planning Committee of NATO issued a communiqué after meeting for two days in Brussels. They criticized the Soviet Union for its invasion of Afghanistan, and they agreed on a number of measures to strengthen NATO's military capabilities. The ministers again supported the 1979 dual-track decision for deploying Pershing II and cruise missiles in Europe to offset the Soviet deployment of SS-20s. (DSB 7/80 13)

May 19 *Captive Nations Week* President Carter designated the week of July 13 "Captive Nations Week." (PP 940)

June 1 *Anti-Soviet Triangle* *Pravda* warned Japan, the People's Republic of China, and the United States against organizing a triangular relationship directed at the Soviet Union. The three nations were accused of embarking on a "path of anti-Soviet confrontation." (CDSP XXXII:22 14)

June 5   Vance at Harvard   Former secretary of state Vance, in a speech at Harvard University, called for the ratification of the SALT II treaty despite the Soviet invasion of Afghanistan. He emphasized the need for the United States to deal with Third World problems, particularly political and economic problems. He disagreed with President Carter's refusal to recognize the communist-dominated government in Angola. (NYT 6/6/80 12)

June 12   Carter on Détente   President Carter, in response to a question asked by a Yugoslav reporter, said that despite the Soviet invasion of Afghanistan, he continued to support a policy of détente with the Soviet Union. (PP 1205)

June 26   North Atlantic Council   The ministers attending the North Atlantic Council meeting in Ankara issued a communiqué at the conclusion of their meeting. They condemned the Soviet Union for its invasion of Afghanistan and claimed the Soviets were seeking to obtain a preponderance of power vis-à-vis the West. The ministers also rejected the Soviet proposal to discuss intermediate-range nuclear weapons only if the NATO nations rescinded their decision to deploy Pershing II and cruise missiles. (DSB 8/80 37)

July 19   Republicans Attacked   An article in *Pravda* attacked the Republican party presidential platform, particularly those provisions calling for strengthening America's military capabilities. The article also attacked Ronald Reagan, the Republican presidential candidate. (CDSP XXXII:29 1)

July 29   Carter and Helsinki   President Carter, in remarks made at the White House to human rights groups, accused the Soviet Union of dishonoring the principles embodied in the 1975 Helsinki Final Act. He criticized the Soviets for their invasion of Afghanistan, the treatment of dissidents, and the refusal to permit Jews to emigrate. (PP 1434)

August 5   Presidential Directive 59   The *New York Times* reported that President Carter had signed Presidential Directive 59 (PD-59). The directive selected targets to be hit in the Soviet Union in case of a nuclear war and, in effect, gave the president more targeting options than he had in the past. On October 7 an article in *Pravda* criticized President Carter for approving PD-59. The Soviets claimed the doctrine was misguided in the belief that a limited nuclear war could be fought. The Soviets maintained that the best way to protect the peace was a return to the détente of the 1970s. (NYT 8/6/80 1)

August 22   Bases in Somalia   The United States signed an agreement allowing it to use air and naval facilities in Somalia. On August 31 Tass, the

Soviet news agency, criticized Somalia for allowing the United States to have access to a military base in Berbera. (NYT 8/22/80 10)

August 29   Brezhnev and the U.S.   General Secretary Brezhnev, in a speech in Kazakhstan, criticized PD-59 and American foreign policy in general. He accused the United States of being unwilling to accept that the balance of power in the world was shifting in favor of the socialist and progressive states. He said President Carter's policies were bringing back the cold war and abandoning détente. (CDSP XXXII:35 1)

September 2   Carter and SALT   President Carter, at a question-and-answer session in Missouri, said he would encourage the United States Senate to ratify the SALT II treaty when the Soviets began to remove their troops from Afghanistan. (PP 1620)

September 18   Carter and Nuclear War   President Carter, in response to a question at a news conference, said, if necessary, the United States would use nuclear weapons against the Soviet Union to defend the United States and its allies. (PP 1830)

September 20   Warning on Poland   *Pravda* warned the United States not to interfere in Poland's internal affairs. At the time there was considerable unrest in Poland because of dissatisfaction with government policies. (CDSP XXXII:38 4)

October 19   Pravda on Carter and Reagan   An article in *Pravda* said there was not much difference between the two presidential candidates, Jimmy Carter and Ronald Reagan. Both candidates were charged with seeking to make America militarily superior to the Soviet Union. (CDSP XXXII:42 21)

November 4   The Presidential Election   Ronald Reagan, a Republican, defeated the incumbent, Democrat Jimmy Carter, in the presidential election. (NYT 11/5/80 1)

November 23   Madrid Conference   *Pravda* accused the United States of waging a psychological war against the Soviet Union at the Madrid CSCE meeting that convened on November 11. (CDSP XXXII:47 19)

December 9   NATO and Poland   Secretary of State Muskie flew to Brussels to win the agreement of NATO allies on punitive economic measures to take if the Soviet Union invaded Poland. (NYT 12/10/80 1)

December 12   North Atlantic Council   The ministers attending the North Atlantic Council meeting in Brussels issued a communiqué. They criticized the Soviet Union for its intervention in Afghanistan, for making threatening gestures toward Poland, and for continuing a military buildup. (DSB 2/81 50)

December 18 *Soviets and Poland* *Pravda* said the Soviet Union had every right to intervene in Poland if the Polish government requested Soviet assistance. The Soviets were reacting to the NATO ministers who had warned the Soviet Union not to intervene. (CDSP XXXII:51 1)

December 19 *Madrid CSCE Conference* The Conference on Security and Cooperation in Europe that was meeting in Madrid recessed. During the first phase of the meeting, sharp differences developed between the United States and the Soviet Union regarding human rights and events in Poland. (NYT 12/20/80 23)

December 24 *Carter and Afghanistan* President Carter issued a statement on the first anniversary of the Soviet invasion of Afghanistan, accusing the Soviets of employing "brutal" military tactics against the Afghan population. As a result, many people fled the country, creating serious refugee problems in neighboring lands. (WCPD 2835)

1981

January 16 *State of the Union* President Carter, in his last State of the Union address, said the Soviet Union now realized it would pay a price for its aggression in Afghanistan. He said Soviet policies in Afghanistan violated international law and the United Nations Charter. (WCPD 2932)

January 19 *Watson on Foreign Policy* Thomas Watson, the American ambassador to the Soviet Union, was interviewed by *U.S. News & World Report*. He said the world was never more dangerous than it was then. He attributed the deterioration in Soviet-American relations to the Soviet intervention in Afghanistan. (DOD 36)

January 28 *Haig on Arms Control* Secretary of State Alexander Haig, in response to a question at a news conference, said the Reagan administration planned to link arms control agreements to Soviet political behavior. Haig had been sworn in as secretary of state on January 22. (DSB 2/81 H)

January 29 *Reagan on Foreign Policy* President Reagan, in response to a question at a news conference, said the Soviets believed they had the "right to commit any crime, to lie, to cheat" to achieve their foreign policy objectives. (PP 57)

February 11 *Madrid Conference* Max Kampelman, the American ambassador to the Madrid CSCE talks, said the Soviet Union has never notified the CSCE members when conducting small-scale military maneuvers, and the Soviets often carried out large maneuvers without proper notification. The United States wanted the representatives at the Madrid conference to strengthen the confidence-building and verification measures agreed to at the 1975 CSCE meeting in Helsinki. (DOD 53)

February 23 *El Salvador White Paper* The State Department issued a white paper entitled "Communist Interference in El Salvador." The Reagan administration alleged that Cuba and the Soviet Union were shipping military supplies to the insurgents in El Salvador via Nicaragua. (DSB 3/81 1)

March 26 *Reagan and Poland* The White House issued a statement expressing President Reagan's concern about possible Soviet military intervention in Poland. The statement said that Poland should be allowed to resolve its problems free of external interference. (PP 293)

April 8 *Nuclear Planning Group* The NATO Nuclear Planning Group, after meeting in Bonn for two days, issued a statement. The ministers took note of increased Soviet troop activity near the Polish border and pointed out that the use of force or the threat to use force violated the 1975 Helsinki Final Act. (DOD 151)

May 5 *North Atlantic Council* The ministers attending the North Atlantic Council meeting in Rome issued a communiqué at the close of their two-day meeting. They criticized the Soviet Union for its intervention in Afghanistan and for undermining the principles of the 1975 Helsinki Final act. The Soviets were warned that any military intervention in Poland would inflame international tensions. (DSB 7/81 39)

May 25 *Brezhnev to Reagan* President Brezhnev, in response to a letter from President Reagan, blamed the United States for the deterioration in Soviet-American relations, but he expressed an interest in meeting with the president to try to resolve some of the outstanding differences between the two countries. (DOD 206)

May 29 *Troop Withdrawals from Europe* Secretary of State Haig, in response to a question at a news conference, said the United States would oppose any plan calling for a total withdrawal of American and Soviet troops from Europe. He said such a plan would upset the balance of power in Europe in favor of the Soviet Union. (DOD 209)

June 16 *Haig in China* Secretary of State Haig announced at a news conference in China that Sino-American perceptions concerning the Soviet threat to international peace were very similar. Among other things, both countries wanted foreign troops removed from Afghanistan and Kampuchea (the former Cambodia). Haig informed the Chinese leaders that President Reagan would request that Congress amend legislation that linked China with the Soviet bloc. He also announced that China would send a military delegation to the United States to confer with the Joint Chiefs of Staff. (DSB 8/81 35)

June 19 *Haig Criticized* *Pravda* criticized Secretary of State Haig for allegedly forging military links with China during his recently concluded visit there. The article charged Beijing with supporting the American desire to gain military superiority over the Soviet Union. (CDSP XXXIII:25 1)

June 30 *Captive Nations Week* President Reagan designated the week of July 19 "Captive Nations Week." (PP 586)

July 9 *Haig on the Soviet System* Secretary of State Haig, in response to a question at an interview for the *Wall Street Journal,* said the Soviet system was suffering from some systemic failures that could grow worse in the future. He said the Soviets should spend less money for military purposes and more for solving the systemic problems. (DSB 9/81 25)

August 13 *The Neutron Bomb* President Reagan, in response to a question during a bill-signing ceremony, said the United States would store neutron weapons but would not deploy them in Europe. He defended his decision by pointing out that the neutron bomb was a defensive weapon. The Soviets criticized the president for his decision. (PP 708)

August (no date) *Reagan Criticized* An article in the Soviet publication *New Times* criticized President Reagan for his decision to produce the neutron bomb. The article pointed out that the president made his announcement at a time when people were remembering the conse-quences of the bombing of Japan in August 1945. (NT 8/81 5)

September 13 *Haig on Chemical Weapons* Secretary of State Haig, in a speech in West Berlin, said the United States had proof the Soviet Union was using "lethal chemical agents" in Afghanistan. (DOD 419)

September 17 *Haig Criticized* *Pravda* said that Secretary of State Haig's accusation that the Soviet Union had used chemical weapons in Laos, Kampuchea, and Afghanistan was a "foul-smelling dish of outrageous anti-Soviet canards." (CDSP XXXIII:37 12)

September 22 *Reagan to Brezhnev* President Reagan sent a letter to General Secretary Brezhnev stating that the United States wanted to have a constructive, stable relationship with the Soviet Union. The president again suggested that the two sides try to reach agreements on arms control, trade, and cultural exchange programs. According to Reagan, Soviet-American relations had deteriorated because of Soviet involvement in various regional disputes and Moscow's determination to increase its military capabilities. (DSB 11/81 51)

October 16 *Reagan on Nuclear Policy* President Reagan, at a question-and-answer session at the White House, said that the Soviet SS-20s were aimed at all of Europe, including the United Kingdom. According to the president, the deployment of Pershing II and cruise missiles was designed to meet the challenge presented by the SS-20s. The president created a controversy when he stated that tactical nuclear weapons could perhaps be used in Europe without igniting an all-out war. (PP 957)

October 20 *Nuclear War* General Secretary Brezhnev, in answer to a question by a *Pravda* reporter, said President Reagan was wrong when he said the Soviet Union expected to win a nuclear war. Brezhnev said no one could win a nuclear war, and he called on the United States to pledge not to be the first to use nuclear weapons. (CDSP XXVIII:42 13)

October 30 *Soviet Treaty Violations* Max Kampelman, the United States ambassador at the CSCE Madrid conference, said the Soviet Union had violated the Helsinki Final Act by imprisoning individuals monitoring the act, giving inadequate information about military maneuvers, and using WTO troops to intimidate Poland. (DOD 518)

November 12 *Nulear War* *Pravda* accused President Reagan of "actively preparing" for a nuclear war. He was criticized for refusing to pledge not to be the first to use nuclear weapons. (CDSP XXXIII:45 18)

November 18 *Reagan and Foreign Policy* President Reagan, in an address to the National Press Club, proposed a "zero option" plan whereby the United States would not deploy Pershing II and cruise missiles in Europe if the Soviet Union would dismantle its SS-20 missiles. (DSB 12/81 10)

November 19 *Nuclear Weapons* *Pravda* was critical of President Reagan's November 18 speech in which he advocated dismantling of the Soviet SS-20s. Reagan was accused of engaging in propaganda. (CDSP XXXIII:46 25)

November 22 *Brezhnev and Reagan* General Secretary Brezhnev, in a letter to President Reagan, accused the United States of pursuing policies that contributed to international tensions, but the Soviet leader said he wanted to begin negotiations to resolve Soviet-American differences. (CDSP XXXIII:47 9)

November 23 *Brezhnev and Nuclear Forces* President Brezhnev, in an address in the Federal Republic of Germany, said the American decision to deploy medium-range missiles in Europe was a very dangerous one. He said the Soviet Union would never accept President Reagan's "zero option" for eliminating all intermediate-range missiles in Europe. (DOD 617)

November 30 *INF Negotiations* The United States and the Soviet Union opened formal negotiations in Geneva on intermediate-range nuclear forces (INF). (DSB 1/82 30)

December 11 *North Atlantic Council* The ministers attending a meeting of the North Atlantic Council in Brussels issued a communiqué. They accused the Soviet Union of pursuing polices around the world that destabilized the peace and increased international tensions. The ministers reaffirmed their support for the 1979 dual-track decision and the strengthening of NATO's military capabilities to check the aggressive policies of the Soviet Union. (DOD 704)

December 13 *North Atlantic Council* *Izvestia* criticized the North Atlantic Council that met in Brussels for continuing to support the decision to deploy Pershing II and cruise missiles. (CDSP XXXIII:50 16)

December 13 *Martial Law in Poland* The Polish government declared martial law and suppressed the activities of Solidarity, the Polish labor union. (DSB 2/82 85)

December 17 *Reagan on Poland* President Reagan, in a statement at a news conference, said the denial of human rights in Poland and the government's reliance on coercive power could not have taken place without the support of the Soviet Union. (PP 1161)

December 22 *Brezhnev and Reagan* General Secretary Brezhnev, in response to a question during a television interview on NBC, said he would be willing to have a summit meeting with President Reagan. The Soviet leader said there had been an increase in the likelihood of war, and he recommended a number of steps to be taken that would help improve Soviet-American relations. (CDSP XXXIII:51 20)

December 23 *Reagan and Martial Law* President Reagan announced he was imposing sanctions on Poland as a result of the government's decision to impose martial law. A week later he also ordered sanctions imposed on the Soviet Union. The president blamed the Soviets for the imposition of martial law in Poland. (DSB 2/82 1)

December 25 *Poland* *Pravda* accused the United States of carrying out subversive activities in Poland to remove it from the communist bloc. (CDSP XXXIII:52 1)

1982

January 10 *Reagan and Poland* *Pravda* criticized President Reagan for imposing sanctions on Poland and accused him of wanting to overthrow Poland's socialist political system. (CDSP XXXIV:2 12)

January 20 *Solidarity Day* President Reagan designated January 30 "Solidarity Day" in the United States. The president criticized the Polish government for imposing martial law, and he accused the authorities of suppressing human rights in Poland. (PP 44)

January 26 *State of the Union* President Reagan, in his State of the Union address, defended the sanctions the United States imposed on Poland and the Soviet Union because of the imposition of martial law in Poland. He said American policy must be rooted in realism, citing as an example the need to know the aims of the Soviet empire. (PP 77)

February 1 *Haig on Linkage* Secretary of State Haig, in response to a question during an interview, said America's negotiations with the Soviet Union on arms control issues would be linked to the situation in Poland, among other things. The Reagan administration thought linkage would help moderate Soviet policies. Former president Carter had opposed the policy of linkage. (DSB 3/82 29)

February 3 *Brezhnev Rejects Reagan Proposal* General Secretary Brezhnev, in a report to an advisory council on disarmament, rejected President Reagan's proposal for eliminating intermediate-range missiles in Europe. Brezhnev again advocated a nuclear freeze. (DOD 21)

February 3 *Germ Warfare* An article in *Literaturnaya Gazeta* accused the United States of using chemical weapons in Cuba against agricultural crops, livestock, and humans. (CDSP XXXIV:5 11)

February 16 *Soviet Treaty Violations* Max Kampelman, the American ambassador to the Madrid CSCE conference, accused the Soviet Union of violating the Geneva Convention of 1925 and the 1972 Biological Weapons Convention because the Soviets had allegedly used chemical weapons in Laos, Kampuchea, and Afghanistan. On February 20 Tass, the Soviet news agency, issued a statement rejecting Kampelman's allegations. (DOD 56)

March 2 *Haig on Soviet Foreign Policy* Secretary of State Haig, in a statement before the House Foreign Affairs Committee, said it would be difficult to improve Soviet-American relations because of Soviet policies in Afghanistan, Cuba, and Poland. (DSB 4/82 33)

March 10 *Afghanistan Day* President Reagan signed a proclamation designating March 21 "Afghanistan Day." The president said he was determined to make the Soviet invasion of Afghanistan a major issue in Soviet-American relations. (PP 272)

March 16 *Brezhnev on Nuclear Arms* General Secretary Brezhnev, in a speech in Moscow, said the Soviet Union would unilaterally introduce a moratorium on the deployment of medium-range missiles west of the Ural Mountains. He said the moratorium would remain in effect unless the NATO nations went ahead with their plans for deploying Pershing II and cruise missiles. (CDSP XXXIV:11 1)

March 16 *Missile Deployment* The White House issued a statement rejecting the Soviet-proposed moratorium on deploying medium-range missiles west of the Ural Mountains. The moratorium would permit the Soviet Union to continue deploying SS-20 missiles east of the Ural Mountains, and the NATO nations would be threatened by the SS-20s already deployed west of the mountains. (PP 307)

March 22 *Chemical Warfare* Secretary of State Haig submitted a thirty-two page report to Congress linking the Soviet Union to the use of chemical weapons in Afghanistan, Laos, and Kampuchea. The report alleged that more than ten thousand people had died as a result of those weapons. (DSB 5/82 57)

March 26 *NATO* *Pravda* criticized the NATO nations for supporting the deployment of Pershing II and cruise missiles in Europe and for responding negatively to General Secretary Brezhnev's proposal for a moratorium on missile deployment. The Soviets were attempting to drive a wedge between the United States and its NATO allies on the missile issue. (CDSP XXXIV:12 18)

March 28 *A Nuclear Freeze* Secretary of State Haig, in response to a question during an interview, said the nuclear-freeze proposal put forward by General Secretary Brezhnev was unacceptable to the United States because a freeze would benefit only the Soviet Union. (DSB 5/82 35)

March 31 *Arms Control* President Reagan, in response to a question at a news conference, said the United States would be ready to begin negotiations with the Soviet Union for strategic arms reduction talks sometime during the summer. The president, however, rejected the idea of a nuclear freeze. He supported a resolution submitted to the House and the Senate calling for major verifiable force reductions to equal levels. (PP 405)

April 2 *Arms Control* *Pravda* accused President Reagan of not supporting efforts to achieve arms control agreements. The criticism was a response to his comments at the March 31 news conference. (CDSP XXXIV:13 8)

April 5 *Nuclear Capabilities* President Reagan, at a question-and-answer session with reporters, said the Soviet Union enjoyed a nuclear superiority over the United States. He cited the Soviet SS-20s as an example because at the time the NATO nations had nothing similar to those weapons. The president indicated he would be happy to meet with General Secretary Brezhnev if he came to New York to address the United Nations. (PP 429)

April 5 *Chemical Warfare* The Soviet Union, in a note to the United States, protested the American accusation, made on numerous occasions, that the Soviet Union was responsible for the use of chemical weapons in Kampuchea, Laos, and Afghanistan. The Soviets denied the accusation and said the United States was conducting a "slanderous campaign" against the Soviet Union. (CDSP XXXIV:14 18)

April 6 *Haig on Foreign Policy* Secretary of State Haig, in a speech at Georgetown University, said the Soviet Union had been building its military might, in part to undermine the credibility of Western deterrent capabilities. He said President Reagan's military buildup was designed to strengthen Western deterrent capabilities, to correct imbalances that had developed, and to support Western military strategies. The secretary supported President Reagan's refusal to make a "no first strike" pledge. He said the NATO nations could not rely exclusively on conventional military capabilities to deter a Soviet attack. (DSB 5/82 32)

April 17 *Nuclear Weapons* President Reagan, in a radio address to the nation, said the United States had to increase its military capabilities to balance the power of the Soviet Union. He again rejected the idea of a nuclear freeze because the Soviets would then retain a military advantage over the United States and its NATO allies. (PP 487)

April 17 *Brezhnev and Reagan* General Secretary Brezhnev, in remarks to a *Pravda* reporter, said he would be willing to meet President Reagan in a third country sometime in October for a summit meeting. President Reagan had suggested a meeting in New York in June while the United Nations General Assembly was in session. (CDSP XXXIV:16 6)

April 27 *Haig on Foreign Policy* Secretary of State Haig, in a speech to the U.S. Chamber of Congress, emphasized the need for a balanced foreign policy toward the Soviet Union, that is, a balance between strength and a willingness to negotiate. The secretary pointed out that Moscow's policies in Afghanistan and Kampuchea angered many of the non-aligned nations and that a backlash was developing in response to Soviet military growth. Economic conditions in the Soviet bloc were not good, said the secretary, and the Soviet people may begin to demand a better life. (DSB 6/82 40)

May 1 *Arms Control* General Secretary Brezhnev wrote to the co-chairmen of the International Physicians for the Prevention of Nuclear War, saying that he favored "radical" arms control agreements including nuclear-free zones and the elimination of medium-range and tactical nuclear weapons in Europe. (CDSP XXXIV:18 14)

May 9 *START Talks* President Reagan, in a speech at Eureka College, announced that he had written to General Secretary Brezhnev suggesting that the two superpowers begin the START negotiations. He called for a one-third reduction in total warheads, and he wanted no more than half to be deployed on ICBMs. The president also wanted to dismantle ICBMs with multiple warheads. (PP 585)

May 11 *Reagan Criticized* *Pravda* was critical of President Reagan's May 9 speech. He was accused of opposing arms control agreements and of seeking military superiority over the Soviet Union. The Soviets rejected the president's proposal to dismantle large land-based missiles with multiple warheads. (CDSP XXXIV:19 7)

May 13 *Nuclear First Use* President Reagan, in response to a question at a news conference, rejected the idea of making a "no first strike" pledge. He also said he would like to reduce the large land-based strategic nuclear missiles in the Soviet arsenal because they were the most destabilizing weapons. (PP 619)

May 13 *Chemical Weapons* The State Department released a report documenting the recent alleged use of chemical weapons by the Soviet Union and its allies in Laos and Kampuchea. (DSB 7/82 93)

May 27 *Soviet Foreign Policy* President Reagan, in response to a question during an interview, said changing its aggressive foreign policies would help the Soviet Union cope with its economic problems. He also expressed the view that Soviet willingness to engage in arms control negotiations was the result of America's growing military might. (PP 696)

June 8 *Crusade for Freedom* President Reagan, in an address to the British Parliament, pointed out that since coming to power nearly thirty years ago, none of the communist regimes in Eastern Europe had permitted free elections. He wanted the Western nations to do more to promote democratic ideals and to build democratic infrastructures. He advocated a "crusade for freedom" and said the Russian people were not immune to the demands for greater freedom. (PP 742)

June 10 *Soviets Criticize Reagan* *Pravda* criticized President Reagan for his June 8 speech, charging that he wanted to launch an anticommunist crusade that could result in a "catastrophe." (CDSP XXXIV:23 7)

June 12 *Brezhnev and Arms Control* General Secretary Brezhnev, in a message to the United Nations session dealing with questions of disarmament, pledged that the Soviet Union would never be the first to use nuclear weapons. He expressed support for the nuclear-freeze movement and said he favored a treaty to abolish chemical weapons. (DOD 349)

June 14 *Baltic Freedom Day* President Reagan designated June 14 "Baltic Freedom Day." The president's proclamation called on the American people to "reaffirm their belief and hope" that the Baltic nations would achieve their independence. (PP 798)

June 17 *Reagan and Disarmament* President Reagan, in an address to the United Nations General Assembly, accused the Soviet Union of engaging in a massive military buildup during the decade of détente, manipulating the peace movement in the West, and preventing the development of a peace movement within the Soviet Union. He said the United States wanted the Soviets to demonstrate by deeds their commitment to arms control and the reduction of international tensions. He advocated a staged reduction in strategic weapons and a common ceiling of 900,000 troops for the NATO and the WTO nations. (PP 784)

June 18 *Soviets Criticize Reagan* Tass, in an analysis of President Reagan's June 17 speech, accused him of seeking to undermine détente and pursing policies that increased international tensions. (CDSP XXXIV:25 20)

June 25 *Shultz Appointed Secretary of State* President Reagan announced that he had accepted the resignation of Alexander Haig as secretary of state. He was succeeded by George Shultz. (PP 819)

July 1 *Reagan on Arms Control* President Reagan, at a question-and-answer session with editors and broadcasters, said the Soviet Union agreed to the INF negotiations in November 1981 only because the

United States intended to deploy Pershing II and cruise missiles to match the Soviets' SS-20s. (PP 837)

July 19   *Captive Nations Week*   President Reagan designated the week of July 18 "Captive Nations Week." (WCPD 920)

July 19   *Reagan and the Captive Nations*   President Reagan, in signing the annual "Captive Nations Week" proclamation, said the extension of communist power had not meant a better life for the people but "forced labor and mass imprisonment, famine and massacre, the police state and the knock at the door at night." (PP 936)

July 22   *Reagan Criticized*   *Pravda* criticized President Reagan for his July 19 comments on "captive nations." The article said his statement was "unprecedented in its crudeness and cynicism." (CDSP XXXIV:29 10)

August 3   *Reagan Criticized*   *Pravda* criticized President Reagan for launching what was described as a crusade to roll back communism. In several recent speeches, the president had criticized communism and praised the virtues of democracy. (CDSP XXXIV:31 16)

September 21   *Helsinki Accords and the Ukrainians*   President Reagan proclaimed November 9 as a day to honor the establishment of the "Ukrainian Public Group to Promote the Implementation of the Helsinki Accords." The group was organized in 1976 to monitor the 1975 Helsinki Final Act. (PP 1191)

September 22   *Forced Labor*   The State Department issued a statement alleging there were reports the Soviet Union was using an estimated four million political prisoners as forced laborers. (DSB 11/82 41)

October 8   *Solidarity Outlawed*   The Polish government outlawed Solidarity, the Polish labor union led by Lech Walesa. President Reagan, in a radio address to the nation the following day, denounced the decision of the Polish government to outlaw Solidarity. The president said he would seek to revoke Poland's most-favored-nation status, and he threatened other actions as well. (PP 1290)

November 8   *Shultz and the Soviet Union*   Secretary of State Shultz, in response to a question during an interview, said that "it is by now very apparent that the Communist type of command economy simply doesn't work very well." Shultz suggested that the command economies be compared with those operating under free-market conditions. (DSB 12/82 19)

November 10   *Death of Brezhnev*   General Secretary Leonid Brezhnev died and was succeeded by Yuri Andropov. (DSB 1/83 58)

November 22 *Arms Control* President Reagan, in a speech to the nation, announced that he had sent a letter to the Soviet government proposing that each side give advance notification of intercontinental ballistic missile launches and major military exercises. The president expressed support for a greater exchange of information on nuclear forces and a possible improvement in the hot line. (DSB 12/82 1)

November 29 *Chemical Warfare* Secretary of State Shultz updated the March report to Congress on the Soviet use of chemical weapons in Afghanistan, Kampuchea, and Laos. The new report contained additional evidence in support of the allegation. (DSB 12/82 44)

December 10 *Prayer for Poland* President Reagan designated December 12 "A Day of Prayer for Poland, Solidarity, and the Polish People." (DSB 2/83 41)

1983

January 1 _The Soviets Warn U.S._ Tass, the Soviet news agency, issued a statement warning the United States and its allies not to tie relations with the Soviet Union to the situation in Afghanistan because such linkage would endanger détente. (CDSP XXXV:1 5)

January 5 _WTO Communiqué_ At the close of a two-day meeting in Prague, the ministers of the WTO nations issued a communiqué accusing the United States of engaging in an arms race to achieve military superiority over the Soviet Union and criticizing the decision to deploy INF weapons in Europe. The ministers called for a new round of arms control talks to help reduce international tensions, and they also recommended that the NATO and WTO nations sign a treaty renouncing the use of military force. (CDSP XXXV:1 6)

January 8 _Reagan and Soviet Union_ President Reagan, in a radio address to the American people, said he hoped the new leadership in the Soviet Union would seek to improve relations with the United States. The president said relations between the superpowers could improve if the Soviets changed their policies toward Poland, Afghanistan, and the Middle East and moderated their arms buildup. General Secretary Andropov gave no indication that his foreign policies would be substantially different from those of previous Soviet leaders. (PP 23)

January 25 _State of the Union_ President Reagan, in his State of the Union address, said the United States had strengthened its military capabilities and was also taking many diplomatic initiatives to resolve outstanding problems. He said he hoped the new Soviet leadership would demonstrate by deeds its willingness to seek solutions to common problems. General Secretary Andropov was just as critical of President Reagan's policies as was General Secretary Brezhnev. During Andropov's term in office, relations between the United States and the Soviet Union remained strained. (PP 108)

January 26 _Tass Criticizes Reagan_ Tass, the Soviet news agency, issued a statement criticizing President Reagan's January 25 State of the Union address. He was taken to task for his emphasis on rebuilding America's military might and for allegedly misrepresenting Soviet foreign policies. (CDSP XXXV:4 22)

January 31 _Reagan and Andropov_ Vice President Bush, while visiting West Berlin, read a letter from President Reagan to the people of Europe in which he proposed to meet with General Secretary Andropov to sign a treaty eliminating all INF weapons in Europe. (DOD 40)

February 1 *Andropov and Nuclear Weapons* General Secretary Andropov, in an interview with a *Pravda* reporter, said the Soviet Union would never accept President Reagan's "zero option" for eliminating INF weapons in Europe. Andropov said he was in favor of having a summit meeting with President Reagan but only if there were no preconditions for such a meeting. (CDSP XXXV:5 6)

February 2 *Reagan Meets Afghans* President Reagan met with six Afghan leaders at the White House to demonstrate American support for the Afghan resistance movement. The Soviets disapproved of President Reagan's support for the resistance movement. (DSB 3/83 87)

February 4 *Soviets and Use of Chemical Weapons* The Soviet Union, in a note to Secretary General Javier Perez de Cuellar of the United Nations, criticized the report by the United States accusing the Soviets of using chemical weapons in Southeast Asia and Afghanistan. (DOD 79)

February 14 *Forced Labor* The State Department sent to Congress a new report on forced labor in the Soviet Union that accused the Soviets of using forced labor as punishment for crimes and to build the economy. (DSB 4/83 92)

February 16 *Lithuanian Independence Day* President Reagan designated February 16 "Lithuanian Independence Day." He accused the Soviet Union of denying the Lithuanian people the right of self-determination. He said Lithuanians deserved to be free and independent. (PP 237)

February 18 *Reagan on Foreign Policy* President Reagan, in a speech to the Conservative Political Action Conference, said that one of his foreign policy goals was to publicize unsavory aspects of Soviet policy. He mentioned the use of forced labor for the building of the Soviet gas pipeline, the use of chemical warfare in Kampuchea, and repressive Soviet policies in Poland. (PP 249)

February 22 *Reagan on Foreign Policy* President Reagan, in an address to the annual convention of the American Legion, said a major Soviet foreign policy objective was to drive a wedge between the United States and its European allies by using the Soviet nuclear arsenal to spread a sense of insecurity among the NATO nations. (PP 264)

February 23 *Reagan on Arms Control* President Reagan, at a question-and-answer session at the White House, said that while the Soviets allegedly wanted to engage in arms control negotiations, they continued their military buildup. He again criticized the SALT II treaty for legitimizing the increase in Soviet military capabilities. (PP 281)

March 8 *Evil Empire* President Reagan, in a speech to the National Association of Evangelicals, referred to the Soviet Union as an "evil empire" and he described Soviet communism as the "focus of evil" in the world. The president stated his opposition to a nuclear freeze, although he knew that the National Conference of Catholic Bishops was about to issue a pastoral letter in support of a freeze. (PP 364)

March 9 *Tass Critical of Reagan* Tass, the Soviet news agency, issued a statement denouncing President Reagan for his comments on March 8. He was accused of using cold war rhetoric to heighten international tensions and of refusing to negotiate with the Soviet Union for the resolution of outstanding problems. (CDSP XXXV:10 19)

March 21 *Afghanistan Day* President Reagan designated March 21 "Afghanistan Day." He hailed the determination of the Afghan people to fight for their freedom despite having been subjected to chemical and biological weapons by the Soviet Union. (PP 429)

March 23 *Strategic Defense Initiative* President Reagan, in an address to the nation, announced a decision to try to develop a system of defense to counter the Soviet missile threat to the United States. This program, officially known as the Strategic Defense Initiative (SDI), became a major source of tension in Soviet-American affairs. (PP 437)

March 27 *Andropov Criticizes Reagan* *Pravda* published General Secretary Andropov's response to President Reagan's March 23 speech in which he proposed the SDI program. Andropov accused Reagan of wanting to make the United States the dominant military power in the world with a first-strike capability. (CDSP XXXV:13 4)

March 29 *INF Deployment* President Reagan, at a question-and-answer session with reporters, said he intended to proceed on schedule for deploying Pershing II and cruise missiles in Europe. He believed the deployment was necessary because of the lack of an agreement with the Soviet Union. (PP 463)

April 11 *Letters to Andropov* *Pravda* reported that General Secretary Andropov was receiving many letters from Americans in support of a nuclear freeze, arms control agreements, and a summit meeting. (CDSP XXXV:15 20)

April 19 *Andropov on Arms Control* General Secretary Andropov, in reply to questions submitted by *Der Spiegel*, a West German magazine, accused the United States of engaging in an arms race to gain superiority over the Soviet Union. He said the United States wanted the Soviet Union to disarm unilaterally while the NATO nations continued to build their military strength. (CDSP XXXV:17 1)

April 20 *Shultz and Nuclear Weapons* Secretary of State Shultz, in a statement before the Senate Armed Services Committee, supported President Reagan's proposal for modernizing America's strategic nuclear arsenal. He said when the United States reduced its military spending in the 1960s and the 1970s, the Soviet Union continued to add to its military capabilities. (DSB 6/83 8)

April 25 *Reagan and Human Rights* President Reagan, in response to a question submitted by *Bunte Illustrierte*, a West German magazine, said the United States would, as often as necessary, raise the issue of Soviet violations of human rights. He said the United States would insist on a strong human rights plank in the concluding document of the Madrid CSCE meeting. (DSB 7/83 23)

April 29 *Andropov and Space Weapons* *Pravda* published a reply from General Secretary Andropov to a letter from a number of American scientists and public personalities regarding space weapons. Andropov said the Soviet Union supported a treaty banning the deployment of weapons in space. He said such a treaty was not in force because of opposition from the United States and some NATO nations. (CDSP XXXV:17 7)

May 3 *Andropov and the U.S.* General Secretary Andropov, at a dinner in the Kremlin, accused President Reagan of wanting to start an anticommunist crusade. Andropov said the United States was interfering in the internal affairs of other nations and was seeking world domination. He proposed that the WTO and NATO nations reduce their nuclear warheads, missiles, and bombers to equal numbers. (CDSP XXXV:18 6)

May 5 *Reagan and the Nuclear Freeze* President Reagan, in response to a resolution passed by the House of Representatives, expressed his opposition to a nuclear freeze. He said he favored a policy of reducing arms rather than maintaining them at the existing high levels. (PP 644)

May 17 *Soviets and SALT* President Reagan, in response to a question at a news conference, said the Soviets may have tested a new ICBM and, if so, they were in violation of the SALT II agreement. He said the United States was seeking additional information about the missile firing, but the Soviet Union would not cooperate. (DSB 7/83 30)

May 18 *Sakharov Day* President Reagan designated May 21 "National Andrei Sakharov Day." The president praised the Soviet dissident for his commitment to peace and freedom. (PP 731)

June 6 *Captive Nations Week* President Reagan designated the week beginning July 17 "Captive Nations Week." The practice of designating one week each year "Captive Nations Week" began in 1959 as the result of a joint congressional resolution. (PP 825)

June 8 *Reagan and START* President Reagan, on the day the START talks resumed in Geneva, said the American goal was to reduce intercontinental ballistic missiles by one-third. The president wanted a more stable strategic balance at reduced force levels. (PP 831)

June 9 *Tass Scores Reagan* Tass, the Soviet news agency, criticized President Reagan for his remarks on June 8 regarding the resumption of the START talks. Tass said Reagan spoke about American flexibility in arms negotiations, but he was more interested in achieving an American military superiority than in reaching an arms agreement. The Soviets rejected Reagan's plan to have the Soviet Union reduce its ICBMs while the United States built the MX missile. (CDSP XXXV:23 14)

June 13 *Baltic Freedom Day* President Reagan designated June 14 "Baltic Freedom Day." The president supported the efforts of the Baltic nations to win independence from the Soviet Union. (PP 857)

June 15 *Shultz and Soviet Policies* Secretary of State Shultz, in a statement before the Senate Foreign Relations Committee, assessed Soviet-American relations. He said the superpowers "have sharply divergent goals and philosophies of political and moral order," but despite their differences, the two nations had to try to resolve their problems to prevent the outbreak of war. (DSB 7/83 65)

June 22 *Shultz on Foreign Policy* Secretary of State Shultz, in response to a question at a news conference, said his comments to the Senate Foreign Relations Committee on June 15 were in part crafted to send two messages to the Soviets. One was the determination of the United States to defend its vital interests, and the other was a willingness to negotiate with the Soviets on foreign policy issues. He emphasized the linkage between strength and diplomacy. (DSB 8/83 6)

June 28 *The WTO* State and party leaders of the WTO nations met in Moscow and issued a communiqué at the conclusion of their talks. They accused the United States of fueling the arms race and increasing international tensions. They called for a nuclear freeze, a pledge by the nuclear powers not to be the first to use nuclear weapons, and the signing of a nonaggression treaty by the WTO and NATO nations. (CDSP XXXV:26 14)

July 16 *Reagan and Arms Control* President Reagan, in a radio address to the nation, said he was committed to achieving verifiable reductions in strategic nuclear weapons with the Soviet Union. He asked Congress to continue to support the production of the MX missile because, he said, having it would make the Soviet Union more willing to negotiate. (PP 1041)

July 18 *Helsinki Final Act Violations* Max Kampelman, the U.S. ambassador to the Madrid CSCE conference, said the arrest and conviction of Soviet dissident Alexander Shatravka violated the 1975 Helsinki Final Act. Kampelman charged the Soviet Union with harassing its citizens who demonstrated for human rights and nuclear disarmament. He also accused the East German and Czech governments of violating provisions of the Helsinki Final Act. (DOD 564)

July 19 *Captive Nations Week* President Reagan, in a ceremony designating the week beginning July 17 "Captive Nations Week," said that two visions of the world were in competition. One was based on the idea of freedom under God and the other was communism. The president said that if communism were the wave of the future, then communist governments would not have to suppress their people the way they do. (PP 1052)

August 26 *Andropov on INF Weapons* General Secretary Andropov, in response to a question from a *Pravda* reporter, said he was making a new proposal on INF weapons in Europe. He said if the United States would agree not to deploy INF weapons in Europe, the Soviet Union would reduce its SS-20s to the same levels as the British and the French tactical nuclear arsenals. Those Soviet missiles exceeding the number held by the British and the French would be destroyed, but he said nothing about verification measures. (CDSP XXXV:34 1)

September 1 *Korean Airliner Downed* The Soviet Union shot down a Korean passenger plane, killing 269 people. The plane had penetrated deeply into Soviet airspace. Two days later, President Reagan, in a radio address to the nation, said the Soviet Union owed the world an explanation and an apology. (PP 1221)

September 2 **Pravda** *and Korean Airliner* *Pravda* charged that the Korean airliner the Soviets shot down on September 1 was on a spy mission for the United States and had deliberately intruded into Soviet airspace. (CDSP XXXV:35 1)

September 5 *Reagan and the Korean Airliner* President Reagan, in a speech to the American people, said there was no justification for the Soviets to shoot down the Korean airliner. He labeled the act a "crime against humanity." (PP 1227)

September 7 *Madrid CSCE* Foreign Minister Gromyko, in an address to the Madrid CSCE conference, justified the downing of the Korean airliner, alleging it was on a spy mission. (CDSP XXXV:36 10)

September 8 *Shultz and Gromyko* Secretary of State Shultz met with Foreign Minister Gromyko in Madrid, where both were attending the CSCE conference. They discussed arms control and Soviet-American relations. Shultz demanded that the Soviet Union accept blame for shooting down the Korean airliner, but Gromyko refused. (DSB 11/83 67)

September 9 *Reagan and the Korean Airliner* President Reagan designated September 11 "National Day of Mourning" for the passengers and crew killed on the Korean airliner on September 1. (DSB 10/83 13)

September 9 *Shultz on Soviet Policies* Secretary of State Shultz, in an address to the Madrid CSCE conference, criticized the Soviet Union for shooting down the Korean airliner on September 1. He also denounced Soviet policies pertaining to Poland and human rights because, he said, the policies violated both the spirit and the letter of the Helsinki Final Act. (DSB 10/83 50)

September 26 *Reagan at the UN* President Reagan, in an address to the United Nations General Assembly, said that the Soviets increasingly resorted to violence for political gains over the last decade. He criticized the Soviet Union for shooting down the Korean airliner, for violating the Helsinki Final Act, and for using chemical weapons in Afghanistan. He said despite Soviet-American differences, he would continue to seek arms control agreements with the Soviets. (PP 1350)

September 28 *Adropov on American Policy* General Secretary Andropov issued a statement critical of all aspects of American foreign policy. He accused the United States of seeking to achieve military superiority over the Soviet Union and said President Reagan was resorting "to what almost amounts to obscenities alternating with hypocritical preaching about morals and humanism." Andropov repeated the Soviet claim that the Korean airliner that was shot down was on a spy mission. (CDSP XXXV:39 1)

October 3 *Reagan and Democracy* President Reagan, in an address to the Heritage Foundation in Washington, said a new willingness to speak out against the evils of communism helped make American foreign policy more effective. He added that a democratic revolution was under way around the world. (PP 1403)

October 4 *Soviets Criticize Reagan* An editorial in *Pravda* criticized President Reagan for his assertion, made at the United Nations General Assembly on September 26, that American policies were flexible on arms control. Reagan was again accused of seeking military superiority for the United States and its NATO allies over the Soviet Union and the WTO nations. (CDSP XXXV:40 16)

October 18 *Reagan and the Soviet Union* President Reagan issued a statement criticizing the Soviet Union for sentencing Isiof Begun, a Soviet dissident, to seven years of imprisonment and five years of internal exile. The president also listed a series of Soviet policies that he said violated the Helsinki Final Act, including Jewish emigration and other anti-Semitic policies as well as the trial of dissidents. (PP 1478)

October 19 *Reagan and Arms Control* President Reagan, in response to a question at a news conference, said the Soviets were engaged in a propaganda effort to prevent the deployment of Pershing II and cruise missiles in Europe. He said the deployment would proceed on schedule and, as a result, the Soviets might then be more willing to negotiate an arms control treaty. (PP 1490)

October 22 *Reagan and INF Weapons* President Reagan, in a radio address to the American people, said the Soviet Union had thirteen hundred warheads on its SS-20s while the NATO countries had no comparable nuclear systems. He accused the Soviets of attempting to intimidate the nations of Europe to prevent the deployment of the Pershing II and cruise missiles. (DOD 883)

October 25 *Grenada* An American military force of about two thousand troops invaded the island of Grenada with military forces from members of the Organization of Eastern Caribbean States (OECS). President Reagan said the intervention was necessary to protect the Americans in Grenada and to restore democracy to the island. Tass, the Soviet news agency, issued a statement condemning the United States for its invasion of Grenada. (PP 1505)

November 23 *INF Talks* The Soviet Union refused to continue the INF talks with the United States because the NATO nations had begun to deploy INF missiles. (NYT 11/24/83 1)

November 24 *Andropov and INF* General Secretary Andropov issued a statement criticizing the United States and its NATO allies for beginning to deploy Pershing II and cruise missiles in Europe. He said the

Soviet Union would not participate in any INF negotiations, would discontinue its moratorium on deploying INF weapons, and would deploy INF weapons in the German Democratic Republic and Czecho- slovakia. He called on the leaders of the United States and the NATO nations to rethink the decision to deploy INF weapons in Europe. (CDSP XXXV:47 3)

December 7 *Surprise-Attack Talks* Soviet and American officials at the START talks agreed to initiate a separate negotiation for the prevention of a surprise military attack. (NYT 12/8/83 6)

December 8 *START Talks* The START talks recessed, and the Soviet Union refused to agree to a date for their resumption. The Soviet refusal was the result of the NATO nations beginning to deploy INF missiles. Arms control negotiations between the superpowers remained suspended for about a year. (NYT 12/9/83 6)

December 19 *Reagan and the Soviet Union* President Reagan, in response to a question from a reporter for *People* magazine, said he did not regret calling the Soviet Union an evil empire. He said he continued to see the Soviets as a source of evil. (PP 1714)

1984

January 1   *Cruise Missiles*   The cruise missiles that had been deployed in the United Kingdom became operational. On January 13 *Izvestia* carried a statement by General Secretary Andropov that the Soviet Union would return to the INF talks only if the United States and its NATO allies agreed to the status quo before the deployment of Pershing II and cruise missiles. The United States rejected Andropov's proposal. (NYT 1/2/84 2)

January 16   *Reagan and Arms Control*   President Reagan, in an address to the nation, said the harsh rhetoric coming out of the Soviet Union was the result of the fact that the United States had succeeded in strengthening its military posture over the last few years. He expressed a desire to establish better bilateral relations. (PP 40)

January 17   *Conference on Disarmament in Europe*   The signatories to the Helsinki Final Act convened a conference in Stockholm, mandated by the Madrid CSCE follow-up conference that met from 1980 to 1983. The conference was officially entitled "Conference on Confidence- and Security-Building Measures and Disarmament in Europe," CDE for short. The CDE mandate called for the conference to negotiate measures militarily significant, politically binding, verifiable, and applicable to the whole of Europe, including the Soviet Union west of the Ural Mountains. (PP 58)

January 18   *Gromyko at Stockholm*   Foreign Minister Gromyko, in an address to the Stockholm CDE conference, criticized American foreign policies. He said the decision of the United States and its NATO allies to deploy intermediate-range missiles in Europe had created a dangerous condition. Gromyko also found fault with American policies in the Middle East, Grenada, and Central America. (CDSP XXXVI:3 1)

January 23   *Soviet Treaty Violations*   President Reagan sent to Congress a list of Soviet violations of arms control treaties. The message was in keeping with the fiscal year 1984 Arms Control and Disarmament Act passed by Congress requiring the president to issue such a report. (PP 72)

January 24   *Andropov on Foreign Policy*   General Secretary Andropov, in an interview with a reporter from *Pravda*, criticized President Reagan's policies and accused him of wanting to negotiate with the Soviet Union from a position of strength. Andropov said the deployment of intermediate-range missiles by the NATO nations increased military and political tensions. (CDSP XXXVI:4 1)

January 25 State of the Union President Reagan, in his State of the Union address, said he wanted to speak to the Russian people and assure them that Americans wanted to live in peace with them. He urged a common effort to build a safer world. (PP 92)

January 30 Soviets Critical of the U.S. *Pravda* published a memorandum that had been recently sent to the United States criticizing President Reagan's decision to implement a "comprehensive strategic program" for the 1980s. The Soviets claimed that Reagan's decision violated several arms control agreements, including the 1968 Nonproliferation treaty, the 1979 SALT II treaty, and the 1972 ABM treaty. (CDSP XXXVI:4 4)

February 6 Reagan on Foreign Policy President Reagan, in a speech at Eureka College, declared that a willingness to draw distinctions between freedom and communism "is the moral center of our foreign policy." He said that speaking out on behalf of human freedom was an important part of the American foreign policy consensus. (PP 174)

February 10 Death of Andropov Yuri Andropov died after leading the Soviet Union for a little more than a year. He was succeeded by Konstantin Chernenko. (NYT 2/11/84 1)

February 11 Reagan on Foreign Policy President Reagan, in a radio address to the American people, said he hoped that changes in the Soviet leadership, because of the death of Yuri Andropov, would lead to better Soviet-American relations. (PP 191)

February 22 Soviet Mission Attacked A Soviet housing complex next to the Soviet United Nations mission in New York was attacked by a group supporting Jewish emigration from the Soviet Union. The State Department issued a statement condemning the attack. (DSB 4/84 83)

March 2 Chernenko on Foreign Policy General Secretary Chernenko, in a speech to the Supreme Soviet, criticized the United States for deploying intermediate-range missiles in Europe, thus creating what the Soviets referred to as an obstacle to negotiating arms control agreements. He called on the United States to demonstrate by deeds a desire for better superpower relations. (NYT 3/3/84 5)

March 13 Reagan and the Soviet Union President Reagan, in a speech to a Young Leadership Conference, criticized the Soviet Union for its treatment of Jews. He said they were denied the freedom to emigrate and Jewish dissidents were imprisoned because of their efforts to promote freedom. (PP 341)

March 15   *Jews in the Soviet Union*   President Reagan officially designated March 15 "International Day of Concern for Soviet Jews." He issued a statement critical of the Soviet Union for its treatment of Jews. (PP 348)

March 20   *Afghanistan Day*   President Reagan designated March 21 "Afghanistan Day," and he called on the Soviet Union to cease its aggression against the Afghan people. (PP 380)

March 24   *Reagan and Central America*   President Reagan, in a radio address to the nation, accused the Nicaraguan government of being a communist dictatorship tied to Cuba and the Soviet Union. Communism, he said, did not permit people the right to have an electoral choice. The president praised El Salvador for the elections to be held the following day. (DSB 5/84 11)

March 27   *Reagan and Arms Control*   President Reagan, in a speech in Washington, pointed out that since the signing of the SALT I treaty in 1972, the Soviets had added 7,950 strategic nuclear warheads to their arsenal. (PP 422)

April 3   *Shultz and Diplomacy*   Secretary of State Shultz, in a speech to the Trilateral Commission, declared that power and diplomacy are not alternatives but are complementary. He said the Soviet Union would not have any incentive to engage the United States in arms control negotiations if the United States did not modernize its forces. (DSB 5/84 12)

April 6   *Reagan on Foreign Policy*   President Reagan, in a speech at the Center for Strategic and International Studies in Washington, said the Soviet Union would have had little incentive to negotiate with the United States if the 1979 dual-track decision were abandoned, the production of the MX missile cancelled, and a nuclear freeze implemented. (PP 477)

April 8   *Chernenko Criticizes Reagan*   General Secretary Chernenko, in answer to a question from a *Pravda* reporter, blamed President Reagan for beginning a new arms race and attempting to upset the existing balance of power. Chernenko said Reagan's policies were responsible for ending the arms control talks. (CDSP XXXVI:14 7)

April 26   *China Summit*   President Reagan arrived in China for a six-day visit. On his first day, he met with Chinese leaders to discuss issues of interest to both countries, including relations with the Soviet Union, trade, and nuclear energy. (PP 577)

April 27   *Reagan in Beijing*   President Reagan, speaking to Chinese community leaders in Beijing, said that China and the United States opposed military expansionism, particularly the Soviet intervention in Afghanistan and Vietnam's domination of Kampuchea. (PP 579)

April 28   Reagan on China Visit   President Reagan, in an address to the American people, said he repeatedly told the Chinese leaders that differences between the United States and China were less important than their common interests. He said China was opposing Soviet aggression, thus contributing to peace in Asia. (PP 593)

May 4   Soviets Accuse China   Tass, the Soviet news agency, accused China of acquiescing in President Reagan's anticommunist crusade. The president was criticized for his derogatory comments about Soviet policies during his visit to China. (CDSP XXXVI:18 1)

May 8   Soviets and the Olympics   The Soviet Union announced it would not participate in the summer Olympics in Los Angeles. (CDSP XXXVI:19 1)

May 9   Reagan and Central America   President Reagan, in a speech to the nation, spoke about efforts to bring freedom and economic well-being to the nations of Central America despite the policies of Cuba, Nicaragua, and the Soviet Union to promote and support communism. On May 10 Tass, the Soviet news agency, issued a statement attacking President Reagan for his May 9 remarks on Central America. (PP 659)

May 14   Shultz on Foreign Policy   Secretary of State Shultz, in a speech to the League of Women Voters, said the United States had four goals it wanted to achieve in arms control agreements with the Soviet Union: a reduction in weapons, equality between the superpowers, a stable deterrence, and verifiable measures to make certain treaties were not violated. (DSB 6/84 28)

June 4   Reagan on Communism   President Reagan, in a speech in Ireland, said the United States wanted to engage the Soviet Union in negotiations regarding arms control, regional issues, and bilateral relations, but the Soviets were not responding. An editorial in *Pravda* on June 7 criticized President Reagan for his June 4 speech. He was accused of building America's military might rather than attempting to improve Soviet-American relations. (PP 808)

June 12   Antisatellite Treaty   *Pravda* published the replies of General Secretary Chernenko to questions asked by J. Kingsbury Smith, an American journalist. Chernenko said he favored a moratorium on antisatellite testing until the United States and the Soviet Union could agree on a treaty. He said that national means of verification would be adequate to monitor the moratorium. (CDSP XXXVI:24 12)

June 14 *Baltic Freedom Day* President Reagan proclaimed June 14 "Baltic Freedom Day." He said the American people supported the desire of the Baltic republics to be free. (PP 850)

June 18 *Ortega to Moscow* President Daniel Ortega of Nicaragua met with General Secretary Chernenko in Moscow. The two leaders expressed their satisfaction with the development of friendly relations between the two countries, and they condemned American policies in Central America. (CDSP XXXVI:25 16)

June 30 *Arms Control* The Soviet Union called on the United States to begin negotiations to prevent the militarization of outer space. The Soviets proposed that a moratorium on testing and deployment of weapons for outer space begin on the first day of negotiations. (CDSP XXXVI:26 6)

July 3 *Soviets Cancel TV Appearance* The Soviet Union refused to allow Ambassador Arthur A. Hartman to deliver a July 4 television address to the Soviet people. The Soviets said the television address was a part of President Reagan's reelection campaign. (DSB 9/84 80)

July 11 *Stockholm Conference* *Pravda* accused the NATO nations of proposing verification measures at the Stockholm CDE conference that would enable them to learn about the structure and operations of Soviet military forces and those of the WTO nations. (CDSP XXXVI:28 12)

July 16 *Captive Nations Week* President Reagan designated the week beginning July 15 "Captive Nations Week." While signing the proclamation, he declared that once communists came to power, freedom disappeared. As an example, he cited the efforts of the Sandinista government in Nicaragua to subjugate the Catholic church. Reagan said the greatest challenge to human rights was "Communist totalitarianism." (PP 1046)

July 17 *Hot-Line Agreement* The United States and the Soviet Union signed an agreement to improve the hot line. (PP 1051)

July 24 *The Senate and Sakharov* The United States Senate passed a resolution, sent to all the signatories of the Helsinki Final Act, calling on the Soviet Union to provide information about the well-being of Andrei Sakharov, the Soviet dissident. (DSB 9/84 81)

August 3 *Sanctions on Poland* The White House announced that some sanctions imposed on Poland in 1981 were being lifted. The Polish state airline was given permission to resume flights to the United States, and Poland's application for membership in the International Monetary Fund was to be reactivated. Sanctions were lifted because the Polish government released and granted amnesty to political prisoners in an effort to bring order and stability to the country. (PP 1121)

August 17 *Reagan and Poland* President Reagan, speaking at a luncheon in the White House, praised Solidarity, the Polish trade union, calling it an inspiration to free people everywhere. The president also said he rejected any interpretation of the 1945 Yalta agreement supporting the division of Europe. (DSB 10/84 16)

August 19 *Reagan Criticized* *Pravda* criticized President Reagan for his August 17 remarks on Yalta. He was accused of being unwilling to accept what was agreed to at Yalta. (CDSP XXXVI:33 5)

August 20 *Shultz and Diplomacy* Secretary of State Shultz, in a speech in Chicago, said the United States engaged in negotiations with the Soviet Union because it was in America's national interest to do so. He said good agreements could contribute to international stability. (DSB 10/84 18)

September 1 *Chernenko Wants Dialogue* General Secretary Chernenko, in an interview with a *Pravda* reporter, said he wanted to have an honest dialogue with President Reagan, but first the United States would have to abandon its policy of seeking military superiority over the Soviet Union. Chernenko said he wanted to negotiate an agreement banning weapons in outer space, which, he said, could lead to other arms control measures. (CDSP XXXVI:35 1)

September 11 *CDE Talks Resume* President Reagan announced that the CDE conference in Stockholm was again in session. He said the Soviet Union had proposed making a series of declaratory statements, but the United States would insist on more specific measures regarding the reduction of the risk of war in Europe. The president was not opposed to a declaratory statement on the nonuse of force, but he wanted it tied to specific measures, including verification procedures. (PP 1271)

September 24 *Reagan at the UN* President Reagan, in an address to the United Nations General Assembly, said the United States had regained its military strength and was now ready for negotiations with the Soviet Union. He suggested several forums that might be used to promote a Soviet-American dialogue. (PP 1355)

September 26 *Gromyko Meets Shultz* Foreign Minister Gromyko met with Secretary of State Shultz in New York to discuss Soviet-American relations. Gromyko blamed American policies for the increased tensions between the two nations. (DSB 11/84 89)

September 28 *Reagan and Gromyko* President Reagan met with Foreign Minister Gromyko in Washington for approximately three-and-a-half hours. The two leaders discussed a broad range of issues, including a resumption of the suspended arms control talks. In a statement to the press after the meeting, Gromyko said he did not see any change in American foreign policies. (PP 1393)

September 29 *Reagan on Foreign Policy* President Reagan, in a radio address to the American people, discussed Soviet-American relations and his meeting with Foreign Minister Gromyko the previous day. Reagan said he emphasized the need for the superpowers to find a way to cope with regional disputes as well as arms control issues. (PP 1393)

October 10 *Soviet Treaty Violations* President Reagan sent to Congress a report entitled "A Quarter Century of Soviet Compliance Practices Under Arms Control Commitments: 1958-1983." The report, in effect a record of Soviet treaty violations and alleged violations, was prepared by the General Advisory Committee on Arms Control and Disarmament, a White House advisory panel. (PP 1493)

October 18 *Chernenko on Foreign Policy* *Pravda* published General Secretary Chernenko's answers to questions asked by *Washington Post* editors on October 16. The Soviet leader complained that when the United States said it wanted to negotiate, the words were not backed by deeds. He expressed the hope that relations between the superpowers would improve and arms control treaties would be negotiated. (CDSP XXXVI:42 1)

October 18 *Soviet-American Relations* Secretary of State Shultz, in a speech in Los Angeles, said that managing the Soviet-American relationship was complicated because the two systems had such different values. He said despite these differences, the United States wanted to have a constructive relationship with the Soviet Union. (DSB 12/84 1)

October 19 *Soviet-American Relations* Secretary of State Shultz, in a speech to the World Affairs Council in Los Angeles, said because of President Reagan's policy of strengthening the United States, there was no longer the perception that the balance of power was shifting in favor of the Soviet Union. He said the Soviets would adjust to this new reality and eventually negotiate with the United States to resolve outstanding issues. (DSB 12/84 5)

October 22 *Shultz on Foreign Policy* Secretary of State Shultz, in a speech to the National Conference on Soviet Jewry, said that Soviet persecution of Jews and other minorities had intensified. The Soviets, he said, were also guilty of launching anti-Semitic campaigns. (DSB 12/84 11)

October 25 *Shultz on Terrorism* Secretary of State Shultz, in a speech in New York City, said there was ample documentation that the Soviet Union and its allies were supporting terrorism. The secretary said the United States might respond with armed force to terrorist activities, even if the evidence against the offender were not absolute. On October 27 *Pravda* criticized Secretary of State Shultz for his October 25 remarks on terrorism. The United States was accused of preparing to carry out military strikes all over the globe, thus endangering world peace. (DSB 12/84 12)

November 15 *UN and Afghanistan* The United Nations General Assembly passed a resolution, supported by the United States, calling for the withdrawal of all foreign forces from Afghanistan. (DSB 1/85 47)

November 16 *Chernenko on Foreign Policy* *Pravda* published the responses of General Secretary Chernenko to a series of questions asked by reporters from NBC News. The Soviet leader said the top priority in Soviet-American relations should be arms control, but he did not think conditions were right for convening a summit meeting with President Reagan. (CDSP XXXVI:46 8)

November 22 *Arms Control* Robert C. McFarlane, assistant to the president for national security affairs, announced that the United States and the Soviet Union had agreed to resume arms control negotiations. Secretary of State Shultz and Foreign Minister Gromyko were to meet in January in Geneva to work out the details. (PP 1834)

December 14 *Soviets Criticize SDI* *Izvestia* warned that if the United States went ahead with its SDI project, future arms control agreements would be more difficult to negotiate, and past agreements might be endangered. (CDSP XXXVI:50 16)

December 14 *North Atlantic Council* The ministers attending the North Atlantic Council meeting in Brussels issued a communiqué at the conclusion of their two-day meeting. They announced their determination to continue deploying Pershing II and cruise missiles unless they could reach an agreement with the Soviet Union on eliminating such weapons. (DSB 2/85 15)

1985

January 21 *Inaugural Address* In his second inaugural address President Reagan said the United States must remain militarily strong and must continue to speak out in support of freedom. He expressed his continued support for the SDI program and pointed out the need to continue seeking agreements with the Soviet Union. (PP 57)

January 26 *Arms Control Talks* The White House announced that the United States and the Soviet Union had agreed to begin negotiations on nuclear and space weapons in March. (DSB 3/85 36)

January 31 *Shultz on Foreign Policy* Secretary of State Shultz, in a statement before the Senate Foreign Relations Committee, said that true friendship between the United States and the Soviet Union could not be achieved while the Soviet system was driven by an ideology always seeking additional power. (DSB 3/85 13)

February 1 *Soviet Treaty Noncompliance* President Reagan, as required by law, sent to Congress a message detailing Soviet noncompliance with arms control agreements. On February 3, *Izvestia* ridiculed the president's report to Congress. According to *Izvestia*, the purpose of the report was to make reaching an agreement at the forthcoming arms control talks in Geneva more difficult. (DSB 4/85 29)

February 6 *State of the Union* President Reagan, in his State of the Union address, said that because of the country's military buildup during his first term in office, the Soviets were now more willing to come to the bargaining table. (PP 134)

February 22 *Shultz on Foreign Policy* Secretary of State Shultz, in a speech in San Francisco, said the Brezhnev Doctrine was being challenged around the world. He mentioned the efforts made to change the communist regimes in Afghanistan, Angola, Cambodia, Ethiopia, and Nicaragua. The secretary advocated supporting those efforts. (DSB 4/85 16)

February 22 *Shultz on Foreign Policy* Secretary of State Shultz, at a question-and-answer session in San Francisco, said there was no doubt that supplies from the Soviet bloc were going to Nicaragua and from there to El Salvador to support the communist insurgency. (DSB 4/85 22)

March 11 *Death of Chernenko* General Secretary Konstantin Chernenko died and was succeeded by Mikhail Gorbachev. (CDSP XXXVII:9 1)

March 11 *Reagan on Communism* President Reagan, in response to a question during an interview with reporters from *Newsweek* magazine, said his comments describing the Soviet Union as an "evil empire" that would end up "on the ash heap of history" were based on the idea that all people cherish freedom, and any system that denied people freedom would eventually disappear. (PP 258)

March 18 *Reagan on Communism* President Reagan, in a speech in Canada, said that freedom movements were rising in many countries dominated by the communists. He also said he wanted to negotiate arms control agreements with the Soviet Union, but its record of complying with treaties was not good. As examples he cited Yalta, the ABM treaty, and the 1975 Helsinki Final Act. (PP 301)

March 21 *Afghanistan Day* President Reagan designated March 21 "Afghanistan Day." In his proclamation, the president deplored the reports of Soviet atrocities and human rights violations in Afghanistan. He said the American people were united in their determination that the Afghan people should be free and independent. (PP 325)

March 25 *Soviets Criticize Reagan* *Pravda* criticized President Reagan for his anticommunist comments made in a speech in Canada on March 18. The article ridiculed the president for his assertion that many nations were struggling to free themselves from communist rule. He was also accused of not wanting the Geneva arms control talks to succeed. (CDSP XXXVII:12 18)

March 30 *Reagan and Central America* President Reagan, in a radio address to the American people, declared that the Soviet Union wanted to establish a beachhead for subversion in Central America. If the Soviets succeeded, he said, they would then be able to expand their influence and power throughout the region. (PP 370)

April 7 *Gorbachev on INF* General Secretary Gorbachev, during an interview with the editor of *Pravda*, called for better Soviet-American relations and said both countries must do their utmost to bring about a relaxation of international tensions. He announced that the Soviet Union would not deploy any more INF weapons until the following November, and he called on the United States to cease deploying Pershing II and cruise missiles. The United States refused. (CDSP XXXVII:14 6)

April 10 *Reagan and Arms Control* President Reagan, during an interview in London, accused the Soviet Union of attempting to drive a wedge between the United States and its NATO allies on the SDI issue. He said it was "disingenuous" of the Soviets to oppose the SDI program when they had the only operational ABM system in the world. (PP 416)

April 15   Reagan and Nicaragua   President Reagan, in a speech in Washington, called on Congress to approve aid for the contras fighting the Sandinista government in Nicaragua. He accused the Nicaraguan government of committing atrocities that he said were the "natural expression" of a communist regime. (NYT 4/16/85 1)

April 16   Reagan on Communism   President Reagan, in a speech to a conference on religious liberty, spoke about the unwillingness of communist regimes to allow freedom of religion. He specifically identified the Soviet Union and Nicaragua as two nations that persistently attacked religious institutions. (PP 438)

April 17   Nuclear Test Moratorium   The Soviet Union announced a willingness to begin a nuclear test moratorium on August 6, provided the United States also ceased testing. The Soviets were endorsing a proposal made by the U.S. Center for Defense Information in Washington. (CDSP XXXVII:16 15)

April 29   Ortega in Moscow   Nicaragua and the Soviet Union issued a communiqué after General Secretary Gorbachev met with President Ortega in Moscow. They accused the United States of interfering in Nicaragua's internal affairs in an effort to overthrow the communist government, and they condemned the United States for the escalating violence in Central America. (CDSP XXXVII:17 14)

May 15   Reagan and Sakharov   President Reagan issued a statement calling on the Soviet Union to end the exile of Andrei Sakharov and to allow his wife to travel abroad for medical treatment. The president said the Soviet effort to isolate Sakharov from the attention of the international community would fail. (PP 617)

June 14   Baltic Freedom Day   President Reagan proclaimed June 14 "Baltic Freedom Day." He pointed out that during a four-day period from June 14 to June 17, 1941, almost one hundred thousand Baltic people were imprisoned, deported, or murdered by the Soviets. (PP 768)

July 2   Gromyko Replaced   The Soviet Union announced that Andrei Gromyko, after serving as foreign minister for twenty-eight years, was to be given new responsibilities. He was succeeded by Eduard Shevardnadze. (CDSP XXXVII:26 1)

July 2   Summit Announcement   The United States and the Soviet Union announced that a superpower summit meeting would take place in Geneva in November. (CDSP XXXVII:27 4)

July 3 *Shultz on the Summit* Secretary of State Shultz, in response to a question at a news conference, said there would be a good deal of preparation before Reagan and Gorbachev met at the summit. He said the meeting was important because there was a new leader in the Soviet Union, and both Reagan and Gorbachev had expressed an interest in improving Soviet-American relations. (DSB 8/85 30)

July 5 *The ABM Treaty* General Secretary Gorbachev called on the United States to reaffirm the ABM treaty by renouncing the decision to proceed with the Strategic Defense Initiative. He said an American reaffirmation would contribute to strategic stability and mutual trust. (CDSP XXXVII:27 5)

July 8 *Reagan on Terrorism* President Reagan, in a speech to the annual convention of the American Bar Association, identified Cuba, Iran, Libya, Nicaragua, and North Korea as countries supporting and sponsoring international terrorism. He said the United States would not tolerate attacks "from outlaw states run by the strangest collection of misfits, loony tunes, and squalid criminals since the advent of the Third Reich." He noted the close ties of all the states sponsoring terrorism to the Soviet Union. (PP 898)

July 19 *Captive Nations Week* President Reagan designated the week of July 21 "Captive Nations Week." He said he would continue to speak out on behalf of the people in Eastern Europe, Afghanistan, and Kampuchea and against those nations that violated provisions of the Helsinki Final Act. (PP 935)

July 30 *Helsinki Final Act* Foreign Minister Shevardnadze, in a speech at the tenth anniversary of the signing of the Helsinki Final Act, criticized the NATO nations for deploying missiles in Europe. He accused the United States of endangering the ABM treaty because of the Strategic Defense Initiative and said the lack of progress in arms control negotiations was attributable to American policies. (CDSP XXXVII:31 1)

July 30 *Shultz on Foreign Policy* Secretary of State Shultz, in a speech in Helsinki in commemoration of the tenth anniversary of the signing of the Helsinki Final Act, said although Europe was divided, the ideals of European civilization were alive in every nation in Europe. The secretary also criticized the Soviet Union for its numerous violations of the Helsinki Final Act. (DSB 10/85 30)

August 5 *Nuclear Testing* President Reagan, at a question-and-answer session with reporters, said the United States would not agree to a nuclear test moratorium as proposed by General Secretary Gorbachev on April 17. The president believed testing was necessary to "ensure the credibility and effectiveness" of the U.S. deterrent forces and the "reliability and safety" of the American nuclear arsenal. He pointed out that the moratorium proposal came after the Soviets completed a series of nuclear tests. (PP 975)

September 11   *Call for Sakharov's Release* The State Department issued a statement expressing concern about the health and whereabouts of Andrei Sakharov and his wife, Yelena Bonner. The United States wanted Bonner and Sakharov released. (DSB 11/85 59)

September 17   *Reagan and SDI* President Reagan, in response to a question at a news conference, declared he would not use the Strategic Defense Initiative as a bargaining chip in negotiations with the Soviet Union. (PP 1103)

September 23   *Shultz at the UN* Secretary of State Shultz, in an address to the United Nations General Assembly, said when the ABM treaty was signed in 1972 it was assumed that limiting defensive measures would help reduce strategic offensive arms, but this did not occur. He accused the Soviet Union of continuing to build an unnecessary number of first-strike ICBMs, thus endangering the basis of nuclear deterrence. (DSB 11/85 8)

September 25   *Soviets Criticize Shultz* *Pravda* criticized Secretary of State Shultz for his September 23 address to the United Nations General Assembly. He was accused of distorting Soviet policies, and his allegations about the ABM treaty were rejected. (CDSP XXXVII:39 9)

September 27   *Reagan and Shevardnadze* Foreign Minister Shevardnadze met with President Reagan at the White House. They exchanged ideas about the forthcoming summit meeting, and Shevardnadze gave the president a letter from General Secretary Gorbachev. (DSB 11/85 53)

October 14   *Shultz on Foreign Policy* Secretary of State Shultz, in a speech in San Francisco, said that differences between the East and West were "grounded in fundamental moral differences about justice and freedom. . . ." (DSB 12/85 20)

October 24   *Reagan at the UN* President Reagan, in an address to the United Nations General Assembly, called on the Soviet Union to help resolve regional conflicts such as those involving Afghanistan, Angola, Cambodia, Ethiopia, and Nicaragua. The president linked improved Soviet-American relations to the resolution of these regional conflicts. (PP 1285)

October 25   *Reagan Speech Criticized* Tass, the Soviet news agency, accused President Reagan of ignoring arms control issues in his address to the United Nations General Assembly on October 24. The president was criticized for his emphasis on regional issues because, according to Tass, American imperialism was a major cause of regional disputes. (CDSP XXXVII:43 17)

October 30 *NATO Nuclear Planning Group* The NATO Nuclear Planning Group issued a communiqué after a two-day meeting in Brussels. The NATO representatives expressed concern over the continued Soviet nuclear buildup and said the increases in Soviet missiles were much more than was needed for a "credible deterrence." (DSB 1/86 61)

November 5 *Shultz in Moscow* Secretary of State Shultz, at a news conference in Moscow, said he had met with General Secretary Gorbachev and Foreign Minister Shevardnadze to exchange views on Soviet-American relations in preparation for the forthcoming summit meeting in Geneva. The secretary said he had a "very vigorous" round of talks with the general secretary that lasted approximately four hours. (DSB 1/86 57)

November 14 *Reagan on the Summit* President Reagan, in an address to the American people, spoke about the forthcoming summit meeting with General Secretary Gorbachev. Among other things, the president stressed the need to affirm the virtues of freedom and democracy. He said the affirmation would contribute to the success of the Geneva summit. (PP 1388)

November 17 *Shultz on Foreign Policy* Secretary of State Shultz, in response to a question on a television show, said that he had noticed a favorable change in the willingness of Soviet leaders to discuss human rights issues. (DSB 1/86 22)

November 18 *Gorbachev and Reagan* President Reagan met with General Secretary Gorbachev for a summit meeting in Geneva. In the evening, the Soviet leader gave a dinner in honor of President Reagan. (CDSP XXXVII:47 1)

November 21 *Soviet-American Statement* The United States and the Soviet Union issued a joint statement at the conclusion of the Reagan-Gorbachev talks. The two sides agreed that "a nuclear war cannot be won and must never be fought." They discussed regional issues, human rights, arms control, risk reduction centers, MBFR, and the CDE meeting in Stockholm. (DSB 1/86 7)

November 21 *Shultz on Foreign Policy* Secretary of State Shultz, in a briefing for the news media, said he thought the United States and the

Soviet Union would have a more stable relationship as a result of the Geneva summit meeting. (DSB 1/86 11)

November 21 *Reagan on the Summit* President Reagan addressed a joint session of Congress on the results of his summit meeting with General Secretary Gorbachev. The president said that he and Gorbachev and their aides met for about fifteen hours and that he and Gorbachev met privately for five hours. The president believed the meetings were constructive because they began a dialogue that would continue. Gorbachev agreed to visit the United States in 1986, and Reagan accepted an invitation to visit the Soviet Union in 1987. (DSB 1/86 13)

November 23 *Reagan on SDI* President Reagan, in a radio address to the American people, said a major Soviet goal at the Geneva summit meeting was to get the United States to abandon the Strategic Defense Initiative. The president said he made it clear to General Secretary Gorbachev the United States was going to continue doing SDI research. (DSB 2/86 23)

November 27 *Gorbachev on Foreign Policy* General Secretary Gorbachev, in an address to the Central Committee of the Communist party, reviewed events at the Geneva summit. He said the Soviet Union was willing to negotiate with the United States for the complete abolition of nuclear weapons. He added that he wanted Soviet troops out of Afghanistan, but a withdrawal of troops would not begin until the United States quit supplying the rebel groups in Afghanistan with arms and other forms of assistance. (VS LII:7 194)

December 10 *Shultz on Foreign Policy* Secretary of State Shultz, in a speech in London, spoke about regional conflicts and their impact on Soviet-American relations. He said Soviet involvement in regional conflicts contributed to the demise of détente in the 1970s, and the resulting increase in Soviet-American tensions disrupted the arms control process and dashed hopes for better superpower relations. The secretary defended giving moral and military support to groups fighting the spread of communist tyranny. (DSB 2/86 24)

December 14 *Shultz on Foreign Policy* Secretary of State Shultz, in a speech in Berlin, said the people of West Berlin knew that armaments were the manifestation rather than the cause of East-West tensions. He said the people in the Soviet bloc did not want to live under governments supported by military power and that the Berlin Wall was a symbol of the differences between East and West Germany. (DSB 2/86 29)

December 23 *Soviet Treaty Violations* President Reagan, as required by law, sent Congress a memorandum on "Soviet Noncompliance with Arms Control Agreements." The president said the evidence supported the conclusion that "there is a pattern of Soviet noncompliance." (DSB 2/86 65)

December 27 *Reagan and Afghanistan* President Reagan issued a statement on the sixth anniversary of the Soviet invasion of Afghanistan. He called on the Soviets to withdraw their troops from Afghanistan and thereby help improve Soviet-American relations. (DSB 2/86 22)

1986

January 15 *Gorbachev and Arms Control* General Secretary Gorbachev issued a statement in support of eliminating all nuclear weapons by the year 1999. He favored a comprehensive nuclear test ban treaty and the abolition of medium-range and tactical nuclear weapons in Europe. He announced an extension of the Soviet nuclear test moratorium for three more months. The United States said it would carefully study the Soviet proposals. (CDSP XXXVIII:3 6)

February 4 *State of the Union* President Reagan, in his State of the Union address, expressed support for the insurgents fighting communist regimes in Afghanistan, Angola, Cambodia, and Nicaragua. He also expressed the hope that relations with the Soviet Union would improve as a result of General Secretary Gorbachev's forthcoming visit to the United States. (PP 125)

February 11 *Shcharansky Released* Anatoly Shcharansky was released from prison, and Soviet authorities gave him permission to emigrate to Israel. He had been jailed in 1978 after having been found guilty of treason and espionage. The White House issued a statement welcoming the Soviet decision. President Reagan said he would continue to support the protection of human rights in the Soviet Union. (NYT 2/12/86 1)

February 25 *Gorbachev on Foreign Policy* General Secretary Gorbachev, in a speech to the Twenty-seventh Congress of the Communist party, called for the complete abolition of nuclear weapons by the end of the century, and he supported adequate verification measures for any arms control treaty. He agreed to discuss the elimination of intermediate-range nuclear weapons without linking the issue to SDI. He said there would have to be some progress in negotiating arms control agreements before he would agree to a date for another summit meeting with President Reagan. (CDSP XXXVIII:8 1)

March 7 *Soviet Treaty Violations* Kenneth Adelman, the director of the Arms Control and Disarmament Agency, made public a list of Soviet violations and probable violations of arms control agreements. He said the violations were a serious problem in negotiating additional arms control agreements with the Soviet Union. (AFPCD 63)

March 7 *Reducing the Soviet Mission* The State Department issued an announcement on reducing the size of the Soviet United Nations delegation from 275 to 170 over a two-year period. The United States alleged that some of the Soviet personnel were engaged in espionage activities. (AFPCD 171)

March 11 *The Soviets Protest* The Soviet foreign ministry made public a protest to the United States about the American decision to reduce the size of the Soviet United Nations delegation. The Soviets said the American demand was not in keeping with the alleged American desire to improve Soviet-American relations. The note also suggested there might be a further delay in arranging a date for a Gorbachev-Reagan summit meeting. (CDSP XXXVIII:10 21)

March 13 *Nuclear Testing* General Secretary Gorbachev issued an announcement extending the Soviet moratorium on nuclear testing that began in August 1985. He said the Soviet Union would conduct no more tests until the United States resumed testing. (CDSP XXXVIII:11 9)

March 14 *Reagan and Regional Conflicts* President Reagan, in a message to Congress, said Soviet involvement in regional conflicts in the 1970s "produced victims on a scale unknown since the genocides of Hitler and Stalin." (PP 341)

March 21 *Afghanistan Day* President Reagan designated March 21 "Afghanistan Day," and he criticized the Soviet Union for its continued military activities in Afghanistan. (PP 382)

March 29 *Gorbachev and Reagan* General Secretary Gorbachev, in a televised address to the Soviet people, proposed meeting with President Reagan somewhere in Europe to negotiate a comprehensive nuclear test ban treaty. (CDSP XXXVIII:13 5)

March 29 *Reagan on Arms Control* The White House issued an announcement on the arms control proposals made by General Secretary Gorbachev that same day. President Reagan repeated proposals he had made in the past regarding verification measures for the Threshold Test Ban treaty and the Peaceful Nuclear Explosion treaty, and he rejected Gorbachev's proposal for another nuclear test ban moratorium. (PP 415)

April 14 *Libya Attacked* President Reagan, in an address to the nation, said that American warplanes had attacked Libya a few hours earlier in retaliation for its alleged terrorist attacks against U.S. military personnel in Berlin on April 5. (PP 468)

April 14 *Shultz on Foreign Policy* Secretary of State Shultz, in response to a question at a news conference, said the Soviet Union had been informed of the American decision to retaliate against Libya because of its terrorist activities. He said the Soviets were told the purpose of the attack and were presented with evidence linking Libya to terrorist activities. (DSB 6/86 4)

April 15 *Soviets Cancel Meeting*   The Soviet Union, in a note to the United States, condemned the American bombing of Libya the previous day, accusing the United States of engaging in "aircraft-carrier diplomacy." As a sign of their displeasure, the Soviets cancelled the scheduled May 14 meeting between Foreign Minister Shevardnadze and Secretary of State Shultz. The purpose of that meeting was to reach an agreement on a date for a Reagan-Gorbachev summit meeting. (CDSP XXXVIII:15 2)

April 24 *A Nuclear-Free Zone*   A Soviet government statement published in *Pravda* called for the establishment of a Pacific nuclear-free zone. The statement suggested that the Pacific Basin nations should convene a conference to discuss ways to reduce tensions and resolve conflicts. The article accused the United States and Japan of promoting conflicts in Asia and of wanting to create another military bloc. (CDSP XXXVIII:17 6)

April 28 *Nuclear Accident*   The Soviet government announced that a nuclear accident had occurred in Chernobyl located in the Ukraine. (NYT 4/29/86 1)

May 13 *Reagan and Shcharansky*   President Reagan met with the Soviet dissident Anatoly Shcharansky at the White House. The latter thanked the president for his support of human rights, and the president promised to continue to speak out for those individuals denied permission to emigrate from the Soviet Union. (DSB 7/86 75)

May 14 *Reaction to Chernobyl*   President Reagan issued a statement on the Chernobyl accident. Among other things, he denied the Soviet allegation that the United States and some allied nations were exploiting the accident by spreading inaccurate information. The president criticized the Soviet Union for its failure to make more information available to the media. (DSB 7/86 75)

May 20 *Sakharov Day*   President Reagan designated May 21 "Andrei Sakharov Day." The president said some progress was made in the protection of human rights in the Soviet Union, but its overall record was unsatisfactory. (PP 633)

May 27 *Russian Emigration*   The Soviet Union announced that it would allow 117 individuals to leave the country so they could be reunited with their families living in other nations. The United States welcomed the Soviet announcement. (NYT 5/28/86 1)

May 27 *Reagan on Arms Control* President Reagan issued a statement on Soviet and American compliance with arms control measures. He accused the Soviet Union of many violations of arms control agreements and an unwillingness to seriously negotiate a START agreement. As a result, he said, the United States would not in the future be guided by the restraints in the SALT II treaty. (PP 678)

June 1 *Shultz on Arms Control* Secretary of State Shultz, in response to a question on the television program "Meet the Press," accused the Soviet Union of violating several parts of the SALT II treaty. He said the Soviets could not select the parts of the treaty they would respect while insisting that the United States abide by the entire treaty. (DSB 8/86 32)

June 1 *Soviets Criticize Reagan* A Soviet government statement published in *Pravda* criticized President Reagan for his announcement on May 27 that the United States would no longer be restrained by the provisions of the SALT II treaty. (CDSP XXXVIII:22 8)

June 12 *Baltic Freedom Day* President Reagan designated June 14 "Baltic Freedom Day." The president said the United States supported the independence of the three Baltic nations. (PP 760)

June 13 *Shultz on SALT* Secretary of State Shultz, in response to a question during an interview, said that President Reagan decided to abandon the SALT II treaty restraints because they were obsolete. He said the president continued to favor a reduction in nuclear weapons, including nuclear warheads. (DSB 8/86 23)

June 13 *Reagan on SALT* President Reagan, at a question-and-answer session at the White House, said the Soviet Union had been violating the SALT II treaty for seven years. He said that in the future the United States would modernize its military arsenal without being guided by the restraints of the SALT II treaty. (PP 769)

June 16 *Reagan and Afghan Resistance Leaders* President Reagan met with a number of Afghan resistance leaders at the White House. He expressed support for their efforts to defeat the communist forces in Afghanistan. (PP 774)

June 23 *Reagan on Foreign Policy* President Reagan, in an interview with reporters from the *Los Angeles Times,* said the United States and the Soviet Union now had a more stable relationship because Soviet policies were viewed within a more realistic framework. As a result, said the president, the United States was no longer deluding itself about Soviet policies. (PP 825)

June 27 *Shultz on Foreign Policy* Secretary of State Shultz, in response to a question at a news conference, said the growing presence of Soviet forces in Southeast Asia was a problem that troubled the ASEAN nations. (DSB 9/86 37)

July 8 *Reagan and Arms Control* President Reagan, in an interview with a reporter for the *New York Daily News,* said he was optimistic about concluding a meaningful arms control agreement with the Soviet Union. He said General Secretary Gorbachev favored reducing nuclear arsenals and had even proposed specific percentage reductions. (PP 931)

July 21 *Captive Nations Week* President Reagan designated the week beginning July 20 "Captive Nations Week." (PP 977)

July 22 *Reagan Discards SALT II Restraints* American and Soviet representatives met in Geneva to discuss President Reagan's decision to no longer abide by the SALT II restraints. The meeting lasted a week, but no agreements were reached. The president's decision was one factor that contributed to Soviet-American tensions during the period between the 1985 and 1986 summit meetings. (NYT 7/23/86 5)

July 25 *Gorbachev and Reagan* President Reagan, in a letter to General Secretary Gorbachev, suggested that the United States and the Soviet Union should share the benefits of SDI research and should negotiate an agreement eliminating all offensive ballistic missiles. The president also suggested that the superpowers agree to abide by the terms of the ABM treaty for seven-and-a-half more years. Gorbachev favored extending the ABM treaty for fifteen years and tied the proposal to reductions of long-range missiles. (NYT 7/26/86 4)

August 1 *Helsinki Human Rights Day* President Reagan designated August 1 "Helsinki Human Rights Day." (PP 1036)

August 5 *Cultural Agreement* The Soviet Union and the United States agreed to a cultural exchange program that was the result of a Gorbachev-Reagan agreement at the 1985 Geneva summit. (AFPCD 325)

August 5 *Arms Control* President Reagan sent to Congress a list of arms control treaty violations committed by the Soviet Union. The president reiterated his policy, announced on May 27, of no longer abiding by the SALT II restraints. (PP 1052)

August 13 *Reagan on Berlin* President Reagan issued a statement on the twenty-fifth anniversary of the Berlin Wall. He said the Berlin Wall must some day come down and the division of Berlin and Europe must eventually end. (PP 1090)

August 18 *Nuclear Testing* General Secretary Gorbachev, in a televised speech in Moscow, announced that the Soviet Union was extending its moratorium on nuclear testing until January 1. He called on the United States to negotiate a treaty banning all nuclear tests. President Reagan refused to join the Soviet moratorium. (CDSP XXXVIII:33 5)

August 23 *Zakharov Arrested* The FBI arrested Gennady Zakharov, a member of the Soviet United Nations delegation, and charged him with spying. (NYT 8/24/86 1)

August 30 *Daniloff Arrested* The Soviet Union arrested Nicholas Daniloff, a correspondent for *U.S. News & World Report*, and charged him with spying. The Reagan administration believed the Soviets were retaliating for the arrest of Zakharov. (CDSP XXXVIII:35 16)

September 5 *Gorbachev and Reagan* President Reagan sent a letter to General Secretary Gorbachev assuring him that Daniloff was not a spy. Gorbachev publicly rejected Reagan's assurance of Daniloff's innocence thus, in effect, accusing President Reagan of lying. The Daniloff affair strained Soviet-American relations and delayed discussions for a second summit meeting. (NYT 9/7/86 1)

September 13 *Daniloff Released* Secretary of State Shultz announced that Nicholas Daniloff had been released by the Soviet authorities into the custody of the American *chargé* in Moscow. The United States released Gennady Zakharov to the custody of the Soviet ambassador in Washington. (AFPCD 326)

September 16 *Daniloff's Arrest* The White House announced that it intended to raise the issue of Daniloff's arrest whenever it was possible to do so. The announcement warned that the Daniloff affair could adversely affect Soviet-American relations. (PP 1193)

September 17 *Soviets Expelled* The Reagan administration decided to expel twenty-five members of the Soviet United Nations delegation. The United States charged that the Soviet delegation was too large and that many of the delegates were KGB agents engaged in espionage activity. (NYT 9/18/86 1)

September 20 *Shultz on Foreign Policy* Secretary of State Shultz, at a news briefing, commented on his two days of talks with Foreign Minister Shevardnadze in Washington. He said the major item on their agenda was the Daniloff affair, but no agreements had been reached. (DSB 11/86 54)

September 22 *Reagan at the UN* President Reagan, in an address to the United Nations General Assembly, criticized the Soviet Union for the arrest of Nicholas Daniloff and accused the Soviets of permitting members of their United Nations mission to engage in espionage activities. (PP 1227)

September 25 *Reagan Criticized* *Pravda* criticized President Reagan's speech to the United Nations General Assembly on September 22. He was accused of opposing a comprehensive ban on nuclear testing and of ignoring the many arms control proposals put forth by General Secretary Gorbachev. (CDSP XXXVIII:39 6)

September 30 *Shultz on Zakharov and Orlov* Secretary of State Shultz announced that Gennady Zakharov, the Soviet national who had been arrested by the FBI, had pleaded nolo contendere in a New York court and had agreed to immediately leave the United States. Shultz also informed the press that the Soviets had agreed to allow Yuri Orlov, one of the founders of the Helsinki Watch Group, to leave the Soviet Union. (AFPCD 329)

September 30 *Daniloff Freed* The Soviet Union released Nicholas Daniloff. His release ended a crisis and paved the way for a Gorbachev-Reagan summit. (NYT 9/30/86 1)

September 30 *Reagan and Gorbachev* President Reagan announced that he would meet with General Secretary Gorbachev for a summit meeting in Reykjavik, Iceland, in October. General Secretary Gorbachev had been scheduled to visit the United States in 1986, but he refused to set a date for his visit because he did not believe sufficient progress had been made regarding arms control to warrant a Washington summit. (PP 1292)

October 11 *Reykjavik Meeting* President Reagan and General Secretary Gorbachev met in Reykjavik, Iceland, for two days of discussions. The United States assumed the meeting was primarily intended to establish a date and an agenda for the Washington summit, but General Secretary Gorbachev arrived in Reykjavik prepared for substantive negotiations on arms control. He called for a 50 percent reduction in strategic nuclear weapons, negotiations to achieve a comprehensive nuclear test ban, the elimination of INF weapons in Europe, a promise by both nations to remain within the ABM treaty for ten years, and a revision of the ABM treaty to take account of SDI research. (AFPCD 76)

October 13 *Reagan on Reykjavik* President Reagan, in an address to the American people, evaluated the results of his meeting with General Secretary Gorbachev at Reykjavik. The president emphasized differences between the United States and the Soviet Union that resulted from Reagan's commitment to SDI. (PP 1367)

October 14 Reagan Criticized General Secretary Gorbachev, in an address to the Soviet people, blamed President Reagan for the failure to reach any substantive agreements at the Reykjavik summit. (CDSP XXXVIII:42 11)

October 19 Diplomats Ousted The Soviet Union expelled five American diplomats in retaliation for the American expulsion of twenty-five Soviet diplomats on September 17. (NYT 10/20/86 1)

October 21 Diplomats Ousted The United States expelled fifty-five Soviet diplomats in retaliation for the Soviet ouster of five American diplomats on October 19. (NYT 10/22/86 1)

October 22 Diplomats Ousted The Soviet Union expelled five American diplomats and announced that the 260 Russian workers at the American embassy would no longer be permitted to work there. (NYT 10/23/86 1)

November 5 UN and Afghanistan The United Nations General Assembly passed an American-supported resolution calling for the withdrawal of all foreign troops from Afghanistan. The same resolution had been passed every year beginning in 1980. The Soviet Union voted against the resolution. (AFPCD 473)

November 5 Shultz in Vienna Secretary of State Shultz, in a speech to the CSCE conference in Vienna, said there were some disappointments in implementing the Helsinki Final Act. He identified groups in the Soviet Union unable to leave the country, and he identified groups in Czechoslovakia being harassed, including Charter 77 members, individuals affiliated with the Catholic church, and jazz musicians. He also accused the Bulgarian and Polish governments of human rights abuses. The secretary said he would do what he could at Vienna to work for full compliance with the Final Act. (DSB 1/87 47)

November 6 Shultz and Shevardnadze Secretary of State Shultz, at a news conference, said he had just concluded five hours of talks with Foreign Minister Shevardnadze in Vienna. They discussed human rights, regional issues, terrorism, and arms control. (DSB 1/87 51)

November 18 Reagan and Communism President Reagan, in a speech in Washington, advocated supporting those groups around the world fighting communist governments that came to power as a result of the use of force, such as the governments in Nicaragua and Afghanistan. He also criticized the failure to aid the rebels fighting the Hungarian government in 1956. (PP 1563)

November 21 Reagan Criticized An article in *Pravda* by Georgy Arbatov, a leading Soviet analyst on American foreign policy, criticized President

Reagan's speech on November 18. Arbatov accused Reagan of wanting to launch an anticommunist crusade and berated him for saying the United States was wrong in not supporting the 1956 Hungarian uprising. (CDSP XXXVIII:47 6)

November 28 *SALT II Exceeded* The United States exceeded the limits imposed by the SALT II treaty by deploying a B-52 bomber capable of carrying cruise missiles. (NYT 11/29/86 1)

December 19 *Sakharov Exile Ended* The Soviet Union ended Andrei Sakharov's internal exile that began in 1980 and allowed him to return to Moscow. The White House issued a statement welcoming his release and that of Yelena Bonner from internal exile. (NYT 12/20/86 1)

1987

January 26 *The CSCE Process* The White House issued a statement on the resumption of the CSCE meeting in Vienna saying the "human rights situation in the Soviet Union and other nations of Eastern Europe remains tragic." (PP 53)

January 27 *State of the Union* President Reagan, in his State of the Union address, emphasized the need to support the Strategic Defense Initiative, maintain an adequate defense budget, and assist the contras fighting the Nicaraguan government. He said that despite the poor quality of life in the Soviet Union, the government had spent $75 billion over the past five years in weapons for various client states. (PP 56)

January 29 Pravda *Criticizes Reagan* *Pravda* criticized President Reagan's State of the Union address, accusing him of wanting to destabilize the existing balance of power between the superpowers and making "cheap anti-Soviet fabrications" at the same time that he called for improving Soviet-American relations. (CDSP XXXIX:4 26)

February 19 *Sanctions Lifted Against Poland* The United States government lifted the trade sanctions against Poland that had been in place since 1982. According to the president, both the Catholic church in Poland and Solidarity favored the lifting of the sanctions. (PP 155)

February 20 *Shultz on Foreign Policy* Secretary of State Shultz, in a speech in Denver, said the sixty-year-old conflict between communism and freedom is essentially over: freedom has won. He said the Soviets remained a global competitor only in a military sense, not in an economic or political one. (AFPCD 1)

February 26 *Nuclear Testing* The Soviet Union announced that it had ended its nuclear test moratorium in effect for eighteen months. The Soviets said American policies necessitated ending the moratorium. (CDSP XXXIX:9 17)

February 28 *INF Weapons* General Secretary Gorbachev announced a plan for separating the INF question from other arms control issues. He proposed that the Soviet Union and the United States each be allowed to keep 100 INF missiles. On March 3 President Reagan said he was pleased with Gorbachev's announcement that progress in completing an INF treaty would not be tied to any other arms control issues. The president hoped that progress could now be made in completing an INF treaty. (CDSP XXXIX:9 12)

March 5 *Reagan on Foreign Policy* President Reagan, at a White House briefing for members of the National Newspaper Association, said the Soviet Union was now willing to negotiate an INF agreement because of America's patience and firmness and the NATO decision to deploy Pershing II and cruise missiles in Europe. (PP 212)

March 7 *Reagan on Foreign Policy* President Reagan, in a radio address to the nation, criticized the Soviet Union for its continued occupation of Afghanistan and for shipping arms to countries such as Angola, Cuba, Libya, and Nicaragua. He said improving Soviet-American relations would be difficult if the Soviets continued their policies in support of regional conflicts. (PP 221)

March 20 *Afghanistan Day* President Reagan designated March 21 "Afghanistan Day." The president said that "despite a 7-year reign of terror," Soviet troops had failed to crush the Afghan desire for freedom. He reiterated America's support for the complete withdrawal of all Soviet military forces from Afghanistan. (PP 267)

March 25 *Soviets Criticize Reagan* *Pravda* published a statement by the Ministry of Foreign Affairs criticizing President Reagan's decision to designate a day in March "Afghanistan Day." The statement accused the United States of seeking a military solution to the Afghanistan conflict and therefore being responsible for the continuation of the war. (CDSP XXXIX:12 10)

April 6 *Reagan and the Soviet Union* President Reagan, in a speech in Ottawa, insisted that the Soviet Union comply with the provisions of the 1975 Helsinki Final Act. He said if the Soviet Union liberalized its society, the Soviet economy would improve, and the Soviet people could then enjoy a better life. (PP 336)

April 10 *Reagan and the Soviet Union* President Reagan, in a speech in Los Angeles, said there had been some improvement in Soviet international behavior, but not much. He cited Soviet support for communist regimes in Nicaragua and Angola that fought their own people. He criticized Soviet aggression in Afghanistan and challenged the Soviet Union to set a date for the withdrawal of its forces. (PP 365)

April 15 *Shultz in Moscow* Secretary of State Shultz, at a news conference in Moscow, commented on his discussions with Soviet leaders. He said the two sides had discussed many issues, including human rights, arms control, intelligence, and nuclear testing, but little progress was made in resolving differences. (DSB 6/87 12)

May 17 *Shultz on Foreign Policy* Secretary of State Shultz, in a speech to the American Israel Public Affairs Committee, said the United States would not negotiate with the PLO or the Soviet Union on Middle Eastern issues because both were committed to the use of violence to achieve their goals. He said the Soviet Union encouraged the radical policies of the PLO, and Soviet Jews were unable to practice their religion. As a result, he said, the Soviets were not yet qualified to help negotiate a Middle East peace. (DSB 7/87 7)

June 12 *Reagan in Berlin* President Reagan, in a speech in Berlin, called on General Secretary Gorbachev to tear down the Berlin Wall. (PP 634)

June 13 *Baltic Freedom Day* President Reagan proclaimed June 14 "Baltic Freedom Day." (PP 642)

June 18 *Soviets on Reagan in Berlin* *Izvestia* criticized President Reagan for urging General Secretary Gorbachev to tear down the Berlin Wall. The article warned that Reagan's comments could endanger peace in central Europe and diminish prospects for an arms control agreement. (CDSP XXXIX:24 16)

July 19 *Captive Nations Week* President Reagan designated the week of July 18 "Captive Nations Week." (WCPD 920)

July 24 *Reagan on Captive Nations* President Reagan, in comments made to participants in a ceremony for "Captive Nations Week," again called on General Secretary Gorbachev to tear down the Berlin Wall, to open the Brandenburg Gate, and to free political prisoners. (PP 868)

July 31 *Helsinki Human Rights Day* President Reagan proclaimed August 1 "Helsinki Human Rights Day." He accused the Soviet Union and the Soviet-dominated governments in Eastern Europe of systematically violating the rights guaranteed in the Helsinki Final Act. (PP 907)

August 26 *Reagan on Foreign Policy* President Reagan, in a speech in Los Angeles, reviewed his policies toward the Soviet Union. He said the United States had developed a doctrine for regional disputes, had directly challenged the Soviet Union about human rights, and had adopted a policy of educating people about the nature of totalitarian governments. (PP 978)

August 27 *Soviets Criticize Reagan* The Soviet Ministry of Foreign Affairs issued a statement criticizing President Reagan's August 26 speech. He was accused of dusting off old anti-Soviet rhetoric that made an improvement in Soviet-American relations more difficult to achieve. (CDSP XXXIX:35 19)

August 29   Reagan on Foreign Policy   President Reagan, in a radio address to the nation, proposed a number of things the Soviets could do to improve relations with the United States, including halting aid to the Sandinista government, publishing an accurate defense budget, and repudiating the use of force to achieve foreign policy goals. (PP 988)

September 13   Arms Control   Secretary of State Shultz, in response to a question on the program "Face the Nation," said the Soviet radar site at Krasnoyarsk violated the ABM treaty. He stated there would be no further agreements pertaining to the ABM treaty until the Krasnoyarsk issue was resolved. (DSB 11/87 19)

September 15   Nuclear Risk Reduction Centers   President Reagan announced that the United States and the Soviet Union had signed a treaty to establish nuclear risk reduction centers in Washington and Moscow. The purpose of the centers is to avoid conflicts that might result from an accident, misinterpretation, or miscalculation. The centers exchange information and issue notifications as required under certain treaties, such as those pertaining to confidence-building measures. (PP 1033)

September 16   Reagan on Foreign Policy   President Reagan, in addressing a conference on public diplomacy, rejected the idea of a moral equivalency between the United States and the Soviet Union. He asserted there could be no moral equivalency between democratic and totalitarian regimes. (PP 1038)

September 18   Soviet-American Statement   The United States and the Soviet Union issued a joint statement at the conclusion of three days of talks between Secretary of State Shultz and Foreign Minister Shevardnadze. The major topic of their talks was various arms control proposals. They agreed in principle to conclude the INF treaty, but there were still details to be completed. They also agreed to expedite negotiations to achieve a 50 percent reduction in strategic offensive weapons. (PP 1048)

October 22   The Stockholm CDE Conference   The Stockholm CDE conference adjourned after agreeing on a set of measures that included prior notification by the CSCE members of any military activities above a threshold of thirteen thousand troops or three hundred tanks. The Soviets agreed that verification procedures could take place in the Soviet Union. (DSB 4/19/87 18)

October 23 *Shultz on Summit* Secretary of State Shultz, after meeting with General Secretary Gorbachev and Foreign Minister Shevardnadze, said no date was set for a Reagan-Gorbachev summit meeting because of lack of agreement on limiting SDI research. He was satisfied with the results of his talks, but the superpowers remained far apart on arms control issues. (CDSP XXXIX:43 9)

October 28 *Reagan on Foreign Policy* President Reagan, in a speech at West Point, said he welcomed the changes taking place in the Soviet Union, but he was disappointed that Soviet policies pertaining to regional conflicts, such as Nicaragua and Afghanistan, had not changed. (PP 1239)

October 30 *Summit Meeting* President Reagan announced that General Secretary Gorbachev had accepted the president's invitation to visit the United States for a summit meeting. (PP 1256)

November 4 *Reagan on Foreign Policy* President Reagan, in a speech to the people of Western Europe transmitted by the Voice of America, said the Soviet Union had a poor record in complying with past arms control agreements. He said the INF treaty, to be signed in December when Gorbachev arrived in Washington for a summit meeting, would have ironclad guarantees to make it enforceable. (PP 1271)

November 12 *Reagan on Afghanistan* President Reagan, in a discussion with Afghan resistance leaders at the White House, said he had encouraged the Soviet Union to withdraw its troops from Afghanistan, but General Secretary Gorbachev had been unwilling to set a date for the withdrawal. (PP 1324)

November 24 *Shultz and Shevardnadze* Secretary of State Shultz and Foreign Minister Shevardnadze held a news conference in Geneva after two days of talks. The two leaders completed the INF treaty, worked out arrangements for a Gorbachev-Reagan summit meeting, and discussed human rights, bilateral issues, and regional issues. (AFPCD 96)

November 28 *Reagan on Foreign Policy* President Reagan, in a radio address to the nation, spoke about the scheduled summit meeting with General Secretary Gorbachev. The president said the four major topics at the summit would be human rights, bilateral issues, regional issues, and arms control. He again said the Strategic Defense Initiative was not a bargaining chip in the arms control negotiations. (PP 1385)

November 30 *Reagan on Foreign Policy* President Reagan, in a speech at the Heritage Foundation, urged the Soviet Union, in the spirit of glasnost, to introduce freedom of religion. He also criticized Soviet policies in Afghanistan, Angola, and Nicaragua. (PP 1392)

December 2 *Arms Control Compliance* President Reagan, as required by law, sent to Congress a record of Soviet noncompliance with arms control agreements. The record demonstrates, said the president, that the Soviets had developed a pattern of noncompliance over the years. He said he intended to raise the subject of treaty violations with General Secretary Gorbachev at the summit. (PP 1408)

December 4 *Shultz on Foreign Policy* Secretary of State Shultz, in a speech in Washington to the World Affairs Council, commented on the changes taking place in the Soviet Union and the nations of Eastern Europe. The secretary said the Soviet leadership had come to realize the disadvantages of a closed society. Shultz said a test of change in the Soviet Union would be measured by the government's attitude toward human rights. (DSB 1/88 3)

December 8 *Gorbachev to Washington* President Reagan welcomed General Secretary Gorbachev to Washington. The president said he hoped the meeting with Gorbachev would result in improved relations with the Soviet Union and a greater degree of cooperation in resolving issues such as arms control, human rights, and regional conflicts. In response to President Reagan's welcoming comments, General Secretary Gorbachev said he hoped the INF treaty would lead to other agreements between the superpowers and contribute to diminishing international tensions. (PP 1452-1453)

December 8 *The INF Treaty* The United States and the Soviet Union signed the INF treaty eliminating intermediate-range missiles. President Reagan, in an address to the American and Russian people, expressed his pleasure at the signing of the treaty. He linked the security of the superpowers to the necessity of having open and free societies that guarantee basic human rights. (PP 1455)

December 10 *Joint Statement* The United States and the Soviet Union issued a joint statement on the results of the summit meeting. The statement listed topics that had been discussed, agreements reached, and negotiations to be continued. General Secretary Gorbachev again invited President Reagan to visit the Soviet Union. (PP 1491)

December 10 *Reagan on the Summit* President Reagan, in an address to the American people, labeled the summit meeting a "clear success," and he said the INF treaty was the most important step since World War II to halt the arms race. (PP 1504)

1988

January 25 *State of the Union* President Reagan, in his State of the Union address, said there could be no settlement of the Afghanistan problem until the Soviets withdrew all their troops. He pledged to continue to work for the reduction of strategic nuclear weapons, and he continued to support the Strategic Defense Initiative. (PP 84)

February 2 *Shultz on Foreign Policy* Secretary of State Shultz, in a statement before the House Foreign Affairs Committee, discussed what he considered important foreign policy priorities for 1988. He said the United States wanted to complete the START treaty, promote the peace process in Central America, and encourage the Soviet Union to remove its troops from Afghanistan. (DSB 4/88 43)

February 5 *Shultz on Foreign Policy* Secretary of State Shultz, in a speech in Seattle, said the "new thinking" in the Soviet Union was increasingly influenced by the community of free nations, but he did not think the United States and the Soviet Union could ever become genuinely friendly because of their many differences. He did suggest that both countries could develop a much better relationship than in the past. (DSB 4/88 38)

February 29 *Reagan and the Soviet Union* President Reagan, in a speech to the Annual Leadership Conference of the American Legion, said the INF treaty was not based on trust, because the Soviets had a record of violating international agreements. He said the United States had learned from experience the importance of verification measures to support international agreements. (PP 273)

March 21 *Afghanistan Day* President Reagan designated March 21 "Afghanistan Day." He said the United States continued to insist that all Soviet military forces should withdraw from Afghanistan. (PP 358)

April 13 *Reagan on Foreign Policy* President Reagan, in a speech to the American Society of Newspaper Editors, said he welcomed the changes taking place in the Soviet Union, but he was critical of the many restraints on freedom that continued to exist. He cited as examples the law making it illegal to teach Hebrew to Jewish children, the Ukrainian Catholic church having to operate underground, and ethnic groups being denied basic rights. (PP 451)

April 14 *The Soviets and Afghanistan* Afghanistan, Pakistan, the Soviet Union, and the United States signed an agreement, worked out under the auspices of the United Nations, for the Soviet Union to withdraw its military forces from Afghanistan by February 15, 1989. (CDSP XL:15 17)

April 14 *Afghanistan Agreement* On April 14, the United States and the Soviet Union signed an agreement to refrain from interfering in the internal affairs of Afghanistan and Pakistan. (DSB 6/88 57)

April 21 *Reagan on Foreign Policy* President Reagan, in a speech in Massachusetts, said the values of the free world gave hope to people everywhere who were denied their freedom. He said his administration had emphasized the moral differences between the United States and the Soviet Union rather than just focusing on arms control issues. He again rejected the idea of a moral equivalence between the superpowers. (PP 489)

May 19 *The Helsinki Accords* President Reagan, at an interview with foreign journalists at the White House, accused the Soviet Union of violating the human rights provisions of the 1975 Helsinki Final Act. He cited Soviet policies pertaining to religion and emigration as examples, but, he said, the Soviet record was improving. (PP 610)

May 23 *Reagan and the Soviet Union* President Reagan, in a speech to the people of Western Europe carried over the Voice of America, said he welcomed the changes in Soviet policies pertaining to human rights but, he said, much more had to be done. He said he was obligated to raise the issue of human rights when he met with General Secretary Gorbachev because the United States and the Soviet Union had signed the 1975 Helsinki Final Act that guaranteed basic freedoms. (PP 631)

May 25 *The Moscow Summit* President Reagan, before leaving for the Moscow summit, said that during each of their three previous summits, he and General Secretary Gorbachev made progress on the four major agenda items: arms control, human rights, regional conflicts, and bilateral relations. He hoped that the Moscow summit would result in more progress. (PP 643)

May 27 *The Helsinki Accords* President Reagan, in a speech in Helsinki, said the 1975 Helsinki Final Act, signed by the United States, the Soviet Union, and thirty-three other nations, established standards for international behavior and mechanisms to measure compliance with those standards. He again called on General Secretary Gorbachev to allow freedom of religion and to tear down the Berlin Wall. (PP 656)

May 29 *Reagan and Gorbachev* President Reagan met with General Secretary Gorbachev in Moscow. (PP 672)

May 30 *Reagan Meets Religious Leaders* President Reagan, in a talk to religious leaders at the Danilov Monastery in Moscow, said he hoped that soon all the Soviet people would enjoy freedom of religion. In a separate meeting with a number of dissidents at the Spaso House in Moscow, he expressed support for their efforts to promote human rights and assured them of the support of the American people. He added that better Soviet-American relations depended on whether the Soviet Union carried out the human rights provisions of international agreements it had signed. (PP 674-675)

May 30 *Gorbachev Toasts Reagan* General Secretary Gorbachev, in a toast to President Reagan, reviewed Soviet-American relations and prospects for the future. He expressed the hope that an international security system linked to the United Nations could be established. He said protecting the environment had become a major global problem, and he advocated a reduction in military budgets so resources could be used to meet human needs. The primary theme of his toast was that better Soviet-American relations would contribute to a more stable and peaceful international order. President Reagan, in a toast to General Secretary Gorbachev, reviewed the progress the two nations had made in resolving their major differences since their first meeting in 1985. The president said that much had been accomplished but much more had to be done. (PP 677)

May 31 *Reagan Talks to Artists* President Reagan, in a talk to artists and cultural leaders in Moscow, said he welcomed the changes in the Soviet Union that permitted greater artistic freedom, and he hoped there would be even more freedom in the future. (PP 682)

May 31 *Reagan at Moscow State University* President Reagan, in a speech at Moscow State University, spoke about the value of freedom and its links to many other aspects of life, such as art and technology. He said that he and Gorbachev wanted to have student exchange programs involving thousands of students a year, but, the president said, he would also like to see individuals having the right to travel free of governmental restrictions. (PP 683)

June 1 *Soviet-American Joint Statement* The United States and the Soviet Union, at the conclusion of the Moscow summit meeting, issued a joint statement reviewing progress that was made and the problems that remained on the four major agenda items of arms control, human rights, regional problems, and bilateral issues. (PP 698)

June 1 *Reagan and the Soviet Union* President Reagan, in response to a reporter, said that Soviet-American relations were quite different now compared to 1981. He attributed the change in part to the leadership of General Secretary Gorbachev and the trust that had developed between the two leaders as a result of their four summit meetings. (PP 707)

June 1 *Reagan Criticized* *Izvestia* criticized President Reagan for his May 30 meeting with Russian dissidents at Spaso House. Soviet officials did not consider the guests attending the Spaso House meeting to be representative of the Soviet population. (CDSP XL:22 1)

June 3 *Reagan on Foreign Policy* President Reagan, in a speech at the Royal Institute of International Affairs in London, discussed the importance of the just-concluded Moscow summit meeting. The president said that cold war barriers were beginning to come down, and he suggested that Soviet-American relations might be entering a new era as a result of changes in the Soviet Union. (PP 715)

June 14 *Baltic Freedom Day* President Reagan designated June 14 "Baltic Freedom Day." He said the Balkan states were brought under Soviet domination as a result of collusion between Adolph Hitler and Josef Stalin. (PP 776)

June 28 *Gorbachev and New Thinking* General Secretary Gorbachev addressed the All-Union Party Congress in Moscow. In his address, the president analyzed the "new thinking" that was influencing Soviet policies. He decried the arms race, minimized the importance of class conflict as an element of international relations, and promoted the idea of a foreign policy based on national interest. The changes recommended by Gorbachev contributed to better Soviet-American relations. (NYT 6/29/88 1)

July 13 *Captive Nations Week* President Reagan designated the week beginning July 17 "Captive Nations Week." (PP 948)

July 17 *Conventional Arms Reduction* *Pravda* published a statement issued by the WTO ministers saying that conventional arms reduction talks should aim for a staged reduction in military forces to equal levels. The ministers also called for an international monitoring commission to observe the carrying out of any agreements reached between the WTO and NATO nations. (CDSP XL:29 24)

July 19 *Krasnoyarsk Radar* A spokesperson for the Soviet Foreign Ministry announced that if the United States were willing to abide by the ABM treaty for at least nine or ten years, the Soviet Union would be prepared to dismantle the Krasnoyarsk radar site that the United States said violated the ABM treaty. (CDSP XL:29 24)

August 20   Reagan on Czechoslovakia   President Reagan issued a statement on the twentieth anniversary of the Soviet invasion of Czechoslovakia. He said there could be no genuine reconciliation between East and West until the Soviet Union dealt with the injustices of the invasion and renounced the Brezhnev Doctrine. (PP 1093)

August 24   ABM Review Conference   The United States, at the ABM review conference in Geneva, raised the question of Soviet violations of the ABM treaty, particularly the Krasnoyarsk radar station. The United States asserted there could be no START agreement until Soviet violations were corrected. (DSB 11/88 19)

August 27   Reagan on Foreign Policy   President Reagan, in a radio address to the American people, reviewed foreign policy events. He welcomed the cease-fire in the Iran-Iraq war, the withdrawal of half the Soviet forces from Afghanistan, and the announcement of Vietnam to withdraw its forces from Cambodia. He attributed some of the favorable changes in world events to America's policy of peace based on strength. (PP 1110)

August 31   ABM Review Conference   The United States, at the conclusion of the ABM treaty review conference, issued a statement about topics that had been discussed. The United States insisted that the Soviet radar site at Krasnoyarsk violated the ABM treaty and should be dismantled, but no progress was made in resolving the issue. (AFPCD 93)

September 23   Shultz and Shevardnadze   Secretary of State Shultz and Foreign Minister Shevardnadze issued a joint statement after two days of talks in Washington. The two leaders reviewed the implementation of past agreements and discussed current problems, including human rights, regional conflicts, arms control, and bilateral issues. (DSB 11/88 28)

September 26   Reagan at the UN   President Reagan, in an address to the United Nations General Assembly, spoke about changes taking place in the communist nations and the growing commitment of many nations to peace and freedom. He welcomed the improvement in Soviet-American relations and said that if reforms in the Soviet Union continued, there would be a further improvement. (PP 1219)

October 28   Reagan on Foreign Policy   President Reagan, in an address to the World Affairs Council in Los Angeles, said that more progress was made in settling regional disputes than expected. He attributed the progress to American support for groups fighting to overthrow or modify Soviet-backed regimes. He said the United States had a "moral duty to resist the international threat to human rights posed by Soviet expansionism." (PP 1403)

October 28 *Shultz on Foreign Policy* Secretary of State Shultz, in a speech in San Francisco, reviewed Soviet-American relations since President Reagan came to office. The secretary said the Reagan administration put human rights on the top of the superpower agenda, restored America's military might, supported "freedom fighters" attempting to overthrow communist governments, and negotiated important agreements with the Soviet Union without compromising American principles. (DSB 1/89 6)

November 2 *Krasnoyarsk Radar* The State Department announced that American and Soviet experts had met to discuss the American charge that the Soviet radar site at Krasnoyarsk violated the ABM treaty, but the talks failed to resolve differences between the two sides. The announcement said the United States would continue to insist that the radar site be dismantled. (DSB 1/89 16)

November 8 *Bush Elected* George Bush, the Republican candidate for president, defeated his Democratic opponent, Michael Dukakis. (NYT 11/9/88 1)

November 14 *Reagan and Sakharov* President Reagan met with Andrei Sakharov, the Soviet dissident. In response to a question before the meeting, the president said human rights remained an irritant in Soviet-American relations. (PP 1499)

December 3 *Reagan on Foreign Policy* President Reagan, in a radio address to the nation, reviewed Soviet-American relations since he took office. He was generally optimistic about the superpower relationship, but he did say he was looking forward to the day when the Berlin Wall would be torn down and the works of Solzhenitsyn would be published in the Soviet Union. (PP 1585)

December 4 *Shultz on Foreign Policy* Secretary of State Shultz, in response to a question on a television program, said the ability to resolve problems with the Soviet Union had improved since President Reagan came to office. The secretary said that when he first brought up the topic of human rights, the Soviets would not discuss it with him. Now, he said, the two sides have a "systematic dialogue" on the topic. (DSB 2/89 7)

December 7 *Gorbachev at the UN* General Secretary Gorbachev addressed the United Nations General Assembly where he announced a reduction of a half-million personnel in the Soviet military forces and cuts in several categories of armaments over a two-year period. The reduction included one-third of the tank divisions in central and Eastern Europe. (CDSP XL:49 1)

December 7 *Bush and Reagan Meet Gorbachev* General Secretary Gorbachev met with President Reagan and President-elect Bush. The meeting was not billed as a summit but simply an opportunity to demonstrate continuity in Soviet-American relations. (PP 1590)

December 7 *Reagan on Foreign Policy* President Reagan, in a speech at the American Enterprise Institute, commented on his meeting earlier in the day with General Secretary Gorbachev. The two leaders agreed that there had been substantial improvement in Soviet-American relations since the first summit meeting in Geneva in 1985. (PP 1594)

December 9 *Shultz on Foreign Policy* Secretary of State Shultz, at a news conference in Brussels, said he welcomed the December 7 speech by General Secretary Gorbachev at the United Nations announcing troop reductions. The secretary pointed out, however, that the Soviet Union would still have a substantial numerical superiority in conventional forces compared to those of NATO even after the Soviet troop reductions took place. (DSB 2/89 47)

December 16 *Reagan on Foreign Policy* President Reagan, in a speech in Virginia, said that some of the changes taking place in the Soviet Union were in part the result of American firmness, a strong defense, healthy alliances, and a willingness to use force when necessary. He also said the United States should not hesitate to point out the differences in the American and Soviet political systems. (PP 1631)

December 22 *Angola and Cuba* President Reagan welcomed the signing of the agreement between Angola and Cuba calling for the withdrawal of Cuban troops to be completed by July 1, 1991. Soviet and Cuban involvement in Angola had been a major cause of Soviet-American tensions. (DSB 2/89 12)

1989

January 4 *Moscow Conference* President Reagan issued a statement in support of holding a CSCE conference on human rights in Moscow in 1991. He said this was a way of encouraging the Soviet Union to continue the progress that had been made over the last three years in protecting human rights. (DSB 3/89 69)

January 15 *CSCE Final Document* The thirty-five nations participating in the Vienna CSCE negotiations, including the United States and the Soviet Union, signed a concluding document containing provisions pertaining to terrorism and human rights and calling for additional negotiations. (DSB 3/89 21)

January 17 *Baker on Foreign Policy* James A. Baker III, President-elect Bush's choice for secretary of state, in an appearance before the Senate Foreign Relations Committee during his confirmation hearings, said the United States must be prudent in dealing with the Soviets. He welcomed the changes that had taken place in the Soviet Union but noted it remained a superpower and retained a force structure, designed to launch an offensive military attack, in support of policies hostile to American values. (DSB 4/89 10)

January 17 *Shultz at the CSCE* In an address to the CSCE conference in Vienna, Secretary of State Shultz welcomed changes that had taken place in the Soviet Union since the signing of the 1975 Helsinki Final Act. Among other things, he mentioned the end to the jamming of radio broadcasts, the release of more than 600 political prisoners, including some Helsinki monitors, and the change in Soviet emigration policies. Shultz did, however, criticize some Eastern European nations for continuing to violate the 1975 Helsinki Final Act. (DSB 3/89 50)

January 19 *Bush and Gorbachev* President-elect Bush, in a question-and-answer session with reporters, said he had received a letter from General Secretary Gorbachev pledging to continue efforts to build a secure peace. The president wanted to continue the progress that had been made in improving Soviet-American relations. (PP 6)

January 25 *Baker Takes Office* James Baker was sworn in as secretary of state. (DSB 4/89 9)

January 27 *Bush on Foreign Policy* President Bush, in response to a question at a news conference, said he did not believe in playing the China card or the Soviet card. He said the United States had strong bilateral relations with both nations, and he did not approve of playing one country off against the other. (PP 23)

February 2 *MBFR Talks* The Mutual and Balanced Force Reduction talks that had been going on since October 1973 concluded. Despite more than fifteen years of negotiations, the talks produced no significant results. A new set of negotiations for force reductions in Europe, now called Conventional Forces in Europe (CFE), replaced the MBFR talks. The United States and the Soviet Union approved the change. (DSB 4/89 25)

February 6 *Bush on Foreign Policy* President Bush, in response to a question at a news conference, said the Soviet Union did not have interests in Central America comparable to those of the United States, but, he said, he would like to have General Secretary Gorbachev cooperate with the United States in seeking solutions to Central American problems. (PP 64)

February 9 *Administration Goals* President Bush addressed a joint session of Congress and said the United States would continue to cooperate with General Secretary Gorbachev in support of the changes taking place in the Soviet Union. Bush did say, however, that the Soviet Union retained a powerful military machine in support of objectives the United States opposed. (PP 74)

February 15 *Soviets Withdraw from Afghanistan* The Soviet Union completed the withdrawal of its forces from Afghanistan. (PP 106)

February 15 *Bush and Afghanistan* President Bush, on the day after the withdrawal of all Soviet troops from Afghanistan, called upon the Soviet Union to stop interfering in the internal affairs of Afghanistan. He said the Soviets had nothing to fear from an independent, non-aligned Afghanistan. At the time, the Soviets were supplying the Afghan government with military assistance. (PP 100)

February 15 *Bush and China* President Bush, at a reception on the first day of a two-day visit to China, said he welcomed improved relations between China and the Soviet Union, and he suggested that their rapprochement could lead to a resolution of the Cambodia problem and greater stability on the Korean peninsula. (PP 139)

February 27 *Bush on Foreign Policy* President Bush, in an address to the nation after returning from his trip to Asia, said the People's Republic of China was dealing cautiously with the Soviet Union in response to General Secretary Gorbachev's efforts to improve Sino-Soviet relations.

The president said he and the Chinese leaders agreed that the Soviets should be judged by deeds, not words. (PP 150)

March 6 Bush on Foreign Policy President Bush, in a speech at the annual convention of the Veterans of Foreign Wars, said he wanted to develop a more stable relationship with the Soviet Union, but the United States could not be sure what would be the result of the changes taking place under Gorbachev's leadership. The president said that because of this uncertainty, the United States must continue to have an adequate defense. (PP 172)

March 6 Baker on Foreign Policy Secretary of State Baker, in a speech in Vienna at the opening of the CFE negotiations, called on General Secretary Gorbachev to clearly renounce the Brezhnev Doctrine, and he also called on the Soviet Union to further reduce its conventional military forces in Europe. (DSB 5/89 56)

March 7 Baker and Shevardnadze Secretary of State Baker met with Foreign Minister Shevardnadze in Vienna for the first high-level talks between the superpowers since President Bush's election. The meeting allowed Secretary Baker to explain President Bush's foreign policy goals and how they might differ from those of President Reagan. (DSB 5/89 59)

March 21 Afghanistan Day President Bush designated March 21 "Afghanistan Day." He said the Soviet leaders had come to realize the Afghan people could not be defeated. (PP 358)

March 24 Bush on Foreign Policy President Bush, in a statement at a news conference, said he would like to see some new Soviet thinking about Central America. He said the Soviet Union was helpful in resolving other regional disputes, but not Nicaragua. (PP 306)

April 14 Baker on Foreign Policy Secretary of State Baker, in an address to the American Society of Newspaper Editors, discussed some problems in Soviet-American relations. He said that General Secretary Gorbachev refused to renounce the Brezhnev Doctrine, was unwilling to tear down the Berlin Wall, was unhelpful in Central America, and sold sophisticated fighter planes to Libya despite that country's support of terrorism. (DSB 6/89 8)

May 4 Baker on Foreign Policy Secretary of State Baker, in a speech at the Center for Strategic and International Studies in Washington, praised the U.S. policy of rejecting a condominium with the Soviet Union whereby the world would be divided into spheres of influence. Instead, the United States decided to aid its European allies, put together a coalition of free nations, and promote freedom. Now, he said, Western values were influencing the Soviet Union. (DSB 7/89 36)

May 11   Arms Control   General Secretary Gorbachev met with Secretary of State Baker in Moscow and told him that the Soviet Union intended to reduce its nuclear forces in Europe by the end of the year. Gorbachev also called for negotiations to reduce the number of short-range nuclear weapons. (CDSP XLI:19 1)

May 11   Baker on Foreign Policy   Secretary of State Baker commented on his two days of talks with Soviet leaders in Moscow. They discussed human rights, arms control, and bilateral and regional issues. A new item was put on the Soviet-American agenda, transnational relations. This included such things as environmental issues, drug trafficking, and natural disasters. (DSB 7/89 30)

May 12   Bush on Foreign Policy   President Bush, in a speech at Texas A & M University, welcomed the changes taking place in the Soviet Union, but he noted that in the past, friendly overtures from the Soviets were usually followed by increased international tensions. The president said he hoped these cycles of tranquility and hostility would cease. He also called upon the Soviet Union to change its policies in Cuba, Nicaragua, and Eastern Europe. (PP 540)

May 12   Soviet Military Might   An article in *Izvestia* said the Soviet Union "overdid it" in building up its military might in Eastern Europe in the past. (CDSP XLI:19 26)

May 21   Bush on Foreign Policy   President Bush, in a speech at Boston University, declared that the "new thinking" in the Soviet Union had not completely overcome the old. The president favored a step-by-step approach toward the Soviet Union because it was not yet clear how much change would actually occur in Soviet foreign and domestic policies. (PP 582)

May 22   Baker on Foreign Policy   Secretary of State Baker, in a speech to the American Israel Public Affairs Committee, said he would like to see some Soviet "new thinking" in resolving Middle East problems. He said Moscow should renew diplomatic ties with Israel and stop selling sophisticated weapons to Libya. He called on the Soviet Union to discard slogans and begin to support seriously a Middle East peace process. (DSB 7/89 24)

May 24   Bush on Foreign Policy   President Bush, in a speech at the Coast Guard Academy, said the strategy of the United States in the past was to contain the Soviet Union, but the task now, he said, was to work to integrate it into the community of nations. (DSB 7/89 19)

May 31 *Bush to West Germany* President Bush, in a major speech in the Federal Republic of Germany, welcomed the foreign policy initiatives introduced by General Secretary Gorbachev, but the president insisted that more had to be done. He made four recommendations that he said would contribute to better relations between the NATO and WTO members. First, he proposed strengthening the Helsinki process that had done so much to promote the protection of human rights in Eastern Europe and the Soviet Union. Second, he recommended tearing down the Berlin Wall, a symbol of European division, to enable glasnost to be brought to East Berlin. Third, he suggested broad cooperation for coping with environmental dangers such as those destroying the Black Forest in West Germany. Finally, the president suggested that a number of steps should be taken to demilitarize Europe. (PP 650)

June 4 *Elections in Poland* Poland held its first free elections since the communists came to power. The candidates supported by Solidarity won a decisive victory over the communists. (NYT 6/5/89 1)

June 8 *Baker on Foreign Policy* Secretary of State Baker, in response to a question at the National Press Club, said the Soviet leaders talked about a European home, but this was unrealistic as long as Europe remained divided and the Berlin Wall intact. President Bush and General Secretary Gorbachev often referred to a "common European home," indicating that the cold war was over and Europe was no longer divided. The two leaders, however, disagreed on the meaning of the term. (DSB 8/89 58)

June 13 *Military Agreement* The United States and the Soviet Union signed an agreement for averting military activity in specified conflict-prone areas. A joint military commission was established to monitor the implementation of the agreement. (CDSP XLI:24 28)

June 14 *Baltic Freedom Day* President Bush designated June 14 "Baltic Freedom Day." (DSB 8/89 80)

June 23 *CSCE Conference* The Paris meeting of the CSCE-mandated Conference on the Human Dimension ended. At the conference, the Soviet Union was praised for the changes made in its human rights policies since 1985. At the conference, the Soviet delegation criticized Romania for erecting a barbed wire fence along its border with Hungary. The criticism was evidence that the Soviets were doing more than they had in the past to carry out the rights protected in the Helsinki Final Act. (NYT 6/25/89 17)

July 3 *Bush on Poland* President Bush, in response to a question at a news conference with correspondents from Poland, said he would like to see Soviet troops leave their country. (PP 886)

July 6 *Common European Home* General Secretary Gorbachev, in an address to the Council of Europe's parliamentary assembly, presented his ideas for a "common European home." Gorbachev rejected the Brezhnev Doctrine formulated to justify Soviet intervention in Czechoslovakia in 1968. Among other things, he stressed the importance of arms control, human rights, the rule of law, and the protection of the environment. (CDSP XLI:27 6)

July 8 *The WTO* The ministers of the WTO nations issued a communiqué at the close of their meeting in Bucharest emphasizing the right of all the member nations to develop their political systems without outside interference. The ministers also called for developing better relations with the NATO nations to improve the European political environment. (CDSP XLI:27 8)

July 11 *Bush in Poland* President Bush, in a speech in Poland, congratulated the Polish people for holding their first free elections since before World War II. The elections took place in June. He said Poland was a good example to prove that the urge for freedom could not be indefinitely denied. (PP 933)

July 12 *Bush in Hungary* President Bush, in a speech at Karl Marx University in Hungary, praised Imre Nagy, the leader of the 1956 Hungarian uprising who was executed by the Soviets. The president said Hungary was leading the way in helping tear down the iron curtain. (PP 940)

July 16 *Bush on Europe* President Bush, in response to a question at a news conference in Paris, said that he and General Secretary Gorbachev had some differences on the concept of a "common European home." The president said his concept was based on freedom, democracy, and market economies. (PP 973)

July 21 *Soviet Military Doctrine* Soviet Marshal Sergei F. Akhromeyev, in an appearance before the House Armed Services Committee in Washington, said the Soviet Union was determined to put into place a defensive military doctrine with as low a level of troop strength as possible. Never before had a Soviet military officer testified before a congressional committee. (NYT 7/22/89 6)

July 21 *Captive Nations Week* President Bush, in ceremonies at the White House commemorating "Captive Nations Week," welcomed the changes taking place in Eastern Europe and the Soviet Union. The president declared that more nations were embracing democracy and free-market economies. (PP 996)

July 29 *Baker and Shevardnadze* Secretary of State Baker and Foreign Minister Shevardnadze met in Paris where they discussed arms control, the situation in Cambodia, regional conflicts, and the agenda for their next meeting in Washington on September 19. (DSB 10/89 39)

August 21 *Czechoslovakia Invasion* The State Department issued a statement on the twenty-first anniversary of the Soviet invasion of Czechoslovakia. The statement called on the Czech government to demonstrate a greater tolerance for freedom and human rights. At the time, the Czech government was cracking down on groups protesting government policies. (DSB 10/89 40)

September 7 *Bush on Soviet Reductions* President Bush, in a speech to the American Legion, said he welcomed the military reductions taking place in the Soviet Union, but he did not think that Soviet deeds matched their verbal commitments. He said the United States had to remain militarily strong if the Soviet Union were to be encouraged to continue reductions. (PP 1154)

September 21 *Bush and Shevardnadze* President Bush met with Foreign Minister Shevardnadze at the White House. The topics they discussed included a summit meeting, internal events in the Soviet Union, human rights, and regional conflicts. Shevardnadze delivered a letter to Bush from General Secretary Gorbachev dealing with arms control. The Soviet leader agreed to dismantle the radar site at Krasnoyarsk, which the United States insisted violated the 1972 ABM treaty. (DSB 11/89 1)

September 23 *Baker and Shevardnadze* Secretary of State Baker and Foreign Minister Shevardnadze issued a statement after meeting for two days in Jackson Hole, Wyoming. The two leaders expressed support for continuing the process of improving Soviet-American relations, and they announced plans for a 1990 summit meeting between President Bush and General Secretary Gorbachev. (DSB 11/89 5)

September 23 *Chemical Weapons* Secretary of State Baker and Foreign Minister Shevardnadze issued a joint statement committing the United States and the Soviet Union to work for the completion of a treaty banning chemical weapons. (DSB 11/89 8)

September 23 *Arms Control* Secretary of State Baker, at a news conference, discussed the accomplishments of his meeting with Foreign Minister Shevardnadze. Among other things, Baker said the Soviets agreed to drop their linkage of a START treaty to SDI, and they agreed to full verification measures in support of arms control agreements. (DSB 11/89 10)

September 25 *Bush at the UN*   President Bush, in an address to the United Nations General Assembly, said that more people were rejecting totalitarianism in favor of freedom and democracy. He discussed the possibility of creating a new international community based on freedom and market economies. Bush alluded to improved Soviet-American relations, and he expressed confidence that more progress would be made in completing arms control agreements. (PP 1248)

September 27 *Bush on Foreign Policy*   President Bush, at a question-and-answer session with reporters, said that as a result of improved relations between the United States and the Soviet Union, contentious issues could be discussed in an open and honest fashion. He added that despite the new superpower relationship, the United States had to maintain its military might because the Soviet Union was modernizing its military forces. (PP 1263)

October 5 *The Soviets and SDI*   Victor Karpov, a deputy minister of foreign affairs, said, in response to a question from an *Izvestia* staff correspondent, that the Soviet Union was no longer as concerned about the Strategic Defense Initiative as it was in the past because President Bush's SDI program was different from the one proposed by President Reagan in 1983. (CDSP XLI:40 21)

October 5 *Aid to Nicaragua*   Foreign Minister Shevardnadze, in a statement issued at a news conference in Nicaragua, said the Soviet Union had discontinued military aid to Nicaragua but would continue to provide economic assistance. Soviet military aid to Nicaragua was a source of tension in Soviet-American relations. (CDSP XLI:40 22)

October 16 *Baker on Foreign Policy*   Secretary of State Baker, in a speech in New York, said Soviet leaders now realized that Brezhnev's expansionist policies of the 1970s did not bring about greater security for the Soviet Union. He said there now existed a historic opportunity to improve Soviet-American relations. (DSB 12/89 10)

October 18 *Hungary's New Constitution*   The Hungarian parliament approved a new constitution that no longer guaranteed the Communist party a monopoly of power. The name of the country was also officially changed from the Hungarian People's Republic to the Republic of Hungary. The United States welcomed the change. (DSB 12/89 39)

October 18 *Honecker Resigns*   Erick Honecker, the leader of the German Democratic Republic for eighteen years and an opponent of

Gorbachev's reforms, was forced to resign. He was replaced by Egon Krenz. (NYT 10/19/89 1)

October 23 *Shevardnadze and Afghanistan* Foreign Minister Shevardnadze, in a report to the Supreme Soviet, said the Soviet intervention in Afghanistan in December 1979 violated Soviet and international law. He also said the radar site in Krasnoyarsk violated the ABM treaty. His comments were, in part, intended to discredit former president Brezhnev and his policies. (CDSP XLI:43 1)

October 23 *Baker on Arms Control* Secretary of State Baker, in a speech at the Commonwealth Club of San Francisco, outlined America's strategy regarding arms control issues. He said the United States wanted to reduce first-strike and surprise-attack capabilities and wanted the Soviets to be more open about their military activities to diminish fear about their intentions. He also advocated expanding the superpower agenda to deal more effectively with regional disputes. (DSB 12/89 14)

October 25 *Brezhnev Doctrine* General Secretary Gorbachev declared that the Soviet Union had no right to intervene in the affairs of the Eastern European nations. He was, more explicitly than in the past, repudiating the Brezhnev Doctrine formulated by the former Soviet leader to justify the invasion of Czechoslovakia in 1968. (NYT 10/26/89 1)

October 26 *Bush and Nicaragua* President Bush, in response to a question at a news conference with Latin American journalists, said the United States would continue to try to convince the Soviet Union that it was not in its interest to continue supplying the Nicaraguan government with military supplies. Nicaragua was still receiving military equipment from the Soviet Union that had been shipped before the October 5 Soviet announcement that no more military aid would be sent. (PP 1387)

October 31 *Bush and Gorbachev* President Bush announced at a news conference that he would meet with General Secretary Gorbachev on December 2 for two days of talks near the island of Malta. The president said the meeting would allow the two leaders to exchange ideas, but he did not expect any major agreements to result from the meeting nor was there going to be a formal agenda. (PP 1423)

November 4 *Resolution for Peace* American and Soviet officials at the United Nations held a news conference to announce their decision to cosponsor a resolution calling for a strengthening of the United Nations to promote peace and cooperation. This was the first time the superpowers had cosponsored a United Nations General Assembly resolution. (CDSP XLI:44 21)

November 9 *Berlin Wall* The German Democratic Republic opened the Berlin Wall and allowed thousands of East Germans to freely travel to West Germany. President Bush, at a question-and-answer session with reporters, said he welcomed the decision of the East German government. (PP 1488)

November 11 *Zhivkov Resigns* Todor Zhivkov, the leader of Bulgaria since 1954, resigned as a result of mass protests against communist rule. Gorbachev sent a congratulatory message to Petar Mladenov, Zhivkov's successor. (CDSP XLI:45 21)

November 17 *Bush on Foreign Policy* President Bush, during an interview with NBC radio, said he would bring up subjects during his meeting with General Secretary Gorbachev about which the two nations differed. As examples, the president mentioned Nicaragua and Afghanistan. (PP 1543)

December 2 *Bush and Gorbachev Meet* President Bush and General Secretary Gorbachev met for two days of discussions on ships near the island of Malta. On the first day of their meeting they talked for five hours on the Soviet vessel *Gorky*. (CDSP XLI:49 20)

December 3 *Discussions on Nicaragua* President Bush, in response to a question at a joint news conference with General Secretary Gorbachev, said he and the Soviet leader had discussed the situation in Nicaragua and Central America. Bush said there were still some Soviet-American differences pertaining to Central American problems, but the differences had been narrowed. (PP 1628)

December 3 *Bush on the Summit* President Bush, at a joint news conference with General Secretary Gorbachev, said that the improvement in Soviet-American relations was a good thing in itself but would also be an instrument to bring about positive changes in the international political system. (PP 1626)

December 4 *Bush and Gorbachev* President Bush, in response to a question at a news conference in Brussels, said he had a much clearer idea of General Secretary Gorbachev's priorities as a result of their recent meeting. Bush also said the meeting gave him an opportunity to demonstrate American concern about Soviet and Cuban policies in Central America. (PP 1648)

December 4 *Bush on Foreign Policy* President Bush, in an address to the ministers representing the NATO nations meeting in Brussels, said the division of Europe was coming to an end, thus bringing about what the United States desired since 1945. He said the NATO nations should take the lead in promoting freedom and reforms throughout Europe. (PP 1644)

December 10 *Husak Resigns* President Gustav Husak of Czechoslovakia resigned after being forced to accept a cabinet with a noncommunist majority. (CDSP XLI:50 21)

December 27 *Ceausescu Executed* *Pravda* reported that President Nicolae Ceausescu of Romania and his wife had been executed after having been found guilty of "crimes against the Romanian people and Romania." (CDSP XLI:52 29)

December 27 *Bush and Romania* President Bush, at a question-and-answer session in Texas, said he welcomed the changes taking place in Romania, although he expressed some reservation about the summary execution of President Ceausescu. (PP 1741)

December 29 *Havel Elected* President Bush sent a message of congratulations to Vaclav Havel on his election as president of Czechoslovakia. He was one of the original signers of Charter 77 and had been jailed by the communist government for his human rights activities. (PP 1747)

1990

January 25 *Bush and Gorbachev* President Bush, at a question-and-answer session, praised General Secretary Gorbachev and hoped he would be successful in implementing his reforms. At the time Gorbachev was being criticized by his opponents, and there was some doubt that he would remain in office. (PP 100)

January 31 *State of the Union* President Bush, in his State of the Union address, praised the improved relations with the Soviet Union and the progress it was making toward democratization. He proposed deep reductions in conventional force levels in Europe, and he wanted Soviet and American military forces in Eastern and central Europe to be reduced to 195,000 and the United States to have the right to station an additional 30,000 troops in other areas of Europe. (PP 133)

February 7 *Bush on Containment* President Bush, in a speech in California, said it took nearly fifty years to vindicate the strategy of containing the Soviet Union, but now the cold war was coming to an end and the Soviet system was undergoing change. He said the United States was taking steps to ensure a lasting peace. (PP 173)

February 7 *Communists Lose Monopoly* The Central Committee of the Communist party accepted General Secretary Gorbachev's proposal to end the communist monopoly of power and accept a multiparty system. (NYT 2/8/90 1)

February 8 *Bush and Arms Control* President Bush, in remarks at a fundraising dinner in Ohio, said General Secretary Gorbachev had responded positively to the January 31 proposal for further reductions in conventional military forces in central and Eastern Europe. (PP 194)

February 10 *U.S.-Soviet Ministerial Meeting* Secretary of State Baker and Foreign Minister Shevardnadze issued a joint statement at the conclusion of their meeting in Moscow. The two leaders discussed arms control, regional issues, and the Bush-Gorbachev summit meeting scheduled to convene in June in Washington. (AFPCD 367)

February 10 *Baker in Moscow* Secretary of State Baker became the first American official to address the International Affairs Committee of the Supreme Soviet. He emphasized the need for the United States and the Soviet Union to continue to improve their relations and to cooperate in resolving global problems. (AFPCD 371)

February 10 *Troop Reductions* Secretary of State Baker said General Secretary Gorbachev would not accept President Bush's proposal for troop reductions in Europe if he insisted on having thirty thousand more troops stationed in Europe than the Soviet Union. Gorbachev insisted on parity. (NYT 2/10/90 1)

February 12 *Bush and Troop Reductions* President Bush rejected the Soviet proposal for lowering conventional military forces in Europe to equal levels. The president insisted on having thirty thousand more troops in Europe than the Soviet Union because he thought they contributed to political stability. On February 13 General Secretary Gorbachev reversed his position and accepted the American proposal for conventional troop reductions in Europe that permitted the United States to maintain thirty thousand troops in Europe outside of central Europe. There was no explanation for the sudden change in Soviet policy. (NYT 2/13/1990 1)

February 13 *German Unity* The ministers of the United Kingdom, France, the United States, the Soviet Union, the German Democratic Republic, and the Federal Republic of Germany, at a meeting in Ottawa, accepted a framework for German unification. The ministers agreed to a two-plus-four process whereby the two German states would negotiate with each other and the Big Four would also negotiate. (NYT 2/14/90 1)

February 13 *Open Skies* The ministers representing NATO and the WTO countries agreed on the need to establish an open-skies regime that would enable nations to conduct flights over other countries to monitor military activities. President Eisenhower had first proposed an open-sky program in 1955, but the Soviets rejected it. (AFPCD 65)

February 14 *Bush and NATO* President Bush, at a question-and-answer session at the White House, said the nations of Europe wanted an American military presence, but the nations of Eastern Europe wanted Soviet troops withdrawn from their countries. He defended NATO membership for a united Germany saying it would contribute to stability in Europe, a position the Soviets rejected. (PP 220)

February 19 *Soviets and Israel* General Secretary Gorbachev rejected a request made by the United States for direct flights from the Soviet Union to Israel to facilitate the emigration of Jews from the Soviet Union. (NYT 2/20/90 1)

February 21 *Havel and the Soviet Union* President Havel of Czechoslovakia addressed a joint session of Congress and endorsed the idea of the United States providing assistance to the Soviet Union to promote the development of democracy. (NYT 2/22/90 1)

February 22 *Germany and NATO* Secretary of State Baker issued a prepared statement for the House Foreign Affairs Committee in which he insisted that a unified Germany must be allowed membership in NATO. The Soviet Union opposed NATO membership for a united Germany. (AFPCD 240)

March 6 *Gorbachev and Germany* General Secretary Gorbachev, in answer to a question, said a united Germany could not join NATO. He said NATO membership for Germany "is absolutely ruled out." (CDSP XLII:10 27)

March 11 *Lithuanian Independence* The Lithuanian parliament declared that Lithuania was now independent and sovereign. The desire of the Lithuanians to free themselves from Soviet control became a contentious issue in Soviet-American relations. (NYT 3/12/90 1)

March 17 *Germany and NATO* Foreign Minister Shevardnadze, at a meeting of the WTO members, said membership for a united Germany in NATO would be "impossible." (NYT 3/18/90 1)

March 20 *Baker and Shevardnadze* Secretary of State Baker met with Foreign Minister Shevardnadze while the two were attending Namibia independence day ceremonies. They discussed German unification, Afghanistan, and arms control issues. (USDSD 10/15/90 188)

March 20 *National Security Strategy* President Bush sent to Congress the annual National Security Strategy Report. In it the president expressed support for integrating the Soviet Union into the international political system. He also favored unifying Germany and permitting it to become a member of NATO. (PP 389)

March 22 *Katyn Massacre* Official Soviet records revealed that the Soviet Union, not Germany, was responsible for the Katyn Forest massacre in 1940. Polish officials alleged that fifteen thousand Polish soldiers were executed. (NYT 3/23/90 9)

March 29 *Bush and Gorbachev* President Bush, in a letter to General Secretary Gorbachev, assured him that the United States did not want to do anything to inflame the crisis that resulted from Lithuania desiring to be free. Bush said he hoped the problem could be resolved peacefully. (NYT 3/31/90 1)

April 4 *Baker and Shevardnadze* Secretary of State Baker and Foreign Minister Shevardnadze met in Washington to continue preparations for the Bush-Gorbachev summit meeting in June in Washington. Baker and Shevardnadze also discussed arms control and Lithuania. (USDSD 10/15/90 188)

April 5 *Bush and Gorbachev* The White House announced that President Bush and General Secretary Gorbachev agreed to convene a summit meeting in Washington on May 30. (PP 464)

April 6 *U.S.-Soviet Ministerial Meeting* Secretary of State Baker, at a news conference, discussed the results of his meetings with Foreign Minister Shevardnadze. The United States insisted that the Soviet Union must try to resolve peacefully its differences with Lithuania regarding the question of secession. The two leaders also focused on arms control, regional issues, human rights, and the possibility of a united Germany joining NATO. Shevardnadze insisted that a united Germany could not be a member of NATO. (AFPCD 379)

May 4 *Strengthening CSCE* President Bush, in a speech at the University of Oklahoma, proposed that the NATO ministers take steps at their forthcoming NATO summit meeting to strengthen the CSCE. He said the "CSCE should offer new guidelines for building free societies including setting standards for truly free elections." (PP 625)

May 5 *Talks on Germany* Secretary of State Baker met in Bonn with Foreign Minister Shevardnadze and the foreign ministers of East and West Germany, France, and the United Kingdom to discuss German unification. The meeting was the first of the two-plus-four talks on German unity. (NYT 5/6/90 1)

May 12 *Citizens Democracy Corps* President Bush, in a commencement address at the University of South Carolina, announced the creation of a citizens democracy corps to function as a clearinghouse for "American private sector assistance and volunteer activities in Eastern Europe." He said the United States would do whatever it could to make certain that elections in Eastern Europe were free and fair. (USDSD 9/3/90 34)

May 19 *Baker in Moscow* Secretary of State Baker, at a press conference in Moscow, commented on the four days of talks he had just completed with General Secretary Gorbachev and Foreign Minister Shevardnadze. Topics discussed included independence for Lithuania, the START negotiations, regional issues, human rights, and the need to resolve the "remaining refusenik cases." Baker expressed some disappointment that more progress was not made regarding the CFE negotiations. (AFPCD 390)

May 31 *Gorbachev in Washington* President Bush welcomed General Secretary Gorbachev to the United States for another summit meeting. (AFPCD 391)

May 31 *Dinner for Gorbachev* President Bush hosted a state dinner for General Secretary Gorbachev at the White House. (PP 737)

June 1 *Soviet-American Agreements* General Secretary Gorbachev and President Bush signed a number of agreements pertaining to chemical weapons, nuclear testing, and the peaceful uses of atomic energy. They also issued a joint statement expressing their satisfaction with the progress being made in completing a START treaty. (PP 740)

June 1 *Bush and Gorbachev* General Secretary Gorbachev hosted a dinner for President Bush. In his toast to President Bush, the Soviet leader said the success of the summit proved there was greater understanding between the Soviet Union and the United States, and that would help promote peaceful changes in Europe. (PP 751)

June 2 *Soviet-American Statements* The United States and the Soviet Union issued joint statements on the need to provide food for Ethiopia and to take steps to protect the environment. (PP 755)

June 3 *Gorbachev and Bush* President Bush and General Secretary Gorbachev, at a news conference, expressed satisfaction with the results of the summit meeting, although they disagreed about whether Germany should become a member of NATO. The two leaders agreed there was now much more trust between the two nations than in the past. (PP 756)

June 4 *Nuclear Proliferation* President Bush and General Secretary Gorbachev issued a joint statement expressing their opposition to the proliferation of nuclear and chemical weapons and of missiles capable of carrying those weapons. (PP 768)

June 4 *Joint Statements* President Bush and General Secretary Gorbachev issued joint statements pertaining to Bering Sea fisheries conservation, the peaceful uses of atomic energy, and technical economic cooperation. (PP 771)

June 7 *Soviet-American Relations* Secretary of State Baker, in an address to the North Atlantic Council meeting in Scotland, said that the United States and the Soviet Union were committed to achieving greater strategic stability and that the superpowers would continue to negotiate arms control agreements after completing the START treaty. (USDSD 9/3/90 43)

June 7 *WTO Meeting* Representatives of the WTO nations meeting in Moscow agreed to study the need to change their alliance in keeping with the improved relations between the members of the WTO and NATO. (CDSP XLII:23 15)

June 12 *Soviet-American Relations* Secretary of State Baker, in a statement before the Senate Foreign Relations Committee, said the ability to promote democracy and make the world more secure was in large part dependent on the continued improvement in Soviet-American relations. (USDSD 9/3/90 45)

June 14 *Baltic Freedom Day* President Bush designated June 14 "Baltic Freedom Day." He said the American people supported the aspirations of the Baltic people for freedom and independence.

June 15 *Nuclear Weapons* The White House issued a statement opposing the Soviet desire to begin negotiations on short-range nuclear weapons in Europe before completing an agreement on conventional forces in Europe. President Bush wanted to begin negotiations on short-range nuclear weapons in Europe after the completion of a CFE treaty. (PP 833)

June 22 *Baker and Shevardnadze* Secretary of State Baker and Foreign Minister Shevardnadze met in Berlin for the second session of the two-plus-four talks regarding German unification. (USDSD 10/15/90 188)

July 6 *Changes in NATO* The heads of states of the NATO nations issued a London Declaration on a Transformed North Atlantic Alliance. The leaders called on the NATO and WTO nations to declare they no longer had an adversarial relationship. The leaders also announced a new force structure and strategy for NATO to adjust to the changes that had occurred in East-West relations. (PP 964)

July 6 *Bush and NATO* President Bush, at a news conference following the NATO summit in London, commented on some of the changes that had taken place regarding NATO. He labeled the changes a "historic turning point." He invited the Soviet Union and the nations of Eastern Europe to "establish regular diplomatic liaison with the alliance." (PP 967)

July 7 *Soviets Hail NATO Change* On July 7, Foreign Minister Shevardnadze welcomed the changes agreed to by the NATO nations in the just-concluded London meeting. (CDSP XLII:26 11)

July 17 *Baker and Shevardnadze* Secretary of State Baker met with Foreign Minister Shevardnadze in Paris for the third session of the two-plus-four negotiations regarding German unification. (USDSD 10/15/90 188)

July 18 *Captive Nations Week* President Bush designated the week of July 15 "Captive Nations Week." He said some nations continued to violate human rights agreements but that in general there were fewer violations than in the past. (WCPD 1114)

July 25 *Captive Nations Week* President Bush, in a ceremony commemorating "Captive Nations Week," praised the changes that had occurred in Eastern Europe since 1989. For thirty-two years presidents had declared one week a year as "Captive Nations Week" as a reminder of the Soviet subjugation of the people of Eastern Europe. (PP 1065)

August 2 *Baker and Shevardnadze* Secretary of State Baker and Foreign Minister Shevardnadze held a press conference at the conclusion of their talks in the Soviet Union. The two leaders agreed that the United States and the Soviet Union were no longer adversaries and therefore would cooperate in resolving Asian problems as they had in Europe. Among other things, the two leaders discussed problems pertaining to Afghanistan, Cambodia, China, and the ASEAN nations. (AFPCD 404)

August 2 *The UN and Iraq* The United Nations Security Council passed a resolution, supported by the United States and the Soviet Union, condemning Iraq for its invasion of Kuwait earlier that day. (AFPCD 455)

August 3 *The Superpowers and Iraq* Secretary of State Baker and Foreign Minister Shevardnadze issued a joint statement in Moscow demanding that Iraq withdraw its forces from Kuwait. (AFPCD 460)

August 6 *The UN and Iraq* The United Nations Security Council approved a resolution, supported by the United States and the Soviet Union, to impose economic sanctions on Iraq. (AFPCD 466)

August 13 *Restrictions on Soviets Lifted* President Bush removed the ceiling on the total number of Soviet business people permitted to work and reside in the United States. (PP 1129)

August 25 *Soviets Support Sanctions* The United Nations Security Council adopted a resolution approving the use of force to implement United Nations sanctions imposed on Iraq because of its invasion of Kuwait. The United States and the Soviet Union supported the resolution. (NYT 8/26/90 1)

September 9 *Bush and Gorbachev* President Bush and General Secretary Gorbachev met in Helsinki to discuss the Persian Gulf crisis. They called on all nations "to adhere to the sanctions mandated by the United Nations." The two leaders expressed the hope that a political solution could be found to resolve the Gulf crisis, but they did not discuss military options should a political solution not be found. (PP 1205)

September 9 *Bush and Gorbachev* President Bush and General Secretary Gorbachev issued a joint statement after their meeting in Helsinki expressing their determination to make certain Iraq's aggression against

Kuwait did not succeed. They called upon Iraq to unconditionally withdraw its forces from Kuwait. (USDSD 9/17/90 92)

September 12 *Agreement on Germany* France, the United Kingdom, the United States, the Soviet Union, and East and West Germany signed an agreement ending Allied occupation rights. Germany was united and its sovereignty fully restored. The United States, since the end of World War II, consistently supported the reunification of Germany, but the Soviet Union just as consistently opposed it. (USDSD 10/8/90 164)

October 1 *Bush at the UN* President Bush, in an address to the United Nations General Assembly, praised the Soviet Union for supporting the United Nations activities in the Persian Gulf. The support, said Bush, indicated a new and different relationship between the superpowers in which they cooperated to solve international problems. Bush expressed the hope that better Soviet-American relations would help to strengthen the United Nations. (PP 1330)

October 15 *Bush and Gorbachev* President Bush congratulated General Secretary Gorbachev on receiving the Nobel Peace Prize. (PP 1414)

October 18 *Soviet-American Statement* The United States and the Soviet Union issued a joint statement expressing support for a peaceful solution to problems in El Salvador. In the past, the superpowers often clashed because of their conflicting policies in Central America. (USDSD 10/22/90)

October 19 *Baker and the Soviet Union* Secretary of State Baker, in an address before the American Committee on U.S.-Soviet Relations, reviewed the many favorable changes taking place in Soviet-American relations and the new spirit of cooperation that permitted the two countries to cooperate in resolving bilateral and multilateral issues. (AFPCD 412)

November 8 *Persian Gulf Crisis* Secretary of State Baker and Foreign Minister Shevardnadze, at a briefing for the press, announced that the two nations were continuing to cooperate to find a political solution to the Persian Gulf crisis. (AFPCD 531)

November 19 *CFE Treaty* The twenty-two members of NATO and the WTO signed the Conventional Forces in Europe treaty, substantially lowering the military forces of the two alliances. President Bush praised the treaty as a means of ending the East-West military confrontation. (USDSD 11/26/90 282)

November 19 *Bush and the Soviet Union* President Bush, in an address to the CSCE meeting in Paris, welcomed the changes that had taken place in the Soviet Union and the nations of Eastern Europe. He expressed support for strengthening the CSCE to enable it to promote more effectively human rights and freedom. He said the CFE treaty signed that morning ended the military confrontation between East and West. (USDSD 11/26/90 283)

November 21   *Charter of Paris*   The heads of state attending the CSCE meeting in Paris signed a Charter of Paris for a New Europe. President Bush said the signing of the charter ended the cold war and the CSCE members could now concentrate on working for peace and stability. (PP 1652)

November 29   *The UN and Iraq*   The United Nations Security Council approved a resolution, supported by the United States and the Soviet Union, authorizing the use of force to compel Iraq to withdraw its forces from Kuwait. (AFPCD 544)

December 11   *The Superpowers and Angola*   Secretary of State Baker and Foreign Minister Shevardnadze issued a joint statement expressing their determination to work together to restore peace in Angola. In the past, the Soviet Union and the United States supported opposing factions in the Angolan civil war. (AFPCD 773)

December 12   *Bush and Shevardnadze*   President Bush, after meeting with Foreign Minister Shevardnadze, announced several policies to assist the Soviet Union, including giving it access to the International Monetary Fund and the World Bank. (USDSD 12/17/90 331)

December 13   *Bush and Gorbachev*   President Bush announced that he would meet with General Secretary Gorbachev in Moscow on February 11. Bush expressed the hope that the START treaty would be completed by that time. (CDSP XLII:50 24)

December 20   *Shevardnadze Resigns*   Foreign Minister Shevardnadze announced his resignation as foreign minister. In his resignation speech he warned of the possibility of a coup d'état in the Soviet Union to oust General Secretary Gorbachev and the reformers. (CDSP XLII:52 8)

December 20   *Baker and Shevardnadze*   Secretary of State Baker issued a statement regarding the resignation of Foreign Minister Shevardnadze. Baker praised the Soviet leader for supporting the many policies that brought about improved Soviet-American relations. (AFPCD 420)

December 29   *Jackson-Vanik Amendment*   President Bush issued an Executive Order waiving the Jackson-Vanik amendment, approved in 1974, thus permitting the Soviet Union to receive credit guarantees to purchase agricultural products. (PP 1824)

1991

January 2 *Shevardnadze on Resignation* Eduard Shevardnadze, in an interview with the editor of *Moscow News,* said he resigned as foreign minister, in part, because he opposed the use of force to restore order in various parts of the Soviet Union. (NYT 1/3/91 3)

January 11 *Bush and Gorbachev* President Bush received a phone call from General Secretary Gorbachev to discuss the Persian Gulf crisis. Bush said the call was symbolic of the close consultations that now took place between the superpowers. (PP 28)

January 13 *Violence in the Baltics* Soviet military forces took control of Lithuania, and a number of people died in the ensuing violence. President Bush criticized the Soviet resort to force and said there was no justification for the Soviet action. Bush said the intervention was inconsistent with efforts to improve Soviet-American relations. (PP 38)

January 15 *A New Foreign Minister* General Secretary Gorbachev appointed Aleksandr Bessmertnykh as foreign minister. He replaced Eduard Shevardnadze, who resigned in December. (CDSP XLIII:3 25)

January 17 *War in the Persian Gulf* The United States and its allies launched an air attack against Iraq because of its invasion of Kuwait. The Soviet Union was not a member of the allied coalition attacking Iraq, but the Soviets supported the American-led coalition. (NYT 1/17/91 1)

January 21 *Bush and the Baltics* President Bush appealed to the Soviet Union "to resist using force" in the Baltic republics. That same day the NATO ministers meeting in Brussels considered imposing sanctions on the Soviet Union if the violence in the Baltics did not cease. (NYT 1/22/91 14)

January 22 *Bush and the Baltics* President Bush met with representatives of the Baltic republics to discuss what could be done to discourage the Soviets from using military force to suppress the freedom movements in the three republics. (NYT 1/23/91 14)

January 28 *Summit Postponed* The United States and the Soviet Union postponed the Bush-Gorbachev summit scheduled to begin on February 11 in Moscow. President Bush was preoccupied with the war in the Persian Gulf, and he was also displeased with the Soviet use of force in the Baltic republics. (NYT 1/29/91 1)

January 29   *State of the Union*   President Bush, in his State of the Union address, said he wanted to continue the process of improving relations with the Soviet Union, but he again expressed disappointment that General Secretary Gorbachev had used force in attempting to retain control of the Baltics. The president supported the aspirations of the Baltic people to be free. (PP 74)

March 15   *Baker and Gorbachev*   Secretary of State Baker met with General Secretary Gorbachev in Moscow. The two leaders reaffirmed their desire for a closer Soviet-American friendship, and they discussed several issues, including the situation in the Persian Gulf. They were unable to reconcile differences regarding data pertaining to the CFE treaty. (CDSP XLIII:11 19)

March 16   *Statement on El Salvador*   The United States and the Soviet Union issued a joint statement on El Salvador. The superpowers expressed support for resolving the civil conflict in El Salvador through negotiations and a cease-fire agreement. In the past, the United States and the Soviet Union were often at odds in dealing with Central American nations. (USDSD 3/25/91 215)

April 3   *Cease-Fire in Iraq*   The United Nations Security Council approved Resolution 687, supported by the United States and the Soviet Union, establishing a cease-fire in Iraq between Iraqi military forces and those of the United Nations coalition. (USDSD 4/8/91 234)

April 5   *Resolution on Iraq*   The United Nations Security Council approved Resolution 688, supported by the United States and the Soviet Union, that condemned the Iraqi government for the repression of the civilian population, including Kurds, in various parts of the country. (USDSD 4/8/91 233)

April 25   *Peace Talks*   Secretary of State Baker and Foreign Minister Bessmertnykh agreed that the United States and the Soviet Union would cosponsor a Middle East peace conference. (CDSP XLIII:17 19)

May 8   *Bush and the Baltic Republics*   President Bush met with the leaders of Lithuania, Latvia, and Estonia and expressed the hope that the three Baltic republics could resolve their problems with the Soviet Union. The three leaders were on a private visit to the United States. (PP 489)

May 31   *Peace Accords in Angola*   Secretary of State Baker visited Lisbon to participate in the signing of peace accords to end the fighting in Angola. The civil war in Angola had been going on since 1975, with the United States and the Soviet Union backing different factions. (USDSD 6/10/91 410)

May 31 *Joint Statement on Africa* The United States and the Soviet Union issued a joint statement expressing satisfaction with their cooperation to peacefully resolve political problems in Africa. (USDSD 5/31/91 409)

June 1 *Baker and Bessmertnykh* Secretary of State Baker met with Foreign Minister Bessmertnykh in Lisbon. The two leaders discussed a number of issues, including the START negotiations, the CFE treaty, and the peace process in the Middle East. (USDSD 6/3/91 394)

June 4 *Strauss to Soviet Union* President Bush announced that he was nominating Robert Strauss to be ambassador to the Soviet Union, replacing Jack Matlock. (PP 603)

June 6 *Baker and the Soviet Union* Secretary of State Baker, in an address to the North Atlantic Council meeting in Copenhagen, said two trends had emerged in the Soviet Union over the past year. One was the loss of legitimacy of Soviet political institutions and second was the emergence of a new pluralism that, combined with economic reforms, could establish a new legitimacy. (USDSD 6/10/91 403)

June 13 *Baltic Freedom Day* President Bush designated June 14 as "Baltic Freedom Day." (PP 652)

June 20 *Bush and Yeltsin* President Bush met at the White House with President Boris Yeltsin of the Republic of Russia. In response to a question, President Yeltsin said the Soviet Union no longer provided other countries, such as Cuba, with foreign assistance. (PP 703)

June 21 *Bush and Gorbachev* President Bush had a telephone conversation with General Secretary Gorbachev. The two leaders discussed reforms in the Soviet Union, economic issues, and the START treaty. (PP 708)

July 12 *Captive Nations Week* President Bush designated the week beginning July 14 "Captive Nations Week." He pointed out that despite the changes in the Soviet Union and Eastern Europe, many people around the world were still denied freedom. (WCPD 951)

July 14 *Baker and Bessmertnykh* Secretary of State Baker and Foreign Minister Bessmertnykh met in Washington and announced that, except for one issue, they had almost completed the START treaty. The two leaders were unable to agree on how to define throw-weight for the purpose of determining whether a missile is a new type of missile that could carry a different number of warheads. (USDSD 7/15/91 503)

July 30 *The Moscow Summit* President Bush arrived in Moscow for a summit meeting with General Secretary Gorbachev. (USDSD 8/12/91 591)

July 30 *Bush in Moscow* President Bush, in an address to the Moscow State Institute for International Relations, discussed the improved superpower relationship and the opportunities that resulted from it. He did, however, point out differences between the two countries regarding the refusal of the Soviet Union to return to Japan the islands taken after World War II, the military aid the Soviets continued to supply to Cuba, and the need to reduce the Soviet military budget. (USDSD 8/12/91 592)

July 31 *The Middle East* The United States and the Soviet Union issued a joint statement pledging their support to reconcile differences between the Arab states and Israel. (USDSD 8/12/91 593)

July 31 *The START Treaty* The United States and the Soviet Union signed the START treaty. The START negotiations began in 1982. (USDSD 8/12/91 596)

August 1 *Bush in the Ukraine* President Bush, in an address to the Supreme Soviet of the Ukrainian Soviet Socialist Republic, said the United States would not choose between supporting General Secretary Gorbachev or leaders in various Soviet republics desiring independence. He said the United States supported freedom, democracy, and economic reforms. (USDSD 8/12/91 596)

August 1 *Helsinki Human Rights Day* President Bush proclaimed August 1 "Helsinki Human Rights Day." (USDSD 8/12/91 611)

August 1 *Central America* Foreign Minister Bessmertnykh and Secretary of State Baker issued a joint statement in which they pledged to cooperate in seeking solutions for the problems confronting the Central American nations. (USDSD 8/12/91 595)

August 19 *Gorbachev Ousted* General Secretary Gorbachev, while vacationing in the Crimea, was ousted in a coup d'état by opponents of his reforms. (CDSP XLIII:33 1)

August 19 *Bush Condemns Soviet Coup* President Bush condemned the coup in the Soviet Union and praised General Secretary Gorbachev as a historic figure promoting domestic reforms and cooperating to solve international problems. Bush demanded that Gorbachev be returned to power. (WCPD 1154)

August 21 *Bush and Yeltsin* President Bush, in comments at a news conference, said he had spoken to President Yeltsin, and the Russian leader said more military units were abandoning support for the leaders of the coup. (WCPD 1169)

August 21 *Bush and Gorbachev* President Bush, in remarks to reporters at a news conference, said he had a phone conversation with General Secretary Gorbachev in which the Soviet leader said that events were under control and that he planned to return to Moscow. The coup had failed. (WCPD 1176)

August 24 *Gorbachev Resigns* President Bush's press secretary read a statement welcoming the decision of Gorbachev to resign as general secretary of the Communist party. Members of the party attempted to oust Gorbachev from power. (WCPD 1187)

August 29 *Aid to the Soviet Union* President Bush, at a joint news conference with British prime minister John Major, said the United States and the United Kingdom were committed to assisting the Soviet Union carry out its reforms. The two leaders also expressed support for the independence of the Baltic republics. (USDSD 9/2/91 648)

August 29 *Nuclear Weapons* President Bush, in response to a question at a news conference, said he was confident the leaders of the various Soviet republics that had nuclear weapons would act responsibly in ensuring they were properly secured. (WCPD 1199)

September 2 *Relations with the Baltics* President Bush announced that the United States "is now prepared immediately to establish diplomatic relations" with the Baltic states. (USDSD 9/2/91 647)

September 4 *Baker to Moscow* Secretary of State Baker, in an opening statement at a news conference in Washington, said he was going to Moscow with a four-part agenda. He wanted to explain the principles guiding American policy toward the Soviet Union, express his support for fundamental economic reforms, continue efforts to promote a Middle East peace process, and discuss security issues. (USDSD 9/9/91 667)

September 6 *Baltics Recognized* The Soviet Union recognized the independence of the three Baltic republics. The United States welcomed the Soviet decision. (NYT 9/7/91 1)

September 6 *Pankin Press Conference* Boris Pankin, who had replaced Aleksandr Bessmertnykh as foreign minister, held his first press conference. He promised to continue the policies of former foreign minister Shevardnadze, with particular emphasis on the protection of human rights. (CDSP XLIII:36 30)

September 10 *Human Rights Conference* The CSCE conference on human rights opened in Moscow. Participants agreed that the major threat to human rights was no longer communism but "violent nationalistic passions." The three Baltic states were admitted as members of the CSCE. (CDSP XLIII:36 33)

September 11 *Baker and Gorbachev* Secretary of State Baker and President Gorbachev, at a news conference in Moscow, reported on their just-completed conversations. They discussed the failed coup attempt, arms control, Soviet relations with Cuba, and economic cooperation. President Gorbachev said he would continue to pursue a foreign policy based on cooperation with the United States to resolve international problems. (USDSD 9/16/91 681)

September 11 *Baker and Yeltsin* Secretary of State Baker met with Russian president Yeltsin, and the two leaders discussed about twenty issues, including control of nuclear weapons in the various republics, the relationship between the central government and the new sovereign republics, and various forms of aid the United States might provide to Russia. (USDSD 9/16/91 682)

September 11 *CSCE in Moscow* Secretary of State Baker addressed the CSCE Conference on the Human Dimension in Moscow. He urged the Soviet Union to promote peaceful change and more democracy and to recognize existing borders, both internal and external. (USDSD 9/16/91 679)

September 11 *Soviet Troops in Cuba* President Gorbachev told Secretary of State Baker that the Soviet Union would begin negotiations with Cuba regarding the withdrawal of Soviet troops and an end to subsidies. Some officials in Washington opposed providing economic assistance to the Soviet Union because of its substantial aid to the Castro government. (NYT 9/12/91 1)

September 13 *Baker and Pankin* Secretary of State Baker and Foreign Minister Pankin issued a joint statement on Afghanistan. They expressed support for a nonaligned Afghanistan free to determine its future without any outside intervention. Both leaders pledged to cease supplying arms to the various factions and called for open and free elections. (USDSD 9/16/91 683)

September 27 *Bush and Nuclear Weapons* President Bush, in an address to the nation, said the United States would eliminate all tactical nuclear weapons in Europe and Asia. He also announced an end to the twenty-four-hour alert for American bombers, and he called on the Soviet Union to negotiate additional arms control measures. (WCPD 1348)

October 1 *Food Situation in the Soviet Union* President Bush announced that Edward Madigan, the secretary of agriculture, would visit the

Soviet Union to study the food situation there. The president said he was making available to the Soviet Union $585 million in credit guarantees for private sales of United States agricultural products. (WCPD 1374)

October 4   *Moscow CSCE Meeting* The Moscow CSCE Conference on the Human Dimension that convened September 10 concluded. Among other things, the conference participants agreed that the protection of fundamental freedoms was a legitimate concern of the international community. In the past, the Soviets claimed that human rights was an internal affair. The participants agreed on norms to be met before a government could declare a state of emergency and on rights that had to be protected during the state of emergency. (CDSP XLIII:40 24)

October 29   *Bush and Gorbachev* President Bush met with President Gorbachev in Spain to begin the Middle East peace process. The two leaders pledged to do whatever they could to help resolve problems in the Middle East. (WCPD 1534)

November 8   *NATO and the Soviet Union* The heads of government and state participating in the North Atlantic Council meeting in Rome agreed to fundamental changes in the alliance in response to the changes in the Soviet Union and the nations of Eastern Europe. The ministers agreed to change NATO's strategic doctrine to reflect the fact that an invasion from the East was no longer likely. The ministers abandoned the doctrine of "forward defense" that had been formulated to cope with a Soviet invasion of the FRG. (WCPD 1598)

November 19   *Foreign Minister Shevardnadze* Eduard Shevardnadze again became foreign minister of the Soviet Union. (NYT 11/20/91 12)

November 20   *Aid to the Soviet Union* President Bush announced that the United States would make available an additional $1.5 million in food assistance for the Soviet Union and the various republics. (USDSD 11/25/91 868)

December 2   *Ukrainian Independence* The White House issued a statement welcoming the Ukrainian vote for independence. (USDSD 12/9/91 880)

December 2   *Agreement on El Salvador* The U.S. Department of State and the USSR Ministry of Foreign Affairs issued a joint statement expressing support for efforts to end the fighting in El Salvador. The statement called for a UN-supervised cease-fire agreement and negotiations to end the conflict between the government and the Farabundo Marti National Liberation Front (FMLN). (USDSD 12/9/91 880)

December 8   *A New Commonwealth*   The leaders of Russia, Ukraine, and Belorussia established the Commonwealth of Independent States that, in effect, abolished the Soviet Union. (NYT 12/9/91 1)

December 16   *The Vote on Zionism*   The United Nations General Assembly voted to repeal the November 1975 resolution equating Zionism with racism. The United States and the Soviet Union supported the repeal, although the Soviets had voted for the resolution when it was first passed. (USDSD 12/23/91 908)

December 18   *Nuclear Weapons*   The leaders of the Soviet republics with nuclear weapons pledged to Secretary of State Baker to honor the nuclear agreements the Soviet Union negotiated with the United States. (NYT 12/19/91 1)

December 20   *Yeltsin and NATO*   President Yeltsin wrote to NATO expressing the desire to have Russia join the military organization. (NYT 12/21/91 5)

December 25   *Gorbachev Resigns*   Gorbachev resigned as president of the Union of Soviet Socialist Republics. (CDSP XLIII:52 1)

December 25   *Bush and Gorbachev*   President Bush issued a statement praising President Gorbachev "for his intellect, vision, and courage." Bush also credited Gorbachev for ending the cold war. (USDSD 12/30/91 911)

December 25   *Bush and the Soviet Union*   On Christmas Day, President Bush, in an address to the American people, said the demise of the Soviet Union was a "victory for democracy and freedom." (USDSD 12/30/91 911)

Index